IN HIS IMAGE, BUT...

IN HIS IMAGE, BUT ...

Racism in Southern Religion, 1780-1910

H. Shelton Smith

Duke University Press
Durham, N. C.
1972

© 1972, Duke University Press

LCC card 72-81338

ISBN 0-8223-0273-x

Printed in the U.S.A.
by Heritage Printers

TO MY GRANDCHILDREN

Alice Jackson   Richard Bowden

Martha Shelton   Carolyn Yancey

Charles Blackwell

Paul Barrett

who will, I hope, work

for a more humane

South

PREFACE

According to biblical anthropology, "God created man in his own image" (Gen. 1:27). From this fundamental doctrine Christian thought derived the claim that all men are equal in the sight of God, and that they therefore owe one another equality of respect and goodwill. Religious leaders of the white South have always theoretically subscribed to the doctrine of the *imago Dei*, yet until at least well into the present century they, with rare exceptions, affirmed the inferiority of the Negro race and defended the traditional regional pattern of white supremacy. It is the purpose of this volume to trace the growth of this anti-Negro movement between 1780 and 1910 and to indicate its impact upon human relations.

The central theme was first presented in the James A. Gray Lectures of Duke University Divinity School in 1965, but the present text, which is entirely new, broadens the scope of inquiry and endeavors to treat more adequately the various aspects of the racial question. The South is the locus of primary attention, but its racial developments are examined in relation to those occurring elsewhere in the nation.

Following an introductory sketch of the attitude of representative churchmen (clerical and lay) toward slavery and the Negro in colonial times, the investigation concentrates upon the period beginning in 1780. Not until that year did any religious communion in the South except the Society of Friends begin to legislate against black servitude. Furthermore, the antislavery legislation of all the non-Quaker churches proved largely ineffective with respect to their own practice. Far from cutting their ties with the institution of human bondage, they actually admitted more and more slaveowners into membership until they became captive to the slavocracy. In the end, therefore, they massively supported a violent revolution in a desperate effort to preserve chattel slavery and Negro subserviency. After the fall of the Confederacy, the church was the first major southern institution to establish the color line; and, tragically, the clergy generally took the lead in justifying it. Leaders of the white church also vigorously denounced the postwar movement to elevate the freedmen to civil and political equality.

The reader may perhaps wonder why I did not make greater use of the official minutes of the regional church judicatories after the end of reconstruction. The answer is that most black communicants had withdrawn from the predominantly white denominations by then, and that those denominations thereafter largely forgot the black people, even though they still occasionally passed a resolution or adopted a report professing interest in the freedmen's spiritual welfare. Hence, in order to ascertain the white churchman's racial attitudes in later years, it was necessary to depend largely upon the published sentiments of representative spokesmen. But such material is abundant, and it indicates that racism in the South, far from subsiding, became increasingly rampant in the late nineteenth and early twentieth centuries.

It is important to understand the meaning of the term racism as used in this book. In short, racism from the Christian standpoint is a response that violates the equalitarian principle implied in the biblical doctrine of the *imago Dei*. If, for example, a person regards another race as an inferior member of the human family and seeks to deny it an equal opportunity for growth and participation in the common life, he is a racist. Racism is two-directional in its evil expression. On the one hand, it impeaches the impartiality of God and, on the other, it breeds social discord.

H. Shelton Smith

Durham, North Carolina
April, 1972

ACKNOWLEDGMENTS

First of all, I am grateful to former Dean Robert E. Cushman and the faculty of Duke Divinity School for the privilege of delivering the James A. Gray Lectures.

Inasmuch as this work is based mainly upon primary sources, I am deeply indebted to far more library specialists than can be identified here. I must, however, express special thanks to the following: Dwight L. Cart, Congregational Library (Boston); Ellis E. O'Neal, Jr., Andover Newton Theological School; L. Franklin Long, University of Notre Dame; Edward C. Starr, American Baptist Historical Society; Nicholas B. Wainright, Historical Society of Pennsylvania; Gerald W. Gillette, Presbyterian Historical Society; Donald N. Matthews, Lutheran Theological Seminary; Mrs. B. D. Aycock, Union Theological Seminary (Richmond); Carlton P. West, Wake Forest University; Kenneth J. Foreman, Jr., Historical Foundation of the Presbyterian and Reformed Churches; Miss Ruth Pritchard, Southeastern Baptist Theological Seminary; Mrs. Reba McMahon, Historical Commission of the Southern Baptist Convention; Miss Carole M. Treadway, Guilford College; Miss Isabel Howell, University of the South; Herbert Hucks, Jr., Wofford College; William B. Tate, University of Georgia; Clifton H. Johnson, Amistad Research Center, Dillard University; and Mrs. John H. Warnick, Southern Methodist University.

The library staffs at Duke University were exceptionally helpful in my research. Of those connected with the Perkins Library, I am especially grateful to Elvin E. Strowd and Miss Gertrude Merritt, assistant librarians; Miss Mattie Russell, curator of manuscripts; John L. Sharpe, curator of rare books; Edwin J. Hicks, newspaper librarian; Misses Florence Blakely and Mary W. Canada, reference librarians; and Emerson Ford, director of interlibrary loan service. Two friends went far beyond the call of duty in their professional assistance: Donn Michael Farris, librarian of Duke Divinity School, and Miss Harriet Leonard, reference librarian of the Divinity School.

Of the numerous professors who helped me to locate or to collect primary documents, I am notably obligated to William R. Hutchison, the Divinity School, Harvard University; Robert T. Handy, Union Theological Seminary (New York); Lefferts A. Loetscher, Princeton Theological Seminary; W. Harrison Daniel, University of Richmond; Louis W. Hodges, Washington and Lee University; H. Burnell Pannill, Randolph Macon College; James L. McAllister, Mary Baldwin College; William Mallard, Jr., Candler School of Theology, Emory University; Charles E. Wynes, University of Georgia; and William A. Clebsch, Stanford University.

During his graduate study at Duke, William B. Gravely, now associate professor of religion at the University of Denver, rendered inestimable service as my research assistant. He was especially helpful as a critic of several versions of my manuscript. Mr. Lawrence O. Kline, also a graduate student at Duke, went the second mile in a wide variety of services which greatly facilitated my research and writing.

For a careful reading of the entire manuscript I am deeply grateful to John Hope Franklin, University of Chicago; David E. Swift Wesleyan University; James H. Smylie, Union Theological Seminary (Richmond); Gordon Harland, Pennsylvania State University; Edwin S. Gaustad, University of California at Riverside; Stuart C. Henry and Frederick Herzog, Duke University. Their perceptive criticisms resulted in important improvements in the substance and style of the manuscript.

During the course of my research, the Research Council of Duke University provided me with several generous financial grants. The Gurney Harriss Kearns Foundation also made a liberal grant toward the publication of the volume.

I owe hearty thanks to Mrs. Jacob Kaplan, an expert typist, for transforming my manuscript into a beautiful copy for the printer. I am also thankful to Ashbel G. Brice, director of the Duke Press, and his colleagues, John W. Dowling and John C. Menapace, for guiding the manuscript through the press. Finally, I am greatly indebted to Miss Doralyn J. Hickey, associate professor of library science at the University of North Carolina in Chapel Hill, for proof-reading assistance and for preparing the comprehensive index.

CONTENTS

Preface vii

Acknowledgments ix

INTRODUCTION 3

I. THE FAILURE OF ANTISLAVERY 23

II. DEBATE AND DIVISION 74

III. IN DEFENSE OF BONDAGE 129

IV. TO THE BITTER END 166

V. NEW PATTERNS ON OLD PREMISES 208

VI. THE TRIUMPH OF RACIAL ORTHODOXY 258

Index 307

IN HIS IMAGE, BUT . . .

INTRODUCTION

"White racism" is a new term for an old American malady. The social disease may have been operative from the moment that "twenty Negars" were put ashore at Jamestown in 1619. At any rate, a Virginia court in 1630 sentenced one Hugh Davis to "be soundly whipped, before an assembly of Negroes and others, for abusing himself to the dishonor of God and shame of Christians, by defiling his body in lying with a negroe; which fault he is to acknowledge next Sabbath day."[1] Ten years later, in 1640, Robert Sweet, a white man, was required "to do penance in church according to the laws of England, for getting a negroe woman with child[,] and the woman [to be] whipt."[2] Both decisions reflected anti-Negro feelings, even though other emotional responses may have been involved. These racial antipathies apparently increased in later years, for in 1691 Virginia enacted a law banishing permanently any white person, male or female, who married a Negro, mulatto, or Indian.[3] Virginia was not unique in passing this type of legislation; other colonies, North and South, were adopting similar laws.[4]

There is no agreement among present-day historians as to what originally generated these and kindred racist responses. Some think that they were the outgrowth and rationalization of slavery.[5] Carl N. Degler, however, reverses the order of causation, saying that racial discrimination preceded and preconditioned slavery. One might,

---

1. William W. Hening, ed., *Statutes at Large: Being a Collection of All the Laws of Virginia* (13 vols., Richmond, 1809-23), I, 146.
2. *Ibid.*, I, 552.
3. *Ibid.*, III, 87.
4. John C. Hurd, *The Law of Freedom and Bondage in the United States* (2 vols., Boston, 1858-62), I, 249-50, 263, 290, 292.
5. Louis Ruchames, ed., *Racial Thought in America*, I: *From the Puritans to Abraham Lincoln: A Documentary History* (Amherst, Mass., 1969), 12-15; Marvin Harris, *Patterns of Race in the Americas* (New York, 1964), 70; Oscar and Mary F. Handlin, "Origins of the Southern Labor System," *William and Mary Quarterly*, 3d ser., VII (April, 1950), 214-18, 221-22.

he thinks, properly "speak of slavery in the English colonies as the institutionalization of a folk prejudice."[6] Neither of these views satisfies Winthrop Jordan, who, after carefully analyzing early black-white relations in Maryland and Virginia, concluded that the enslavement of the black man and white antipathy toward him "appeared at the same time." Accordingly he argues that neither prejudice caused slavery, nor slavery prejudice, but that they generated each other. More precisely, "both were . . . twin aspects of a general debasement of the Negro. Slavery and 'prejudice' may have been equally cause and effect, continuously reacting upon each other, dynamically joining hands to hustle the Negro down the road to complete degradation."[7]

But while differing in their theories of the original causation of slavery, those historians would all agree that the enslavement of the Negro greatly reinforced the white man's belief in the black man's inferiority. They would also likely agree that success in reducing Negroes to an abject status goes far to explain why American slavery, in the evolution of black-white relations, got identified exclusively with the Negro, and consequently became racial slavery.

I

Precisely what attitude the clergy generally took toward slavery in seventeenth-century Anglo-America is largely conjectural, because of the paucity of documentary evidence. But by the early decades of the next century, when printed sermons and tracts on the subject began to appear in considerable numbers, it is clear that church leaders, with rare exceptions, viewed Negro bondage as compatible with the Christian faith. Nor was this notion peculiar to the South or to any particular religious tradition.

We find it, to begin with, in New England Puritanism. Since

---

6. *Out of Our Past: The Forces That Shaped Modern America* (New York, 1959), 38. See also Degler, "Slavery and the Genesis of American Race Prejudice," *Comparative Studies in Society and History*, II (October, 1959), 49–66.

7. *White Over Black: American Attitudes Toward the Negro, 1550–1812* (Chapel Hill, N. C., 1968), 80. For an earlier statement of essentially the same view, see Jordan, "Modern Tensions and the Origins of American Slavery," *Journal of Southern History*, XXVIII (February, 1962), 18–30.

Boston by 1708 had four hundred Negro slaves,[8] one would expect the ministers of that city to express themselves on the subject of slavery. One such was Samuel Willard of South Church (Congregational), who in 1703 devoted an entire lecture to servitude, including chattel slavery.[9] "All Servitude," he declared, "began in the Curse," but had been so ordered by divine providence as to be beneficial to mankind. Yet why only Indians and Negroes should have been cursed with perpetual slavery Willard left unexplained, except to say that it was "so ordered in the Providence of God."[10] He exhorted masters to deal humanely with their slaves, but at the same time he cautioned the slave "not to rise up against his Master," even if treated harshly. The bondsman was to bear such punishment with total subjection, remembering "that Servitude itself was bro't on by Sin."[11] The Boston churchman held that the soul of the slave was "of as much worth, as the Soul of his Master, having the same noble Faculties and Powers, . . . and being alike Precious to Christ."[12] Even so, he nowhere even hinted that the slave had an equal right to freedom.

At least as early as 1689 Cotton Mather charged that masters were keeping their bondsmen "Strangers to the *Way of Life*" and treating them "only as *Horses* or *Oxen*." In seeking to excuse themselves, they claimed that their slaves were too dull to respond to religious instruction. All such pretexts merely revealed the master's "desperate Wickedness."[13] "You deny your *Master in Heaven*," Mather told owners of Negroes, "if you do nothing to bring your Servants unto the Knowledge and Service of that glorious *Master*."[14] Appealing to their self-interest, he urged that Christianized blacks would make more efficient slaves. He also told the masters that they

8. Lorenzo J. Greene, "Slave-Holding New England and its Awakening," *Journal of Negro History*, XIII (October, 1928), 496.
9. "Sermon CLXXIX [August 24, 1703]," in *A Compleat Body of Divinity in Two Hundred and Fifty Expository Lectures on the Assembly's Catechism* (Boston, 1726; reprint ed., New York, 1969), 613–17.
10. *Ibid.*, 614.
11. *Ibid.*, 616–17.
12. *Ibid.*, 616.
13. *Small Offers towards the Service of the Tabernacle in the Wilderness* . . . (Boston, 1689), 58.
14. *The Negro Christianized: An Essay to Excite and Assist that Good Work, the Instruction of Negro-Servants in Christianity* (Boston, 1706), 5.

need have no fear of losing their slaves on account of baptism, since Christianity contained no law forbidding servitude. Mather urged that masters were duty-bound to teach their bondsmen "that it is GOD who has caused them to be *Servants,* and that they serve JESUS CHRIST, while they are at Work for their *Masters.*"[15] Nowhere did he give the slave any hope of ever becoming a free man. Perhaps this was too much to expect of the Boston Puritan, especially since he himself owned slaves.[16]

The Society of Friends was the pioneering antislavery church in America; nevertheless, it must be noted that up until the eve of the American Revolution many, if not most, of the prosperous Friends in all the colonies still held slaves. Unlike churchmen in most of the other denominations, Quakers did not publish pamphlets or sermons in support of slavery, but the fact that they bought and kept Negroes spoke more loudly than the printed word. Since Pennsylvania was Quaker-ruled throughout the first half of the eighteenth century, its sentiment on slavery would seem to be representative of Quakerism in general. In any case, William Penn, founder of the "holy experiment" on the Delaware, was still a slaveowner at his death in 1718.[17] During the first third of the century, Philadelphia's Quaker merchants were busily engaged in importing and selling West India blacks, and some of them persisted in that trade well into the 1750's.[18] According to a cautious historian, Friends were "the principal slaveholders" in many sections of southeastern Pennsylvania. "At many different periods during the eighteenth century," he further observed, "[they] probably held from a half to a third of all the slaves in the colony."[19]

Nor was the colony free of anti-Negro sentiment. In 1725, for instance, it passed a law which (1) prohibited free Negroes from trading with slaves, (2) stipulated that if a black and a white should

15. *Ibid.,* 32.
16. Henry W. Haynes, "Cotton Mather and His Slaves," *American Antiquarian Society Proceedings,* N.S., VI (1890), 191–95. Mather did, however, condemn the slave trade as "a spectacle that shocks humanity." Mather, *Bonifacius: An Essay upon the Good* (1710), ed. David Levin (Cambridge, Mass., 1966), 54.
17. Thomas E. Drake, *Quakers and Slavery in America* (New Haven, 1950), 4, 23–24.
18. Harold D. Wax, "Quaker Merchants and the Slave Trade in Colonial Pennsylvania," *Pennsylvania Magazine of History and Biography,* LXXXVI (April, 1962), 144–50, 157–59.
19. Edward R. Turner, *The Negro in Pennsylvania: Slavery—Servitude—Freedom, 1639–1861* (Washington, 1911), 58.

cohabit, the former would be sold into servitude and the latter fined, and (3) levied a penalty of one hundred pounds upon any magistrate or minister who married a black and white couple.[20] The city of brotherly love also buried the black dead outside its corporate limits.[21] In sum, the Negro in colonial Pennsylvania bore the brunt of discrimination, regardless of whether his status was that of indentured servant, chattel slave, or freeman.[22]

During the colonial era, Roman Catholics were concentrated overwhelmingly in Maryland. In his report of March 1, 1785, to Cardinal Antonelli of Rome, Father John Carroll, future archbishop of Baltimore, put the Maryland faithful at about 15,800. This figure included some 3,000 Negro slaves.[23] The slaves, he noted, were "kept so constantly at work" that their spiritual nurture was neglected, with the result that they were "very dull in faith and depraved in morals." Catholic priests as well as laymen held property in slaves. Carroll himself owned several.[24] The practice did not contravene Catholic doctrine, which taught that slavery, as distinct from its abuses, violated neither divine nor natural law.[25] Hence Catholic spokesmen sharply dissented from the radical abolitionist doctrine that slavery was inherently sinful. On the other hand, many American Catholics lamented the existence of Negro servitude and wished to see it ended. This was notably true of the great Catholic patriot and signer of the Declaration of Independence, Charles Carroll of Carrollton, who in 1797 introduced a bill in the Maryland legislature to abolish slavery.[26] In 1817 he manumitted thirty of his own bondsmen.[27] Like most Protestant

20. Hurd, *The Law of Freedom and Bondage*, 289–90.
21. Turner, *The Negro in Pennsylvania*, 47.
22. *Ibid.*, 26–30, 37, 100–101, 109–14.
23. The text of Carroll's report is in John Tracy Ellis, ed., *Documents of American Catholic History* (Milwaukee, 1956), 151–54. Shortly before submitting his report, Carroll had been appointed as superior of American Catholic Missions.
24. John T. Gillard, S.S.J., *Colored Catholics in the United States* (Baltimore, 1941), 63.
25. John Tracy Ellis, *American Catholicism* (Chicago, 1956), 87.
26. C. J. Nuesse, *The Social Thought of American Catholics, 1634–1829* (Westminster, Md., 1945), 75.
27. Ellen Hart Smith, *Charles Carroll of Carrollton* (Cambridge, Mass., 1942), 267. However, none of the manumissions took effect before 1824, and some of them did not become effective until 1856. Kenneth L. Carroll, "Religious Influences on the Manumission of Slaves in Caroline, Dorchester, and Talbot Counties," *Maryland Historical Magazine*, LVI (June, 1961), 196.

churchmen of this period, he favored sending free blacks out of the United States, and consequently heartily endorsed the American Colonization Society, which was formed in 1816 with the exclusive aim of settling free Negroes in Africa.[28] The society's first president was Bushrod Washington, and he was succeeded in 1830 by Charles Carroll.[29]

Colonial Anglicanism, like New England Puritanism and Roman Catholicism, held that human bondage was compatible with Christianity. This is clearly verified by the teaching and policy of the Society for the Propagation of the Gospel in Foreign Parts (S.P.G.) and also by the sentiments expressed by its missionaries. Founded by Commissary Thomas Bray of Maryland, the society was chartered in London in 1701. Within a few years it placed missionaries in all the American colonies, giving preference to colonies in which the Church of England was most in need of assistance.[30] From the outset the missionaries endeavored to evangelize Indian and Negro slaves, but their efforts displeased many masters. Writing to Henry Compton, bishop of London, Francis Le Jau, missionary in Goose Creek parish in South Carolina, reported that "the Generality of the Masters" objected to the conversion of their bondsmen.[31] This was also the judgment of his fellow missionaries in the colony.[32] In fact, the S.P.G. missionaries everywhere else were encountering either indifference or outright opposition on the part of masters toward those who were seeking to preach the gospel to their slaves.[33]

---

28. Philip J. Staudenraus, *The African Colonization Movement, 1816–1865* (New York, 1961), 29–30. A basic assumption of virtually all colonizationists was that the Negro could never be accorded equality among white Americans. This was the opinion, for example, of the Rev. Robert Finley of New Jersey, a foremost leader in the movement to organize a colonization society. *Ibid.*, 19.

29. Smith, *Charles Carroll of Carrollton*, 270.

30. H. P. Thompson, *Into All Lands: The History of the Society For the Propagation of the Gospel in Foreign Parts, 1701–1950* (London, 1951), 13–18, 47–91. See also William Warren Sweet, *Religion in Colonial America* (New York, 1942), 57–65.

31. Le Jau to Compton, May 27, 1712, in Frank J. Klingberg, ed., *The Carolina Chronicle of Dr. Francis Le Jau, 1706–1717* (Berkeley and Los Angeles, 1956), 116. See also *ibid.*, 60, 121, 124–25, 129.

32. Frank J. Klingberg, *An Appraisal of the Negro in Colonial South Carolina: A Study of Americanization* (Washington, 1941), 6–7, 32, 34.

33. Frank J. Klingberg, *Anglican Humanitarianism in Colonial New York* (Philadelphia, 1940), 130, 133, 155, 166–67; Lorenzo J. Greene, *The Negro in Colonial New England, 1620–1776* (New York, 1942), 270; William Stevens Perry, ed., *Historical Collections Relating to the American Colonial Church* (5 vols. in 4, Hartford, 1870–78), III, 231.

Faced with this discouraging situation, Le Jau and other missionaries urged the S.P.G. to send them suitable tracts or sermons with which to soften the resistance of slaveowners. Their plea was not in vain, for frequently some distinguished clergyman would preach an anniversary sermon before the "Venerable Society" which was later printed for general circulation. A notable discourse of this type was delivered in 1711 by William Fleetwood, bishop of Asaph.[34] In his earnest plea for Negro evangelization, the bishop told masters that Christianity posed no threat to slavery. Taking issue with the traditional notion that a baptized slave was entitled to freedom, he declared that masters "are neither prohibited by the Laws of *God*, nor those of the *Land*, from keeping Christian slaves; their slaves are no more at Liberty after they are Baptized, than they were before. . . . The Liberty of Christianity is entirely spiritual."[35] As if to clinch his argument, the bishop observed that the S.P.G. itself was a slaveholder, thanks to Colonel Christopher Codrington, who in 1710 had willed to the Society two Barbadian plantations and some three hundred slaves to be used in "promoting Learning and Religion."[36] Despite the fact that Fleetwood maintained that Negroes were "equally the Workmanship of God," and were "endued with the same Faculties and intellectual Powers" as whites, he nowhere as much as intimated that the Society should liberate any of its slaves. Its only obligation, besides keeping the blacks busy and healthy, was to "instruct them in the Faith of Christ, bring them to Baptism, and put them in the way that leads to everlasting Life."[37]

Although the missionaries made full use of the Fleetwood sermon, it seems to have had little impact upon slaveowners in the colonies. Hence in 1727 Edmund Gibson, bishop of London, appealed directly to the Christian masters, saying that he was "loath to think" that any of them would "*deliberately hinder*" his Negroes from being instructed in the Christian Faith." Like the bishop of

---

34. The sermon is reprinted in Klingberg, *Anglican Humanitarianism*, 197–212. For decades this sermon "was widely used by the missionaries in trying to win over the whites to a program of Negro conversion." *Ibid.*, 20.

35. *Ibid.*, 205–6.

36. *Ibid.*, 210. The text of the will is reprinted in Frank J. Klingberg, "British Humanitarianism at Codrington," *Journal of Negro History*, XXIII (October, 1938), 454.

37. Klingberg, *Anglican Humanitarianism*, 211.

Asaph, he insisted that slavery was in no danger from Christianity, since the only freedom demanded by it was "Freedom from the Bondage of Sin and Satan." Far from being an enemy of slavery, the gospel of Christ would actually place slaves "under stronger Obligations to perform" their duties "with the greatest Diligence and Fidelity."[38] But even though ten thousand copies of this pastoral document were distributed throughout the colonies, most masters still remained apathetic if not hostile toward the religious instruction of Negroes.[39]

One may well doubt that the master's unwillingness to permit his slaves to attend religious instruction resulted mainly from fear that their baptism would require him to manumit them. In fact, that question had been settled many years earlier by legislative action. In 1667 Virginia flatly declared "that conferring of baptisme doth not alter the condition of the person as to his bondage or freedome."[40] Similar laws were passed in most other colonies, including Maryland (1671), New York (1706), and South Carolina (1712).[41] When, in 1713, the clergy of South Carolina sent a letter to the S.P.G. spelling out the obstacles to their work with Negroes, they did not even mention baptism. In their opinion, the major impediments were (1) the master's refusal to grant his slaves any time for religious instruction, (2) fear that if slaves were allowed to assemble in considerable numbers, they might "be tempted to recovery their liberty," and (3) the general tendency of masters to "malign" those who sought to convert their slaves, on the ground "that a slave grows worse by being a Christian."[42]

Yet another factor that fostered coolness toward the conversion

38. Edmund Gibson, *Two Letters of the Lord Bishop of London: the First, to the Masters and Mistresses of Families in the English Plantations abroad; Exhorting them to Encourage and Promote the Instruction of their Negroes in the Christian Faith. The Second, To the Missionaries there; Directing them to distribute the said Letter, and Exhorting them to give their Assistance towards the Instruction of the Negroes within their several Parishes* (London, 1727), 7, 11.
39. Klingberg, *An Appraisal of the Negro*, 34.
40. Helen T. Catterall, ed., *Judicial Cases Concerning American Slavery and the Negro* (5 vols., Washington, 1929-37), I, 57.
41. William H. Browne, ed., *Archives of Maryland*, II (Baltimore, 1884), 272; Hurd, *The Law of Freedom and Bondage*, I, 281, 300-301.
42. Klingberg, *An Appraisal of the Negro*, 6. See also Marcus W. Jernegan, "Slavery and Conversion in the American Colonies," *American Historical Review*, XXI (April, 1916), 517, 520, 522; Alexander Hewat, *An Historical Account of the Rise and Progress of the Colonies of South Carolina and Georgia* (2 vols., London, 1779), II, 99-101.

of blacks was the equalitarian implications of Christian fellowship. On becoming a Christian, the slave joined a community that professed oneness in Christ. As Paul put it, "There is neither slave nor free, ... for you are all one in Christ Jesus" (Gal. 3:28). This spiritual unity, this Christian equality, implicitly challenged the dogma of Negro inferiority. Morgan Godwyn, a graduate of Oxford University, who came to Virginia about 1665 and served parishes in York and Stafford counties, and who later spent some time on the island of Barbados, recognized this as a real hurdle to the evangelization of blacks. Thus in his remarkable book he pointed out that when masters were exhorted to encourage the conversion of their bondsmen, they would commonly exclaim, *"What, such as they? What, those black Dogs be made Christians? What, shall they be like us?"*[43] In 1711 Francis Le Jau cited two instances in which whites revealed their superiority attitude toward Negroes. "Is it Possible," asked a mistress of slaves, "that any of my slaves could go to Heaven, & must I see them there?" A young man announced that he had "resolved never to come to the Holy Table while slaves are Recd there."[44] On his return from Rhode Island, where he had "resided a considerable time," Dean George Berkeley (later bishop) preached the anniversary sermon of the S.P.G., in which he charged that a main obstacle to converting blacks in that colony was "an irrational contempt" for Negroes "as creatures of another species, who had no right to be instructed or admitted to the sacraments."[45] The dean might well have added that even when blacks were received into the church, they were usually assigned pews that marked them off as inferior to their white brethren.[46]

Far more serious than being segregated in worship, however, was the fact that black Christians were constantly told that their bondage to the white man had been decreed by God. This fact was made clear, for example, in two sermons which the Rev. Thomas Bacon

43. *The Negro's & Indians Advocate, Suing for their Admission into the Church: Or a Persuasive to the Instructing and Baptizing of the Negro's and Indians in our Plantations.... To which is added, A Brief Account of Religion in Virginia* (London, 1680), 61.
44. *The Carolina Chronicle*, 102. See also Godwyn, *The Negro's & Indians Advocate*, 138.
45. "A Sermon Preached Before the Society for the Propagation of the Gospel [February 18, 1732]," *Works of George Berkeley* (4 vols., Oxford, 1901), IV, 404.
46. Klingberg, *An Appraisal of the Negro*, 71–72 n.; Klingberg, *Anglican Humanitarianism*, 136.

of Maryland preached to a congregation of Episcopal slaves.[47] "Almighty God," he declared, "hath been pleased to make you slaves here, and to give you nothing but Labour and Poverty in this world."[48] Far from giving them any hope of earthly freedom, he said: "If you desire *Freedom*, serve the Lord here, and you shall be his *Freemen* in Heaven hereafter."[49] After telling his "*dear* BLACK *brethren* and *Sisters*" that their owners were "GOD'S OVERSEERS," he warned them that whatever wrongs they committed against their masters and mistresses were "done against GOD himself," and that unless they repented and served their overseers faithfully, God would punish them severely in the world to come.[50]

The evangelical upsurge of the 1740's, generally known as the Great Awakening, engulfed the colonies from Massachusetts to Georgia, and kindled a much greater response from Negroes than had either Puritanism, Quakerism, Catholicism, or Anglicanism. In his triumphant tours of the colonies, George Whitefield, the most influential evangelist of his time, was instrumental in converting droves of blacks. At the close of a preaching mission in and around Philadelphia, in May, 1740, almost fifty Negro converts trailed him to his lodging house to thank him "for what God had done to their souls." "I believe," he wrote in his journal, "masters and mistresses will shortly see that Christianity will not make their negroes worse slaves."[51]

During his travels through the South, Whitefield became so distressed over the cruel treatment of the slaves that in 1740 he published a caustic letter against slavemasters. The "generality" of masters, he feared, drove their Negroes as hard as horses and often punished them like beasts. "Your Dogs," he observed, "are caress'd and fondled at your Tables: But your Slaves, who are frequently stiled Dogs and Beasts, have not equal privilege. They are scarce permitted to pick up the Crumbs which fall from their Masters

---

47. *Two Sermons Preached to a Congregation of Black Slaves, at the Parish Church of S. P. in the Province of Maryland* (London, 1782). This pamphlet was originally published in 1749.
48. *Ibid.*, 16.
49. *Ibid.*, 69.
50. *Ibid.*, 28.
51. *George Whitefield's Journals* (new ed., Guilford and London, 1960), 422. This edition of the *Journals* contains an excellent map of Whitefield's evangelistic journeys in the American colonies.

Tables."⁵² The evangelist particularly condemned those masters who were deliberately depriving their slaves of the benefit of Christianity on the pretext that it "would make them proud" and "unwilling to submit to Slavery." Only a false or superficial religion would produce any such result. "I challenge the whole World," said Whitefield, "to produce a single Instance of a Negroe's being made a thorough Christian, and thereby made a worse Servant."⁵³

Even though Whitefield held that blacks, if born and brought up in America, were naturally as capable of improvement as whites, he did not advocate their freedom; indeed, by 1747 he himself owned eight slaves whom he used to cultivate his South Carolina plantation for the benefit of his orphanage at Bethesda, Georgia.⁵⁴ Naturally, then, he opposed the original antislavery policy of Georgia, contending that that province never would be prosperous until Negro slavery was permitted there.⁵⁵ In 1750 the trustees repealed the antislavery law of that colony, and the famed evangelist lost little time in buying blacks for his Bethesda plantation. Writing to a Mr. B. in 1751, he defended the lawfulness of slavery on biblical grounds, noting especially that Abraham bought bondsmen. He conceded that the slave trade was wrong, but then went on to say that since it would be carried on anyhow, he would consider himself "highly favoured" if he "could purchase a good number" of Negroes and bring up their offspring "in the nurture and admonition of the Lord." The proslavery evangelist further rationalized his position by remarking that while liberty was "a sweet thing" to those who were born free, slavery might not be so irksome to those who "never knew the sweets" of liberty.⁵⁶

Of native evangelicals in this period, the foremost preacher to blacks was Samuel Davies, who was born in New Castle County, Pennsylvania, in 1723. Ordained to the ministry in the "new side" branch of Presbyterianism, he shared the evangelistic zeal of the

52. "Letter III. To the Inhabitants of Maryland, Virginia, North and South-Carolina," *Three Letters of the Reverend Mr. George Whitefield* (Philadelphia, 1740), 13.
53. *Ibid.*, 15.
54. Stuart C. Henry, *George Whitefield: Wayfaring Witness* (Nashville, 1957), 117.
55. Whitefield to the Trustees of Georgia, December 6, 1748, in *Works of the Reverend George Whitefield, M.A.* (6 vols., London, 1771–72), II, 209.
56. Whitefield to Mr. B., March 22, 1751, *ibid.*, II, 404–5. Luke Tyerman's *Life and Times of the Rev. John Wesley* . . . (3 vols., London, 1870–71), II, 132, mistakenly identified Mr. B. as John Wesley.

Great Awakening.[57] Settling in Virginia in 1748, he continued his great ministry there until 1759, when he became president of the College of New Jersey (Princeton). Although Davies started his ministry in Hanover County, he quickly organized thriving congregations in three adjoining counties. Owing largely to his labors, Hanover Presbytery was constituted in 1755, the first permanent presbytery to be launched in the South.[58]

From the outset of his Virginia ministry, Davies took a keen interest in instructing "the poor Negroes," whose spiritual welfare was almost universally neglected. By 1751 he reportedly had "baptized about forty" blacks.[59] While in Great Britain (1753–55) soliciting funds for the College of New Jersey, Davies also pleaded the cause of his black parishioners so effectively that the London Society for Promoting Religious Knowledge Among the Poor later sent him a generous supply of instructional materials, including Isaac Watts's *Psalms and Hymns*. In a letter to Robert Crutenden, a member of the London Society, he reported that the Negroes were delighted with the books, and that some of them had actually stayed up all night singing Watts's gospel hymns. "Two Sundays ago," Davies wrote, "I had the pleasure of seeing 40 of their black faces around the table of the Lord." He estimated that "more than a thousand Negroes" were then attending churches under his care.[60]

Samuel Davies unquestionably cared deeply for the slave's immortal soul, but he showed no concern to change the slave's earthly status. This of course followed logically from his medieval theory that God's appointments "not only admit, but require, that there should be civil Distinctions among Mankind; that some should rule, and some be subject; that some should be Masters, and some Servants [slaves]."[61] In pleading with masters to give more

---

57. The rise of "new side" Presbyterianism is treated ably in Leonard J. Trinterud, *The Forming of an American Tradition: A Re-examination of Colonial Presbyterianism* (Philadelphia, 1949), especially Chaps. 3, 5, 7, 10.

58. Ernest Trice Thompson, *Presbyterians in the South*, I: *1607–1861* (Richmond, 1965), 52–61; Wesley M. Gewehr, *The Great Awakening in Virginia, 1740–1790* (Durham, N. C., 1930), Chap. 4.

59. "Old Documents," *Evangelical and Literary Magazine*, IV (October, 1821), 541.

60. Davies to Crutenden, March 2, 1756, *ibid.*, 544–49. See also George W. Pilcher, "Samuel Davies and the Instruction of Negroes in Virginia," *Virginia Magazine of History and Biography*, LXXIV (July, 1966), 293–300.

61. *The Duty of Christians to propagate their Religion among Heathens, Earnestly recommended to the Masters of Negroe Slaves in Virginia. A Sermon Preached in Hanover, January 8, 1757* (London, 1758), 23.

attention to their bondsman's salvation, Davies told them that liberty, although "the sweetest and most valuable" of earthly blessings, was "not essential" to a slave's happiness. If liberated from the tyranny of sin and Satan, the slave would possess a freedom "more noble and divine" than civil liberty, for he would be "the Lord's Free Man."[62]

II

The Negro's liberation came hard in America, especially in the plantation South, where slavery seemed indispensable to maintaining a dependable labor force. But even in the North prior to about 1750, antislavery pioneers encountered massive indifference, and sometimes bitter hostility. No churchmen knew this better than the Quakers, who constituted the antislavery vanguard. When, for instance, four Germantown Quakers presented their antislavery protest of 1688 to "the monthly meeting of Richard Wa[o]rrell's," they received no encouragement whatever. Finding that document too sensitive to handle, the meeting merely referred it to the Philadelphia Quarterly Meeting, which in turn passed it on to the Philadelphia Yearly Meeting. None of the three bodies would touch it, even though the Germantown protest was gentle in spirit and relatively mild in substance.[63]

During the next half-century, a few other Friends, such as George Keith (a Quaker schismatic), John Hepburn, William Southeby, Ralph Sandiford, and Benjamin Lay, published antislavery papers and tracts, but their appeals went unheeded.[64] In some instances, indeed, they were persecuted. Sandiford and Lay were expelled from the Society of Friends, and Southeby barely escaped the same

62. *Ibid.*, 20.
63. The text is reprinted in Samuel W. Pennypacker, "The Settlement of Germantown, and the Causes Which Led to It," *Pennsylvania Magazine of History and Biography*, IV, No. 1 (1880), 28–30; H. Shelton Smith, Robert T. Handy, and Lefferts A. Loetscher, *American Christianity: An Historical Interpretation with Representative Documents* (2 vols., New York, 1960–63), I, 181–82. See J. Herbert Fretz, "The Germantown Anti-Slavery Petition of 1688," *Mennonite Quarterly Review*, XXXIII (January, 1959), 42–59, for a critical evaluation of traditional interpretations, including that of "the Pastorious legend."
64. For illuminating reviews of these pamphlets, see Thomas E. Drake, *Quakers and Slavery in America*, 14–16, 28–47; David Brion Davis, *The Problem of Slavery in Western Culture* (Ithaca, N.Y., 1966), 309–26.

fate.[65] These antislavery pioneers did not suffer in vain; still, it was not until the emergence of John Woolman at midcentury that American Quakerism underwent a decisive awakening to the iniquity of Negro slavery.

At least one New England Puritan, Judge Samuel Sewall of Boston, advocated Negro freedom as vigorously as the Quakers. In his celebrated tract, *The Selling of Joseph*, he urged that since Negroes were of the seed of Adam and the children of God, they had "equal Right unto Liberty, and all other outward Comforts of Life."[66] Sewall flatly rejected the traditional doctrine that slavery was brought on by the Fall of Man. Through "the Indulgence of God to our First Parents after the Fall," he declared, "the outward Estate of all and every of their Children, remains the same, as to one another. So that Originally and Naturally, there is no such thing as slavery." Consequently, Joseph "was rightly no more a Slave to his Brethren, than they were to him: and *they* had no more Authority to *Sell* him, than they had to *Slay* him."[67]

The judge brushed aside the current arguments for bondage as of questionable validity. Against the claim, for instance, that the Negro race was condemned to slavery for Ham's having seen the nakedness of his father Noah, he replied that, according to the Bible (Gen. 9:25, 27), the curse fell upon Canaan, not Ham. And Negroes, he added, were not descendants of Canaan, but of Cush. In answer to those who justified slavery on the ground that Africans had thereby been introduced to Christianity, he said, "Evil must not be done, that good may come of it." Even though God's people did benefit from the selling of Joseph into slavery, this "did not rectify his brethrens Sale of him." To those who defended slavery by saying that Abraham purchased slaves, he rejoined that, even so, God expected Christians to show a more benevolent spirit toward mankind.[68]

Yet it must be noted that Sewall's desire to get rid of slavery did

65. Drake, *Quakers and Slavery in America*, 39–47; Kenneth L. Carroll, "William Southeby, Early Quaker Antislavery Writer," *Pennsylvania Magazine of History and Biography*, LXXXIX (October, 1965), 26–27.
66. "The Selling of Joseph: A Memorial [Boston, 1700]," Massachusetts Historical Society *Proceedings, 1863–1864*, VII (Boston, 1864), 161.
67. *Ibid.*, 162.
68. *Ibid.*, 163–65.

not spring from a belief in Negro equality, despite his recognition that all human beings were God's offspring and "Brethren and Sisters of the Last ADAM." "There is," he observed, "such a disparity in their Conditions, Colour & Hair, that they can never embody with us, and grow up into orderly Families, to the Peopling of the Land: but still remain in our Body Politick as a kind of extravasat Blood."[69] That statement reflected a racist spirit which was to taint the antislavery movement from start to finish.

Nonetheless, Samuel Sewall was far more benevolent toward the Negro than John Saffin, a Boston merchant and also, like Sewall, a judge of the Superior Court. In 1701 Saffin attacked the *Selling of Joseph* in a starkly proslavery tract.[70] His onslaught was doubly caustic because Sewall had been largely instrumental in legally forcing him to abide by an agreement to manumit his black slave Adam. Sewall's equal-right theory, he charged, would subvert the divinely established social order, inasmuch as God had "ordained different degrees and orders of men," appointing some to be masters and others to be slaves.[71] Saffin buttressed his argument with the biblical texts (including Leviticus 25:44–46) that would be recited *ad nauseam* by all future defenders of Negro slavery. In his opinion, it was "no Evil thing" to pluck Africans out of heathenism and put them in a land "where they may have the Knowledge of the true God, [and] be Converted and Eternally saved." Yet even though they might be "saved," they were to be held in bondage. If, however, added Saffin, they should ever be freed, they "must all be sent out of the Country, or else the remedy would be worse than the Disease."[72] Thus John Saffin was perhaps the first American to advocate the colonization of free Negroes.

Puritan sentiment being overwhelmingly on the side of Saffin, it is no wonder that Sewall had to endure much criticism. Even so, he stood his ground and continued to present his unpopular tract to

---

69. *Ibid.*, 162.
70. *A Brief and Candid Answer to a Late Printed Sheet, Entituled, The Selling of Joseph* ... (Boston, 1701), reprinted in part in George H. Moore, *Notes on the History of Slavery in Massachusetts* (New York, 1866), 251–56. For an account of the factors that provoked the Saffin pamphlet, see Lawrence W. Towner, "The Sewall-Saffin Dialogue on Slavery," *William and Mary Quarterly*, XXI (January, 1964), 40–52.
71. *A Brief and Candid Answer*, 252.
72. *Ibid.*, 253, 254.

numerous clergymen and laymen of influence. The intrepid Quaker, Benjamin Lay, valued it so highly that he incorporated it in his own antislavery pamphlet of 1737.[73]

The antislavery impulse did not catch fire in America until the beginning of the Revolutionary crisis. This fact suggests that there was a close relationship between the movement to throw off the yoke of Great Britain and the movement to liberate the black man from his white overlord. Certainly the same natural-rights ideology informed both endeavors. It is even very probable that the powerful wave of natural-rights philosophy was a major factor in awakening clergymen to the antislavery implications of the Christian religion. In any case, from the outset of the Revolutionary crisis churchmen drew upon the doctrine of natural rights as well as the insights of Christianity in their indictment of human bondage. "For God's sake," exclaimed the Rev. Samuel Webster of Salisbury, Massachusetts, in 1769, "break every yoke and let these oppressed ones [Negroes] *go free without delay*—let them taste the sweets of that *liberty*, which we so highly prize, and are so earnestly supplicating God and man to grant us: nay, which we claim as the natural right of every man."[74] Four years later, in 1774, Nathaniel Niles of Newbury, Massachusetts, preached a ringing discourse on liberty, saying: "God gave us liberty, and we have enslaved our fellow-men. . . . For shame, let us either cease to enslave our fellow-men, or else let us cease to complain of those that would enslave us."[75]

In 1776, shortly before the adoption of the Declaration of Independence, Samuel Hopkins, Congregational minister in Newport, Rhode Island, published an exceptionally perceptive indictment of domestic bondage in the form of a dialogue between a slaveholder and himself.[76] The robust Edwardean Calvinist demolished current

---

73. *All Slave-Keepers, That Keep the Innocent in Bondage, Apostates* . . . ([Philadelphia], 1737), 199–207. See Moore, *Notes on the History of Slavery in Massachusetts*, 82–83 n.

74. *An Earnest Address to My Country on Slavery* [1769], quoted in Joshua Coffin, *A Sketch of the History of Newbury, Newburyport, and West Newbury, from 1635 to 1845* (Boston, 1845), 338. Alexander Hewat, pastor of a Scotch Presbyterian Church in Charleston, South Carolina, from 1763 to 1775, also argued forcefully that the Negro had a natural right to freedom. *An Historical Account . . . of the Colonies of South Carolina and Georgia*, II, 92, 94.

75. *Two Discourses on Liberty: Delivered at the North Church, in Newburyport, on Lord's Day, June 5th, 1774* . . . (Newburyport, Mass., 1774), Discourse I, 38–39.

76. "A Dialogue Concerning the Slavery of the Africans, Showing it to be the Duty

proslavery arguments. To the claim, for instance, that slavery was a good thing since it brought heathen Africans into a land of "gospel light," he replied, witheringly, that most Africans were impervious to the gospel because of "the treatment they receive from professed Christians." Besides, this method of evangelizing the heathen was contrary to the teaching of Christ, who commanded his followers to carry the gospel to them in their own homeland.[77] Hopkins was particularly enraged by those who argued against universal emancipation on the plea that freed blacks would not only be unable to look after themselves but would be a menace to society. If this should turn out to be a fact, retorted Hopkins, the blame would rest, not upon the Negro, but upon the institution of slavery. For it was the nature of slavery not merely to deprive the black man of all opportunity for mental growth, but to sink him into the pit of sloth and degradation. Consequently it was no wonder that the bondsman easily fell into vices of all kinds. "And shall we, because we have reduced them to this abject, helpless, miserable state by our oppression of them, make this an argument for continuing them and their children in this wretched condition? God forbid!"[78]

In his search for an explanation as to why whites generally were not more concerned to see Negroes become freemen, the Newport churchman reached a conclusion that revealed his unusual insight. White people, he observed, regarded Negroes as "fit for nothing but slaves." They did not consider Negro people as "in any degree on a level" with themselves; indeed they regarded them "as quite another species of animals, made only to serve" the white man and his family. Not until whites abandoned their superiority posture and viewed Negroes "as by nature and by right on a level" with themselves would they strive zealously to abolish slavery.[79]

Except within Quakerism, southern ministers did not enlist in the antislavery cause until near the end of the Revolutionary struggle. Interestingly, the non-Quaker pioneer critics of human bondage in the South were lay churchmen and leading statesmen,

---

and Interest of the American Colonies to Emancipate all the African Slaves [Norwich, Conn., 1776]," in Edwards A. Park, ed., *Works of Samuel Hopkins, D.D.* (3 vols., Boston, 1854), II, 551–88. In 1785 the New York Manumission Society published a second edition of this tract, a copy of which it sent to each member of Congress.

77. *Ibid.*, 557.   78. *Ibid.*, 581.
79. *Ibid.*, 573–74.

such as Charles Carroll of Carrollton and William Pinkney of Maryland, George Mason and Thomas Jefferson of Virginia, and Henry Laurens of South Carolina. Clement Eaton has rightly characterized them as "aristocrats with liberal views."[80]

None of them equaled Jefferson as a critic of chattel slavery. While he had often condemned slavery long before the Revolution, it was in his *Notes on the State of Virginia*—written during 1780–81, but not published in an authorized edition for general distribution until 1787—that he revealed his most profound reason for wanting to abolish the institution of human bondage. "The whole commerce between master and slave," he wrote, "is a perpetual exercise of the most boisterous passions, the most unremitting despotism on the one part, and degrading submissions on the other."[81] Under these circumstances, he observed, the morality of masters necessarily underwent deterioration. Nor could the younger generation be nurtured in this school of tyranny without taking the same odious attitude toward slaves. Moral depravity, however, was not the only result of a slave society; the industry of white people was also adversely affected by a slave labor system. Work was viewed as primarily a Negro's job. Actually, only "a very small proportion" of slavemasters were "ever seen to labour."

Predicating liberty as God's gift to all men, Jefferson felt certain that Negroes were absolutely destined to be free some day, but he was wistful as to how this might come to pass. According to the *Notes*, he entertained a cautious hope that, "under the auspices of heaven," a total emancipation might be accomplished "with the consent of the masters." On the other hand, he greatly feared that such a social revolution would not take place short of a bloody race war; and he warned his fellow whites that in the event of a violent upheaval, "the Almighty has no attribute which can take side with us in such a contest." The Anglican churchman thus broodingly confessed, "I tremble for my country when I reflect that God is just."[82]

But while Jefferson sincerely wished to see all blacks freed from the yoke of bondage, he was by no means ready to incorporate them

---

80. *Freedom of Thought in the Old South* (Durham, N.C., 1940), 3–31.
81. William Peden, ed., *Notes on the State of Virginia* (Chapel Hill, N.C., 1955), 162.
82. *Ibid.*, 163.

into the common life of America. In fact he explicitly declared that, when liberated, the freedmen should be colonized somewhere outside the American nation.[83] Inasmuch as the Declaration of Independence had proclaimed unequivocally "that all men are created equal," the desire of its chief author to get rid of all emancipated Negroes strikes one as glaringly inconsistent. The foremost colonial equalitarian nevertheless essayed a rationalization. His apologetic proceeded on the belief that whites and blacks were racially so variant that if they remained together after the latter gained their freedom, growing tensions would ultimately result in the extermination of one or the other race. Those racial variants, according to Jefferson, were both physical and intellectual. The Negro's figure, hair texture, and "a very strong and disagreeable odour" proved that he was strikingly different from the white man. His very blackness, moreover, rendered him less beautiful than white folk. With respect to intellectual faculties, blacks appeared "much inferior" to whites; scarcely a single black would be "found capable of tracing and comprehending the investigations of Euclid." While apparently equal to whites in memory, blacks were "dull" and "tasteless" in imagination. The poems of Phillis Wheatley, for example, were "below the dignity of criticism."[84]

Yet, in the very next paragraph of the *Notes*, Jefferson proceeded to cast doubt upon the validity of that demeaning image of the Negro, thus leaving one uncertain as to just where he really stood.[85] Fearing lest that image should "degrade a whole race of men from the rank in the scale of beings which their Creator may perhaps have given them," he wrote: "I advance it therefore as a suspicion only, that the blacks, whether originally a distinct race, or made distinct by time and circumstances, are inferior to the whites in the endowments both of body and mind."[86]

In later years Jefferson occasionally returned to the question of Negro ability, always professing a desire to find indubitable evidence that blacks were in fact as well endowed physically and

83. *Ibid.*, 143.
84. *Ibid.*, 138–40. The poetical compositions to which Jefferson referred are in Phillis Wheatley, *Poems on Various Subjects, Religious and Moral* (London, 1773).
85. Daniel J. Boorstin, an able analyst of the Virginian's assessment of the Negro, has observed that Jefferson "perhaps designedly" stated his position ambiguously. See his *The Lost World of Thomas Jefferson* (Beacon paperback ed., Boston, 1960), 92.
86. *Notes on the State of Virginia*, 143.

mentally as whites. In 1791, following an inspection of Benjamin Banneker's almanac, he wrote the black mathematician, saying: "No body wishes more than I do to see such proofs as you exhibit, that nature has given to our black brethren, talents equal to those of other colors of men, and that the appearance of a want of them is owing merely to the degraded condition of their existence, both in Africa & America."[87] Evidently the Virginian never satisfied himself that Negroes were natively equal to whites, for within about six months of his death he replied to a letter from William Short, saying: "The plan [you proposed] of converting blacks into Serfs would certainly be better than keeping them in their present [enslaved] condition, but I consider that of expatriation to the governments of the W[est] I[ndies] of their own colour as entirely practicable, and greatly preferable to mixture of colour here. To this I have a great aversion."[88]

Thus Jefferson to the very end of his life feared the "mixture of colour" if the Negro stayed in the United States as a freeman. While deeply concerned to erase the blot of slavery from his country, he at the same time wanted to shove the black man out of it. As his letter to Short implied, he would still free the Negroes even if they were not to be deported. Yet if they were not deported, he would hold them in serfdom or in some other form of subjection to white Americans. The celebrated apostle of human equality never knew how accurately he had prophesied the later plight of Negro Americans.

The sage of Monticello may well have done more than any other American of his time to foster doubt with respect to the Negro's native capacity and to generate public sentiment for his expatriation. Certainly the anti-Negro *Notes* stirred an immense ferment in the Old Dominion,[89] and its influence doubtless became a prime factor in prompting Virginians to play a leading role in organizing the American Colonization Society.

87. Jefferson to Banneker, August 30, 1791, in Paul L. Ford, ed., *Writings of Thomas Jefferson* (10 vols., New York, 1892–99), V, 377. See also Jefferson to Henri Grégoire, February 25, 1809, *ibid.*, IX, 246.
88. Jefferson to Short, January 18, 1826, *ibid.*, X, 362. See also Jefferson to Edward Coles, August 25, 1814, *ibid.*, IX, 478; Jefferson to David Barrow, May 1, 1815, *ibid.*, IX, 515–16.
89. Jordan, *White Over Black*, 551–65.

Chapter I

THE FAILURE OF ANTISLAVERY

It was characteristic of southern statesmen of the Revolutionary era to condemn domestic slavery, but still cling to most of their slaves. If they did manumit any of them, they usually did so only in token numbers. Despite his antislavery convictions, Jefferson was holding about two hundred slaves by the end of the American Revolution,[1] and he never freed more than a few of them. In 1773 Patrick Henry confessed to his Quaker friend Robert Pleasants, a Virginia antislavery crusader, that traffic in slaves was an "abominable Practice" and that slavery itself was a "lamentable Evil." The famed orator freely acknowledged that in view of such sentiments it would be hard for any one to believe "that I am Master of Slaves of my own purchase!" He had been "drawn along," he wrote, "by ye general Inconvenience of living without them."[2] His fellow patriots were like-minded; they agreed that slavery was a baleful institution, yet they found it too inconvenient to live without Negroes at their command. Henry heartily applauded the antislavery labors of the Friends, but did not lend them a hand. He believed that the time would come when there would be an opportunity to abolish human bondage. "Everything we can do, is to improve it if it happens in our day, if not, let us transmit to our descendants together with our Slaves a pity for their unhappy Lot, and an abhorrence for Slavery."[3] In this respect also, Henry expressed the sentiment of many of his fellow statesmen. They wished to see slavery abandoned, but they found it imprudent or untimely to participate in any organized movement to overthrow it. They tended to believe that the system of servitude would eventually be

---

1. Dumas Malone, *Jefferson and His Time*, Vol. III: *Jefferson and the Ordeal of Liberty* (Boston, 1962), 207.
2. Henry to Pleasants, January 18, 1773, in George S. Brookes, *Friend Anthony Benezet* (Philadelphia, 1957), 443–44.
3. *Ibid.*, 444.

eliminated by the progress of rational enlightenment and the growth of a benevolent spirit. Aggressive antislavery action in the meantime might actually retard or frustrate this humanitarian development. Interestingly, however, men of this outlook, including especially Jefferson, actively shared in the organized campaign to colonize free blacks.

The more effectual antislavery leaders in the South were not the Jeffersons and Henrys, but predominantly Friends, Methodists, Baptists, and Presbyterians.[4] Yet even they, except in the case of the Society of Friends, fatefully undermined their witness by failing to exclude slaveholders from their respective communions. As a result of this morally compromising action, they contributed substantially to the failure of southern antislavery.

I

In the South, as in the North, the antislavery pioneers were Quakers; and they alone of our four religious bodies cleansed their communion of the taint of slaveholding. The great antislavery awakening within American Quakerism was due in large measure to the leadership of Anthony Benezet and John Woolman. They played distinctive roles, yet their labors were complementary.

Born in France of an affluent Huguenot family, Benezet came to Philadelphia with his parents in 1731, when eighteen years of age.[5] After considerable vocational vacillation, he settled down to teaching school and soon became one of America's distinguished educators. Yet his supreme dedication was to Negro freedom.[6] From the late 1750's until his death in 1784 the renowned schoolmaster lost few opportunities to plead the cause of the oppressed bondsman. His chief antislavery mission, he announced, was to put an end to the slave trade.[7] His ultimate goal, of course, was to abolish slaveholding itself, but he held that the immediate need was to cut

---

4. This point is emphasized with respect to antislavery leadership in Virginia by Robert McColley, *Slavery and Jeffersonian Virginia* (Urbana, Ill., 1964), 148–62.

5. Roberts Vaux, *Memoirs of the Life of Anthony Benezet* (Philadelphia, 1817); Brookes, *Friend Anthony Benezet*, 1–7.

6. Jean S. Straub, "Anthony Benezet: Teacher and Abolitionist of the Eighteenth Century," *Quaker History*, LVII (Spring, 1968), 3–16.

7. Benezet to John Fothergill, London, March 28, 1773, in Brookes, *Friend Anthony Benezet*, 302–3.

off the supply of Negroes from Africa. In 1772 he estimated that "the English alone" were "violently" bringing out of Africa "at least an hundred thousand" Negroes each year.[8] Thus, to accomplish his mission he had to enlist the cooperation of the British as well as his fellow Americans.

The Philadelphia Quaker's major weapon against the slave trade was the tract. Of nine or more such productions, three became especially influential: *A Short Account of That Part of Africa, Inhabited by the Negroes* (1762); *A Caution and Warning to Great Britain and Her Colonies* (1766); and *Some Historical Account of Guinea* (1771). Reprinted again and again on both sides of the Atlantic, they aroused deep hatred of slavery and the slave traffic. The *Short Account*, for example, greatly moved London's Granville Sharp, who in 1772 won a celebrated legal battle in the court of Lord Chief Justice Mansfield to free James Somerset, a slave. The *Historical Account* was a major factor in leading Thomas Clarkson to dedicate his life to the overthrow of the British slave trade, which was finally accomplished in 1807.

In addition to publishing and circulating powerful antislavery tracts, Benezet was adept at enlisting the aid of key laymen outside the Quaker fold. It was at his behest that the able Philadelphia patriot and physician, Benjamin Rush, published *An Address to the Inhabitants of the British Settlements in America, Upon Slave-Keeping* (1773). He also exerted great influence upon Benjamin Franklin. Through his good offices, both Rush and Franklin established friendly relations with Granville Sharp, and they actively supported the London barrister's antislavery crusade. Beyond these services, Benezet lobbied effectively on behalf of petitions against the slave trade and slaveholding in the colonial assemblies.[9]

John Woolman's role was more restricted than that of Benezet; his distinctive task was to induce his fellow Quakers to give up their Negroes. In a sense he was the Hosea of American Quakers, tenderly suffering with the oppressed bondsmen, on the one hand, and sharing in the guilt of their owners, on the other. When twenty years old, in 1740, he left the family farm in West Jersey to take a

---

8. Benezet to Granville Sharp, London, May 14, 1772, *ibid.*, 293.
9. Benezet to Robert Pleasants, April 8, 1873, *ibid.*, 298–302; Edward R. Turner, *The Negro in Pennsylvania: Slavery—Servitude—Freedom, 1639–1861* (Washington, 1911), 77–78.

position as clerk and accountant at Mount Holly. About the time he left home he was undergoing a deeper sense of God's presence that persisted during his early years at Mount Holly. Referring to this experience in his fascinating *Journal,* he wrote: "I looked upon the works of God in this Visible Creation, and an awfullness covered me: my heart was tender and often contrite, and a universal Love to my fellow Creatures increased in me."[10] Since this universal love included the black man, it is no wonder that when, in 1743, the young clerk's employer sold a Negro woman and told him to write a bill of sale, he was thrown into moral shock. Against a smiting conscience he obeyed his master's order, albeit protesting that slaveholding was "inconsistent with the Christian Religion."[11] This crisis produced a moral milestone in Woolman's life. He never again wrote a bill to sell a fellow creature, and he went forth to expel the sin of slaveholding from the Society of Friends.

Inasmuch as Woolman's main strategy was to encounter slaveholders personally, he had to travel much of his time. Between 1743 and 1768 almost no year passed when he did not take one or more extended journeys—usually on horseback, but occasionally on foot—in order to plead the Negro's case with his fellow churchmen.[12] In 1746 he spent nearly three months visiting Quaker meetings in Maryland, Virginia, and North Carolina. Eleven years later he repeated that mission. He went on long journeys to New England in 1747 and 1760. On numerous occasions he crisscrossed the middle colonies. These personal contacts gave the Mount Holly mystic a better understanding of the slaveholding situation within American Quakerism than any other Friend of his time.

Woolman's *Journal* for these years clearly shows that his antislavery message often fell upon deaf ears, and that he was deeply troubled on many occasions by the failure of his Quaker brethren to recognize the iniquity of human servitude. During his 1760 journey through Rhode Island, for instance, he was deeply troubled to see so many slaves in that colony. He was especially distressed to find that the Negro slave traffic was still thriving there, even among

10. "The Journal of John Woolman," in Amelia Mott Gummere, ed., *The Journal and Essays of John Woolman* (Philadelphia, 1922), 157.
11. *Ibid.,* 161.
12. For a calendar of Woolman's travels, see Janet Whitney, *John Woolman, Quaker* (London, 1943), 417–19.

Friends. Understandably, he went to the yearly meeting at Newport "in Bowedness of Spirit." While there he learned, to his consternation, that a large number of Negroes had been imported from Africa and were "then on Sale by a member of our Society." Upon hearing that, said Woolman, paraphrasing Habakkuk (3:16), "my Belly trembled, my lips quivered."[13]

It was, however, Woolman's journey of 1757 through Maryland, Virginia, and North Carolina that gave him most intense "inner suffering." Again and again what he saw and heard left him in "tears."[14] Although he told his fellow Quakers "that Liberty was a Natural right of all men equally," and that the souls of their slaves were "as precious as ours," he apparently failed to make any converts to his antislavery doctrine. Hence the weeping reformer often bordered on despair. Two things weighed especially heavy upon his mind. One was the neglected condition of the slaves, many of whom, he said, had scarcely enough clothes to hide their nakedness. Furthermore, he found that the whites generally took "little or no care of Negro marriages." Some even broke up marriages by selling man and wife "far asunder."[15] The other thing that burdened the sensitive Quaker was the easygoing life of the planter families, who often lived in luxury "on the hard toyl of their slaves."[16] This "gain of Oppression" made him so "uneasie" when he was given lodgment by these affluent Friends that he adopted a novel tactic by which to warn them of their injustice. Just before leaving a host's house he took a few coins from his pocket and asked him to give them to those Negroes who would make the best use of them.[17]

These firsthand experiences enabled Woolman to produce a profoundly perceptive essay, *Some Considerations on the Keeping of Negroes*. Published in two parts, the first part—written shortly after the author returned from his first southern mission—appeared in 1754, and the second in 1762. Among other things, he laid down the basic articles of his antislavery creed, which may be summarized as follows: first, that men of all races are brethren because they all partake of the same God-given Pure Principle or Inner Light;

13. "The Journal," Gummere, ed., *The Journal and Essays of John Woolman*, 234.
14. See, for example, *ibid.*, 189, 193, 199.
15. *Ibid.*, 194.
16. *Ibid.*, 167.
17. *Ibid.*, 189. Sometimes Woolman himself gave the money directly to the slaves.

second, that liberty is the gift of God to all his children; third, that whosoever is truly motivated by God's universal love will find his own heart enlarged toward all mankind; and fourth, "that all Men by Nature are equally entitled" to treatment according to the Golden Rule (Matt. 7:12).[18]

During his second visit to the South, Woolman met Quakers who appealed to the Bible in defense of slavery, and he answered them at length in *Some Considerations*. In a spirited passage he ridiculed the Hamitic myth, saying: "To suppose it right that an innocent Man shall at this Day . . . be deprived of that Liberty which is the natural Right of human Creatures; and be a Slave to others during Life, on Account of a sin committed . . . by *Ham*, the Son of *Noah*, is a Supposition too gross to be admitted into the Mind of any Person, who sincerely desires to be governed by solid Principles."[19] He also disagreed sharply with those who tried to justify human bondage by noting that God's chosen people, the Jews, held bondsmen. That was true, he said, but even so it was "far from being a clear Case" that this was "the genuine Design of their inspired Lawgiver." For did not the prophets often condemn the Jewish rulers for oppressing the poor? "The great Men amongst that People were exceedingly oppressive; and, it is likely, exerted their whole Strength and Influence to have the Law construed to suit their Turns."[20]

Many years before Thomas Jefferson described the manner in which slavery perverted the attitude of the enslaver, Woolman had anticipated him in a more penetrating analysis of the same phenomenon. Woolman was more realistic in his doctrine of man, and he perceived the corrupting effect of self-love more keenly than did the Virginia rationalist. Whenever self-loving men, he warned, held absolute control over their fellowmen, such control always had "a direct Tendency to vitiate their Minds, and make them more unfit for Government." This tendency became all the greater when those under their command were called slaves, clothed in unseemly garments, and confined to menial labor, for thereby the enslaved were made to appear "a Sort of People below us in Na-

---

18. "Some Considerations on the Keeping of Negroes," in Gummere, ed., *Journal and Essays of John Woolman*, 380, 378, 338, 362, 340.
19. *Ibid.*, 355.
20. *Ibid.*, 359, 360.

ture."[21] The color black, moreover, had become so completely identified with the idea of slavery that blackness itself implied inferiority and invited the white man's aggression.[22] This very aggressiveness, however, tended to incite the spirit of revenge in the black man. Consequently, said Woolman, unlimited power and oppression contain "the Seeds of War and Desolation."[23]

Largely as a result of the writing and personal work of Benezet and Woolman, American Quakerism experienced a notable growth of antislavery sentiment during the third quarter of the eighteenth century. A significant start was made in 1754, when the Philadelphia Yearly Meeting passed down to all its constituent meetings *An Epistle of Caution and Advice*, drafted by Woolman,[24] advising Friends to cease buying Negroes, whether imported or native-born. "To live in ease and plenty by the toil of those whom violence and cruelty have put in our power is neither consistent with Christianity nor common justice," the document declared. It also warned that those who violated Christianity in this manner might well suffer "the displeasure of Heaven."[25] We are told that wherever the *Epistle* was read, "it roused the people."[26]

In 1755 the yearly meeting followed up the *Epistle of Caution* with a minute in which it advised monthly meetings to admonish any Friend who continued to import or buy blacks.[27] When this action failed to get significant results, Philadelphia Yearly Meeting then had to decide what to do next. The problem could not be sidestepped, for most Friends had disregarded the minute of 1755. In the summer of 1758, for instance, some Philadelphia Quakers, Woolman reported, "had bought Negro Slaves."[28] This slave-

21. *Ibid.*, 363.
22. *Ibid.*, 366–67.
23. *Ibid.*, 370.
24. Until recently the authorship of the *Epistle* of 1754 had been assigned to Anthony Benezet, but Janet Whitney, *John Woolman*, 183–84, has shown conclusively that Woolman wrote it.
25. The essential parts of the *Epistle* are in Thomas E. Drake, *Quakers and Slavery in America* (New Haven, 1950), 58–59.
26. Whitney, *John Woolman*, 182.
27. Rufus M. Jones, *The Quakers in the American Colonies* (paperback ed., New York, 1966), 516.
28. "The Journal," Gummere, ed., *The Journal and Essays of John Woolman*, 215. See Harold D. Wax, "Quaker Merchants and the Slave Trade in Colonial Pennsylvania," *Pennsylvania Magazine of History and Biography*, LXXVI (April, 1962), 145, 158–59.

buying question got much attention at the yearly meeting's September session. Some Friends wanted to revoke the minute of 1755; others were for doing nothing. After shedding many tears of indignation over the temporizing spirit of his brethren, Woolman delivered a blistering speech, which demonstrated once more that his saintliness was not soft. "Many Slaves on this continent are oppressed, and their cries have reached the ears of the Most High!" he proclaimed. Openly charging that "self-interest" was the roadblock to decisive action, the reformer, as on many other occasions, warned that failure to press the cause of Negro freedom could well bring down upon procrastinating Quakers the judgment of a righteous God.[29]

Woolman's scathing words had a catalytic effect; the meeting, following "weighty" deliberation, adopted a minute which (1) enjoined Friends to follow the Golden Rule and liberate their slaves, with "a Christian provision" for them as freemen; (2) approved a committee, headed by Woolman, to visit and urge slaveowning Quakers to free their Negroes; and (3) directed monthly meetings within the yearly body to discipline recalcitrant slave importers, sellers, and buyers "by refusing to permit them to sit in meetings for discipline, or to be employed in the affairs of Truth, or to receive from them any contribution towards the relief of the poor, or other services of the meeting."[30]

This was a great victory for the Woolmanites, and it presaged similar victories throughout colonial Quakerism. With renewed zeal, Woolman and his fellow committeemen took to the road, and during the next two years they visited numerous meetings in Pennsylvania and New Jersey, pleading for obedience to the minute of 1758.[31] During the next twenty years, antislavery sentiment within the bounds of the Philadelphia Yearly Meeting gained great strength, and manumissions occurred in increasing numbers. Not every Quaker, to be sure, favored the movement, and therefore Philadelphia had to apply additional pressure as time went on. In 1774 the yearly body voted to disown unyielding buyers and sellers

---

29. "The Journal," Gummere, ed., *The Journal and Essays of John Woolman,* 216–17.
30. The minute is in Jones, *The Quakers in the American Colonies,* 517–18.
31. "The Journal," Gummere, ed., *The Journal and Essays of John Woolman,* 219–31.

of blacks. Two years later, in 1776, it applied the same penalty to those who refused to free their slaves.[32] Hesitating Quakers got the message, and most of them eventually complied with the rules. Consequently by 1780 the yearly meeting had virtually disentangled itself from the slaveholding iniquity.[33]

In the meantime New England and New York yearly meetings were also moving against slavery. The former adopted a minute in 1773 outlawing slaveholding, and committees visited the various local meetings to bring Friends into obedience. Sometimes the ultimate weapon, disownment, had to be used, as in the case of Stephen Hopkins, former governor of Rhode Island. After he had refused frequent requests to free a Negro woman, Smithfield Monthly Meeting, in 1773, finally expelled him.[34] Such pressure was effective, and by 1782 New England Friends could report themselves rid of the burden of human bondage. John Woolman's visit to Long Island in 1760 prompted Friends there to take more seriously the injustice of slavery. After considerable foot-dragging the New York Yearly Meeting, in the decade of the 1770's, took more effective steps, first, to stop Friends from importing and selling Negroes, and then to require them to give up slaveholding itself. As a result, the yearly meeting reported in 1787 that none of its members had any connection with slavery.[35]

In the South, where Quaker planters felt that slave labor was indispensable to their economic survival, antislavery spokesmen understandably met with more resistance. However, even there the Society of Friends finally cut loose from slavery. In Maryland, the man who did most to light the fires of Negro freedom within the Society was once again the Mount Holly reformer. During three successive summers (1766–68) Woolman walked to numerous Maryland meetings. He went afoot, he said, because this mode of travel would generate "a more lively feeling of the Condition of the Oppressed slaves," and it would also set "an example of lowliness" to masters of Negroes.[36] He also wore undyed clothes, a custom he

32. Sydney V. James, *A People Among Peoples: Quaker Benevolence in Eighteenth-Century America* (Cambridge, Mass., 1963), 130; Drake, *Quakers and Slavery*, 72.
33. Jones, *The Quakers in the American Colonies*, 520.
34. *Ibid.*, 164–65; Drake, *Quakers and Slavery*, 79.
35. Drake, *Quakers and Slavery*, 80; Jones, *The Quakers in the American Colonies*, 255–58.
36. "The Journal," Gummere, ed., *The Journal and Essays of John Woolman*, 271.

had observed ever since 1762 and would continue until his death ten years later in York, England. In his first journey (1766), with John Sleeper, he covered much of Maryland's Eastern Shore, though focusing chiefly upon meetings in Caroline and Talbot counties. The second trip embraced meetings along the Western Shore. The third was short and did not reach far into Maryland. None of the three visitations gave him much satisfaction from the standpoint of antislavery conversions, and he sat through many meetings "with bowedness of Spirit."[37] Nevertheless, the seeds that he scattered abroad produced a bountiful harvest in later years, especially during the Revolutionary War. By 1790, for example, Friends in three Eastern Shore counties—Caroline, Dorchester, and Talbot—had liberated over three hundred blacks.[38]

Virginia Friends were also at first far from joyful over the prospect of losing their slaves. John Woolman might tell them, as he did during his visit of 1757, that slaves were "a burthensome Stone" around their necks, and that vital religion declined wherever slavery prevailed, but they beheld him with skeptical eyes. Thus in their yearly meeting of 1757, held at Western Branch (Isle of Wight County), they declined to agree to discontinue buying Negroes altogether; they merely agreed not to buy any more for trading purposes. This meant that they would continue to purchase them as needed for use on their own farms. Still, the rising tide of antislavery sentiment would not let them stop there for long. At their yearly meeting of 1768 they were told in a report that Virginia Friends, with few exceptions, were clear of importing or buying blacks.[39]

To bring Friends to give up slaveholding itself was much more difficult. This difficulty, furthermore, was compounded by the fact that a Virginia law, enacted in 1723 and re-enacted in 1748, did not permit manumissions except for some meritorious service, such as

37. *Ibid.*, 272–77.
38. Kenneth L. Carroll, "Religious Influences on the Manumission of Slaves in Caroline, Dorchester, and Talbot Counties," *Maryland Historical Magazine*, LVI (June, 1961), 183. See also Drake, *Quakers and Slavery*, 81–82.
39. Stephen B. Weeks, *Southern Quakers and Slavery* (Baltimore, 1896), 204. To get entirely clear of slave purchasers, however, the yearly meeting was forced to adopt a rule in 1772 to disown those who could not be persuaded to abandon the practice. *Ibid.*, 205.

would meet the approval of the Governor and Council.[40] After a new law was enacted in 1782, permitting masters to free their slaves provided they agreed to support those who were children, or who were aged or infirm,[41] the Society of Friends intensified its antislavery campaign. One of Virginia Quakerism's most zealous opponents of slavery was Robert Pleasants, a prosperous planter on the upper James River. He demonstrated the depth of his convictions by liberating eighty blacks of his own.[42] Over many years he and Anthony Benezet exchanged letters and collaborated in efforts to curtail slave importations into the colonies.[43] Undoubtedly he was a major factor in prodding the yearly meeting into outlawing slaveholding in 1788. In that same year Cedar Creek Monthly Meeting disowned thirteen Friends, when they could not be persuaded to free their slaves.[44] As a result of such discipline, the yearly meeting was able to announce in 1798 that only two Virginia Quakers still owned blacks.[45]

Quaker antislavery sentiment grew more slowly in North Carolina than it did in Virginia. By 1758 the yearly meeting went only so far as to recommend that Friends use their slaves humanely and that they "encourage them to come to meetings as much as they reasonably can."[46] The first significant step was taken in 1776, when this body "earnestly and affectionately advised" all who held slaves "to Cleanse their Hands of them as soon as they possibly can." The yearly meeting also ruled "that none of the members of this meeting shall be permitted to buy or sell any slaves or hire any from such who are not in membership with us."[47] Five years later, in 1781, the yearly meeting permitted monthly meetings to disown such Friends as could not be persuaded to liberate their slaves.[48]

40. William W. Hening, ed., *Statutes at Large: Being a Collection of All the Laws of Virginia* (13 vols., Richmond, 1809–23), IV, 132; VI, 112.
41. *Ibid.*, XI, 39–40.
42. Weeks, *Southern Quakers and Slavery*, 214.
43. Brookes, *Friend Anthony Benezet*, 255–56, 298–302, 351–53, 425–26.
44. Weeks, *Southern Quakers and Slavery*, 213.
45. *Ibid.*, 214 n.
46. MS Minutes of the North Carolina Yearly Meeting of the Society of Friends, 13th to 15th of 10th Month, 1758, 67 (Quaker Collection, Guilford College, Greensboro, N.C.)
47. *Ibid.*, 28th of 10th Month, 1776, 148.
48. *Ibid.*, 26th of 10th Month, 1781, 197.

When, however, Quakers began to free their Negroes, they ran up against a North Carolina law, first enacted in 1741 and re-enacted in substance in 1777, prohibiting the manumission of any slave except for meritorious service acceptable to a county court.[49] For the next three decades the yearly meeting repeatedly petitioned the legislature to liberalize the legal terms of manumission, but to no avail.[50] Finally, between 1808 and 1810 the North Carolina Yearly Meeting, with the legal aid of the distinguished Catholic jurist, William Gaston,[51] created a special agency by which to accomplish manumissions without violating state law. In effect, the Society of Friends itself served temporarily as a slaveholder. Specifically, the yearly meeting appointed a holding committee to receive such slaves as Quaker masters might turn over to it, with the understanding that these slaves would be employed under the committee's direction on a wage basis until they could be sent to free territory. This peculiar agency remained active until the Civil War. By 1830 the committee had received into its care 1,054 slaves, of whom 652 had been transported to free governments at an expense of more than twelve and a half thousand dollars.[52] North Carolina Friends doubtless preferred a more ideal method of ridding themselves of slavery, but this novel plan enabled them to liberate hundreds of Negroes who otherwise would have remained in servitude.

By the dawn of the nineteenth century, then, Quakerism as a whole had forever cut its ties with the system of Negro bondage. This achievement is all the more significant because the Friends in numerous instances not only set their bondsmen free but assisted them financially, educationally, and otherwise to establish themselves as freemen.[53]

In view of this unparalleled ministry to the Negro race, one

49. Weeks, *Southern Quakers and Slavery*, 209.
50. *A Narrative of Some of the Proceedings of North Carolina Yearly Meeting on the Subject of Slavery Within Its Limits* (Greensboro, N.C., 1848), 13–23.
51. Between 1800 and 1832, William Gaston, a native of North Carolina, served several terms in each house of the legislature, and from 1832 till his death in 1844 was a justice of the state supreme court. In an address delivered at the University of North Carolina in 1832, he pronounced slavery "the worst evil" afflicting the South, and urged its ultimate extirpation. C. J. Nuesse, *The Social Thought of American Catholics, 1634–1829* (Westminster, Md., 1945), 209.
52. Weeks, *Southern Quakers and Slavery*, 224–28.
53. James, *A People Among Peoples*, 291–96, and *passim*; Drake, *Quakers and Slavery*, 77; William C. Dunlap, *Quaker Education in Baltimore and Virginia Yearly Meetings* (Philadelphia, 1936), 451–87.

would have expected the Society of Friends to reap a bountiful harvest of black members. Yet extremely few joined the Society. A common explanation is that Quakerism was not adapted to the African temperament. However, in Jamaica many Negroes were at one time Quaker communicants.[54] Another reason sometimes given is that the freedmen were too limited in educational equipment to appreciate the central doctrines of Quakerism. Both of these claims are plausible, but they alone do not account for the scarcity of black Friends. Actually most leaders of colonial Quakerism neither put forth any effort to make disciples of Negroes nor did they really welcome them into the Society. "Not until 1796," wrote a well-informed historian of American Quakerism, "did Philadelphia Yearly Meeting grudgingly concede that Negroes were eligible for membership."[55] In instances where blacks applied for membership, their qualifications were scrutinized with meticulous care, and they were usually kept in suspense as to the outcome for a very long time. William Bowen was refused membership in the Mount Holly Monthly Meeting for several years, despite John Woolman's persistent pleading on his behalf. It took Isaac Linegar more than two years to gain membership in North Carolina's Deep River Monthly Meeting.[56] Joseph Drinker, a staunch Quaker equalitarian, deplored this anti-Negro sentiment and entreated the Society of Friends to open its doors freely to black people, but to little avail.[57]

Quaker discrimination against Negroes did not stop with denying most of them membership in the Society. When blacks went to Friends' meetings for worship, whether as members or as visitors, they were not received on terms of social equality. As a distinguished Quaker scholar has observed, they "usually sat in a special place,— against the wall, under the stairs, or in the gallery."[58] Furthermore, their dead bodies were often denied a resting place in Quaker

54. Henry J. Cadbury, "Negro Membership in the Society of Friends," *Journal of Negro History*, XXI (April, 1936), 151 n.
55. James, *A People Among Peoples*, 234. See also Drake, *Quakers and Slavery*, 120–21.
56. Cadbury, "Negro Membership in the Society of Friends," *Journal of Negro History*, XXI, 177, 194–96. See also Weeks, *Southern Quakers and Slavery*, 223 n.
57. Thomas E. Drake, "Joseph Drinker's Plea for the Admission of Colored People to the Society of Friends, 1795," *Journal of Negro History*, XXXII (January, 1947), 110–12.
58. Cadbury, "Negro Membership in the Society of Friends," *Journal of Negro History*, XXI, 168.

II

American Methodism began with a goodly antislavery heritage from John Wesley. On February 12, 1772, according to his journal, he read a book "by an honest Quaker, on the execrable sum of all villanies, commonly called the Slave-Trade."[60] That honest Quaker was none other than Anthony Benezet, and the book was *Some Historical Account of Guinea*. Three years later, when Wesley published *Thoughts upon Slavery*, he drew freely upon Benezet's description of Guinea.[61]

While the First Methodist devoted most of his fifty-one page pamphlet to a vigorous attack upon the slave traffic, he by no means spared the slaveholder. "Liberty," he insisted, "is the right of every human creature, as soon as he breathes the vital air. And no human law can deprive him of that right, which he derives from the law of nature."[62] In answer to the master's claim that slavery was justifiable on the ground that the African was stupid, Wesley replied: "Allowing them to be as stupid as you say, to whom is that stupidity owing? Without question it lies altogether at the door of their inhuman masters: who give them no means, no opportunity of improving their understanding. . . . The inhabitants of *Africa* where they have equal motives and equal means of improvement, are not inferior to the inhabitants of *Europe*. . . . Their stupidity therefore in our plantations is not natural; otherwise than it is the natural effect of their condition. Consequently it is not their fault, but yours: you must answer for it, before God and man."[63]

As soon as he read the *Thoughts*, Benezet wrote Wesley that he was so impressed with it that he was immediately having it re-

---

59. *Ibid.*, 160–62.
60. Nehemiah Curnock, ed., *The Journal of the Rev. John Wesley, A.M.* (8 vols., London, 1909–16), V, 445–46.
61. Brookes, *Friend Anthony Benezet*, 84–85.
62. *Thoughts upon Slavery* (London, 1774), 51. See also *ibid.*, 31.
63. *Ibid.*, 40–41.

printed in Philadelphia.[64] The assurance that his tract would be reprinted in the colonies gratified Wesley, for, as he told William Wilberforce many years later, he regarded American slavery as "the vilest that ever saw the sun."[65]

Wesley's antislavery contribution to American Methodism was not limited to the writing of a widely read tract. Of far greater impact was his appointment to the American field of two advocates of Negro freedom: Francis Asbury (1771) and Thomas Coke (1784). Of the two men, Asbury did much more than Coke to determine the direction of antislavery thought in American Methodism. Since he often visited Maryland's Eastern Shore, he became greatly impressed with Quakerism's antislavery achievements in that region. "I find," he wrote in his journal in 1778, "the more pious part of the people called Quakers, are exerting themselves for the liberation of the slaves. This is a very laudable design; and what the Methodists must come to, or, I fear the Lord will depart from them."[66]

Very likely, therefore, Asbury prodded his fellow preachers into taking their first step against slavery. In any case, at a conference held in Baltimore in 1780 they condemned slavery as "contrary to the laws of God, man, and nature, and hurtful to society." Despite the validity of that judgment, however, the preachers merely advised Methodist laymen who held slaves to liberate them. Furthermore, they did not require their fellow traveling ministers who owned slaves to promise to free them. They went only so far as to say that the conference "ought" to require such a promise of them.[67] As measured by Quaker antislavery demands, these rules were remarkably mild. Nevertheless, they were a start in the right direction.

In a spring conference of 1784, the preachers stiffened Method-

64. Benezet to Wesley, May 23, 1774, in Brookes, *Friend Anthony Benezet*, 318. Interestingly, the Quaker interspersed the tract with many comments of his own. During the next decade, the two churchmen often exchanged letters on the slavery question.

65. Wesley to Wilberforce, February 24, 1791, in John Telford, ed., *Letters of John Wesley* (8 vols., London, 1931), VIII, 265.

66. Elmer T. Clark, J. Manning Potts, and Jacob S. Payton, eds., *The Journal and Letters of Francis Asbury* (3 vols., Nashville, 1958), I, 273–74.

67. *Minutes of the Annual Conferences of the Methodist Episcopal Church, For the Years 1773–1828* (New York, 1840), I, 12. No preachers from North Carolina and Virginia attended the Baltimore conference, but even if they had been present it is not likely that they would have objected to these rather gentle regulations.

ism's antislavery rules by passing legislation (1) to expel (after due warning) any member of a society who bought a Negro for his own use, or who, under any circumstances, sold one; (2) to grant a year of grace to Virginia's local preachers who declined to emancipate their slaves, but to suspend all local preachers in Maryland, Delaware, Pennsylvania, and New Jersey; and (3) to discontinue the employment of all traveling preachers who refused to free their slaves.[68] On their face, these regulations seem extremely rigorous; however, they contained built-in qualifications that considerably weakened their force. For instance, in Virginia, Methodism's stronghold, the slaveholding local preachers were left free to ignore the rules for a year, and apparently those in North Carolina might do as they pleased indefinitely. Furthermore, the insertion of the words "where the law permits" afforded slaveholding preachers (both local and traveling) a very convenient escape hatch.

At the historic Christmas Conference of 1784, when the Methodist Episcopal Church was organized, and when Asbury and Coke became superintendents (bishops), the preachers felt a "most bounden duty to take immediately some effectual method to extirpate this abomination [slavery] from among us." Accordingly, the conference voted to expel all slaveholding members of Methodist societies—except those in Virginia, where, in "consideration of their peculiar circumstances," they were granted two years of grace—who would not, within twelve months after due notification, perfect a legal document to manumit all their slaves when they reached certain specified ages.[69] The conference also voted to expel immediately all Methodists who bought (except for the purpose of liberation) or sold slaves.[70]

Since these new regulations struck directly at lay slaveholders,

68. *Ibid.*, I, 20–21.

69. However, a *nota bene* was appended, saying: "These rules are to affect the members of our society no farther than is consistent with the laws of the states in which they reside."

70. *Minutes of Several Conversations Between the Rev. Thomas Coke, LL.D., the Rev. Francis Asbury, and Others, at a Conference, Begun in Baltimore, in the State of Maryland, on Monday, the 27th of December, in the Year 1784, Composing a Form of Discipline For the Ministers, Preachers and Other Members of the Methodist Episcopal Church in America* (Philadelphia, 1785), 15–17. According to Donald G. Mathews, Thomas Coke was chiefly responsible for the new rule on slavery. *Slavery and Methodism: A Chapter in American Morality, 1780–1845* (Princeton, N.J., 1965), 11.

the public reaction to them would soon indicate whether it would be possible to purge Methodism of slavery. Thus when Bishop Coke, immediately after the Christmas Conference closed, began a journey that lasted about five months and covered Methodist territory from New York to North Carolina, a major purpose may well have been to size up the attitude of his brethren, especially in the South, toward the new rules. After a short time in New York and New Jersey, he rode southward into the heartland of both Methodism and human bondage. On March 30, 1785, he preached to "attentive people" at Roanoke Chapel (Virginia). There he met Devereaux Jarratt, an Anglican clergyman and warm friend of Methodism. Going to "brother *Seaward's*" house after service, they "talked largely on the minutes concerning slavery"; but Jarratt "would not be persuaded." "The secret is," said Coke, "he has twenty-four slaves of his own: but I am afraid he will do infinite hurt by his opposition to our Rules."[71] The bishop had good reason to be apprehensive, for Jarratt was highly respected by Virginia Methodists, and he vigorously assailed the unpopular rules.[72]

Despite Jarratt's opposition, Coke defended the antislavery regulations with increasing vigor and exhorted the societies to abide by them. On April 7 he spent almost half a day in helping "a dying friend" draw up a will to emancipate his eight slaves. "This is a good beginning," he recorded in his journal. But two days later he ran into a hornet's nest, when he preached against slavery at Martin's barn. "A high-headed lady . . . told the rioters (as I was afterward informed) that she would give fifty pounds, if they would give that little doctor one hundred lashes."[73] The angry mob might well have flogged the preacher if a friendly justice of the peace had not intervened. Yet on April 11 another mob showed up for his sermon at "brother Baker's," armed "with staves and clubs." Their attack was frustrated only because the "little doctor" did not touch on the offensive subject. Not everybody, however, rejected the bish-

71. *Extracts of the Journals of the Late Rev. Thomas Coke, LL.D.* (Dublin, 1816), 61.
72. See, for example, Jarratt to Edward Dromgoole, May 31, 1785 (Edward Dromgoole Papers, University of North Carolina Library at Chapel Hill). In a letter of March 22, 1788, to Dromgoole, Jarratt expressly contended that the Bible authorized slavery.
73. *Extracts of the Journals of the Late Rev. Thomas Coke,* 64.

op's antislavery message. For his preaching was partly responsible for a total of fifty-four manumissions since he entered Virginia.[74]

During his short visit to North Carolina, Bishop Coke refrained from preaching against slavery on the ground that the law made emancipations difficult. While there, however, he held a three-day conference at "Brother Greenhills," with about twenty preachers in attendance. The conference petitioned the state General Assembly to relax the laws restricting manumissions.[75]

On returning to Virginia, the game crusader renewed his attack upon human bondage, but soon again found himself in trouble, despite an effort to be more tactful in handling the sensitive subject. The most serious conflict took place at the Virginia Conference (May 1–4), which he and Asbury held at "Brother Mason's," with some twenty preachers on hand. While the conference was in session, a large group of influential laymen appeared, demanding an outright repeal of the obnoxious slavery rules. The encounter became extremely heated, and the ringleaders "drew in their horns" only after the bishops had threatened to withdraw all the preachers from the disaffected district.[76]

By June 1, when the bishops and preachers gathered in conference at Baltimore, they were so shaken by the uproar that they hastily voted to "suspend the execution of the minute on slavery till the deliberations of a future Conference."[77] Commenting on their retreat, Coke wrote: "We thought it prudent to suspend the minute concerning slavery, on account of the great opposition that had been given to it, our work being in too infantile a state to push things to extremity."[78] Even though the churchmen had backed down, they contended in a *nota bene* to the minutes that they still

74. *Ibid.*, 62–64.
75. *Ibid.*, 65–66. Bishop Asbury interviewed the governor on behalf of the petition, and reportedly "gained him over."
76. *Ibid.*, 67.
77. *Minutes of the Annual Conferences, 1773–1828*, I, 24. William Warren Sweet was therefore mistaken when he said: "For a number of years the rules adopted in the Conference of 1784 remained in force and were quite largely complied with." *The Methodist Episcopal Church and the Civil War* (Cincinnati, 1912), 16. See also Hunter D. Farish, *The Circuit Rider Dismounts: A Social History of Southern Methodism, 1865–1900* (Richmond, 1938), 5.
78. *Extracts of the Journals of the Late Rev. Thomas Coke*, 74. According to the Virginian Jesse Lee, the antislavery rules adopted by the conference of 1784 "were offensive to most of our southern friends." *A Short History of the Methodists* (Baltimore, 1810), 102.

deeply abhorred slavery and would "not cease to seek its destruction by all wise and prudent means." Since, however, no future conference revived the vexed question for more than ten years, it is clear that the preachers were actuated more by prudence than by courageous commitment to the cause of Negro freedom. Thus while the new church grew in membership from 18,000 in 1785 to 56,664 in 1796, its doors remained wide open to slaveholders. Naturally, therefore, the institution of Negro servitude increased its strangling grip upon Methodism.

There were, however, a few Methodist preachers who stoutly resisted the tendency to compromise with slavery during this decade of denominational silence.[79] One of the most outspoken members of this group was James O'Kelly, a native of Ireland, who probably migrated to Virginia during his youth. One of eleven preachers ordained at the Christmas Conference of 1784, he served for many years as a presiding elder in south central Virginia, where slaves were numerous. Precisely when he became a convert to the antislavery movement is unknown, but it was not later than 1785, for on March 5 of that year he emancipated Dianna, his only slave.[80] Within the next four years he published a blistering attack upon slavery. He expressed astonishment that white Americans who treasured so highly their own recently won liberty should enslave Africans, "who have as much right to their natural liberty as to the common air." O'Kelly was particularly troubled by the fact that most of his fellow Methodists favored black servitude. "Be well assured," he nevertheless warned, "that slavery is a work of the flesh, assisted by the devil; a mystery of iniquity, that works like witchcraft, to darken your understanding, and harden your hearts against conviction."[81] But had not God ordained slavery? Reply-

---

79. See, for examples, Freeborn Garrettson, *The Experience and Travels of Mr. Freeborn Garrettson* (Philadelphia, 1791); William K. Boyd, ed., "A Journal of James Meacham," *Historical Papers*, Trinity College Historical Society, Ser. X (1914), *passim*; George A. Phoebus, comp., *Beams of Light on Early Methodism in America. Chiefly Drawn from the Diary, Letters, Manuscripts, Documents, and Original Tracts of the Rev. Ezekiel Cooper* (New York, 1887), 316–28; William B. Gravely, "A Preacher's Covenant Against Slavery, 1795," *South Carolina United Methodist Advocate* (Columbia), March 18, 1971.

80. Certificate of emancipation, Mecklenburg County Court House, Boydton, Virginia, Deed Book 6, p. 471. Dr. William T. Scott, Elon College, North Carolina, kindly made available to me a copy of O'Kelly's certificate of emancipation.

81. *Essay on Negro Slavery* (Philadelphia, 1789), 10.

ing to that query, O'Kelly said: "If there be such a being in existence as may be called God, who was the author of this tragedy, it must be one of those gods that ascend from the bottomless pit. Such a god I defy in the name and strength of Jesus, and proclaim eternal war against him!"[82]

Two things were especially odious to O'Kelly. One was the claim, already almost a commonplace, that the Bible authorized slavery. "When Christ insists that we must observe his laws, . . . you fly to Moses for protection; but there is no shelter there. . . . We are not Jews nor Moses' disciples."[83] But did not slavery harmonize with the spirit of Christ? Any such claim, he replied, was sheer "blasphemy."[84] The second thing that offended the Methodist emancipationist was the general practice of hiring out bondsmen as a means of raising preachers' salaries. "The primitive Christians," he observed, "did not support their ministers upon the hire of slaves procured for that purpose. . . . This hath more the appearance of wolves than shepherds."[85]

Those pungent criticisms often prompted angry outcries, and sometimes even kindled threats of violence. "Say, brethren," pleaded O'Kelly, "have not I gone through perils concerning this thing [slavery]? Twice the clubs have been raised to beat me; once the pointed dagger was presented against me . . . . Now my life is threatened; yet I must defend this truth."[86] The plucky Irishman could not be silenced.[87]

Nevertheless, as O'Kelly himself acknowledged, only a very few Methodists in Virginia had manumitted their Negroes. Apparently only in Maryland did they liberate a significant number of them.[88] Despite this scanty antislavery harvest, the General Conference of 1796 affirmed that it was "more than ever convinced of the great

82. *Ibid.*, 11–12.
83. *Ibid.*, 21.
84. *Ibid.*, 23.
85. *Ibid.*, 18.
86. *Ibid.*, 20.
87. In 1792 O'Kelly was diverted from antislavery activity by a controversy over the power of the episcopacy, in consequence of which he withdrew from the Methodist Episcopal Church. *Journal of the General Conference of the Methodist Episcopal Church, 1792* (New York, 1899), 2–4. He became a principal founder of the Christian Church, which in 1931 merged with the Congregationalists.
88. Kenneth L. Carroll, "Religious Influences on the Manumission of Slaves in Caroline, Dorchester, and Talbot Counties," 187–92. Both Freeborn Garrettson and Francis Asbury frequently preached in these three Eastern Shore counties.

evil of" slavery.[89] If, however, this conference was really "more than ever" convinced of "the great evil" of domestic servitude, it is strange that its own antislavery rules marked a significant retreat from those adopted at the Christmas Conference in 1784. The contrast is especially conspicuous in two respects. For one thing, the rule of 1784 had required the immediate expulsion of any church member who either bought or sold a slave, but the rule enacted in 1796 made expulsion mandatory only if a member sold a slave. A Methodist in good standing might now freely purchase a slave, if he executed a legal instrument to free him at the expiration of a period of years to be determined by the quarterly meeting. This meant that an acceptable Methodist could buy all the Negroes needed for his own personal use. For another thing, the rule of 1784 had denied church membership to all future slaveholders, but the rule of 1796 permitted a slaveholder to unite with a Methodist church after the preacher in charge had merely "spoken to him freely and faithfully on the subject of slavery."[90] Since these provisions comprised the heart of the antislavery rules as adopted in 1796, it is clear that the conference had basically retreated from the antislavery regulations established by the Christmas Conference eleven years earlier.

Methodism's tendency to compromise with slavery increased with each succeeding quadrennial conference during the next twenty years.[91] The General Conference of 1800, for example, defeated a motion to the effect "that from this time forth no slaveholder shall be admitted into the Methodist Episcopal Church." It also defeated a motion to require all Methodist slaveholders to emancipate, at a certain age, all children born to their bondsmen after July 4, 1800.[92] The question of what to do with slaveholding itinerant ministers was revived after a silence of sixteen years, and the conference declared, "[T]hey shall forfeit their ministerial character in the Methodist Episcopal Church, unless they execute, if it be practicable, a legal emancipation of such slave or slaves, agreeably to the laws of the state wherein they live."[93] That rule was so

89. *Journals of the General Conference of the Methodist Episcopal Church*, I: *1796–1836* (New York, 1855), 22.
90. *Ibid.*, 23.
91. William Warren Sweet, *Virginia Methodism* (Richmond, 1945), 197.
92. *Journals of the General Conference of the Methodist Episcopal Church*, I, 40.
93. *Ibid.*, 44.

skillfully framed that a preacher could hold slaves without running much risk of losing his ministerial orders. Besides, no attempt was made to discipline slaveholding local preachers.

The next General Conference (1804) not only took no further action against slavery; it actually exempted all members of Methodist churches in the two Carolinas and Georgia from observing the rule with respect to buying and selling Negroes.[94] The conference now for the first time included in its rules the admonition: "Let our preachers from time to time, as occasion serves, admonish and exhort all slaves to render due respect and obedience to the commands and interests of their respective masters."[95] This instruction encouraged ministers to use their influence to tighten the master's moral grip upon his bondsmen. In 1808 the General Conference yielded still further to the slavocracy. Upon the motion of Bishop Asbury, it authorized the printing of one thousand copies of the *Discipline* without the section and rule on slavery for use in the South Carolina Conference, which then embraced Georgia and a part of North Carolina. It also authorized annual conferences to set their own rules with respect to buying and selling blacks.[96] These two actions indicated that Methodism no longer expected to maintain a uniform system of antislavery discipline.

During the ensuing quadrennium, there was a growing disposition to cease agitating the slavery question, accompanied by the feeling that abolitionism, even within Methodism itself, was a lost cause. Accordingly, when, at the General Conference of 1812, a motion was made by a member of the Western Conference, requesting the delegates "to inquire into the nature and moral tendency of slavery," it was tabled.[97] Four years later, in 1816, there was evidently a desire to see the vexing question settled once and for all. Thus the General Conference of that year asked a nine-member committee, consisting of a representative from each annual conference, to examine the slavery question exhaustively and recommend appropriate action. The only positive result of the

---

94. *Ibid.*, 63. The *Discipline* of the Methodist Episcopal Church for 1804 also included Tennessee in the list of exempted states. *The Doctrines and Disciplines of the Methodist Episcopal Church* (New York, 1804), 216.
95. *Journals of the General Conference of the Methodist Episcopal Church*, I, 63.
96. *Ibid.*, 93.
97. *Ibid.*, 121.

committee's labor was a single resolution that was merely designed to provide a uniform rule in place of a confusing variety of regulations then operative in the various annual conferences. "No slaveholder," said the resolution, "shall be eligible to any official station in our Church hereafter where the laws of the state in which he lives will admit of emancipation, and permit the liberated slave to enjoy freedom."[98] Clearly, this rule was too full of loopholes to prove effective. The most significant aspect of the committee's report was confessional in nature.

> The committee . . . are of opinion that, under the present existing circumstances in relation to slavery, little can be done to abolish a practice so contrary to the principles of moral justice. They are sorry to say that the evil appears to be past remedy.... Your committee find that in the South and West the civil authorities render emancipation impracticable, and ... they are constrained to admit that to bring about such a change in the civil code as would favour the cause of liberty is not in the power of the General Conference.[99]

Despite the defeatist confession, the problem of slavery was revived at the next General Conference (1820). But it was injected into that conference because of a controversy in the Tennessee Conference, where a vigorous antislavery party had been dominant for several years.[100] The Tennessee body, in its session of 1819, had refused to admit on trial Gilbert T. Taylor because he held slaves. On the same ground, it declined to ordain Dudley Hargrove. A minority of sixteen ministers, led by Henry B. Bascom, strongly protested these decisions, saying: "We deprecate the *course* taken, as oppressively severe in itself, and ruinous in its consequences, and we disapprove of the *principle* as contrary to and a violation of the order and discipline of our church."[101] Bishops William McKendree and Enoch George, who were present for the conference, opposed the antislavery party, even to the extent of advising

---

98. *Ibid.*, 170.
99. *Ibid.*, 169–70.
100. R. N. Price, *Holston Methodism,* II (Nashville, 1906), 213–17, 240–45, 249–50, 252–56; Henry B. Bascom, *Methodism and Slavery* (Frankfort, Ky., 1845), 7.
101. Quoted in Moses M. Henkle, *The Life of Henry Bidleman Bascom* (Louisville, 1854), 118.

the dissidents to present their protest to the General Conference of 1820.[102] With this encouragement, Bascom went before that conference with his complaint, and he urged, among other things, that the power of an annual conference to form its own rules on the subject of buying and selling bondsmen be revoked.[103] Once again a select committee wrestled with the slavery question, but the conference could agree to nothing except to withdraw the authority of a yearly conference to make slave rules of its own.[104] This action of course gratified the Bascomites, for it tended to curb the antislavery movement in Tennessee Methodism.

American Methodists enacted their most stringent antislavery rules in 1784, but they suspended them within six months. After an interval of eleven years they renewed their legislative efforts to extirpate the demon of slavery within their church, but none of the rules subsequently enacted measured up to those of 1784. As early as 1808 there was little prospect that Methodism would succeed in disentangling itself from Negro bondage. Bishop Asbury himself reflected the compromising tendency in his journal for February 1, 1809: "Would not an *amelioration* in the condition and treatment of slaves have produced more practical good to the poor Africans, than any attempt at their *emancipation?* . . . What is personal liberty of the African which he may abuse, to the salvation of his soul; how may it be compared?"[105] This represented a far cry from Asbury's attitude in 1778, when he warned Methodists that unless they, like the Quakers, took up the antislavery cause, he feared the Lord would depart from them. The masters, said the bishop in the same journal entry, "are afraid of the influence of our [antislavery] principles," and "keep the blacks from us." As a result, the preachers had been hampered in their evangelistic work with the slave population. Inasmuch as it was far more important to save the slave's soul than to liberate him from his master,

---

102. In his episcopal address to the General Conference, Bishop McKendree, anticipating the Bascom protest, said: "It may be proper for you to examine our relation to the subject of slavery—particularly in reference to the transfer of power to make rules and regulations respecting the buying and selling of slaves." Robert Paine, *The Life and Times of William McKendree* (2 vols., Nashville, 1874), I, 408.

103. Henkle, *The Life of Henry Bidleman Bascom,* 119-20.

104. *Journals of the General Conference of the Methodist Episcopal Church,* I, 202.

105. Clark, Potts, and Payton, eds., *The Journal and Letters of Francis Asbury,* II, 591.

Methodists could do "the poor Africans" more good if they would cease their attempts at emancipation. The most striking thing about Asbury's conclusion is that he was seeking to rationalize Methodism's increasing compromise with human bondage.

III

In 1790 there were approximately 65,000 Baptists in the United States. Of that number, a little over 20,000 were in Virginia, and about 18,000 more were scattered over Kentucky, the two Carolinas, and Georgia.[106] As they, like the Methodists, were numerically strong in the South, they soon became involved in the antislavery agitation that followed in the wake of the American Revolution. This was especially the case in Virginia, the center of southern Baptist strength. In 1785 the Baptist General Committee of that state acknowledged that slavery was "contrary to the word of God," and it solicited the judgment of both local churches and associations with respect to the question.[107] Two years later, in 1787, the Ketocton Association seemed bolder than the General Committee; in addition to pronouncing slavery "a breach of the divine law," it endorsed a plan of gradual emancipation. When, however, its member churches raised a storm of objection, the association at its next session meekly "resolved to take no further steps in the business."[108]

After a silence of five years, the Virginia General Committee in May, 1790, once again revived the slavery question and appointed a committee to draft a resolution on the subject. The committee, however, found itself so divided that it could only agree to place the burden of preparing a resolution upon John Leland, a native of Massachusetts, who had been in Virginia since 1776, and who meanwhile had proven to be a powerful evangelical preacher. He was recognized as a leading Jeffersonian apostle of political and religious liberty.[109] Being a strong foe of slavery, he submitted a

106. John Asplund, *The Annual Register of the Baptist Denomination, in North America; To the First of November, 1790* (n.p., n.d.), 47.
107. *Minutes of the Virginia Baptist General Committee, . . . 1791* (Richmond, n.d.), 5. (The action taken in 1785 was published in the minutes of the General Committee for the year 1791.)
108. Robert B. Semple, *A History of the Rise and Progress of the Baptists in Virginia* (Richmond, 1810), 303–4.
109. Leland, "The Virginia Chronicle," in L. F. Greene, ed., *The Writings of the Late Elder John Leland* (New York, 1845), 92–124. See also Bernard H. Cochran, "An

resolution saying: "[S]lavery is a violent deprivation of the rights of nature, and inconsistent with a republican government; and therefore [we] recommend it to our brethren to make use of every legal measure, to extirpate the horrid evil from the land, and pray Almighty God, that our honourable legislature may have it in their power, to proclaim the general Jubilee, consistent with the principles of good policy."[110] The General Committee adopted this resolution, but it failed to meet with general approval in the associations.

The Roanoke Association, meeting a month later, took the position that in view of the "complex circumstances" attending the subject of slavery, the General Committee had no right to take any action on it. That question, said the association, should be left entirely to each man's discretion.[111] The Strawberry Association in 1792 warned the General Committee "not to interfere" with the institution of servitude.[112] Reading the signs of the times, the General Committee, at its next regular session in 1793, voted (though not unanimously) to drop the divisive question on the claim that, after all, it fell within the political rather than the religious sphere.[113] In thus deferring to the state as the agency to determine whether slavery was to be maintained, the Virginia Baptists took an evasive course which most other churches in the South would sooner or later follow. By the end of the century, the Baptists of the Old Dominion found themselves too deeply entangled in the system of Negro slavery to emulate the Quakers.

A more significant antislavery movement among Baptists emerged on the Kentucky frontier. Of the approximately 74,000 inhabitants there in 1790, 12,430 were slaves.[114] Baptist preachers, mostly from

---

Examination of the Influence of John Leland (1754–1841) on Baptist Life and Thought" (typed Th.M. thesis, Southeastern Baptist Theological Seminary, 1957), Chap. 2.

110. *Minutes of the Virginia Baptist General Committee, . . . 1790* (Richmond, n.d.), 7.

111. MS Minutes, Roanoke Association, June, 1790, 39 (Virginia Baptist Historical Society, University of Richmond).

112. MS Minutes, Strawberry Association, May, 1792, unpaginated (Virginia Baptist Historical Society, University of Richmond).

113. *Minutes of the Virginia Baptist General Committee, . . . 1793* (Richmond, 1793), 4.

114. Asa Earl Martin, *The Anti-Slavery Movement in Kentucky Prior to 1850* (Louisville, 1918), 16 n.

Virginia, arrived there early, and by 1781 they had organized two churches, Severn's Valley and Cedar Creek. Four years later, in 1785, Elkhorn and Salem asociations were formed. The total Baptist membership had grown to more than three thousand by 1790. Since both proslavery and antislavery preachers migrated to Kentucky, the bondage question was bound to produce tensions. By far the most influential leader of the antislavery faction was David Barrow, a native of Virginia. In 1784, according to his Circular Letter of 1798, he had become so convinced that slavery was "contrary to the laws of God and nature" that he manumitted all his bondsmen.[115] After a Virginia ministry of twenty-four years, he set out for Kentucky in the fall of 1798, seeking both better farmland and less competition with slaveowners. One of his parting wishes was that the bondsmen would soon "be delivered from the iron talons of their *task-masters.*"[116]

Long before Barrow arrived in Kentucky the antislavery forces were active among Baptists. In the fall of 1789 the church of Rolling Fork (Nelson County) demanded that Salem Association say whether it was lawful in the sight of God for a member of Christ's church to hold his fellow men in perpetual servitude. On receiving the evasive reply that it was "improper" to discuss that question, the church simply withdrew from the association. Within the next few years several other churches, including Severn's Valley, left the Salem body for the same reason. Joshua Carmen and Josiah Dodge, the two chief ministerial leaders of the antislavery faction, also bolted the association.[117] Even those churches which kept their connection with Salem were sharply torn by arguments over slavery.

The Elkhorn Association also soon felt the shock of bitter factionalism among its member churches. After an unsuccessful effort in 1791 to resolve the tensions, the association ignored the agitation for more than a decade. In 1805, however, the Elkhorn body adopted a resolution declaring it "improper for ministers, churches or associations to meddle with emancipation from slavery, or any other

---

115. Charles R. Allen, Jr., "David Barrow's *Circular Letter* of 1798," *William and Mary Quarterly*, 3d ser., XX (1963), 445. The text of the *Letter* is reprinted in full on pages 443–51.
116. *Ibid.*, 450–51.
117. J. H. Spencer, *A History of Kentucky Baptists, from 1769 to 1885* (2 vols., Cincinnati, 1885), I, 183–84.

political subject."[118] This merely made the emancipationists all the more aggressive in their crusade. The generally irenic William Hickman was so indignant that he preached a vehement sermon to his church (Forks of Elkhorn), avowing non-fellowship with slaveholders.

The antislavery spirit soon spread to churches that were connected with other associations. In 1805 Bracken Association dropped two of its member churches and three of its ministers in consequence of their antislavery sentiments and activities.[119] The Bracken victors were not content to stop at this point; they brought pressure to bear upon North District Association to oust David Barrow for preaching emancipationism. After considerable maneuvering, they attained their objective. Going still further, the North District leaders sent a committee to Barrow's church, Mount Sterling, seeking to bring about his dismissal. Commenting on that extraordinary step, David Benedict wrote: "How ardent and blind must have been that zeal, which hurried a large and respectable body into such overbearing and inconsistent measures!"[120] Although North District, in 1807, rescinded its action against Barrow, it did so not out of love to emancipationists but because it had violated standard Baptist polity.

By then it was clear to Barrow and his fellow abolitionists that they could no longer hope to fulfill their mission within the existing associations, and in September, 1807, messengers from nine churches formed an association of their own, calling it "Baptized Licking-Locust Association, Friends of Humanity."[121] As the published Circular Letter indicated, the distinctive feature of the new association was its commitment to the abolition of slavery. "One would think," said the letter, "that no human being could look at this system but with abhorrence . . . . But . . . there are professors of christianity in Kentucky, who plead for it as an institution of the God of mercy; and it is truly disgusting to see what pains they take to drag the holy scriptures of truth, into the service of this heaven

---

118. *Ibid.*, 185.
119. *Ibid.*, II, 97.
120. *A General History of the Baptist Denomination in America and Other Parts of the World* (2 vols., Boston, 1813), II, 249.
121. For minutes of the organizing meeting, see William W. Sweet, *Religion on the American Frontier: The Baptists, 1783–1830. A Collection of Source Material* (New York, 1964), 564–70.

daring iniquity."[122] A basic rule of the association was non-fellowship with slaveholders.

Since these antislavery messengers needed a propaganda weapon, their chief mentor, David Barrow, had one to suggest. After hearing him read the document, they unanimously approved it for publication. The result was a fifty-page pamphlet that easily ranked as one of the strongest antislavery tracts of its time.[123] Barrow argued, first, that the harmony-working laws of nature, as established by God, were alien to slaveholding. Hence, the introduction of slavery into God's orderly universe "is an *unnatural* and devilish *usurpation*."[124] Second, God in the original creation did not give one man dominion over another human creature. Consequently, property in man was both unreasonable and unjust.[125] Third, slavery was a radical violation of the natural rights of man as set forth in the Declaration of Independence and as fought for in the American Revolution. "Now if *liberty* be such an inestimable blessing, and the *birth right* of all *mankind*, can that be honest policy especially in America, which withholds the blessing from one million of our fellow creatures!"[126] Fourth, the teaching of Jesus stood in radical opposition to slavery. Furthermore, slavery in Old Testament times was more humane than the American type.[127]

Barrow held that the objections commonly raised against emancipation were "very trifling." To the claim that Negroes were too limited in capacity to be set free, he replied that considering their lack of education and their "pinched situation," they revealed vastly more ability than might be expected. "Indeed I believe I may venture to say, their talents or natural abilities, are not inferior to the whites in any respect." To the contention that race mixture would follow emancipation, he expressed doubt that freedom would accelerate the present rate of race mixture under "*illicit embraces*." Thus "if it [race mixture] must take place, it

---

122. *Ibid.*, 567.
123. David Barrow, *Involuntary, Unmerited, Perpetual, Absolute, Hereditary Slavery, Examined; on the Principles of Nature, Reason, Justice, Policy, and Scripture* (Lexington, Ky., 1808). The titlepage contains the statement, "This pamphlet is not to be sold, but given away."
124. *Ibid.*, 11.
125. *Ibid.*, 13.
126. *Ibid.*, 18. See also *ibid.*, 19.
127. *Ibid.*, 28-37.

had better be on lawful grounds." Intermarriage, he argued, was preferable to the common practice of concubinage.[128]

While Barrow certainly wanted to rid the country of slavery, he did not advocate immediate total abolition. "I do not know one among us [the Friends of Humanity]," he added, "who is in favor of an *immediate general emancipation*."[129] Barrow did not propose any plan of emancipation in his essay, for he urged that the first step was not to put forward a specific plan but to awaken the public to the iniquity of slavery.

The Friends of Humanity could not have found a more persuasive antislavery creed than the one framed by David Barrow. They adopted it enthusiastically and entered upon their apostleship with wholehearted dedication. Nevertheless, their mission proved increasingly difficult, for the friends of slavery were many and the friends of abolition, few. They could expect no encouragement from the regular Baptist associations, from which they had separated. To what extent they found new recruits is obscure, and the estimates seem to be largely guesswork.[130] However, such fragmentary information as is available indicates that their growth was extremely slow. When David Benedict, a Baptist historian, made a journey through Kentucky about 1810, he reported that the zeal of the Friends of Humanity had already "in some measure abated."[131] In any case, soon after the death of Barrow in 1819 the movement disintegrated.[132]

On moving southward from Virginia and Kentucky, one enters a region in which Baptist antislavery sentiment was, during the

---

128. *Ibid.,* 45.

129. *Ibid.,* 42. William Birney, *James G. Birney and His Times* (New York, 1890), 17, was thus mistaken in saying that Barrow "advocated immediate abolition."

130. J. H. Spencer, *History of Kentucky Baptists,* I, 186, has told us that David Benedict estimated that at one time "twelve churches, twelve ministers, and 300 members" belonged to the Friends of Humanity. Such an estimate, however, does not appear in Benedict's discussion of the Kentucky emancipationists. See his *A General History of the Baptist Denomination in America and Other Parts of the World,* II, 245–50.

131. *A General History of the Baptist Denomination in America and Other Parts of the World,* II, 249.

132. In this connection, it may be observed that the Rev. James Lemen, a native of Virginia, led a similar Friends of Humanity movement in Illinois that played a strategic role in preventing the slavery interests from gaining control in that key western territory. Sweet, *Religion on the American Frontier: The Baptists,* 88–101, 570–607.

post-Revolutionary period, virtually nonexistent. By 1790, some 15,000 Baptists were located in the Carolinas and Georgia, and yet apparently not one of their churches or associations in that vast area lifted an official voice against human bondage. In the year 1799, Cedar Spring Church in back-country South Carolina did ask its association (Bethel) whether or not slaveholding was "agreeable to the gospel," but no answer was ever forthcoming.[133] In none of these three states, moreover, did a David Barrow emerge.[134] This lack of antislavery interest did not mean that the Baptists showed no concern for Negroes. On the contrary, they had gathered thousands of them into their churches before the end of the eighteenth century. In South Carolina, for instance, some of the most prestigious churches, as in Charleston and Welch Neck, had large black memberships.[135] But this zeal to convert the Negro was accompanied with a tacit or explicit advocacy of his servitude.

As many Baptist preachers in this period held property in Negroes, their proslavery sentiments are not surprising. That slaveholding widely prevailed among Baptist preachers in South Carolina prior to 1805 has been authoritatively demonstrated by Leah Townsend, who explored exhaustively such primary documents as local church books and minutes of district associations. In one of her arresting conclusions, she wrote: "Of the 100 preachers or licentiates of 1780–1800 listed in the 1790 census, one had 55 slaves, one 19, one 17, and thirty-seven from one to 11, a total of 40 slave owners, or two-fifths of the whole."[136] These facts become all the more significant when it is noted that the most influential preachers, such as Richard Furman, Peter Bainbridge, and Edmund Botsford, were among the larger slaveholders. They generally owned sizable plantations as a means of supplementing their salaries.

---

133. Leah Townsend, *South Carolina Baptists, 1670–1805* (Florence, S.C., 1935), 242. At this time Cedar Spring had twenty Negro members. *Ibid.*, 258.

134. John Asplund did say in *The Annual Register*, 57, that slavery was "a violation of the rights of nature, and inconsistent with a republican government," but his testimony apparently had little effect upon his brother ministers.

135. Townsend, *South Carolina Baptists*, 29, 47, 71, 256–57. Two independent Negro Baptist churches were formed in South Carolina soon after the American Revolution. *Ibid.*, 70, 259–60. See also Edward D. Holmes, "George Liele: Negro Slavery's Prophet of Deliverance," *Foundations*, IX (October–December, 1966), 333–45.

136. Townsend, *South Carolina Baptists*, 281.

By the dawn of the nineteenth century, Baptist leaders in South Carolina were upholding human bondage with growing unanimity. This was clearly revealed in the wake of the Vesey crisis of 1822. In the summer of that year Charleston whites were greatly shocked by news that Denmark Vesey, a free Negro carpenter of the city, was plotting an insurrection to liberate the slaves. Discovering the plot in the nick of time, city officials arrested one hundred and thirty-one black suspects, of whom sixty-seven were found guilty. Of the latter, thirty-five were hanged and the remainder sentenced to banishment beyond the limits of the United States.[137] In sentencing Vesey, the court charged, among other things, that he had been "totally insensible of the divine influence of the Gospel," which in fact "was to reconcile us to our destinies on earth." Had he, added the court, searched the scriptures "with sincerity" he would have found that Paul's words, "Servants obey in all things your masters," were "applicable to the deluded victims of your artful wiles."[138]

Since Vesey and his principal confederates belonged to a local congregation of the African Methodist Episcopal Church, the city government suppressed that congregation and had its house of worship demolished.[139] The minister in charge, Morris Brown, abandoned Charleston and returned to the North, where he later became a leading bishop in his denomination.

Soon after the Vesey episode, Richard Furman, pastor of the First Baptist Church in Charleston and president of the South Carolina Baptist State Convention, submitted an important paper to Governor John L. Wilson, in which he set forth the convention's attitude toward Negro slavery. After observing that some churchmen in the state had employed the Bible in criticizing human bondage, Furman said: "These sentiments the Convention, on whose behalf I

---

137. Lionel H. Kennedy and Thomas Parker, *An Official Report of the Trials of Sundry Negroes, Charged with An Attempt to Raise An Insurrection in the State of South Carolina* . . . (Charleston, 1822), 47, 188. The authors were the presiding magistrates of the first court. For a critical reassessment of the traditional view, see Richard C. Wade, "The Vesey Plot: A Reconsideration," *Journal of Southern History*, XXX (May, 1964), 143–61.

138. Kennedy and Parker, *An Official Report*, 178.

139. *Ibid.*, 22, 24; Ulrich B. Phillips, *American Negro Slavery* (Baton Rouge, 1966), 420–21. The Charleston A.M.E. church reported a membership of 1,848 in May, 1818. Daniel A. Payne, *History of the African Methodist Episcopal Church*, ed. C. S. Smith (Nashville, 1891), 27.

address your excellency, cannot think well founded: for the right of holding slaves is clearly established in the Holy Scriptures, both by precept and example."[140] At no point did the Charleston churchman even imply that a master was under any moral obligation to manumit his bondsmen. While he remarked incidentally that the convention "would be happy" to see the slaves emancipated if they should ever become fitted for freedom, he at the same time said that "a considerable part" of mankind would always be slaves, either de jure or de facto.[141]

Furman earnestly admonished masters and slaves alike to fulfill their respective duties to one another as necessary to preserving the existing social order. He particularly warned Christian slaves that they would neither be obedient to God "nor be held as regular members of the Christian Church" if they failed to serve their masters faithfully.[142] By thus making the slave's obedience to God and his right to church membership contingent upon faithful service to his owner, Furman gave great comfort to South Carolina masters. Governor Wilson received the Baptist communication with great joy, and in his reply said "that such doctrines, from such a source, will . . . tend to make our servants not only more contented with their lot, but more useful to their owners."[143]

IV

Like the Methodist and Baptist churches, the Presbyterian communion did not take action against domestic slavery until after the American Revolution. A cautious beginning was made in 1787, when the Synod of New York and Philadelphia (then the supreme judicatory of American Presbyterianism) endorsed the principle of universal liberty. Yet, since the synod feared that the manumission of servile blacks might be "dangerous to the community," it

---

140. *Rev. Dr. Furman's Exposition of the Views of the Baptists, Relative to the Coloured Population of the United States, in a Communication to the Governor of South-Carolina* (Charleston, 1823), 7. A substantial portion of this paper is reprinted in H. Shelton Smith, Robert T. Handy, and Lefferts A. Loetscher, *American Christianity: An Historical Interpretation with Representative Documents* (2 vols., New York, 1960–63), II, 183–86.
141. *Rev. Dr. Furman's Exposition*, 15.
142. *Ibid.*, 18.
143. *Ibid.*, 2.

adopted a twofold recommendation to Presbyterian masters: first, that they provide their slaves with "such good education as to prepare them for the better enjoyment of freedom"; second, that they give their more responsible slaves "a *peculium* [private property], or grant them sufficient time and sufficient means of procuring their own liberty at a moderate rate, that thereby, they may be brought into society with those habits of industry that may render them useful citizens." Finally, the synod recommended that all Presbyterians "use the most prudent measures, consistent with the interest and the state of society . . . to procure eventually the final abolition of slavery in America."[144] Inasmuch as the rights-of-man spirit had been vibrating throughout the country for twenty years, this resolution appears remarkably conservative. Since it in effect postponed actual abolition of slavery to an indefinite future, few masters would feel any urgency to give their slaves either property or an education. But despite the mildness of this first resolution, the Presbyterian Church waited until 1818 before taking substantially stronger action against domestic servitude.

In the meantime Kentucky Presbyterians became aggressive in their antislavery witness. David Rice, their major spokesman, after a twenty-year ministry in Virginia, settled permanently in that frontier region in 1783. Three years later, in 1786, he and four other Virginia missionaries organized the pioneer Presbytery of Transylvania.[145] Rice also founded a grammar school, out of which grew Transylvania University. One of his greatest desires, however, was to uproot slavery in the Kentucky territory. Thus in 1792, on the eve of the constitutional convention (to which he and six other ministers were delegates), he published, under the name of "Philanthropos," a forceful pamphlet in which he argued that both justice and good policy demanded the total abolition of slavery. His fundamental contention was that inasmuch as all men were created in the image of God, every man, regardless of race, had a God-given right to freedom. Consequently, no man could justly enslave a human being.[146] Neither could slavery be good policy, either political-

144. *Records of the Presbyterian Church in the United States of America* (Philadelphia, 1841), 540.
145. Ernest Trice Thompson, *Presbyterians in the South*, I: *1607–1861* (Richmond, 1963), 116–17.
146. *Slavery Inconsistent with Justice and Good Policy* (facsimile ed., University of Kentucky Library Associates, Lexington, 1956), 4–6, 12.

ly or socially. Politically, it radically contradicted the American creed of freedom and equality. Socially, its evils were manifold. Slavery, charged Rice, bred an idle class of whites; it sowed the seeds of discord between slaves and freemen; it inflated the white man's feeling of superiority over the black man; and it exposed the bondwoman to her master's lust.[147]

With courage and candor, Rice laid bare the superficiality of the objections being raised against emancipation. To the claim that it would deprive owners of their legal property, he rejoined that no legislature had a right to treat a man as a piece of property. "The owners of such slaves then are the licensed robbers, not the just proprietors, of what they claim: freeing them is not depriving them of property, but restoring it to the right owner. . . . The master, it is true, is wronged, . . . but this is his own fault, and the fault of the inslaving law."[148] To those who argued that abolition would result in interracial marriage, he replied that the presence of mulattoes everywhere indicated that racial amalgamation was already taking place "in a way much more disgraceful, and unnatural, than [by] intermarriages."[149] Responding to those who argued against abolition on scriptural grounds, he observed sharply that the Bible had "been wickedly pressed into the service of Mammon."[150]

The only objection to abolition that carried much weight with Rice was the plea that the slaves were unprepared for a life of freedom. Yet since he held that slavery had been the main cause of the Negro's unpreparedness for freedom, he argued that the constitutional convention's first step was "to *resolve* UNCONDITIONALLY to put an end to slavery" in Kentucky. After that action was taken, it would then be the duty of the legislature to devise a feasible plan of emancipation. While he did not sketch a detailed blueprint, he did propose (1) that no new importations of slaves into the state be permitted, (2) that the process of emancipation be gradual, and (3) that the state institute a program that would prepare the slaves as quickly as possible for their freedom.[151]

When the convention met, the churchman delivered a vibrant address in favor of abolition, stressing the points already made in

147. *Ibid.*, 12–20.
149. *Ibid.*, 29.
151. *Ibid.*, 38–39.

148. *Ibid.*, 22.
150. *Ibid.*, 30.

his pamphlet. But despite the strenuous pleas of Rice and his fellow emancipationists, slavery was written into the constitution by a vote of twenty-six to sixteen.[152] The result was a body blow from which the Kentucky antislavery movement never recovered.[153]

Although Rice continued to fight the proslavery forces in the state, he thereafter apparently worked mainly through the channels of his church. Within his own Transylvania Presbytery, divergent views had arisen. Many highly dedicated antislavery church members were troubled by the fact that some of their brethren, although acknowledging that slavery violated God's law, continued to hold slaves and also to condone the practice by others. Now, ought the former to hold Christian communion with the latter? The presbytery overtured the General Assembly in 1795 for an answer. In reply, the assembly recommended that inasmuch as Presbyterians in various other similar situations were living together "in peace and charity," the Kentuckians should do the same. At the same time the assembly referred them to the resolution passed by the Synod of New York and Philadelphia in 1787 as primary evidence that the Presbyterian Church viewed slavery "with deepest concern."[154] The assembly's advice evidently satisfied a majority of the Kentucky churchmen, for in 1796 the Presbytery of Transylvania adopted a resolution saying "that altho Presby[tery] are fully convinced of the great evil of slavery[,] yet they ... do not think that they have sufficient authority from the word of God to make it a term of church communion; they therefore leave it to the consciences of the brethren to act as they may think proper."[155]

Four years later, in 1800, the same issue arose in the newly organized West Lexington Presbytery. Two of its member churches, Cane Ridge and Concord, believed that slaveholders should be ex-

---

152. Martin, *The Anti-Slavery Movement in Kentucky Prior to 1850*, 16. Rice had resigned his seat in the convention before the final vote was taken, but the other six preachers—three Baptists, two Presbyterians, and one Methodist—voted solidly against slavery.

153. At another convention, held in 1799, the fight to outlaw slavery was renewed, but it was in vain. *Ibid.*, 31.

154. *Minutes of the General Assembly of the Presbyterian Church, ... 1789-1820* (Philadelphia, [1847]), 103. A special committee, headed by David Rice, presented a letter to the Transylvanians appealing for "forbearance and peace." *Ibid.*, 104.

155. Typescript of the Minutes of Transylvania Presbytery (1786-1837), April 15, 1796, 149 (Historical Foundation of the Presbyterian and Reformed Churches, Montreat, N.C.).

cluded from Christian fellowship, and they presented a memorial to West Lexington, requesting its opinion on the matter. Considering it "not prudent" to decide "a matter of such moment," the presbytery asked its superior judicatory, the Synod of Virginia, for advice. In a letter submitting the memorial, West Lexington informed the synod that the views of the Cane Ridge and Concord churchmen were shared by "a large majority of this presbytery."[156]

In its reply, the Synod of Virginia, although lamenting the existence of slavery, firmly opposed the principle of denying Christian fellowship to slaveholders, calling it "unwarrantable," a "direct" violation of the decision of the General Assembly, and "a manifest departure" from the practice of the apostles and the early church. In addition to cautioning emancipationists to avoid militancy, the synod implicitly called into question the memorial's contention that slaveholding was necessarily sinful.[157]

This advice was evidently unacceptable to at least the Concord Presbyterians, for in 1809 the session excluded one John Moore from church privileges for having offered a slave for sale at public auction. On appeal by Moore, West Lexington Presbytery reversed the decision on the ground that it found nothing in the Bible or in the "directory" of the Presbyterian Church which applied to the case.[158] From this judgment the session of the Concord Church appealed to the synod. Though momentarily reversing West Lexington's decision, the synod, on further reflection, returned the case to Concord's session for reconsideration. Moore's final ecclesiastical fate seems uncertain. It may be noted, however, that in 1815 the General Assembly of the Presbyterian Church adopted a resolution condemning the buying and selling of slaves "as inconsistent with the spirit of the gospel."[159]

Presbyterians in the Carolinas were in this period far less responsive to the antislavery spirit than were their Kentucky breth-

---

156. Typescript of the Records of West Lexington Presbytery, I (1799–1810), August 6, 1800 (Historical Foundation of the Presbyterian and Reformed Churches, Montreat, N.C.), 38–39.
157. MS Minutes of the Synod of Virginia, II (September 25, 1800), 54–58 (Union Theological Seminary Library, Richmond, Va.).
158. Typescript of the Records of West Lexington Presbytery, I, October 10, 1809, 159.
159. *Minutes of the General Assembly of the Presbyterian Church . . . 1789–1820*, 586.

ren. Their general attitude was reflected in the case of James Gilliland, a native of South Carolina. In 1796 the Presbytery of South Carolina refused to ordain him unless he would promise not to preach publicly against slavery. On appealing from that decision to the Synod of the Carolinas, he received a severe jolt, for the synod fully concurred with the presbytery. Like the presbytery, the synod agreed that Gilliland might air his views privately, but it warned that "to preach publicly against slavery, in present circumstances, and to lay down as the duty of every one, to liberate those who are under their care, is that which would lead to disorder, and open the way to great confusion."[160] Gilliland presumably acquiesced, for in 1796 he was installed as minister of Bradaway Church in his native state. Nevertheless, about eight years later he removed to Brown County in Ohio, where he preached to Red Oak Church for almost forty years. In the meantime he and other southern exiles played an important role in transforming Chillicothe Presbytery into a militant agent of abolitionism.

The antislavery timidity of North Carolina Presbyterianism was revealed in the attitude of Henry Pattillo, pioneer missionary-educator in the eastern and central sections of the state. In a slender volume, published in 1787, Pattillo condemned the slave trade as "wicked," but he warned that anyone "who put freedom" into the heads of slaves was "by no means" a friend to them. "This is an event," he continued, "that all the wisdom of *America* seems at present unequal to; but which divine providence will accomplish in time."[161] Twelve years later, in 1799, he seemed especially fearful of any discussion of emancipation on the part of churchmen. "The subject of manumission will greatly injure our interest as a church," he said in a letter to a South Carolinian. "I once touched it with caution: it offended some, & pleased none; tho' I mentioned it as a very distant object."[162]

The Synod of Virginia was more willing to speak out in favor of Negro freedom than Henry Pattillo. In 1800 this body urged Pres-

---

160. Quoted in William H. Foote, *Sketches of North Carolina; Historical and Biographical Illustrations of the Principles of a Portion of Her Early Settlers* (3d ed., Dunn, N.C., 1965), 294.
161. *The Plain Planter's Family Assistant* (Wilmington, N.C., 1787), 23.
162. Pattillo to Wm. Williamson, South Carolina, December 4, 1799 (MS in Presbyterian Historical Society, Philadelphia).

byterian slaveholders to prepare their blacks for ultimate liberty, and to manumit them as soon as they were "duly qualified for that high privilege."[163] Yet, as already noted, the synod cautioned churchmen in Kentucky to avoid all radical antislavery measures, lest they do more harm than good.

It is no wonder, then, that Virginia Presbyterians revolted against the militant abolitionist, George Bourne. Born at Westbury (Wiltshire), England, in 1780, Bourne came to America about 1805 and was for several years engaged in journalism in Baltimore.[164] Around 1809 he began preaching as an independent in the western part of Virginia; but on April 24, 1812, he was admitted to the Lexington Presbytery, and on the following December 26 was ordained pastor of South River Congregation.[165] At first he must have been generally esteemed, for in 1813 and again in 1815 he served as a commissioner from his presbytery to the General Assembly. His downfall began in 1815, when he presented a paper to the assembly of that year in which he and several other churchmen asked how to deal with Presbyterians who held slaves.[166] Since, in reply, the assembly did not meet Bourne's expectations, he sharply condemned its softness on slaveholders.[167]

When Bourne returned to South River, he encountered an irate people who soon demanded his resignation. Thus on September 29, 1815, at the request of the session and with the concurrence of Bourne, Lexington Presbytery dissolved the pastoral relation between South River and the minister. The next day two charges were preferred against Bourne, and he was cited to answer them at the next meeting of the presbytery.[168] The accusations were (1) that at the General Assembly of 1815 Bourne had "brought very heavy charges against some ministers of the gospel in Virginia whom he refused to name, respecting their treatment of slaves, the tendency of which was to bring reproach upon the character of

163. MS Minutes of the Synod of Virginia, II (September 25, 1800), 54–55.
164. Theodore Bourne, "George Bourne, The Pioneer of American Antislavery," *Methodist Quarterly Review*, LXIV (January, 1882), 71–73.
165. MS Minutes, Lexington Presbytery, V (1811–13), 27, 65 (Union Theological Seminary Library, Richmond, Va.).
166. *Minutes of the General Assembly of the Presbyterian Church, . . . 1789–1820*, 582.
167. *Ibid.*, 585–86, 601.
168. MS Minutes, Lexington Presbytery, VI (1814–17), 52–55.

the Virginia clergy in general"; and (2) that since his return to the state he had "made several unwarrantable and unchristian charges against many of the members of the Presbyterian Church in relation to slavery."[169]

When Lexington Presbytery met on December 27, 1815, only four of its thirteen ministers and four elders were present; nevertheless, Bourne was placed on trial. Two witnesses supported the first charge. The Rev. John D. Paxton testified that the defendant told the General Assembly of 1815 that "he had seen a professor of religion, perhaps he said a preacher[,] driving slaves through a certain town in Virginia." However, when asked to name the person, Bourne refused to do so. The second witness, Mr. Robert Herron, testified that Bourne said that he had cited an instance at the last assembly of a preacher who tied up his slave and repeatedly whipped him.[170] In response to the first charge, Bourne presented as a witness the Rev. John McCue, and put to him the following question: "Did you about three years ago ride to Madison County, and purchase two Negro men[,] one woman[,] and two children, and with the latter one before and the other behind you, stop at my house in Port Republic; alight with the two children; and did I not walk with you thence to Wm Craig's in company with these Negroes? Answer[:] I did all this."[171]

In support of the second charge, one witness and three letters were offered. The same Robert Herron "testified that he thinks he has heard Mr. Bourne say he believed it to be impossible that any one could be a Christian and a slaveholder; that slaveholders were all a set of Negro thieves."[172] Then three letters which Bourne had written to the Rev. A. B. Davidson during July and August of the preceding summer were read. In them the author argued that according to the Bible, no person could be a Christian and yet hold slaves. He further maintained that a slave-trader was a thief.[173] In reply to the second charge, Bourne appealed not only to the Bible; in particular, he cited a note appended to the 142d question in the

169. *Ibid.*, 54–55.
170. *Ibid.*, 59–62.
171. *Ibid.*, 63.
172. *Ibid.*, 63–64.
173. *Ibid.*, 64–94. At one time A. B. Davidson, a slaveholder, had apparently agreed in principle with Bourne's antislavery views. *Ibid.*, 75.

Larger Catechism, in which it was plainly affirmed that, according to several biblical texts cited, those who bought, sold, or owned slaves were men-stealers.[174]

In light of the testimony given, Lexington Presbytery concluded that George Bourne was unfit to remain one of its members, and therefore immediately deposed him "from the office of the Gospel Ministry."[175] From this decision Bourne appealed to the next General Assembly, which was to meet in May, 1816.

In the meantime, the deposed churchman published a vehement indictment of human bondage.[176] He climaxed a detailed analysis of slavery with the assertion that it was "a flagrant violation of every law of God, nature, and society."[177] Bourne's sharpest criticisms were directed against church leaders who professed to follow Jesus and yet owned their fellow men. "The most obdurate adherents of Slavery," he said, "are Preachers of the Gospel and Officers and Members of the church. A Son of Belial is easily convinced; he offers no palliative; he denounces, although he perpetuates the evil; . . . but Christians defend *Negro-stealing*."[178] Bourne contended that any churchman who owned slaves and would not emancipate them "ought . . . to be excommunicated from the Church of God."[179] He also argued that no congregation should tolerate a minister who would not abandon slaveholding.

When it came to getting rid of human bondage, Bourne was no less radical. To the question, "How shall we expel the evil?" he replied, "Colonization is wholly impracticable."[180] Nor did he believe that the remedy lay in what was called gradual emancipation. "The system is so entirely corrupt," said Bourne, "that it admits of no cure, but by a total and immediate, abolition."[181]

This pungent attack upon Virginia slaveholders, with special attention to Presbyterian preachers (many of whom owned slaves), infuriated members of Lexington Presbytery, and they earnestly

---

174. *Ibid.*, 96. Interestingly, the presbytery explicitly denied that the note in question formed any part of the Westminster Confession of Faith.
175. *Ibid.*, 97.
176. *The Book and Slavery Irreconcilable* (Philadelphia, 1816). Among other antislavery writings, Bourne made extensive use of David Rice's tract, *Slavery Inconsistent with Justice and Good Policy*.
177. *The Book and Slavery Irreconcilable*, 106.
178. *Ibid.*, 8.   179. *Ibid.*, 88.
180. *Ibid.*, 134 n.   181. *Ibid.*, Postscript, 10.

hoped that the General Assembly of 1816 would uphold their action against Bourne. That assembly, however, did not act upon the appeal, because Lexington had not transmitted to that judicatory a certified copy of its proceedings in the case. But on hearing the case in 1817, the assembly reversed the presbytery's sentence on the ground "that the charges ... were not fully substantiated, and that, if they had been, the sentence was too severe."[182] Accordingly, Lexington Presbytery was instructed to "commence the trial anew."[183]

A few days after that decision was rendered, Bourne wrote a letter from Germantown, Pennsylvania, to Lexington Presbytery, contritely apologizing "for everything" in his attitude or statements which might have offended his Virginia brethren. "I hope," he added, "the Presbytery will receive this acknowledgement, both as the proof of my regret and as ample reparation, that the whole subject may forever be obliterated." He then requested dismissal to some other presbytery "which chuses to receive me into their communion."[184] The churchmen of Lexington completely disregarded the apology, and at their session of September 1, 1817, reinstated the case, added four new charges to the two original charges, and cited Bourne to appear for retrial at the next session of the presbytery. Among the new charges was the claim, of which much was made, that the defendant in June, 1815, had authorized the purchase of a horse for which he later refused to pay.[185]

Bourne gave two reasons for not attending a retrial: first, that his life would be in danger if he returned to Virginia; second, that even if he did attend he would not receive a fair trial.[186] Lexington

182. *Minutes of the General Assembly of the Presbyterian Church,* ... *1789–1820*, 646.

183. Writing to the Rev. Samuel Houston of Natural Bridge, Virginia, the Rev. Conrad Speece reported that Lexington Presbytery had been "severely handled at the General Assembly [of 1817] for deposing him [Bourne] formerly [1815] by a very small number of our members," and he added, "I have pretty well made up my mind to have nothing to do in Bourne's [second] trial at a very thin meeting of Presbytery." Speece to Houston, December 23, 1817 (MS Collection, Pennsylvania Historical Society). I am indebted to Professor David E. Swift of Wesleyan University for bringing this letter to my attention.

184. MS Minutes, Lexington Presbytery, VI, 153–54.

185. *Ibid.,* 152, 155–60. Inasmuch as this horse deal was considered highly important, it seems strange that it received no attention in the first trial.

186. Bourne did, however, reply to the charges in a letter, which he asked to have recorded in the minutes. *Ibid.,* 25, 31–35.

Presbytery devoted much of its next three meetings to hearing testimony against Bourne, and finally, on April 23, 1818, once more deposed him from the ministry.[187] This time, to the great relief of Virginia Presbyterians, the General Assembly of 1818 sustained Lexington's verdict.[188]

Although an outcast from the Presbyterian Church, George Bourne became a powerful force in the northern abolitionist crusade of the 1830's. Long before William Lloyd Garrison proclaimed the doctrine of immediate universal emancipation, he had explicitly espoused it. Furthermore, while Garrison was still pinning his hopes to colonization, Bourne had renounced it. Writing to George Bourne's son, Theodore, in 1858, Garrison said:

> I confess my early and large indebtedness to him for enabling me to apprehend, with irresistible clearness, the inherent sinfulness of slavery under all circumstances, and its utter incompatibility with the spirit of Christianity. . . . Mightily did he aid the Antislavery cause in its earliest stages by his advocacy of the doctrine of immediate and unconditional emancipation. . . . Never has slavery had a more indomitable foe or freedom a truer friend.[189]

It has sometimes been said that even though the General Assembly of 1818 did uphold Bourne's conviction, it at the same time passed a special committee's report which took a strong antislavery position.[190] From this some seem to have drawn the conclusion that Bourne's dismissal from the Presbyterian ministry was due less to his antislavery views than to other factors. Unquestionably Bourne was a polemicist who, as his *The Book and Slavery* reveals, often employed highly abrasive rhetoric, especially against "Negro-stealing" clergymen. Nevertheless, the assembly's antislavery stance was considerably less rigorous than has generally been assumed.

---

187. *Ibid.*, VII, 47.
188. *Minutes of the General Assembly of the Presbyterian Church, . . . 1789–1820*, 682.
189. Theodore Bourne, "George Bourne, The Pioneer of American Antislavery," *Methodist Quarterly Review*, LXIV, 69.
190. For the report in full, see *Minutes of the General Assembly of the Presbyterian Church, . . . 1789–1820*, 692–94. Members of the committee were Ashbel Green (Philadelphia), George A. Baxter (Virginia), and Dyer Burgess (Ohio). Both Green and Baxter were conservative on the slavery question.

The report denounced chattel slavery "as a gross violation of the most precious and sacred rights of human nature; as utterly inconsistent with the law of God, . . . and as totally irreconcilable with the spirit and principles of the gospel of Christ." However, the rest of the report was predominantly concessive in spirit toward slaveholders. Churchmen in the free states were urged "to forbear harsh censures" of their southern brethren who were "really using all their influence, and all their endeavours" to abolish the slave system as soon as it could safely be accomplished in the interest of all concerned. The report particularly emphasized the danger to both masters and slaves that would result from immediate and wholesale emancipation. The closing portion of the report contained three recommendations to Presbyterians: (1) that they persevere in instructing slaves in the tenets of Christianity; (2) that they seek to prevent all cruelty in the treatment of bondsmen; and (3) that they heartily cooperate with the American Colonization Society. The third recommendation was highly significant, since it implicitly predicated the widely held belief that the freedmen could never be granted equality with whites in America.

It is clear therefore that, except for its theoretical arraignment of slavery, the assembly's antislavery action was, on the whole, gentle and cautious. Even though it looked with favor upon eventual total abolition of the slave system, it revealed no burning desire to bring it about in the near future. In short, the assembly's moderate platform fell far short of what Bourne had advocated in *The Book and Slavery*.

At least one southerner, who served as a commissioner in the General Assembly of 1818, came back to his native Virginia with an increased desire to hasten the process of emancipation. That man was John D. Paxton, then pastor of a church in Norfolk. In 1823 he accepted the pastorate of Cumberland Church (South Appomattox), which owned some seventy Negroes, who were hired out as the main means of paying the minister's salary.[191] With the approval of several of his leading members, Paxton tried to secure the manumission of these slaves, but his efforts were fruitless. He

---

191. John D. Paxton, *Letters on Slavery; Addressed to the Cumberland Congregation, Virginia* (Lexington, Ky., 1833), 11 n.

then endeavored to organize an auxiliary of the American Colonization Society, but this too met with opposition. In 1826 he and his wife freed all of their slaves and sent them to Liberia, and this act met with even more objection. With the hope of clarifying his position and allaying criticism, Paxton began a series of articles in the Richmond *Family Visitor*, a Presbyterian weekly, but by the time the third article appeared the dissent was so widespread that the editor secured his consent to stop the series.[192]

This did not close the issue for the embattled minister. Important officials of the church subjected him to so much harassment that he finally submitted his resignation and moved to Kentucky. Several years later Paxton published *Letters on Slavery*, which he addressed to the Cumberland Congregation. His antislavery reasoning was profound, but it probably convinced few of his former parishioners.

The capitulation of Virginia Presbyterians to the system of Negro slavery is strikingly illustrated in the attitude of John Holt Rice, a distinguished preacher, educator, and journalist.[193] As editor of the *Christian Monitor* (1815–17) and of its successor, the *Virginia Evangelical and Literary Magazine* (1818–28), Rice exerted great influence upon his fellow churchmen for many years. These journals mirror a remarkable change in his antislavery attitude. In January, 1817, when he published a spirited challenge to bondage by a Quaker, he prefaced the essay with a note demanding immediate action to remove the cancerous institution from southern society. Spurning a prevalent idea that the evil of slavery would somehow cure itself, he said: "We must make exertion to procure amendment. It is folly to delay, while the disease is becoming every hour more inveterate."[194] By July, 1819, Rice had lost his aggressive spirit. In introducing an article by "C" (Conrad Speece), entitled "Thoughts on Slavery," he spoke of bondage as "a subject of great delicacy and difficulty." While he would not flinch from dealing

---

192. *Ibid.*, 13. The text of the third article, which was especially unpalatable to slaveholders, is reprinted in Appendix A, 195–204.

193. William Maxwell, *A Memoir of the Rev. John Holt Rice, D.D.* (Philadelphia, 1835); P. B. Price, *The Life of the Reverend John Holt Rice, D.D.* (Richmond, 1963).

194. *Christian Monitor*, II (January 18, 1817), 147. For the Quaker's essay, see *ibid.*, 147–54. Rice himself had been a slaveholder since 1804.

with it out of a fear of the consequences, neither would he "rush into measures equally ruinous to ourselves and our bondsmen."[195]

The bitter debate over the Missouri Question (1819–20) made the Virginia editor still more reluctant to denounce the bondage system. "We freely confess," he wrote in 1821, "that it is beyond our powers to point out the way of deliverance from this evil."[196] By December, 1825, Rice was virtually a captive to the established order. "We are no advocate of slavery," he once more insisted. "But we do wish that christian philanthropists would observe the wise caution of the Apostles on this subject.... It is most obvious that immediate emancipation would be madness. It would be turning loose on society fifteen hundred thousand lawless, ignorant and depraved beings, who have never been accustomed to reflection and self-government. Gradual emancipation would mend the matter but little, unless measures be adopted to improve the moral condition of the race."[197] In 1827 Rice argued that it was a mistake for preachers to discuss the slavery question. They should, he said, confine their attention to Christianizing masters and slaves and leave the slavery question entirely to the state. "I believe," he wrote a close friend, "that it never has fared well with either church or state, when the church meddled with temporal affairs."[198] Undoubtedly the eminent churchman had retreated basically from his antislavery views of 1817.

On the other hand, Rice remained a zealous believer in the desirability of sending all free Negroes to Africa.[199] While he was moderator of the General Assembly, in 1819, that judicatory adopted a resolution strongly commending the American Colonization Society. A particularly significant portion of the resolution expressly claimed that black people could never be elevated to a plane of equality with whites in America.[200] An "insuperable ob-

---

195. *Virginia Evangelical and Literary Magazine,* II (July, 1819), 293. For Speece's article, see *ibid.,* 293–303.

196. "On the Moral Condition of Slaves," *Evangelical and Literary Magazine,* IV (June, 1821), 309. After Vol. III, "Virginia" was dropped from the title of the *Magazine.*

197. "Reflections on the Close of the Year," *Literary and Evangelical Magazine,* VIII (December, 1825), 663–64. This form of the title of the *Magazine* began in 1824.

198. Maxwell, *A Memoir of the Rev. John Holt Rice, D.D.,* 307.

199. Louis Weeks III, "John Holt Rice and the American Colonization Society," *Journal of Presbyterian History,* XLVI (March, 1968), 26–41.

200. *Minutes of the General Assembly of the Presbyterian Church, . . . 1789–1820,* 710.

stacle" to such equality, said the assembly, was the African's "distinctive" color.

V

It is certain, then, that no communion in the South except the Society of Friends succeeded in disentangling itself from human bondage. The Baptist, Methodist, and Presbyterian bodies seriously compromised with domestic bondage from the outset of their antislavery efforts. They passed laudable resolutions against slavery, but at the same time continued to receive into membership owners of Negroes, and even to ordain slaveholders to the ministry. Inevitably this compromising process undermined their antislavery witness. There was, indeed, a small remnant of ministers in all three communions who stoutly contested this compromising policy, but they seemed powerless to change it. Despairing finally of achieving a slaveless church in the South, most of them migrated to the middle western frontier—especially Ohio, Indiana, and Illinois—where they helped to prevent the further spread of human servitude.

This exodus of antislavery churchmen left southern Christianity all the more vulnerable to the leavening influence of the proslavery factions within the churches. In January, 1798, Bishop Asbury observed in his *Journal* that slavery in Virginia would perhaps last "for ages," because there was "not a sufficient sense of religion nor of liberty to destroy it." Pointing an accusing finger at his fellow Protestants, he continued: "Methodists, Baptists, and Presbyterians, in the highest flights of rapturous piety, still maintain and defend it."[201] The bishop's valid criticism of religion in Virginia was no less applicable to religion in all the other slave states. In truth, the demon of slavery was already steadily capturing the ecclesiastical bodies in the South before the advent of the nineteenth century.

But even though the churches increasingly yielded to slavery, did not the South's manumission societies, most of which were led by dedicated Christians, generate and maintain an effective witness against the bondage system? Many historians have so believed, and in support of their belief have often appealed to a statistical report

201. Clark, Potts, and Payton, eds., *The Journal and Letters of Francis Asbury*, II, 151.

which the great abolitionist Quaker, Benjamin Lundy, published in *The Genius of Universal Emancipation*. In the year 1827, according to Lundy, there were "about" 106 antislavery societies, with 5,150 members, in the slave states, as against 24 such societies, with 1,475 members, in the free states.[202]

In assessing the significance of the Lundy statistics (assuming their general reliability), one must bear in mind some pertinent facts. First, not a single one of the 106 manumission societies in the slave states was located below North Carolina and Tennessee. This means that the great cotton states in the lower South, where proslavery sentiment was overwhelming, were untouched by these societies. But even in the states of the upper South the antislavery societies were confined mainly to areas in which the system of bondage was comparatively limited. North Carolina's fifty societies were concentrated almost entirely in four Piedmont counties— Alamance, Guilford, Chatham, and Randolph—where slaves were proportionately fewer than in the eastern counties of the state. Likewise Tennessee's twenty-five societies were largely confined to its eastern counties, where, on the average, there was roughly only one slave to twelve whites.[203] Thus 75 of Lundy's 106 manumission societies were, in these two states, located outside the main orbit of slaveholders. There is no reason to believe that most of the remaining 31 societies—scattered widely over Delaware, Maryland, the District of Columbia, Virginia, and Kentucky—were any less isolated from the major zones of slavery.

Second, the chief organizers and leaders of the 106 societies were predominantly Quakers, such as Lundy and Charles Osborn, and not the spokesmen of the large slaveholding denominations.[204] Osborn was chiefly instrumental in organizing the North Carolina Manumission Society. Throughout its history (1816–34) every an-

202. *Genius of Universal Emancipation*, October 14, 1827. It should be noted that Lundy laid no claim to statistical accuracy. "It appears," he stated in his preface to the report, "that the number of antislavery societies, together with their members, are about as follows." This was fair warning that his figures were merely rough estimates.

203. Asa Earl Martin, "The Anti-Slavery Societies of Tennessee," *Tennessee Historical Magazine*, I (December, 1915), 279.

204. Merton L. Dillon, *Benjamin Lundy and the Struggle for Negro Freedom* (Urbana, Ill., 1966), Chaps. 2–3; Ruth Anna Ketring, *Charles Osborn in the Anti-Slavery Movement* (Columbus, Ohio, 1937).

nual state convention met in a Quaker church, a fact which clearly indicates that the moving spirits of the organization were Friends.[205] A further indication of Quaker influence is the fact that the society's local auxiliaries were confined overwhelmingly to what was known as the "Quaker District," with greatest density in Guilford and Randolph counties. Osborn, a vigorous antislavery crusader, also took the lead in organizing, in 1815, the Tennessee Manumission Society, which was second in strength only to its sister society in North Carolina. Significantly, all eight of its original members were Friends.[206] Although several Presbyterian ministers (notably John Rankin and Jesse Lockhart) lent their full support to the society, it always remained largely dependent upon Quaker leadership.

Third, the manumission organizations (both state and local) rarely maintained sufficient numerical strength to exert much influence upon public opinion. They occasionally issued petitions and published pamphlets, but little ever came of them. Their memberships were not only generally small, but were in almost constant flux. This was true even of the strongest state body, the North Carolina Manumission Society. In 1822, six years after it began, this society failed to muster a quorum in its two conventions of that year. Two years later the convention voted by eleven to six to dissolve the state organization. Owing to the tenacity of a few members, however, it managed to weather the crisis, and even to gather considerable strength over the next four years.[207] Nevertheless, it began to decline sharply after 1829 and went out of business in 1834.

Fourth, many of the manumission societies, especially after the organization of the American Colonization Society in 1816, contained members who favored the idea of sending blacks, when freed, to another country. For a time at least, even Benjamin Lundy favored colonization. For a short while, colonizationists dominated the North Carolina Manumission Society, causing a temporary split in the organization. We are told by a leading historian of

---

205. Henry M. Wagstaff, ed., *Minutes of the North Carolina Manumission Society, 1816–1834* (Chapel Hill, 1934), 4.
206. Ketring, *Charles Osborn*, 24.
207. Wagstaff, ed., *Minutes of the North Carolina Manumission Society*, 69.

Quakerism that "most American Friends of the early republic" shared the belief that blacks and whites alike would fare better if the former could go somewhere else.[208]

Fifth, the manumission societies generally maintained that slavery should be abolished gradually, not suddenly and universally. The Quakers had employed the gradualistic method successfully in eradicating slavery from their church, and they assumed that it would be effective also in ridding the nation of the bondage system. But a method that was effective in their own small and highly self-disciplined Society proved largely ineffective in a socially heterogeneous South that was massively expanding its slave institution.[209]

In view of such limitations, one could hardly expect the manumission societies to check significantly the growth of slavery. At any rate, they failed to do so, even in North Carolina and Tennessee, where 75 of Lundy's 106 societies were operating in 1827. Between 1810 and 1830 North Carolina's slave population increased by 76,777, but its free Negro population had an increase of only 9,277. During the same period, Tennessee added 97,068 slaves as against 3,258 free blacks. A similar situation is evident if one includes a larger number of slave states. Consider, for example, the South Atlantic states—Delaware, Maryland, District of Columbia, Virginia, North and South Carolina, Georgia, and Florida—where more than sixty per cent of the nation's slightly more than two million bondsmen were located in 1830. Between 1790 and 1810 those states had a gain of 342,306 slaves, whereas only 64,755 blacks were added to the free Negro population. During the next two decades (1810–30), there was an increment of 392,199 slaves as against an increase of only 56,284 free Negroes.[210] Significantly, moreover, free Negroes increased at a slower rate in the last two decades than in the first two.[211]

Consequently, neither the churches nor the manumission so-

208. Drake, *Quakers and Slavery*, 121.
209. After I had written this evaluation of the southern manumission societies, Gordon E. Finnie published his "The Antislavery Movement in the Upper South Before 1840," *Journal of Southern History*, XXXV (August, 1969), 319–42, revealing that both of us had arrived at similar conclusions, though working independently.
210. *Negro Population, 1790–1915* (Department of Commerce, Bureau of the Census, Washington, 1918), 57.
211. In the United States as a whole, according to John Hope Franklin, the rate of free Negro growth "fell sharply" after 1810, and this trend "continued down to 1860." *From Slavery to Freedom* (3d ed., New York, 1967), 217.

cieties were stemming the rising tide of slavery in the South. Yet until well into the twentieth century many historians held that the southern antislavery movement was continuing to gather strength until it was arrested by the emergence of radical abolitionism in the free states. "During the two decades following the establishment of the Federal Union in 1787 the abolition movement almost prevailed," said Thomas E. Drake in 1950.[212] So far as the South was concerned, that claim is open to serious question. Actually, as already demonstrated, southern emancipationism was, on the whole, losing its vitality in those two decades. Aside from Quakerism, the leading communions were increasingly surrendering to the growing proslavery movement. Antislavery in the South was thus a lost cause long before the rise of radical abolitionism above the Potomac.

---

212. *Quakers and Slavery,* 100. See also Theodore M. Whitfield, *Slavery Agitation in Virginia, 1829–1832* (Baltimore, 1930), 58, 133; Martin, "The Anti-Slavery Societies of Tennessee," *Tennessee Historical Magazine,* I, 261.

Chapter II

DEBATE AND DIVISION

The South's "peculiar institution" increased dramatically after 1800. Within the next three decades, more than one million blacks were added to the region's population.[1] In the meantime, however, neither the churches nor the manumission societies offered effective resistance to the growth of human bondage. The system of Negro slavery was thus destined to continue indefinitely unless some powerful extra-southern force could be pitted against it.

Therein lay the significance of the antislavery movement that arose in the free states in the 1830's. The single most powerful agent in that dynamic movement was the American Anti-Slavery Society, launched in Philadelphia on December 4, 1833, with Arthur Tappan, a New York merchant, as its first president. Those playing leading roles in organizing the body included William Lloyd Garrison, Lewis Tappan, Samuel J. May, Elizur Wright, George Bourne, and John Greenleaf Whittier. Vitally important to the society's special mission was the ringing Declaration of Sentiments, drafted by Garrison, militant editor of the *Liberator* and organizer, in 1831, of the New England Anti-Slavery Society.[2]

Fundamentally, the Declaration proclaimed, first, that slavery was a sinful and criminal institution for which the nation ought immediately to repent; second, that the slaves "ought instantly to be set free, and brought under the protection of law"; third, that colonization could be no substitute for the immediate and total abolition of slavery; and, fourth, that black Americans should be accorded the same privileges and opportunities as white Americans.

The Declaration eschewed violence as a method of eradicating human bondage. Instead, it maintained that the people of the free states were obligated "to remove slavery by moral and political ac-

1. *Negro Population, 1790–1915* (Department of Commerce, Bureau of the Census, Washington, 1918), 57.
2. The Declaration of Sentiments is reprinted in H. Shelton Smith, Robert T. Handy, and Lefferts A. Loetscher, *American Christianity: An Historical Interpretation with Representative Documents* (2 vols., New York, 1960–63), II, 186–90.

tion, as prescribed in the Constitution of the United States." Nor did the Congress have any right to interfere with slavery within the bounds of a slaveholding state. On the other hand, "Congress has a right, and is solemnly bound, to suppress the domestic slave trade between the several states, and to abolish slavery in those portions of our territory which the Constitution has placed under its exclusive jurisdiction."

To deliver the land "from its deadliest curse . . . and to secure to the colored population of the United States all the rights and privileges which belong to them as men, and as Americans," the organizers of the American Anti-Slavery Society resolved, "under the guidance and by the help of Almighty God," to set afoot local abolition societies wherever possible; to enlist pulpit and press in the cause of Negro freedom; to place in the field a band of antislavery agents; and to circulate unsparingly antislavery tracts and periodicals. To a remarkable degree they kept the faith, despite fierce opposition. By May, 1835, two hundred and twenty-five auxiliary societies were in operation.[3] The leaders of this movement, especially prior to 1840, were predominantly Protestant evangelicals. Some of the most dedicated antislavery evangelicals, moreover, were ex-southerners, such as William Henry Brisbane, John Rankin, and James G. Birney.[4]

Even though the agents of the American Anti-Slavery Society were non-violent in their attack upon human bondage, leaders of the South, both political and religious, mounted an intensive campaign to persuade the people of the North to curb their activities. The South Carolina legislature, for instance, adopted a committee report on December 16, 1836, charging that abolitionism was "treason against the Union." The legislators thus called upon northern governments to "suppress all those associations within their respective limits purporting to be Abolition Societies," and to "make it highly penal to print, publish and distribute" any

---

3. Austin Willey, *History of the Antislavery Cause in State and Nation* (Portland, Maine, 1886), 35. See also, Gilbert H. Barnes, *The Anti-Slavery Impulse, 1830–1844* (New York, 1933), Chaps. 8, 10; Louis Filler, *The Crusade Against Slavery, 1830–1860* (New York, 1960), 66–70; Dwight L. Dumond, *Antislavery: The Crusade For Freedom in America* (Ann Arbor, 1961), Chaps. 18, 21, 23, 32.

4. Gordon E. Finnie, "The Antislavery Movement in the South, 1787–1836: Its Rise and Decline, and Its Contribution to Abolitionism in the West" (typed Ph.D. dissertation, Duke University, 1962), Chaps. 5–6.

newspaper or tract which tended to incite slave insurrections.[5] Within the next three months, six other southern states passed similar measures. Virginians were so excited that thirty-six counties and several cities enacted resolutions against abolitionism.[6]

Significantly, these southern protests met with much sympathy in the North. From Boston to Philadelphia many cities passed spirited resolutions denouncing abolitionists as irresponsible agitators. For example, in the fall of 1835 a group in Syracuse, New York, resolved "that we look upon the abolitionists as misguided men, and many of them as fanatics and incendiaries of a dangerous order, whose exertions threaten to involve us in a state of anarchy, disorder, disunion." These Syracusians also maintained "that the people of the north rest under the most solemn obligations of duty to their southern brethren to adopt the most efficient measures to arrest the mad course of the abolitionists."[7] In view of such outbursts from angry northerners, it is not surprising that militant abolitionists were often given rough receptions in the 1830's.[8]

The growth of abolitionism, despite vigorous northern resistance, signaled southern churchmen that trouble lay ahead for friends of human bondage. Nor did they fail to recognize the challenge involved in the fact that the antislavery reformers were basing their crusade upon democratic and religious conviction. "With entire confidence in the overruling justice of God, we plant ourselves upon the Declaration of our Independence and the truths of divine revelation as upon the Everlasting Rock," proclaimed the Declaration of Sentiments. Consequently any effective reply to abolitionists had to be essentially moral and religious in nature, and therefore southern ministers were drawn into the controversy, even though they had insisted for a generation that slavery fell exclusively within the jurisdiction of the state. Northern and southern ministers of the gospel thus early became embroiled in debate, a debate so acrid

5. "Committee on Federal Relations," *Acts and Resolutions of the General Assembly of the State of South Carolina* (Columbia, S.C., 1836), 26–28.
6. *Journal of the House of Delegates of the Commonwealth of Virginia, 1835* (Richmond, 1835), Document No. 12, 5–24.
7. *Ibid.*, 29. For many similar resolutions, see *ibid.*, 25–38.
8. Bertram Wyatt-Brown, *Lewis Tappan and the Evangelical War Against Slavery* (Cleveland, 1969), 151–62; Leonard L. Richards, *"Gentlemen of Property and Standing": Anti-Abolition Mobs in Jacksonian America* (New York, 1970).

on both sides that three of Protestantism's largest denominations split apart before midcentury.

I

In 1818 the General Assembly of the Presbyterian Church denounced slavery "as utterly inconsistent with the law of God" and "as totally irreconcilable with the spirit and principles of the gospel of Christ," and then fell silent on the subject for the next seventeen years. From the late 1820's onward, judicatories in Ohio, Indiana, and Illinois had urged the assembly to take more resolute action against human bondage, but a coalition of southerners and northern conservatives had always been able to block any further consideration of the vexing subject.[9] Emerging abolitionism, however, became an increasing threat to this policy of repression. Theodore Dwight Weld, a Congregationalist and an antislavery lobbyist in the General Assembly of 1835, estimated that almost a fourth of the commissioners (delegates) were avowed immediate abolitionists.[10] They and their allies managed to get the antislavery memorials and petitions read before the assembly of that year. One petition alone had been signed by more than a thousand women of the city of New York.[11] The most radical document came from the Presbytery of Chillicothe in Ohio.[12] Of its nine resolutions, three were especially significant. One charged that to buy, sell, or own a slave was "a heinous sin," and it urged church courts to proceed against those guilty of such acts. Another declared that it was "unjust and cruel" to offer Negroes their freedom only on the condition that they leave America, and that any Presbyterian who

9. Victor B. Howard, "The Anti-Slavery Movement in the Presbyterian Church, 1835–1861" (typed Ph.D. dissertation, Ohio State University, 1961), 13–16; C. Bruce Staiger, "Abolitionism and the Presbyterian Schism of 1837–1838," *Mississippi Valley Historical Review*, XXXVI (December, 1949), 392.
10. Weld to Elizur Wright, Jr., June 6, 1835, in Gilbert H. Barnes and Dwight L. Dumond, eds., *Letters of Theodore Dwight Weld, Angelina Grimké Weld, and Sarah Grimké, 1822–1835* (2 vols., New York, 1934), I, 224.
11. Charles Hodge, "The General Assembly of 1835," *Biblical Repertory*, VII (July, 1835), 451.
12. Since the late 1820's Chillicothe had been adopting radical antislavery resolutions almost annually. Robert C. Galbraith, *History of the Chillicothe Presbytery. From its Organization in 1799 to 1889* (Chillicothe, Ohio, 1889), 103, 105, 124, 130. Among this presbytery's more militant abolitionists were John Rankin, James Gilliland, and James H. Dickey, all native southerners.

did this should be censured by his church. Still another affirmed that any Presbyterian who refused to sit with blacks in church or at the communion table "ought, upon conviction, to be suspended from the Lord's table until he repent."[13]

To determine what response should be made to the memorials, the General Assembly formed a special committee, with the Rev. James Hoge as chairman. In due course this committee submitted a report, declaring that slavery was "an evil of immense magnitude" and that Christians were obligated "to use all proper means" for its abolition as speedily as it could be done consistent with the good of all concerned.[14] After brief discussion, the whole matter was referred to a committee, of which Samuel Miller of Princeton Theological Seminary was chairman, with instructions to report to the next General Assembly.[15]

The prospect that human bondage would be a topic of discussion at the next assembly aroused immediate apprehension among both northern conservatives and southerners. As the months passed, a major denominational crisis appeared imminent. Abolitionists were denounced in the North as well as the South. The Philadelphia *Presbyterian*, an outspoken organ of social and religious conservatism, had long believed that colonization was "the only hope for Africans," and it deplored the American Anti-Slavery Society's opposition to sending blacks out of the country. While professing to "hate the system of bondage as the offspring of hell," the journal reserved its chief anathemas for abolitionists, who, in its judgment, were a disruptive force in both church and state.[16] The Synod of Philadelphia shared the antiabolitionist sentiments of the *Presbyterian*.[17] Despite the attacks of the conservatives, abolitionism made steady headway in Presbyterian judicatories, notably in western New York and the Middle West.[18]

13. Hodge, "The General Assembly of 1835," *Biblical Repertory*, VII, 451. All nine resolutions are printed in this essay.

14. *Ibid.*, 452.

15. *Minutes of the General Assembly of the Presbyterian Church in the United States of America*, . . . *1835* (Philadelphia, 1836), 33. Besides Miller, members of the committee were James Hoge (Ohio), Nathan S. S. Beman (New York), James H. Dickey (Ohio), and John Witherspoon (South Carolina).

16. *Presbyterian* (Philadelphia), June 5, 1833; August 13, 1835.

17. Howard, "The Anti-Slavery Movement in the Presbyterian Church," 19.

18. *Ibid.*, 20–21; Zebulon Crocker, *The Catastrophe of the Presbyterian Church in 1837* (New Haven, 1838), 65–66.

Southern Presbyterians, alarmed by antislavery developments within the denomination, fiercely assailed the doctrine and tactics of abolitionism. Taking the lead, the Synod of Virginia in the fall of 1835 bluntly repudiated the claim that slavery was necessarily sinful and ought to be abolished immediately, dubbing it a "dogma" contrary "to the plainest principles of common sense and common humanity and to the clearest authority of the word of God." The synod also maintained that it was the duty of ministers to follow the example of Jesus and his apostles "in abstaining from all interference" with slavery as established by the state and to confine themselves "strictly to their province" of inculcating the respective duties of masters and slaves as taught in the Bible.[19]

By the opening months of 1836, Presbyterian spokesmen in Georgia and South Carolina were frantic over what might happen at the approaching assembly. Early in April, Hopewell Presbytery (embracing Atlanta and much other Georgia territory), after having put forth a biblical, apostolical, and confessional apology for human bondage, argued that slavery, being a political institution, was "not a lawful, or constitutional subject of discussion, much less of action by the General Assembly." The presbytery instructed its delegates "to use all Christian means to prevent the discussion of domestic slavery in the Assembly," and to walk out if proabolitionist legislation should be passed. Hopewell also warned that if the assembly enacted any laws which interfered with domestic slavery, it would "regard itself independent of the General Assembly of the Presbyterian Church."[20] A few days later Charleston Union Presbytery likewise voted that slavery was "a political Institution, with which Ecclesiastical Judiciaries have not the smallest right to interfere," and instructed its commissioners to withdraw from the General Assembly if, despite their opposition, the slavery question should be injected into its deliberations. Charleston furthermore advised southern delegates as a whole to take counsel together "as to the course most suitable to be pursued in this crisis."[21]

19. MS Minutes of the Synod of Virginia, October 24, 1835, 138–39 (Union Theological Seminary Library, Richmond, Va.).
20. *Charleston Observer*, April 16, 1836.
21. *Ibid.*, April 9, 1836. On April 30, 1836, an anonymous contribution appeared in the *Observer*, entitled "The South One and Indivisible," in which the author elaborated fifteen reasons why the General Assembly should not discuss "the subject of the morality of slavery." Reportedly the document had "been extensively examined

Presbyterian leaders in North Carolina and Virginia did not appear as distraught as their brethren in the lower South, but they were no less determined to block debate on the slavery question at the next assembly. Amasa Converse, editor of the *Southern Religious Telegraph,* reflected their prevailing sentiment when he said that southern Presbyterians would "never permit the Assembly or any other judicatory, to regulate their consciences on the morality of slavery." He predicted that if they were challenged to debate the slavery question with their northern brethren, they would "unanimously withdraw from the Assembly."[22]

By this time many northern spokesmen of the denomination had come to fear that if the Miller committee should take a stand against slavery, southern delegates might well bolt the General Assembly. The powerful Charles Hodge of Princeton Theological Seminary evidently shared this anxiety, for just before the assembly of 1836 convened he published an able article in the *Biblical Repertory,* expressly warning that if that judicatory were to adopt the doctrine of abolitionism a division of the church would result forthwith.[23] He argued at length that abolitionism was erroneous in doctrine and evil in its impact upon both church and nation. He insisted that slavery was indubitably biblical and that consequently abolitionism erred in pronouncing it necessarily sinful. To take that position amounted to "a direct impeachment of the word of God." Hodge even contended that "the great duty of the South is not emancipation; but improvement" of the life and lot of the slave.[24]

That remarkable deliverance on the eve of the assembly was as manna from heaven to proslavery southerners; they could not have wished for anything better at this crucial moment. Other influential northerners were also expressing opinions which would incline the assembly to beware of taking any action on the slavery question. Like presbyteries in the South, the Presbytery of New Brunswick (New Jersey) declared that slavery was "a civil" relation with which

---

and approved in the South, as a paper suitable to be handed in by the Southern delegation, in case the next Assembly shall show a disposition to discuss the subject of the morality of slavery."

22. *Southern Religious Telegraph* (Richmond), April 1, 1836.
23. "Slavery," *Biblical Repertory,* VIII (April, 1836), 301–2. Reportedly reprints of Hodge's article were circulated in the General Assembly of 1836.
24. *Ibid.,* 274–79, 297–98, 301.

the church had "no right to interfere."[25] The First Presbytery of New York considered it "highly inexpedient for the next General Assembly ... to adopt any measure whatever touching the question of slavery."[26] Only five days before the assembly opened, the editor of the *Presbyterian*, William M. Engles, told his readers that Presbyterians of the South were unalterably convinced that church judicatories had no right to interfere with the institution of slavery.[27]

This widespread pressure had its effect. When the General Assembly gathered at Pittsburgh in May, 1836, the Miller committee, with one exception, was ready with a report that capitulated to the South. Acknowledging that domestic bondage was too inseparably connected with state laws for a church judicatory properly to interfere with it, and conceding that any action on slavery by the assembly "would tend to distract and divide our churches," a majority of the committee "Resolved, That it is not expedient for the Assembly to take any further order in relation to this subject."[28] The dissenting member, James H. Dickey of Chillicothe Presbytery, countered with a minority report declaring that "the buying, selling, or holding of a human being as property, is, in the sight of God, a heinous sin, and ought to subject the doer of it to the censures of the church."[29] When the discussion began, John McElhenny of Virgina offered as a substitute for both reports a resolution which had been framed by the southern delegation, affirming "that the General Assembly have no authority to assume or exercise jurisdiction in regard to the existence of Slavery."[30] In the furious debate that followed it soon became clear that none of the three reports had enough support for adoption, and at this point James Hoge moved "that this whole subject be indefinitely postponed." His motion carried by a vote of 154 to 87.[31]

The assembly's evasive action greatly vexed southern spokesmen, who wanted a showdown decision on the question of supreme con-

25. *Presbyterian*, May 7, 1836.
26. *Ibid.*, April 30, 1836.
27. *Ibid.*, May 14, 1836. The editor may very well have read the document, "The South One and Indivisible," as published in the *Charleston Observer*, April 30, 1836.
28. *Minutes of the General Assembly of the Presbyterian Church in the United States of America, ... 1836* (Philadelphia, 1836), 248.
29. *Ibid.*, 250.   30. *Ibid.*, 271.
31. *Ibid.*, 272–73.

cern to them. "The decision to *postpone*," complained Amasa Converse, "settles nothing; it places the question on the ground of *expediency*, and it admits *the right* of the church to exercise jurisdiction on this subject [slavery]."[32] The crisis was by no means over; in fact, it might well have led to an early southern secession from the General Assembly if there had not been drastic ecclesiastical surgery performed by a coalition of northern conservatives and southerners. Two factors produced this surgical operation: faith and order, and slavery.

Over the past decade, northern Presbyterians had been increasingly agitated by two schools of thought, commonly styled "old school" and "new school."[33] The former demanded a strict subscription to Calvinism as set forth in the Westminster Confession of Faith, while the latter advocated a moderate version of Calvinism, of which Nathaniel Taylor of Yale was the leading exponent.[34] Several doctrines were bones of contention, but they stemmed mainly from conflicting theories of original sin.[35] Whereas the old school maintained that all mankind really sinned in Adam's first sin, the new school rejected that view as being incompatible with human freedom and moral responsibility.

The old school partisans complained that Taylorism was being filtered into Presbyterianism as a result of the Plan of Union, a plan which had been adopted in 1801 by the General Association of Connecticut (Congregational) and the General Assembly of the Presbyterian Church in order to promote a more effective missionary program in western New York and in the western states of the Union.[36] Under the Plan, a church of either communion might employ a minister from the other. Both communions were served

32. *Southern Religious Telegraph,* June 17, 1836.
33. Samuel J. Baird, *A History of the New School* (Philadelphia, 1868), Chaps. 22–27; Crocker, *The Catastrophe of the Presbyterian Church, in 1837,* Chaps. 10–11; Ezra H. Gillett, *History of the Presbyterian Church in the United States of America* (rev. ed., 2 vols., Philadelphia, 1864), II, Chap. 39; Ernest T. Thompson, *Presbyterians in the South,* I: *1607–1861* (Richmond, 1963), Chaps. 23–24.
34. For an excellent introduction to Taylor's religious thought, see Sidney E. Mead, *Nathaniel William Taylor, 1786–1858: A Connecticut Liberal* (Chicago, 1942).
35. Crocker, *The Catastrophe of the Presbyterian Church, in 1837,* Chaps. 9, 11–12; Baird, *A History of the New School,* Chap. 12; H. Shelton Smith, *Changing Conceptions of Original Sin: A Study in American Theology Since 1750* (New York, 1955), Chaps. 5–6.
36. The full text of the Plan is reprinted in Baird, *A History of the New School,* 155–57.

by the American Home Missionary Society and the American Education Society. Under these circumstances, new school doctrines inevitably penetrated Presbyterian churches. This fact became especially galling to rigid Calvinists because they had been a minority party in recent sessions of the General Assembly, and thus could not purge the denomination of alleged heretics. Twice they had been frustrated in their efforts to depose Albert Barnes, a bold Taylorite, from the ministry. Their second defeat came in the assembly of 1836.[37]

Henceforth northern leaders of the old school were determined to get rid of the new school element, either by separating from the General Assembly and organizing a new one of their own or by expelling their opponents from the existing body. They of course preferred the latter solution, but since this would require them to control the assembly they would need the full support of southern Presbyterians. Hitherto their southern brethren had been largely indifferent toward the doctrinal controversy, believing that it was chiefly a dispute over words or a power struggle. But in the last assembly the debate over slavery had disclosed to southern delegates that most of the abolitionists belonged to the new school party. Obviously it was clear to them that if the Taylorites were separated from the denomination, future assemblies would be less troubled by antislavery agitators.

On the afternoon that the assembly of 1836 adjourned, old school delegates from both sections met in conference to devise future tactics. They formed a committee of correspondence to consult conservatives and to take whatever steps seemed necessary. When the moderator of the assembly, John Witherspoon of South Carolina, emerged from the conference he reportedly told a friend, "The die is cast: the Church is to be divided."[38] Had he and other Southern delegates entered into some sort of agreement with old school leaders in the North to seek a division of Presbyterianism along doctrinal rather than geographical lines with a view to getting rid of Taylorism and abolitionism at a single stroke? Speculations vary at this point.[39]

37. *Minutes of the General Assembly of the Presbyterian Church in the United States of America, . . . 1836*, 268–70.
38. Gillett, *History of the Presbyterian Church*, II, 496 n.
39. For divergent opinions, see Staiger, "Abolitionism and the Presbyterian

But even if there was no such agreement at that time, the fact is that between then and the assembly of 1837 old school leaders in both sections seized every opportunity to prepare the way for united action against new schoolmen. As early as July, 1836, the committee of correspondence issued a call for a pre-assembly convention to frame measures by which to put an end to doctrinal controversy within the denomination.[40] About the same time the *Presbyterian*, a leading watchdog of orthodoxy, proposed a division of the church and urged a North-South thrust against Taylorism.[41] The suggestion was welcomed by at least two southern journals, the *Southern Christian Herald* of Columbia, South Carolina, and the Nashville *American Presbyterian*.[42]

During the fall of 1836 judicatories of the South continued to lambaste abolitionism as their major foe, but they now included new school theology as also a disturbing element in the church. Representative of this trend was an action taken by the Synod of Virginia in response to a paper drawn up by an able committee, of which George A. Baxter, professor of theology in Union Theological Seminary, was chairman. Whereas this body had previously refrained from taking sides in the doctrinal controversy raging in the North, it now expressly charged that the new school was introducing "ruinous error" into Presbyterianism by propagating unorthodox theories of original sin, regeneration, justification, and human ability.[43] The synod implicitly conceded, however, that Taylorism did not trouble the South nearly so much as abolitionism.[44] After quoting 1 Timothy 6:1–5 as decisive proof that human bondage was sanctioned by the word of God, Virginia declared that the General Assembly had no right to pronounce slaveholding sinful. Charging that abolitionism was criminal in its doctrines, the

---

Schism of 1837–1838," *Mississippi Valley Historical Review*, XXXVI, 402–3; Elwyn A. Smith, "The Role of the South in the Presbyterian Schism of 1837–38," *Church History*, XXIX (March, 1960), 49–50.

40. Staiger, "Abolitionism and the Presbyterian Schism of 1837–1838," 403.
41. *Presbyterian*, July 23, 1836.
42. *Ibid.*, August 13 and October 7, 1836.
43. MS Minutes of the Synod of Virginia, November 7, 1836, 176–79 (Union Theological Seminary Library, Richmond, Va.).
44. In fact, the South was solidly old school in doctrine with the exception of a handful of preachers located mostly in eastern Tennessee. Thompson, *Presbyterians in the South*, I, 353–61.

synod concluded that if the abolitionist could not be convinced of his error "the only scriptural remedy" was "to withdraw from such."[45] In specifying that remedy, the Virginians clearly implied that they already favored a division of the church on an ideological rather than a geographical basis. They further implied this by observing that "the likelihood of the necessity of any geographical division" was "not so great as it was some time ago."[46]

Shortly before the next General Assembly, northern old school spokesmen studiously courted their brethren of the South, assuring them of their own antiabolitionist sentiments. Notable in this respect was Samuel Miller's open letter of April 15, 1837, addressed to John McElhenny of Virginia. "I believe as fully as you do," said Miller, "that our *Abolition brethren* . . . are every day deeply wounding the cause of religion . . . and madly indulging in conduct adapted to plunge both the Church and the State into calamities which they can never repair." He expressed the hope that "a large part of our Church will frown on the conduct of those brethren, and refuse to take another step in concurrence with a course so dementive and destructive."[47] That widely publicized statement, together with many similar antiabolitionist declarations by other key northern conservatives, encouraged some influential southerners to explore still further the possibility of reaching an agreement whereby they might remain in the General Assembly without being exposed to the charge that slavery was a criminal institution.

By mid-April of 1837, correspondent "M" reported in the *Presbyterian* that "the Southern portion of our Zion" had undergone "a prodigious" change of mind since the last assembly and now stood "ready to act harmoniously and energetically with their Old-school brethren."[48] The author probably overstated the shift in sentiment; nevertheless, there was a growing inclination to seek a united front with the old school North. Accordingly, when the pre-assembly convention gathered at Philadelphia in May, many of the South's influential leaders were on hand, including Robert J. Breckinridge of Baltimore, father of the anti-new-school "Act and Testimony" of 1834; George A. Baxter and William Swan Plumer

45. MS Minutes of the Synod of Virginia, November 7, 1836, 173–76.
46. Ibid., 176.
47. *Presbyterian*, April 22, 1837. See also the *Charleston Observer*, April 15, 1837.
48. *Presbyterian*, April 15, 1837.

of Virginia; John Witherspoon of South Carolina, moderator of the last assembly; and James Smylie of Mississippi, author of a recent tract emphatically challenging the abolitionist's key doctrine that slaveholding was "a heinous sin."[49] Far from being passive observers, the leading southerners played a dominant role in the proceedings from the outset.[50] Baxter served as president of the convention, and he, Breckinridge, and Plumer gave most of the major addresses. They also exerted great influence in the planning and executing of strategy.

The main purpose of the convention was to frame an anti-new-school memorial for presentation to the General Assembly, scheduled to meet in the same city on May 18. "We are a Convention met about doctrine and order—the very quintessence of Presbyterianism," declared Breckinridge in a masterly address. While recognizing that the slavery question deeply concerned many members, he refused to discuss it, warning that if that question were injected into the discussion it would completely submerge the faith and order issue. Nevertheless, Plumer later in the same day gave a lengthy address on human bondage, expounding seventeen reasons why the General Assembly should not legislate on that subject.[51] He argued, among other things, that such legislation would be unconstitutional, would involve the church in politics, would violate the teachings of Christ and his apostles, and would necessarily arraign the people of the slaveholding states as guilty. He solemnly declared that if the assembly should undertake such legislation and should decide that slaveholding was a sin, the southern portion of the church would withdraw from it.

So far as the proceedings show, no member took issue with Plumer, even though such men as Breckinridge and Joshua L. Wilson of Cincinnati were on record as opposed to slavery. Two considerations probably dictated their silence. For one thing, they did not want to do or say anything at this critical juncture that

---

49. *A Review of A Letter from the Presbytery of Chillicothe to the Presbytery of Mississippi on the Subject of Slavery* (Woodville, Miss., 1836).

50. The proceedings of the convention are reprinted in the *Western Presbyterian Herald* (Louisville), June 1, 1837.

51. *Ibid.* It is worth noting that Plumer's speech followed substantially the points developed in the paper entitled "The South One and Indivisible," which had been widely circulated in the South during the spring of 1836. *Charleston Observer*, April 30, 1836.

might alienate the South and thus torpedo the old school's chance of controlling the ensuing assembly. For another, many old school conservatives had come to believe that abolitionism was a greater danger to the church and the nation than slavery. This was certainly true of Breckinridge.[52]

At the last General Assembly John McElhenny and other southern delegates had endeavored to persuade that body to disclaim all authority to legislate on the subject of slavery, but they were not successful. Perhaps some members of the present convention still wanted such a judicatorial decision, but they did not demand it as a condition of cooperating with the old school party. "All we ask," said Plumer, "is that the Supreme Judicatory do nothing in the way of legislation on this subject." Baxter expressed his agreement with Plumer. Breckinridge refused to recede from the antislavery legislation already passed by previous general assemblies, but at the same time he assured his southern brethren that he would "not lay another burden" on them.[53] Taking this to mean that slavery would be relatively free from interference if the old school should succeed in its "reforming" mission, the southern bloc gave its hearty support to the convention's "Testimony and Memorial" calling into question the doctrine and order of the new school party.[54]

Upon finding themselves a majority in the General Assembly of 1837, the old school delegates took drastic action against the new school party. Their two most radical measures were: (1) the abrogation of the Plan of Union of 1801 on the claim that it "was originally an unconstitutional act" on the part of the General Assembly, since the plan was never submitted to the presbyteries; and (2) the excision of the synods of Western Reserve, Utica, Geneva, and Genesee, thereby separating from the denomination more than five hundred ministers and nearly sixty thousand communicants.[55] In a less crucial, though not unimportant, action the assembly advised the American Home Missionary Society and the American Education Society to cease their operations within all Presbyterian

52. Edmund A. Moore, "Robert J. Breckinridge and the Slavery Aspect of the Presbyterian Schism of 1837," *Church History*, IV (December, 1935), 286–88.
53. *Western Presbyterian Herald*, June 1, 1837.
54. The gist of the "Testimony and Memorial" is reprinted in William H. Foote, *Sketches of Virginia: Historical and Biographical*, Ser. 2 (Philadelphia, 1855), 514–19.
55. *Minutes of the General Assembly of the Presbyterian Church in the United States of America, . . . 1837* (Philadelphia, 1837), 420–22, 440, 444–45.

churches. Those two agencies were said to be "exceedingly injurious to the peace and purity of the Presbyterian Church."[56] The southern bloc voted overwhelmingly for all three of these measures.

The assembly did nothing at all about slavery, despite numerous memorials pleading for stronger antislavery legislation. As Baxter later observed, "All these papers were handed over to the Committee of Bills and Overtures [of which John Witherspoon, a slaveholder, was chairman], by whom they were suppressed . . . without reading."[57] This procedure foreshadowed the fact that proslavery churchmen would have little to fear from old school Presbyterianism.

The old school party had been victorious in 1837, but a final test lay ahead, inasmuch as commissioners from the presbyteries of the ousted synods would claim seats in the next assembly. To be sure of being in full command at that time, the reformers kept up a steady drumfire against new schoolmen. Baxter and Plumer were especially vigilant. They defended the exscinding acts on doctrinal and governmental grounds, but at the same time they made it clear that if those acts were not sustained by the assembly of 1838, slavery would be imperiled. "Should the New School Party gain ascendancy in the next General Assembly," warned Plumer, "abolitionism will unquestionably be in the ascendant also."[58] In his campaign to discredit the new school, Baxter charged that it was a hotbed of abolitionism. He reported that when the George Bourne case was before the General Assembly of 1818 there were in that body between twenty and thirty abolitionist delegates, all of whom came from the disowned synods.[59] As for the General Assembly of 1837, he claimed that with the exception of two delegates from the Presbytery of Chillicothe, "there was [not] a single abolitionist among the orthodox [old school party], whilst nearly the whole of the New-school were of that description." Consequently he argued that if the exscinding acts were finally upheld, "the Presbyterian Church,

---

56. *Ibid.*, 442–43.
57. *Charleston Observer*, August 26, 1837.
58. *Southern Religious Telegraph—Extra*, August 8, 1837. On August 31, 1837, Plumer founded the *Watchman of the South*, through which to promote the old school cause.
59. *Watchman of the South* (Richmond), September 14, 1837.

by getting clear of the New-school, will at the same time, get clear of abolition."[60]

Plumer and Baxter plainly exaggerated the strength of abolitionism in the new school party, but they shrewdly played upon southern fears. By the time southern delegates gathered at the General Assembly of 1838, most of them were ready to stand shoulder to shoulder with northern conservatives to block the enrollment of delegates from the exscinded synods. Within short order the new schoolmen, recognizing the futility of their efforts, withdrew from the old school body and formed an independent General Assembly, although retaining their original denominational name. From then until 1869, when the two bodies in the North reunited, it was necessary to employ the term "old school" or "new school" to distinguish the two branches of Presbyterianism.

Much has been written on the cause of the schism. At the time of the rupture, old schoolmen usually claimed that slavery had nothing to do with it; that the schism grew out of conflicting views of theology and church government.[61] New schoolmen, on the other hand, contended that slavery, as well as theology and polity, prompted the split.[62] Historians of today tend to agree with the latter.[63] Bruce Staiger, in an able essay, declared that "slavery was undoubtedly the deciding factor" in producing the rupture.[64] That assessment seems rather too sweeping, and yet it contains much truth. Questions of faith and order had agitated Presbyterianism long before slavery became a controversial subject, and the dispute over those questions might well have issued in schism sooner or later even if slavery had never existed. Nonetheless, slavery was a

60. *Charleston Observer*, August 26, 1837.
61. Baird, *History of the New School*, 534–36; Howard, "The Anti-Slavery Movement in the Presbyterian Church, 1835–1861," 50–51.
62. Crocker, *The Catastrophe of the Presbyterian Church, in 1837*, 56–70; Charles Beecher, ed., *Autobiography, Correspondence, etc., of Lyman Beecher* (2 vols., New York, 1865), II, 429; Howard, "The Anti-Slavery Movement in the Presbyterian Church, 1835–1861," 48, 57.
63. Moore, "Robert J. Breckinridge and the Slavery Aspect of the Presbyterian Schism of 1837," *Church History*, IV, 293–94; William W. Sweet, *Religion on the American Frontier*, II: *The Presbyterians, 1783–1840* (New York, 1936), 111; Thompson, *Presbyterians in the South*, I, 394, 397, 399, 411; Smith, "The Role of the South in the Presbyterian Schism of 1837–38," *Church History*, XXIX, 60–61.
64. "Abolitionism and the Presbyterian Schism of 1837–1838," *Mississippi Valley Historical Review*, XXXVI, 414.

crucial factor in determining how and by whom the split of 1837 was accomplished. Slavery, more than anything else, cemented the North-South coalition, and it was the coalition that enabled the General Assembly of 1837 to annul the Plan of Union and cut off the offending synods. If the old school commissioners of that assembly had not maintained an intersectional coalition, no rupture would have occurred at that time unless they themselves had withdrawn from their new school brethren. Certainly, then, Negro bondage was a basic factor in a complex of factors which brought about the schism of 1837-38.

While the vast majority of southern Presbyterians endorsed the assembly's reforming acts of 1837, a significant minority refused to do so. As a result, many new school judicatories were organized in the slave states, including six synods.[65] However, these secessions from the old school church were not the outgrowth of antislavery sentiments; they generally resulted from the conviction that the assembly of 1837 had violated the constitution of the Presbyterian Church.[66]

Inasmuch as new school Presbyterianism included a southern constituency, it contained the seeds of conflict over slavery from the beginning. Keenly aware of this danger, the General Assembly was at first extremely careful not to offend that section of the church. In 1838 it remained entirely silent on the explosive subject, despite piles of memorials pleading for tough antislavery legislation. A year later the antislavery pressure was so great, especially from the western presbyteries, that some form of action became imperative; accordingly, the General Assembly adopted a report referring the slavery issue to the lower judicatories, "leaving it to them to take such order thereon as in their judgment will be most judicious and adapted to remove the evil."[67] Yet the high tribunal tried to restrain the lower courts if they passed rigorous measures against "the evil." By the late 1830's an increasing number of presbyteries were adopting resolutions which excluded slaveholders

---

65. Thompson, *Presbyterians in the South*, I, 399-411. For illustrative documents, see Sweet, *Religion on the American Frontier*, II: *The Presbyterians, 1786-1840*, 844-87.

66. See, for example, the *Pastoral Letter of the Synod of Virginia* (N.S.) (Washington, September 28, 1839).

67. *Minutes of the General Assembly of the Presbyterian Church in the United States of America, 1838-1858* (reprint ed., Philadelphia, 1894), 61.

from their pulpits and communion tables. The General Assembly of 1840 requested that all such regulations be rescinded.[68] The eastern judicatories generally agreed with that decision, but those in the West were for the most part critical of it, and refused to rescind their rules.[69]

Not until 1846 did the new school General Assembly pass even a moderately critical judgment upon slavery. After prolonged and heated debate, it reaffirmed the antislavery testimony of the Presbyterian Church as expressed in resolutions from 1787 to 1818, and charged that the existing system of servitude was "opposed to . . . the law of God, to the spirit and precepts of the Gospel, and to the best interests of humanity." At the same time, as though to placate the conservatives, the court expressed doubt that slaveholders were necessarily so destitute of Christian principle as to justify excluding them from the Lord's table or withholding from them ecclesiastical fellowship.[70]

Despite the relative mildness of that action, the new school Synod of Virginia took vehement exception to it. It was "wrong in principle," complained that body, "because predicated upon the ground, that slaveholding is sin *per se*," when in fact "*God's every word recognizes the existence of slaveholding.*"[71] Singling out abolitionists, the synod denounced them as blind fanatics and archfoes of government and religion. They had done more than anything else to cripple the American Colonization Society, "the noblest institution ever projected for the welfare of the man of color."[72]

Since antislavery sentiment grew rapidly in the northern portion of the church during the next decade, the supreme judicatory had to enact stronger and stronger measures against human bondage or suffer increasing numerical losses to more radical antislavery bodies, such as the newly organized Free Presbyterian Synod.[73]

68. *Ibid.*, 104.
69. Howard, "The Anti-Slavery Movement in the Presbyterian Church, 1835–1861," 91–94.
70. *Minutes of the General Assembly of the Presbyterian Church in the United States of America, 1838–1858*, 162.
71. MS Minutes of the Synod of Virginia, October 15, 1846, 100, 104 (Union Theological Seminary Library, Richmond, Va.).
72. *Ibid.*, 101–6.
73. Organized in 1847 on the premise of non-fellowship with slaveholders, the Free Presbyterian Synod became a haven of refuge for abolitionists from both old school and new school Presbyterianism. It eventually numbered over sixty churches

These stronger measures, however, increased the friction between churchmen of the two sections. This was notably the case when the General Assembly of 1853 voted "to request the Presbyteries in each of the slaveholding States" to submit to the next assembly full reports on "the number of slaveholders in connection with the churches under their jurisdiction, and the number of slaves held by them." The presbyteries were also asked to state "whether [Presbyterian] slaves are admitted to equal privileges and powers in the church courts."[74]

That measure infuriated the southern delegates, eleven of whom signed a protest accusing the assembly of having exceeded its legal authority.[75] This was not the end of the issue, for in the following July ruffled new schoolmen from slave territory held a convention at Murfreesboro, Tennessee, and denounced the action as wholly unconstitutional. They also advised their fellow churchmen of the South to refuse the assembly's request.[76]

Four years later, in 1857, the new school communion was caught up in a decisive crisis. Shortly before the General Assembly of that year met, the Presbytery of Lexington, South, in Mississippi, gave official notice that many churchmen within its jurisdiction, including a number of ministers and ruling elders, held bondsmen "from principle" and "of choice," "believing it to be according to the Bible right." Lexington left no doubt that it would sustain them in their position. In reply, the assembly by a vote of 169 to 26 denounced this "new doctrine" as "at war with the whole spirit and tenor of the Gospel of love and good will," and called upon the presbytery "to review and rectify their position."[77]

Speaking on behalf of twenty-two southern commissioners, the Rev. James G. Hamner of Virginia vigorously protested the assem-

---

and covered territory from Pennsylvania to Iowa. Its periodical organ was the *Free Presbyterian* (Yellow Springs, Ohio), edited from 1850 to 1857 by Joseph Gordon, a crusading abolitionist. Andrew E. Murray, *Presbyterians and the Negro—A History* (Philadelphia, 1966), 118–26; Howard, "The Anti-Slavery Movement in the Presbyterian Church, 1835–1861," 139.

74. *Minutes of the General Assembly of the Presbyterian Church in the United States of America, 1838–1858*, 392.

75. *Ibid.*, 393.

76. Howard, "The Anti-Slavery Movement in the Presbyterian Church, 1835–1861," 190.

77. *Minutes of the General Assembly of the Presbyterian Church in the United States of America, 1838–1858*, 574–75.

bly's action, charging that it was "such an assertion of the sin of Slavery, as degrades the whole Southern church—an assertion without authority from the word of God, or the organic law of the Presbyterian body." Furthermore, the action amounted to "the virtual exscinding of the South," and as such it was "oppressive, cruel," and "destructive of the unity of our branch of the Church."[78]

This was the last straw. Instead of acknowledging that human bondage was a sinful system, new school Presbyterians in the slaveholding region decided to secede from the present assembly and form an independent body. Their representatives therefore gathered at Knoxville, Tennessee, in April, 1858, and organized "The United Synod of the Presbyterian Church in the U.S.A."[79]

Those southern Presbyterians who had remained within the old school church after the schism of 1837–38 were spared the agony of their new school brethren in the South. Between that rupture and the Civil War, only in 1845 did the old school General Assembly take a significant stand with respect to human bondage, and in that instance it gave aid and comfort to slaveholders. Among the memorialists of that year were some who, believing that slavery was "a heinous sin in the sight of God," called upon the assembly to enact measures in support of disciplinary action against those Presbyterians "who persist in maintaining or justifying the relation of master to slaves." This demand touched a highly sensitive nerve. Replying energetically, the assembly declared that inasmuch as Christ and his apostles "did not denounce the [master-slave] relation itself as sinful," it could not do so either "without charging the Apostles of Christ with conniving at such sin." Likewise, "since Christ and his inspired apostles did not make the holding of slaves a bar to communion," the assembly had "no authority to do so."[80] This clearly proslavery decision passed in the assembly by a lopsided vote of 168 to 13. All thirteen of the dissenters were from the West.[81]

78. *Ibid.*, 576–77.
79. Thompson, *Presbyterians in the South*, I, 544–46. In 1859, the synod comprised 108 ministers, 187 churches, and 10,877 communicants. Howard, "The Anti-Slavery Movement in the Presbyterian Church, 1835–1861," 221.
80. *Minutes of the General Assembly of the Presbyterian Church in the United States of America, . . . 1845*, XI (Philadelphia, 1845), 16, 17.
81. Howard, "The Anti-Slavery Movement in the Presbyterian Church, 1835–1861," 135 n. The assembly's action prompted considerable criticism in the lower judica-

Old school leaders in the South had every reason to rejoice, for their church had at last taken the moral position for which they had long contended. No one seemed happier than James Henley Thornwell, a delegate from South Carolina and destined to become moderator of the General Assembly in 1847. Before the report on slavery came before the assembly, he had written his wife that it "vindicates the South, and will put the question at rest." He spoke truly; the question was laid to rest in the assembly until the guns of Sumter inaugurated the Civil War.[82]

II

As a denomination, Methodists were no less opposed to abolitionism in the 1830's than the Presbyterians. Having conceded by 1816 that the evil of slavery appeared "to be past remedy," they had turned their main attention to evangelizing the slaves and to promoting the colonization movement.

Negro evangelization had always been a vital concern of American Methodists. By 1817 the denomination had a black membership of 43,000. Negroes constituted 40 per cent of Carolina and Georgia Methodists in 1826.[83] In the late 1820's, Methodism enlarged its ministry to blacks by appointing missionaries to slaves who worked on the larger plantations, where white residents were few and where therefore churches were located far apart. Within two decades, these missionaries were at work in every southern state.[84] The movement originated in South Carolina, and by 1839 the various missions in that state were being served by three general superintendents and seventeen missionaries. The territory of the mission extended from Waccamaw Neck and the Pee Dee River on the east to Savannah River on the west, and embraced two hundred and

---

tories and lost many old school members, especially in the West, to the Free Presbyterian Church. *Ibid.*, 136–39.

82. Benjamin M. Palmer, *The Life and Letters of James Henley Thornwell, D.D., LL.D.* (Richmond, 1875), 287. Though not a member of the committee on slavery, Thornwell submitted a paper to it which seems to have been substantially incorporated in the report. *Ibid.*, 286–87.

83. Donald G. Mathews, *Slavery and Methodism: A Chapter in American Morality, 1780–1845* (Princeton, N.J., 1965), 68.

84. *Ibid.*, 70. See also Mathews, "The Methodist Mission to the Slaves, 1829–1844," *Journal of American History*, LI (March, 1965), 615–31; W. P. Harrison, *The Gospel Among the Slaves* (Nashville, 1893), 189–96.

thirty-four plantations. The workers were ministering to 5,556 church members and catechizing 2,525 children.[85]

The moving spirit of the South Carolina mission was a slaveholder, William Capers, who in 1846 became a bishop of the Methodist Episcopal Church, South.[86] Since he generally served as president of the Missionary Society of the South Carolina Conference, he probably drafted most of the annual reports of the society's board of managers. In any case, those reports clearly reveal the mission's commitment to a proslavery policy. "We denounce the principles and opinions of the Abolitionists, *in toto*," declared the managers in 1836. "We consider and believe that the Holy Scriptures, so far from giving any countenance to this delusion, do unequivocally authorize the relation of master and slave. . . . We would employ no one in the work, who might hesitate to teach thus, nor can such a one be found in the whole number of preachers of this conference."[87] Planters had good reason to welcome such a mission, for it tended to keep the slaves subservient to their masters. There is no evidence that the missions in other states were any less committed to supporting the bondage system.

By the middle 1820's, Methodist leaders were also active colonizationists. Whereas the mission to the slaves was of special interest to one section of the church, the movement to settle free blacks in Africa appealed to Methodists everywhere. The General Conference of 1828 heartily endorsed the American Colonization Society and urged churches to make annual contributions toward the advancement of its work. The conference viewed with favor the settlement in Liberia, believing that it would open the door for the evangelization of the continent of Africa.[88] Some of Methodism's foremost clergymen served as agents of the society. One of the most influential agents was Henry Bidleman Bascom, who, after serving

85. *Minutes of the South Carolina Conference of the Methodist Episcopal Church, For the Year 1839* (Charleston, 1839), 17.
86. William M. Wightman, *The Life of William Capers, D.D.* (Nashville, 1859), 291–92.
87. *Minutes of the South Carolina Conference of the Methodist Episcopal Church, For the Year 1836* (Charleston, 1836), 20–21. According to Wightman, *The Life of William Capers*, 295–96, Capers wrote the 1836 report. For similar sentiments in other reports, see *Minutes* of the conference for 1839, 14–17; for 1840, 12–13; and for 1841, 12–14.
88. *Journals of the General Conference of the Methodist Episcopal Church*, I: *1796–1836* (New York, 1855), 357.

as president of Transylvania University for seven years, was elected to the episcopacy of the Methodist Episcopal Church, South, in 1850.[89] The magic orator captivated audiences all across the nation in 1832–33 with his dramatic lecture on "Claims of Africa." "Liberia is even now a Pharos of light to Western Africa," he proclaimed. He gave many reasons why the people should sustain the American Colonization Society, but the reason that probably drew the most sympathetic response was racial in nature. He acknowledged that free blacks were treated unjustly by whites, but at the same time held out no hope for them in America. "This unhappy people," said Bascom, "are rapidly spreading a fearful taint,—an alarming virus, through all the relations of general society. This taint, this virus, [is] not only affecting the morals, but even the blood" of the American people. Consequently the American Colonization Society *"may prevent incalculable mischief and ruin to this country."* [90]

While Bascom and many other churchmen of all communions sincerely believed that colonization would advance the cause of Christianity in Africa, they also believed, with few exceptions, that it would relieve America of "a fearful taint." This moral ambiguity always clouded the motivation of the colonization movement.[91]

Just when Methodism's mission to the slaves and its colonization drive seemed most successful, a handful of militant abolitionists in New England launched a crusade that within ten years had split the church into northern and southern denominations. In the vanguard of this group were three preachers: La Roy Sunderland, George Storrs, and Orange Scott. Sunderland, a member of the New England Conference, was one of the first Methodist ministers to align himself with abolitionism, and he took part in the Philadelphia convention of 1833 which organized the American Anti-Slavery Society. As editor of *Zion's Watchman* (founded in January,

89. Moses M. Henkle, *The Life of Henry Bidleman Bascom, D.D., LL.D.* (Louisville, 1854), Chap. 16.

90. "Claims of Africa; or An Address in Behalf of the American Colonization Society," in Thomas N. Ralston, ed., *Posthumous Works of the Rev. Henry B. Bascom, D.D.*, (2 vols., Nashville, 1856), II, 281.

91. For clear evidence that the American Colonization Society operated on the premise that free blacks could not be integrated into American society on terms of equality with whites, see the *Sixteenth Annual Report of the American Society for Colonizing the Free People of Colour of the United States* (Washington, 1833), vii–viii, xiv.

1836), he was a thorn in the side of Nathan Bangs, editor of the New York *Christian Advocate and Journal* and a staunch colonizationist. George Storrs of the New Hampshire Conference was an indefatigable antislavery lecturer and organizer. Orange Scott, however, was the high priest of Methodist abolitionists.[92] Converted at a Vermont camp meeting in 1820, he became a presiding elder in the New England Conference twelve years later. By the opening of 1835 he was a zealous emancipationist.[93] In a recruiting campaign, he gave one hundred of his fellow preachers a three-month subscription to the *Liberator*. "Before the three months expired," recalled Scott many years later, "a majority of the N.E. Conference (150 members in all), was converted to Abolitionism." As a result, "the Abolitionists had everything their own way" at the conference of 1835.[94]

The first major controversy over abolitionism within the Methodist Episcopal Church was initiated in February, 1835, when La Roy Sunderland, George Storrs, and three other antislavery radicals published an "Appeal" to members of the New England and New Hampshire conferences.[95] Predicating liberty as "the inalienable gift of the infinite God to every human being," they declared that the system of slavery was "a sin in the sight of Heaven, and ought to cease at once, NOW and FOREVER." Although they regarded any person who held property in a human being as guilty of a criminal act, they believed it to be "the more criminal for a Christian or Christian minister to do this."

The "Appeal" provoked a vigorous "Counter Appeal," drafted by Daniel D. Whedon of Wesleyan University and signed by eight prominent churchmen, including the president of Wesleyan, Wilbur Fisk, and Abel Stevens.[96] These critics of the "Appeal" denied

92. Donald G. Mathews, "Orange Scott: the Methodist Evangelist as Revolutionary," in Martin B. Duberman, ed., *The Antislavery Vanguard: New Essays on the Abolitionists* (Princeton, N.J., 1965), 71–101.

93. Lucius C. Matlack, *The Life of Orange Scott: Compiled from His Personal Narrative, Correspondence, and Other Authentic Sources of Information. In Two Parts* (New York, 1848), 8–9, 25, 33.

94. *Ibid.*, 34. According to Scott's contemporary, Lucius C. Matlack, *The Antislavery Struggle and Triumph in the Methodist Episcopal Church* (New York, 1881), 86–87, the subscription to the *Liberator* was "for six months."

95. *Zion's Herald—Extra* (Boston), February 4, 1835. Sunderland wrote the document.

96. *Zion's Herald—Extra*, April 8, 1835. The "Appeal" was addressed to ministers

the abolitionist doctrine of the necessary sinfulness of slaveholding on two grounds: first, the general spirit of the gospel; second, the specific directions of the New Testament. From the law of love (Matt. 22:39) and the golden rule (Matt. 7:12) they derived the "simple rule" that the abolition of slavery would not be justified unless there were "rational grounds to believe that such a process would add to the sum of happiness." While not saying so flatly, they clearly implied that the general liberation of the slaves would not increase human happiness.

Turning to the specific directions of the New Testament, the counter appellants piled text upon text as proof that the apostolic churches, as at Colossae, contained both masters and slaves with Paul's full permission. Ephesians 6:5–9, for instance, proved "beyond doubt or debate, that the Apostle [Paul] *did permit slaveholders in the Christian church.*" Futhermore, if all the rest of the New Testament were silent on the subject of human servitude, 1 Timothy 6:1–4 alone would provide "an impregnable demonstration that *slaveholding is not in all cases and invariably, sinful;* ... and that it *does not, of itself, form ground of exclusion from the Christian church.*"

Nevertheless, these conservative churchmen observed that the spirit of the gospel had an "irresistible tendency" to destroy the system of slavery, and that it would be a sin to perpetuate the system "beyond the time of its practical removal."

Sunderland and his fellow abolitionists replied at length to their critics in a "Defense of the Appeal."[97] In addition to reinforcing their original antislavery arguments with much new factual data, they exposed vulnerable aspects of the "Counter Appeal." That document, they charged, had aligned the New Testament both with and against slavery. It also had failed to demonstrate that evil would be increased and human happiness diminished by the abolition of slavery. "The question upon which we join issue with our brethren," repeated the abolitionists, "is nothing more or less than this:

---

only, but the "Counter Appeal" was directed to laymen as well as ministers in the New England and New Hampshire conferences. In a postscript, Bishop Elijah Hedding expressed agreement with the argument of the "Counter Appeal" and admonished abolitionists "to desist" from their present course.

97. *Zion's Herald–Extra,* June 3, 1835.

—Is it a sin against God to hold property in the human species?" Since their "brethren" made no further response to that question, the debate ended.

The antislavery crusaders, however, did not lapse into silence, for when the New England and New Hampshire conferences met in the summer of 1835, they were present in strength and demanded that those bodies take stronger action against human bondage. Owing to Bishop Elijah Hedding's adept blocking tactics, the preachers of the New England Conference did not succeed in passing antislavery resolutions, but they made themselves felt in other respects. For one thing, they defeated Wilbur Fisk's drive to get the conference to sever its official connection with *Zion's Herald* for having published the "Appeal." For another, they engineered the election of six abolitionists out of a seven-man delegation to the ensuing General Conference.[98] The cause of abolitionism got attention also in the New Hampshire Conference. Even though Bishop John Emory entered a protest, the conference, acting as a committee of the whole, adopted a radical antislavery report, the first resolution of which charged that the holding of a human being as a species of property was "a sin against God, and a violation of the inalienable rights of humanity."[99] That action shows why only one of the nine preachers chosen as delegates to the next General Conference was not a confirmed abolitionist.

Deeply alarmed by this concerted attack upon slavery, Bishops Hedding and Emory at once issued a pastoral letter to the ministers of the two conferences, warning them that their abolitionist activities would not only defeat the cause of emancipation and subject the bondsmen to more rigorous discipline, but would cripple if not destroy Methodism's ministry to both masters and slaves. In an obvious move to curb the antislavery lecturing of such preachers as Orange Scott and George Storrs, the bishops wrote: "If any, of whatever class, go beyond their own bounds, or leave their proper appointments, . . . to agitate other societies or communities on this subject [slavery], we advise the preachers, the trustees, and the offi-

98. Mathews, *Slavery and Methodism*, 132.
99. Lucius C. Matlack, *The History of American Slavery and Methodism, From 1780 to 1849: and History of the Wesleyan Methodist Connection of America* (New York, 1849), 41.

cial and other members . . . to refuse the use of their pulpits and houses for such purposes."[100] This heavy-handed use of episcopal authority merely threw fat into the abolitionist fire.

Yet, far from agreeing with the antislavery militants, Methodist preachers outside New England overwhelmingly shared the sentiments of Hedding and Emory. This was typically reflected in the reaction of the Ohio Conference, which convened in August, 1835. Responding to the recommendations of a special committee, of which Thomas A. Morris, editor of the *Western Christian Advocate*, was chairman, the conference castigated abolitionists as fomenters of intersectional strife and enemies of Negro evangelization. On the other hand, it commended the American Colonization Society "as a noble, benevolent institution." The churchmen viewed abolitionism as repugnant in that it not only favored immediate emancipation of the blacks but wanted them "to remain among and commingle with the white population." Thus abolitionism in effect fostered racial amalgamation, an outcome "highly offensive to most of the American family." The Ohio preachers paid lip service to gradual emancipation, but their dominant concern was to crush abolitionism. All except four of the one hundred and thirty ministers present voted for the Morris document.[101]

Less than a month later, the Kentucky Conference took similar action on recommendation of a committee, of which Henry B. Bascom was chairman.[102] The methods of abolitionism, complained the preachers, were "ill-selected, unjust, and directly calculated to endanger public tranquility." They would, however, favor gradual emancipation, provided the number of Negroes freed did "not greatly exceed" the nation's ability to send them to some place where they might share "a perfect parity of rights and privileges with the rest of mankind." Like their Ohio brethren, the leaders of Kentucky Methodism warmly applauded the American Colonization Society. Not a single member of the conference voted against the report.

In view of the mounting animosity toward antislavery radicalism,

100. *Christian Advocate and Journal*, September 25, 1835.
101. *Christian Sentinel* (Richmond), September 25, 1835.
102. Charles Elliott, "Documents," *History of the Great Secession From the Methodist Episcopal Church in the Year 1845* (Cincinnati, 1885), Document XXI, columns 908–13.

it is no wonder that when the General Conference met at Cincinnati in May, 1836, nearly all its delegates were spoiling to censure such disturbers of the Methodist peace as Orange Scott. Their opportunity came when two delegates from the New Hampshire Conference, George Storrs and Samuel Norris, attended a meeting of the Cincinnati Antislavery Society and spoke in favor of abolitionism. Stephen G. Roszel of the Baltimore Conference ignited the emotional fireworks by offering two resolutions: first, that the delegates "disapprove in the most unqualified sense the conduct of two members of the General Conference, who are reported to have lectured in this city recently upon and in favour of modern abolitionism"; and second, that the delegates "are decidedly opposed to modern abolitionism, and wholly disclaim any right, wish, or intention to interfere in the civil and political relation between master and slave as it exists in the slave-holding states of this union."[103]

Although from the outset the verdict of the Conference was a foregone conclusion, the tirade against abolitionism lasted two days, with southerners monopolizing the discussion.[104] William Winans of Mississippi and William A. Smith of Virginia, both slaveholders, excelled all others in caustic rhetoric. Far from condemning human servitude, Winans, a native of Pennsylvania, told the conference that he was a slaveholder on principle. A slaveholding minister, he added, had a distinct advantage in the South, because he could preach to the slaves without arousing the suspicions of their masters.[105] Both Winans and Smith bitterly assailed Orange Scott. At one point Smith completely lost his temper and said of Scott, "I wish *to God,* he were in Heaven."[106]

As expected, the Roszel resolutions were overwhelmingly adopted.[107] The fourteen abolitionists of the New England and New Hampshire conferences drafted a protest, charging that the action

103. *Journals of the General Conference of the Methodist Episcopal Church*, I, 447.
104. [James G. Birney], *Debate on "Modern Abolitionism," in the General Conference of the Methodist Episcopal Church, Held in Cincinnati, May, 1836* (Cincinnati, 1836), 5–29.
105. *Ibid.*, 19.
106. *Ibid.*, 27. For Scott's reply to his critics, see *ibid.*, 30–35.
107. *Journals of the General Conference of the Methodist Episcopal Church*, I, 446–47.

taken against George Storrs and Samuel Norris violated the *Discipline* and was therefore unconstitutional, but the document was refused a place in the conference journals.[108]

Although the General Conference lambasted "modern abolitionism," it carefully avoided saying anything against human servitude. Sundry memorials urged that the antislavery rules of the *Discipline* be strengthened, but the conference replied that it was "inexpedient to make any change in our book of Discipline respecting slavery."[109] The bishops' pastoral address, which was drawn up by three prominent colonizationists—Nathan Bangs, Thomas A. Morris, and William Capers—was equally silent on the slavery question. On the other hand, it admonished Methodists everywhere "to abstain from all abolition movements and associations, and to refrain from patronizing any of their publications."[110]

During the following quadrennium, the Methodist "establishment" threw its full weight against abolitionism. From Michigan to New York, and from Maine to Maryland, annual conferences became battlegrounds between conservatives and abolitionists. Everywhere except in New England the conferences were dominated by preachers who tried to check antislavery militancy within Methodism. Any candidate for the ministry would usually be rejected if he were known to be an abolitionist. Lucius C. Matlack, for example, was twice refused admission to the Philadelphia Conference because of his abolitionist activity.[111] Many preachers were suspended from the ministry merely because they would not cease their antislavery efforts.[112] A preacher exposed himself to proscription if he so much as circulated an antislavery pamphlet, joined an antislavery society, or attended an antislavery convention.

No bishop was more energetic in suppressing abolitionists than

---

108. For the complete text of the able protest, see Birney, *Debate on "Modern Abolitionism,"* 90–91.

109. *Journals of the General Conference of the Methodist Episcopal Church*, I, 475.

110. *Christian Advocate and Journal*, June 17, 1836. The pastoral address was signed by bishops Robert R. Roberts, Joshua Soule, Elijah Hedding, and James O. Andrew.

111. Lucius C. Matlack, *Narrative of the Anti-Slavery Experience of a Minister in the Methodist Episcopal Church* (Philadelphia, 1845).

112. Matlack, *The History of American Slavery and Methodism, From 1780 to 1849: and History of the Wesleyan Methodist Connection of America*, 259–93; *Autobiography of the Rev. Luther Lee, D.D.* (New York, 1882), Chap. 16.

Elijah Hedding.[113] In 1836 he deposed Orange Scott from the presiding eldership because of his antislavery crusading. In the same year he refused to appoint George Storrs to that office on the same grounds. Two years later he preferred charges against Scott and La Roy Sunderland. The New England Conference, however, acquitted them, much to the disgust of the bishop.[114]

Hedding regularly refused to permit annual conferences to adopt proabolitionist resolutions, claiming that this was not the proper business of a conference.[115] On this account, the preachers accused him of denying their "conference rights." To this accusation the bishop replied in a forceful address, first delivered at the Oneida Conference in August, 1837, and repeated shortly afterwards at the Genesee Conference.[116] He argued that slavery fell outside the proper business of a conference unless there were slaves and slaveowners within its bounds. In reality, however, Hedding had a more fundamental reason for seeking to prevent conferences from passing radical antislavery resolutions. In short, he did not believe that Methodists necessarily sinned if they held property in Negroes. Posing the question, "What right has any member of our Church to own a slave?," he answered: "The right to hold a slave is founded on this rule, 'Therefore, all things whatsoever ye would that men should do to you, do ye even so to them: for this is the law and the prophets (Matt. 7:12).'" But did any Methodist master act in accordance with that rule? "That there are many such cases among our brethren in the southern states, I firmly believe," replied the bishop. His belief that slavery was not necessarily incompatible with the golden rule clashed sharply with the moral conviction of the famed Christmas Conference of 1784, which explicitly proclaimed that slaveholding per se was "contrary to the Golden Law of God on which hang all the Law and the Prophets."[117]

In the meantime, southern conferences were boldly expressing

113. D. W. Clark, *Life and Times of Rev. Elijah Hedding*, D.D. (New York, 1855), Chap. 16.
114. *Ibid.*, 524–26.
115. Matlack, *The History of American Slavery and Methodism, From 1780 to 1849: and History of the Wesleyan Methodist Connection of America*, 55–57, 60–61.
116. The address is in the *Christian Advocate and Journal*, October 20, 1837.
117. *Minutes of Several Conversations Between the Rev. Thomas Coke, LL.D., the Rev. Francis Asbury, and Others, at a Conference, Begun in Baltimore, in the State of Maryland, on Monday, the 27th of December, in the Year 1784* (Philadelphia, 1785), 15.

proslavery sentiments without any restraint from the presiding bishops. A notorious example was the action taken by the Georgia Conference in December, 1837. After observing that there was a clause in the *Discipline* affirming that Methodists were "as much as ever convinced of the great evil of slavery," the Georgia preachers unanimously "resolved that it is the sense of the Georgia Annual Conference that slavery, as it exists in the United States, *is not a moral evil.*"[118] Despite this glaring flouting of the *Discipline*, the presiding bishop, Thomas A. Morris, permitted the resolution to pass without raising his voice against it.

When news of the Georgia declaration drifted northward, Scott and his fellow abolitionists were all the more incensed over the fact that their own conferences had been denied the opportunity of adopting antislavery resolutions. But not to be outdone, they were already conducting Methodist antislavery conventions, which drew together laymen as well as clergymen. As a propaganda medium, these gatherings were highly effective. Their two major purposes were to provide a platform for distinguished antislavery evangelists and to pass resolutions against slavery. In these respects the convention held at Lynn, Massachusetts, in October, 1837, was typical. After listening to soul-stirring addresses, the members of that assembly adopted resolutions for general circulation. "We believe," they said, "that holding the human species as property, is a most FLAGRANT SIN, and that NO CIRCUMSTANCES can make it otherwise." As against temporizing gradualists and colonizationists, they declared: "We believe that immediate emancipation, without expatriation, is the duty of the master, and the right of the slave." These sensitive churchmen also bore testimony against white racism in the free states. "We fear," they confessed, "the negro-hating spirit is as prevalent in the North as in the South! Colored people are excluded from most of our colleges and academies—from our trades and professions; and from the inside of our steamboats and stage coaches. They are put into one corner of our churches, and are seldom permitted to sit either at the Lord's table, or at any other with the whites!"[119]

By the time the General Conference met at Baltimore in 1840,

118. *Southern Christian Advocate* (Charleston), January 5, 1838.
119. Scott, *An Appeal to the Methodist Episcopal Church*, 138–39.

there may have been as many as fifty thousand abolitionists in Methodism.[120] According to one of their prominent leaders, the antislavery memorials submitted to that body "contained the names of over ten thousand private members, and represented at least five hundred traveling preachers."[121] They eagerly hoped that steps would be taken to advance the cause of abolitionism. However, they were doomed to shattering disappointment. From the outset the bishops, in their official address, deplored the fact that some conferences in the Northeast had agitated the slavery question contrary to the counsel of the last General Conference. They also frowned upon those "self-created [antislavery] conventions" in which Methodist preachers had complained of being deprived of their "conference rights." Wishing to preserve the peace and unity of the church, they wanted no new legislation with respect to Negro bondage. Going even further, they advised the preachers "at this eventful crisis" to refrain from all interference with the master-slave relation as "established by the civil laws" and seek "to bring both master and servant under the sanctifying influence" of the gospel.[122]

In expressing those views, the bishops in effect invited the General Conference to vote down all measures that would encourage the antislavery movement. A coalition of northern conservatives and southerners responded to the episcopal wishes with alacrity. The preachers held that the bishops over the past quadrennium had been correct in so administering the annual conferences as to frustrate the adoption of abolitionist resolutions.[123] On the other hand, they tabled a motion charging that the Georgia Conference of 1837 had contradicted the sense of the *Discipline* when it declared that slavery in the United States was *"not a moral evil."*[124] In a far-reaching resolution, which Henry B. Bascom had adroitly framed, they declared that "under the provisional exception" of the church's general rule on human bondage, "the . . . mere own-

120. *Ibid.*, 135–36. According to Mathews, *Slavery and Methodism*, 168, "The Methodists probably had about 700 ministers out of over 3,000 who would be willing to preach and vote against slavery, and perhaps as many more lay or 'local' preachers."
121. Matlack, *The Antislavery Struggle and Triumph in the Methodist Episcopal Church*, 134.
122. *Journal of the General Conference of the Methodist Episcopal Church, . . . 1840* (New York, 1844), 134–38.
123. *Ibid.*, 99. 124. *Ibid.*, 106.

ership of slave property, in states or territories where the laws do not admit of emancipation, . . . constitutes no legal barrier to the election or ordination of ministers to the various grades of office known in the ministry of the Methodist Episcopal Church."[125] Despite the mass of abolitionist memorials laid before the conference, the delegates blocked all efforts to adopt any new antislavery measures. At the same time, they praised the American Colonization Society "as exerting a most beneficial influence upon the coloured population of our country, and more especially upon the inhabitants of Africa."[126] Finally, in a flagrant manifestation of racism, they responded to the Silas Comfort appeal[127] by resolving "that it is inexpedient and unjustifiable for any preacher among us to permit coloured persons to give testimony against white persons, in any state where they are denied that privilege in trials of law."[128]

Taken together, those decisions signified that Methodism had fallen to a new low in subserviency to its proslavery faction. Understandably, Orange Scott left Baltimore in deep despair for his church. Nor was he cheered in spirit when he visited the annual conferences in which abolitionism had once abounded. "Not a few faltered and fell back from the ranks which Orange Scott had led," lamented one of his closest friends.[129] By February, 1841, the valiant antislavery crusader had virtually lost all hope that Methodism would ever be converted to abolitionism.[130] Scott thus found himself in a baffling dilemma. If he stayed in the old church he would compromise his antislavery convictions, but if he should leave it and organize an independent body in harmony with those convic-

---

125. *Ibid.*, 171.
126. *Ibid.*, 59.
127. While pastor of a church in St. Louis, Silas Comfort had relied upon the testimony of a Negro in persuading his church board to convict one of his parishioners of conduct unbecoming of a Christian. On being accused of an "error of Judgment" by the Missouri Conference, he appealed to the General Conference. Mathews, *Slavery and Methodism*, 200–201.
128. *Journal of the General Conference of the Methodist Episcopal Church*, . . . *1840*, 60. The "official members" of two black Methodist Episcopal churches in Baltimore branded the resolution as "soul-sickening" and "calculated to foster . . . that unholy pride of caste," and petitioned the General Conference to revoke it. The petition was delivered to one of the bishops, but it was never presented to the conference. For text of the document, see Matlack, *The History of American Slavery and Methodism, From 1780 to 1849: and History of the Wesleyan Methodist Connection of America*, 218–20.
129. Matlack, *The Life of Orange Scott*, 182.
130. *Ibid.*, 186.

tions he would be called a schismatic.[131] Neither alternative was completely satisfactory to him. However, by late September, 1842, he had "at last fully decided" to leave the Methodist Episcopal Church.[132] On the following November 8, he, Jotham Horton, and La Roy Sunderland signed a historic document in which they explained why they were withdrawing from the old body. Two major factors had prompted their decision: first, the failure of Methodism to disentangle itself from slavery; and second, the limitations of the episcopal form of church government.[133]

Ever since 1839, a trickle of Methodist abolitionists had been breaking with the parent communion, but Scott's secession precipitated a mass exit, which, in May of 1843, resulted in the organization of the Wesleyan Methodist Connection of America, with a charter membership of six thousand. Nine months later the new church had fifteen thousand members.[134] The Wesleyans rejected episcopacy, required the participation of laymen as well as ministers in both annual and general conferences, elected their conference officials, prohibited fellowship with slaveholders, and adopted a restrictive rule forbidding their church to abridge the rights and privileges of any member or preacher on account of race.[135]

This dramatic exodus from their communion signaled Methodist leaders in the North that they had made a tactical mistake in seeking to crush their abolitionist brethren. It warned them, moreover, that unless they soon took a firmer stand against slavery, they would run the risk of losing many more members to the Wesleyans. On the other hand, they feared that a stronger antislavery stance would provoke a massive southern defection. This was their crucial dilemma when the General Conference convened in New York on May 1, 1844.

131. Wilbur Fisk had often predicted that the abolitionist tactics of Scott and his associates would result in dividing the Methodist Episcopal Church. *Christian Advocate and Journal*, March 2, 9, 23, 30, 1838.

132. Matlack, *The Life of Orange Scott*, 202.

133. Orange Scott, *The Grounds of Secession from the M.E. Church, or, Book For the Times: Being an Examination of Her Connection with Slavery, and also of Her Form of Government. Revised and Corrected. To Which is Added Wesley Upon Slavery* (New York, 1848), 3–16. On December 12, 1842, another leading abolitionist, Luther Lee, also withdrew from the M.E. Church on essentially the same grounds. *Ibid.*, 16–24.

134. Orange Scott, *Church Government: A Work For the Times* (Boston, 1844), 87.

135. Matlack, *The History of American Slavery and Methodism, From 1780 to 1849: and History of the Wesleyan Methodist Connection of America*, 44.

Fatefully, that conference had to dispose of the cases of two slaveholders, one of which involved a bishop. Francis A. Harding, having been suspended from the ministry by the Baltimore Conference for refusing to manumit his slaves, had appealed from that decision to Methodism's supreme tribunal. William A. Smith of Virginia, manager of his trial, argued strenuously that the defendant had in no respect violated the regulations on slavery as contained in the *Discipline*, and he therefore urged the conference to reverse the decision of the lower body.[136] From the outset, however, he fought a losing battle; after three days of bitter debate the delegates upheld the verdict of the Baltimore Conference by a vote of 117 to 56.[137]

The more important case was that of Bishop James O. Andrew of Georgia. Although not a slaveowner when elected to the episcopacy in 1832, he had subsequently fallen heir to bondsmen by inheritance, bequest, and marriage. By 1840 there were four slaves in the Andrew household, and in January, 1844, the bishop married widow Leonora Greenwood, who owned fourteen or fifteen blacks.[138] In response to an inquiry, Andrew admitted that he was legally a slaveowner in "two instances," but he contended that emancipation was "impracticable" under Georgia law.[139]

Despite that explanation, Alfred Griffith of the Baltimore Conference moved "that the Rev. James O. Andrew be, and he is hereby affectionately requested to resign his office as one of the Bishops of the Methodist Episcopal Church."[140] That motion touched off a debate that shook the church to its very foundations. After the first day, James B. Finley of the Ohio Conference offered a substitute motion, declaring "that it is the sense of this General Conference that he [Bishop Andrew] desist from the exercise of his office so long as this impediment remains."[141]

The milder Finley motion, however, fell far short of appeasing

---

136. Robert A. West (official reporter), *Report of Debates in the General Conference of the Methodist Episcopal Church, Held in the City of New York* (New York, 1844), 22–31.

137. *Journal of the General Conference of the Methodist Episcopal Church, . . . 1844* (New York, 1844), 33.

138. Joseph Mitchell, "Traveling Preacher and Settled Farmer," *Methodist History*, V (July, 1967), 7. In 1850, Andrew owned a Georgia farm of 550 acres which was being cultivated by twenty-four slaves.

139. *Journal of the General Conference of the Methodist Episcopal Church, . . . 1844*, 63–64.

140. *Ibid.*, 64. 141. *Ibid.*, 66.

southern delegates, and they defended Andrew to the last ditch.[142] They argued mainly that the bishop held his slaves in full accordance with the provisions of the *Discipline*, and that therefore it would be illegal as well as unjust to condemn him. No delegate maintained this position more stubbornly than William A. Smith, a slaveholder. "We of the south," said the Virginian, "maintain that he [Bishop Andrew] stands acquitted by the Discipline, and that to condemn him without the forms, or the authority of our rules, is not only unjust, but extra-judicial."[143] He contended, furthermore, that the proposed action would have a disastrous impact upon southern Methodists, in that it would diminish the usefulness of their ministers and jeopardize their mission to the slaves. To prevent such a calamity, said Smith, "a division of our ecclesiastical confederation would become a high and solemn duty."[144]

One of the strongest supporters of the Finley motion was John P. Durbin of the Philadelphia Conference. He reminded the conference that the Methodist Episcopal Church had been compromising more and more with slavery almost ever since its organization in 1784. Now the episcopacy itself was in danger of being encumbered with it. However necessary may have been previous concessions to slavery, northern Methodists would never permit the episcopacy, which was "common to all parts" of the church, to be burdened with human bondage. "On that point, sir, our minds are as the mind of one man, and the brethren of the south will find it so," proclaimed Durbin.[145] He briskly contested the claim, advanced by some delegates, that the General Conference had no power to remove a bishop or to suspend the exercise of his functions except by impeachment and trial on the basis of preferred charges.[146]

The battle lines were thus clearly drawn, with both parties equally adamant. Midway in the bitter debate, Bishop Andrew took the floor in his own behalf, saying: "I am a slaveholder, . . . and I cannot help myself. . . . I have no confession to make—I intend to

142. West, *Report of Debates*, 109–15, 138–44, 162–66, 177–83.
143. *Ibid.*, 138.
144. *Ibid.*, 143. Ever since 1836 William A. Smith had been raising the specter of southern Methodist secession to defeat antislavery measures. William W. Sweet, *Virginia Methodism: A History* (Richmond, 1955), 207–8; Mathews, *Slavery and Methodism*, 177–78.
145. West, *Report of Debates*, 173.
146. *Ibid.*, 174–75.

make none. I stand upon the broad ground of the Discipline on which I took office, and if I have done wrong, put me out."[147]

Interestingly, the bishop's critics had not chosen to try him under the *Discipline*'s rules with respect to slavery. Their major reasons were probably two. In the first place, the *Discipline* did in fact permit ministers to hold slaves in states where the laws did not allow the owners to manumit them on terms of real freedom.[148] Such was the case in Georgia, where Bishop Andrew lived. Hence, as the northern Methodist leaders must have recognized, it would have been difficult, if not impossible, to convict the bishop of violating the *Discipline*. In the second place, if Andrew had been tried under the charge that he had violated the *Discipline* with respect to slaveholding, the resulting debates might well have widened the breach between the northern conservatives and their abolitionist brethren and thus have prompted still further defections to the new Wesleyan church. In view of these contingencies, the Finley resolution seemed to be the safer mode of censuring Bishop Andrew, although it clearly exposed its defenders to the charge of violating the slavery regulations of the *Discipline*.

After many days of passionate controversy, the bishops, who from the first had shown no sympathy for the proceedings against their colleague, presented a paper "recommending the postponement of further action in the case of Bishop Andrew" until the next General Conference. Since, however, nothing came of this proposal, the acrimonious charges and countercharges continued until the Finley resolution was finally adopted by a vote of 110 to 68.[149] The split was almost entirely sectional.

Five days later, Henry B. Bascom, who had been strangely silent throughout the public debate, presented a scathing southern protest against the decision.[150] The protest was basically threefold: first,

---

147. *Ibid.*, 148–49.

148. As already observed, the General Conference of 1840 had voted that "the simple holding of slaves . . . in states or territories where the laws do not admit of emancipation, and permit the liberated slave to enjoy freedom, constitutes no legal barrier to the election or ordination of ministers to the various grades of office known in the ministry of the Methodist Episcopal Church." *Journal of the General Conference of the Methodist Episcopal Church, . . . 1840*, 171. This action obviously covered bishops as well as traveling preachers.

149. *Journal of the General Conference of the Methodist Episcopal Church, . . . 1844*, 83–84. According to West, *Report of Debates*, 191, the vote was 111 to 69.

150. *Journal of the General Conference of the Methodist Episcopal Church, . . .*

that in censuring Bishop Andrew, the majority had performed an extra-judicial act; second, that the General Conference had exceeded its authority in taking action against Andrew, since the episcopacy and the conference were coordinates in the organizational structure of the church; and third, that the majority had scuttled "the compromise law of the church" (as finalized in 1816) with respect to slavery. The protesters acknowledged that the third point formed "their principal ground of complaint and remonstrance." "If the compromise law [of the *Discipline*] be either repealed or allowed to remain a dead letter," they warned, "*the south cannot submit, and the absolute necessity of division is already dated.*"[151]

A committee, consisting of John P. Durbin, George Peck, and Charles Elliott, replied to the protest. The committeemen argued—not very convincingly—that the slavery regulations of the *Discipline* did not contain any rule or law specifically applicable to a bishop and that consequently the General Conference was justified in censuring Bishop Andrew on other grounds.[152] On the other hand, they clearly showed that it was idle fancy to claim that the two sections of Methodism had at any time formed a "compact" or "compromise law" with respect to slavery. They also demolished the theory that the episcopacy and the General Conference were coordinate bodies in the Methodist Episcopal Church.[153]

Neither the protest nor the reply to it did more than merely confirm the conflicting parties in their settled opinions. The Finley resolution seems as mild as could have been passed by the conference without producing disastrous division within northern Methodism, and yet the southern delegates fiercely resented it. As they fully perceived, the condemnation of Bishop Andrew included by implication the condemnation of all other slaveholding ministers. Inasmuch, then, as the southern delegates were predominantly slaveholders,[154] it is not surprising that they were furious. For-

---

1844, 186-98. Signers of the protest were overwhelmingly southerners, although a few were from the North.
151. *Ibid.*, 198.
152. *Ibid.*, 204-5.
153. *Ibid.*, 203-4.
154. "According to the census records of 1850," says Joseph Mitchell, "34 of the 47 delegates to the 1844 General Conference who were still living in the South, owned a total of 422 slaves." "Traveling Preacher and Settled Farmer," *Methodist History*, V,

tunately for them, the General Conference of 1844 agreed upon a plan of division (although it was later repudiated by northern Methodism), but even if no plan had emerged southern Methodists would have severed relations with their brethren of the free states.[155]

In May, 1845, delegates from the annual conferences of Methodism within the slaveholding states met at Louisville, Kentucky, where they organized the Methodist Episcopal Church, South, with some 500,000 members. In explaining why this new branch of Methodism had become necessary, the Committee on Organization, of which Henry B. Bascom was chairman, not only repeated the points of conflict between the two sectional parties, as put forward in the southern protest of 1844, but raised a new point of "irreconcilable" difference to which it attached primary importance. Northern Methodists, said the committee, claimed the right of the church to agitate the slavery question, whereas southern Methodists contended that slavery was "a strictly civil institution exclusively in the custody of the civil power," and that the church should leave that institution strictly alone and merely inculcate the several duties arising out of the master-slave relationship.[156] This noninterventionist role of the church, added the committee, squared with the views of Jesus, the Apostles, and John Wesley.

In assigning slavery to the custody of the state, Methodism South played into the hands of Caesar and at the same time entangled itself all the more inextricably in the bondage system. "The true character and actual relations of slavery in the United States are *so predominantly civil and political,*" declared the Bascom report, "that any attempt to treat the subject or control the question upon purely moral and ecclesiastical grounds, can never exert any salutary influence South, except in so far as the moral and ecclesiastical

---

13. Five of those delegates owned twenty or more slaves each, and twelve more owned between ten and nineteen each. Shortly after the General Conference of 1844, a prominent South Carolina delegate to that body, William M. Wightman, a slaveowner, observed that "the Methodist ministry in the Southern Conferences are for the most part slaveowners." *Southern Christian Advocate,* July 26, 1844.

155. For a standard account of the division, see John N. Norwood, *The Schism in the Methodist Episcopal Church, 1844* (Alfred, N.Y., 1923).

156. Henry B. Bascom (chairman), *Report of the Committee on Organization, Presented to the Convention of Delegates from the Annual Conferences of the Methodist Episcopal Church in the Southern and South-Western States, May 14, 1845* (Louisville, 1845), 5–7.

shall be found strictly subordinate to the civil and political."[157] That is plainly an implicit admission of southern Methodism's moral surrender to the civil power. Consequently when the clergymen of this new branch of Methodism exhorted bondsmen to be obedient to their masters, they in effect bowed the knee to Caesar and acknowledged their subordination to his rule.[158]

Traditionally, southern Methodist leaders have usually claimed that the rupture of 1844 was caused less by slavery than by divergent doctrines of church polity.[159] To be sure, the question of the power of the bishop as against that of the General Conference was discussed to some extent. Nonetheless, the ultimate and decisive cause was unquestionably slavery. As William A. Smith was a leading participant in the controversy of 1844, his view on the matter is worth recalling. In August, 1849, during a newspaper debate with Norval Wilson, a northern Methodist minister, he affirmed unequivocally that slavery "was the *cause* of the [Methodist] rupture, and ... other things were the occasions only."[160] That verdict is fully sustained by the scholarly research of Donald G. Mathews.[161] It is a reasonably safe wager that if southern Methodists had not been deeply entangled in the institution of Negro bondage, they would have remained in organic communion with their northern brethren. Symbolic of their continuing entanglement in it after the schism is the fact that every clergyman whom they elected to the episcopacy between 1846 and the Civil War was a slaveholder.

Despite the North-South split, it would be a mistake to infer that

---

157. *Ibid.*, 12.
158. For a provocative interpretation of southern Methodism's theory of church-state responsibilities in relation to slavery, see Lewis M. Purifoy, "The Southern Methodist Church and the Proslavery Argument," *Journal of Southern History*, XXXII (August, 1966), 325–41.
159. This traditional notion still persists. See, for example, Norman W. Spellman, "Interpreting the Conference [of 1844]," in Emory Stevens Bucke, ed., *The History of American Methodism* (3 vols., New York, 1964), II, 65–85. Spellman, in minimizing the importance of the slavery question, mistakenly claims that "the Southern leaders refused to debate the slavery issue," and that only one southerner, Samuel Dunwody of South Carolina, did actually debate it. *Ibid.*, 65, 66, 84.
160. *Correspondence Between Rev. Wm. A. Smith, D.D., President of Randolph-Macon College, and Rev. Norval Wilson, Pastor of the Methodist Episcopal Church, North, in the Town of Fredericksburg, As Published in the "Fredericksburg News"* (Fredericksburg, 1849), 6.
161. Mathews, *Slavery and Methodist*, 250 n.

the leadership of northern Methodism had gone abolitionist. Actually, that leadership remained surprisingly conservative on the bondage question for the next twenty years.[162] At least two cardinal tenets marked a true Methodist abolitionist: first, that to hold a human being as property was a sin under all circumstances; and, second, that slaveholding necessarily disqualified one for church membership.[163] The "Counter Appeal" of 1835 stoutly denied the validity of those two tenets, and yet that document contained the basic platform upon which the conservatives prevented four general conferences (1848–60) from so revising the general rule on human bondage as to exclude all owners of Negroes from the Methodist Episcopal Church. In the meantime the border conferences of the church went undisciplined, even though many of their local and itinerant preachers remained slaveholders throughout the antebellum period.[164]

During the decade of the 1850's, antislavery sentiment grew rapidly in Methodism under the impetus of such militant abolitionists as Gilbert Haven in New England and William Hosmer in western New York.[165] Even so, not until 1864 did the General Conference so amend the general rule on slavery as to deny church membership to all slaveholders.[166] But by that time, thanks largely to the success of Union arms, the measure was superfluous.

III

Baptist abolitionism, like that of Methodism, arose in New England. The early movement was led by Maine, where Baptists num-

162. Milton P. Powell, "The Abolitionist Controversy in the Methodist Episcopal Church, 1840–1864" (typed Ph.D. dissertation, State University of Iowa, 1963), Chap. 6.

163. This twofold conviction was clearly expressed in a set of resolutions passed by the Methodist antislavery convention held at Boston in January, 1843. These resolutions are reprinted in Smith, Handy, and Loetscher, *American Christianity*, II, 198–200.

164. For documentary evidence of ministerial slaveholding in the border conferences, see Hiram Mattison, *The Impending Crisis of 1860; Or the Present Connection of the Methodist Episcopal Church with Slavery, and Our Duty in Regard to It* (New York, 1859), Chaps. 5–7.

165. Gilbert Haven, *National Sermons: Speeches and Letters on Slavery and Its War* . . . (Boston, 1869); William B. Gravely, "Gilbert Haven, Racial Equalitarian: A Study of His Career in Racial Reform, 1850–1880" (typed Ph.D. dissertation, Duke University, 1969); William Hosmer, *The Higher Law* (Auburn, N.Y., 1852).

166. *Journal of the General Conference of the Methodist Episcopal Church, . . . 1864* (New York, 1864), 167.

bered over thirteen thousand by 1830.[167] As early as 1833 the Kennebec Association condemned human bondage as an inherently sinful institution. Eastern, York, Waldo, and Washington associations soon expressed similar sentiments.[168] Some associations went so far as to exclude slaveholders from Christian fellowship. Hancock Association, for example, in 1837 voted to "have no fellowship or communion with those who, under the character of Christians, continue to hold their fellow-men in bondage."[169] By January, 1841, over one hundred and eighty of Maine's two hundred and fourteen Baptist ministers were said to be "decided abolitionists."[170] Three of the most influential abolitionist ministers were Edwin R. Warren, James Gilpatrick, and Samuel Adlam.

Baptist leaders in New Hampshire and Vermont also soon caught the abolitionist fever. In a letter of January, 1837, addressed to W. H. Murch, secretary of the Baptist Union of England, Baron Stow reported that "all but three or four" of New Hampshire's approximately fifty Baptist ministers were "*known* to be abolitionists."[171] A hotbed of Baptist abolitionism in Vermont was the Shaftsbury Association, which in 1837 scattered its antislavery resolutions throughout the South. Shaftsbury also told southern slaveholders that they could not be admitted to Baptist pulpits and communion tables in Vermont.[172]

In Massachusetts, Salem and Worcester associations were in the Baptist antislavery vanguard.[173] A leading spokesman in the Salem body was Cyrus Pitt Grosvenor, who served as pastor of that town's

167. Fay M. Graham, "Maine Baptists and the Antislavery Movement, 1830–1850" (typed M.A. thesis, University of Maine, 1962), 7. This figure does not include the Freewill Baptists, of whom there were more than nine thousand in 1830. Taken together, the Baptists were far stronger than any other denomination in the state. *Ibid.*, 7–8.
168. *Ibid.*, 35–38, 40.
169. Austin Willey, *The History of the Antislavery Cause in State and Nation*, 109–10.
170. *Ibid.*, 155; Graham, "Maine Baptists," 60.
171. Baron Stow to W. H. Murch, January 7, 1837, in A. T. Foss and Edward Mathews, compilers, *Facts For Baptist Churches: [Original Documents] Collected, Arranged and Reviewed* (Utica, N.Y., 1850), 35.
172. Robert A. Baker, "The American Baptist Home Mission Society and the South, 1832–1894" (typed Ph.D. dissertation, Yale University, 1947), 66–67.
173. *Minutes of the Salem Baptist Association, . . . 1836* (Salem, Mass., 1836), 18; *Minutes of the Salem Baptist Association, . . . 1841* (Boston, 1841), 15; *Minutes of the Worcester Baptist Association, . . . 1834* (Worcester, Mass., 1834), 6; *Minutes of the Worcester Baptist Association, . . . 1838* (Worcester, Mass., 1838), 9.

Second Baptist Church from 1831 to 1834. The Anti-Slavery Society of Salem and Vicinity, which was organized in January, 1834, elected him as its first president. In a vibrant speech before that society he denounced slavery as an "ungodly institution" and insisted that "universal emancipation ought to be entered upon immediately."[174]

The response of southern Baptists to their antislavery brethren in New England was caustic. The Charleston Baptist Association told the "deluded and mischievous fanatics" that their efforts to convince southerners that slavery was sinful would be fruitless as long as the latter had their Bibles. At the same time the association issued a solemn warning, saying: "We cannot but regard any interference with this [slavery] question from others, not only as officious and unfriendly, but incendiary and murderous in its tendency, highly injurious to the interests of the slaves themselves, and fatal to the feelings of a common brotherhood."[175] Similar resolutions were passed by many other Baptist bodies in the South.[176]

Fortunately for slaveholding Baptists, many of their northern coreligionists also opposed the abolitionists. This was notably true of the influential Baptist educator, Francis Wayland, president of Brown University. Although opposed to slavery, he wrote William Lloyd Garrison in November, 1831, that he did not wish to receive any more issues of the *Liberator*, as in his opinion immediate abolition was neither wise nor just.[177] This was no fleeting notion, for in an important essay, published in 1838, he argued that abolition societies were harmful to both sections of the nation. By angering southern masters, they had increased the misery of the slaves. In the North, they had "become the tools of third rate politicians." Furthermore, these societies did not offer any plan whereby slavery could be constitutionally abolished.[178]

---

174. *Address Before the Anti-Slavery Society of Salem and Vicinity, in the South Meeting-House, in Salem, February 24, 1834* (Salem, Mass., 1834), 7.

175. *Minutes of the Charleston Baptist Association, at the Eighty-Fifth Anniversary, ... 1835* (Charleston, 1835), 6.

176. Willie Grier Todd, "The Slavery Issue and the Organization of a Southern Baptist Convention" (typed Ph.D. dissertation, University of North Carolina at Chapel Hill, 1964), 90–95.

177. The letter is reprinted in Wendell P. and Francis J. Garrison, *William Lloyd Garrison, 1805–1879* (4 vols., Boston, 1885–89), I, 242–44.

178. *The Limitations of Human Responsibility* (Boston, 1838), 183–86. The Maine Anti-Slavery Society charged that this work was "inaccurate in statement, sophistical and deceptive in reasoning." The society also asserted that it had been "widely cir-

During this period, antiabolitionists like Wayland were in command of the Baptist General or Triennial Convention and of its Board of Foreign Missions.[179] This fact was made perfectly clear, first of all, in response to a letter from English Baptists. On December 31, 1833, the Board of Baptist Ministers in And Near London had directed a letter to the president of the General Convention, Spencer H. Cone of New York, branding slavery "a sin to be abandoned, and not an evil to be mitigated," and appealing to Baptist clergymen throughout the United States "to seek, by all legitimate means, its speedy and entire destruction."[180] Eight months later, on September 1, 1834, the Board of Foreign Missions replied to that communication through its corresponding secretary, Lucius Bolles of Boston. In short, the board told the Englishmen that it could not interfere with slavery, since it was "not among the objects for which the Convention and the Board were formed."[181] In his letter transmitting the board's resolutions, Bolles presented an extended apology for maintaining a hands-off policy toward slavery. He urged, for one thing, that slavery could never be abolished without the free consent of slaveholders. For another, he and many other Americans were of the opinion that immediate emancipation would benefit neither the blacks nor the whites. Far from even intimating that owning Negroes was sinful, he said: "We have the best evidence that our slaveholding brethren are Christians, sincere followers of the Lord Jesus."[182]

For several months the board's action was unknown to Baptist abolitionists in America, but when they learned about it they were highly indignant. Fifty Baptist ministers held a convention at Boston in May, 1835, and endorsed a letter, as drafted by Cyrus Gros-

---

culated and adopted as a text book at the South by slaveholders." Willey, *The History of the Antislavery Cause in State and Nation*, 68.

179. The convention was organized in 1814 as "The General Missionary Convention of the Baptist Denomination in the United States of America For Foreign Missions." It is commonly called the General Convention, though also often referred to as the Triennial Convention, since it met every three years. Its executive agent, the "Acting Board of Foreign Missions," had its office in Boston.

180. The entire long letter is in Foss and Mathews, compilers, *Facts For Baptist Churches*, 17–20.

181. "A Letter From the Baptist Board of Foreign Missions in America in Answer to One From the Board of Baptist Ministers in and Near London, Dated December 31, 1833," in Foss and Mathews, compilers, *Facts For Baptist Churches*, 21.

182. *Ibid.*, 22–23.

venor, to be sent to the London Board of Baptist ministers. By the time the letter was dispatched, it bore the signatures of more than one hundred and eighty persons. "Slaveholding is now the most heinous sin with which America is chargeable," said the abolitionists.[183] Assuring the London churchmen that their letter of 1833 would "produce a good and powerful result" in America, they added, "it is now going out through the length and breadth of our extensive country."[184]

Another national denominational agency equally opposed to abolitionism was the Baptist General Tract Society, founded in 1824. When, in 1835, some "friends in the South" complained that an agent of the society had been sowing the seeds of antislavery in their region, the Board of Managers promptly ruled that agents of the society "shall abstain from all interference with the agitating question of slavery." The board also voted to require all its agents to take a pledge not to interfere with human bondage. In submitting the board's resolutions to southern Baptist papers, the general agent of the tract society, Ira M. Allen, was careful to point out that he himself had never done anything, directly or indirectly, to give the least encouragement to abolitionism.[185]

Nevertheless, southern Baptist leaders had an increasingly uneasy feeling that, despite the precautions taken by northern conservatives, abolitionism was getting a foothold in the general agencies of their church.[186] Their apprehensions were soon fully confirmed, for when one hundred and ten abolitionists met in New York City on April 28–30, 1840, and organized the American Baptist Anti-Slavery Convention, they elected as president of that body Elon Galusha, a vice president of the Board of Foreign Missions. On top of that, the convention sent a pungent address to Baptist slaveholders in the South signed by Galusha.[187] After denouncing

---

183. "Letter to England From a Baptist Convention Held in Boston, May 26 and 27, 1835," in Foss and Mathews, compilers, *Facts For Baptist Churches*, 26.

184. *Ibid.*, 27.

185. For the resolutions of the Board of Managers and a portion of Allen's letter, see Todd, "The Slavery Issue and the Organization of a Southern Baptist Convention," 98–99.

186. Indeed, Baron Stow of Boston, writing to W. H. Murch of England in January, 1837, acknowledged that "several members of the Board [of Foreign Missions] are sincere and pledged abolitionists." Stow to Murch, January 7, 1837, in Foss and Mathews, compilers, *Facts For Baptist Churches*, 34.

187. The entire address is in the *Christian Reflector* (Worcester, Mass.), May 20,

slavery as "a violation of the instincts of nature,—a perversion of the first principles of justice,—and a positive transgression of the revealed will of God," the address closed with a stern warning, saying: "If you should . . . remain deaf to the voice of warning and entreaty . . . we cannot and we dare not recognize you as consistent brethren in Christ; we cannot . . . hear preaching which makes God the author and approver of human misery and vassalage; and we cannot, at the Lord's table, cordially take that as a brother's hand, which plies the scourge on woman's naked flesh,—which thrusts a gag into the mouth of man,—which rivets fetters on the innocent,— and which shuts up the Bible from human eyes."

That "voice of warning," far from being heeded, doubly enraged the southern "brethren," and they retaliated with a spate of resolutions from churches and other bodies castigating abolitionists in general and Elon Galusha in particular.[188] Smarting under the charge that slaveholders were unfit for Christian fellowship, they warned that unless aspersions upon their character ceased they would cut off their benevolent funds to the general Baptist agencies, and, if necessary, even separate from them altogether. As they obviously wanted the Board of Foreign Missions to remove Galusha from its membership, they anxiously awaited a response from that body.

Yet the Boston board kept quiet for many months, despite the southern uproar. Finally, on November 2, 1840, a response was made in the form of an address, which was printed and widely circulated.[189] The exclusive purpose of the Board of Foreign Missions, said the address, "was to 'send the glad tidings of salvation to the heathen.'" Although studiously avoiding the term slavery, the document made it clear that this subject fell entirely outside the board's constitutionally assigned function. The membership of the board, added the address, was not determinable by the board

---

1840. This abolitionist paper began publication in 1838, with Cyrus P. Grosvenor as editor.

188. Todd, "The Slavery Issue and the Organization of a Southern Baptist Convention," 154–56, 163–71; Mary B. Putnam, *The Baptists and Slavery, 1840–1845* (Ann Arbor, 1913), 25–26; Baker, "The American Baptist Home Mission Society and the South, 1832–1894," 82–83.

189. "Address," *Baptist Missionary Magazine*, XX (December, 1840), 281–84. The address was signed by Daniel Sharp, president of the board, and Baron Stow, recording secretary.

further than to fill its vacancies. In particular, the board had "no power of excision." The General Convention "appoints its own Board, triennially, in view of the qualifications which itself prescribes; and appoints whom it pleases."[190]

That communication sorely disappointed southern spokesmen of the church, for they were seeking allies, not neutralists. Georgia Baptists, among others, made this fact unmistakably clear when they were notified in January, 1841, that the Board of Foreign Missions was sending its treasurer, Heman Lincoln of Boston, to explain why the lately published address had refrained from taking a position on the slavery question. Anticipating that visit, the chairman of the executive committee of the Georgia Baptist State Convention, B. M. Sanders, wrote bluntly: "Between us and the abolitionists we know no neutrals. Those who are not for us are against us. If the object of the Board in sending their delegate to us, is to try to steer between us and the abolitionists, and maintain the cooperation of both, they might well have spared themselves the *expense* and *trouble*. In this crusade against *us*, if they think to court the alliance of our enemies and conciliate our favor, they must be grossly ignorant of our feelings."[191] When Lincoln met the executive committee, he tried to convince it that the Boston board "had no sympathies with the late proceedings of the Northern Abolitionists, nor with the spirit of their publications, denouncing and excommunicating Southern Brethren," but he did not succeed in clearing up "several material points."[192]

During this period, the American Baptist Home Mission Society was also seeking to placate disgruntled members of its southern constituency. With this objective in view, the executive committee on February 16, 1841, issued a circular in which it, like the Boston board, argued strenuously that the society would be violating its constitution if it entered the slavery controversy. But even if the constitution authorized such a step, the society would make a mistake to enter the contest, since neither the abolitionists nor the southerners would be satisfied with the decisions reached.[193] Once

190. *Ibid.*, 281, 283.
191. *Christian Index* (Penfield, Ga.), February 19, 1841.
192. *Ibid.*, March 12, 1841.
193. For text of circular, see *Christian Index*, April 9, 1841. The circular was

again, however, Georgia Baptist spokesmen did not relish the posture of neutrality on the bondage question. Noting that the authors of the circular wished to be nonpartisan in the current controversy, the editor of the *Christian Index*, William H. Stokes, asked, "Have they no opinion which party is in the wrong?"[194]

These and other communications from the general agencies of the denomination did little to cool the tempers of the aroused proslavery Baptists. A major crisis loomed, and many leaders in both sections feared a division of their communion was imminent. Could a rupture be avoided? The ensuing General Convention, which was scheduled to meet at Baltimore in late April, 1841, would likely determine the answer to that question. Southern delegates to that gathering were in no concessive mood on the "vexing question." Some fifty of them met in Baltimore for a pre-convention caucus to frame their demands. Anticipating their probable demands, seventy-four influential northern conservatives and southerners, meeting secretly, had approved and signed a so-called "compromise" paper, drafted by Spencer Cone, president of the convention.[195] The kernel of the document was contained in the statement "that no new tests unauthorized by the Scriptures, and by the established usage of the great body of our churches, should be suffered to interfere with the harmonious operations of our benevolent associations, as originally constituted."[196] The new tests went unspecified, but everyone understood that they referred to the position of Baptist abolitionists who, predicating the inherent sinfulness of man's ownership of a fellow being, contended that slaveholders should be denied Christian fellowship and refused appointment as missionaries.

As soon as this remarkable paper was laid before the southern delegates, it soothed their ruffled spirits and gave them hope that, after all, a reconciliation might be achieved largely on their own terms. As the Georgia delegation later reported, it "determined the

---

signed by Spencer H. Cone, chairman of the executive committee of the Home Mission Society, and Benjamin M. Hill, recording secretary.

194. *Ibid.*, April 9, 1841.

195. "Compromise Article," in Foss and Mathews, compilers, *Facts For Baptist Churches*, 75–76.

196. *Ibid.*, 76. For a scathing attack upon this document by Nathaniel Colver of Boston, one of the ablest Baptist abolitionists, see *ibid.*, 77–81.

Southern delegates to take no action until after the election of the Board of Managers."[197] That election went well for the South. Elon Galusha, a vice president of the board, was replaced by Richard Fuller of South Carolina, a slaveholder. Baron Stow, recording secretary of the board, had also been marked for the axe, but at the eleventh hour he wrote a letter to Solomon Peck, foreign secretary, saying that he had never favored the address which the Baptist Anti-Slavery Convention of 1840 sent to southern Baptists, and that he had refused to distribute it among them. "I have never been able to satisfy myself from the New Testament," he added, "that I ought to deny any courtesy to a Christian brother because he is a slaveholder." This timely overture to the proslavery party saved Stow's official neck. In the words of two prominent Dixie delegates, "this communication induced the Southern delegates to believe it would be impolitic to oppose his re-election."[198]

Still another change in the convention's official leadership helped to placate the South. When Spencer H. Cone of New York declined re-election as president, the convention chose William B. Johnson of South Carolina, a slaveholder, as his successor.

The convention's "happy adjustment," as the Georgia delegation called it, was generally hailed with joy by southern Baptists. And why not? For the "adjustment" or "compromise" was fundamentally a capitulation to the proslavery faction of the denomination. Reportedly, abolitionist delegates "took their leave of the Convention in wrath."[199] They were the more wrathful because the "adjustment" could not have been achieved without the cooperation of northern conservatives. "Let it not be said that this was the work of the South alone," observed two incensed abolitionists. "No, it was northern votes that accomplished this guilty deed. For not more than one-third of the delegates to the Convention were from the South."[200]

The "happy adjustment," however, proved to be of short duration, because the Baptist antislavery movement was already gathering momentum every year.[201] Although abolitionist delegates were

197. "Report of the [Georgia] Delegates," in *Minutes of the Twentieth Anniversary of the Georgia Baptist Convention, . . . 1841* (Penfield, Ga., 1841), 7.
198. *Ibid.*, 8.
199. *Ibid.*
200. Foss and Mathews, compilers, *Facts For Baptist Churches*, 82.
201. Putnam, *The Baptists and Slavery*, 30–31, 46–47.

pained by the Baltimore reverses, they did not despair; on the contrary, they soon held conventions in New York and Boston which fired them with new zeal.[202] As a result, when the General Convention met at Philadelphia in April, 1844, the struggle was renewed under conditions more favorable to antislavery Baptists. Yet once again the powerful coalition of northern conservatives and southerners fought stubbornly to stem the tide of "fanaticism." Repeating their old strategy, Richard Fuller promptly offered a resolution declaring in substance that, under its constitution, the convention could not transact any business except that relating to Christian missions. But he soon withdrew it in favor of one presented by George B. Ide of Philadelphia, saying "that, in cooperating together as members of this Convention in the work of Foreign Missions, we disclaim all sanction, either express or implied, whether of slavery or of anti-slavery; but, as individuals, we are perfectly free both to express and to promote, elsewhere, our own views on these subjects in a Christian manner and spirit."[203] This resolution "was adopted with great unanimity."

The situation was entirely different in the Home Mission Society, which was holding its sessions in Philadelphia at the same time. In that body a heated controversy went on for days. The debate was touched off by a foremost Maine abolitionist, Samuel Adlam, who surprised conservative members of the society by offering a resolution saying that "a minister being a slaveholder should present no barrier to his being employed as a missionary by this Society."[204] Adlam himself of course was opposed to the resolution, but he presented it in order to compel the society to say unequivocally whether it would or would not appoint a slaveholder as a missionary. To forestall discussion and to give the coalition of northern conservatives and southerners time to meet this unexpected resolution, the session was immediately adjourned. After an interval of some two days, the Adlam resolution was debated "with much animation" for an entire morning. When the meeting re-

202. Foss and Mathews, compilers, *Facts For Baptist Churches*, 86. The New York convention brought together Baptist abolitionists from nine states.
203. "Minutes of the Eleventh Triennial Meeting [1844]," *Baptist Missionary Magazine*, XXIV (July, 1844), 158.
204. *Twelfth Report of the American Baptist Home Mission Society, Presented by the Executive Board at the Anniversary in Philadelphia, April 23, 1844* (New York, 1844), 5.

sumed after a weekend, Richard Fuller, an adroit tactician, offered an amendment to Adlam's resolution the most important part of which affirmed, first, that the introduction of the slavery question into the work of the Home Mission Society was a violation of its constitution, and, second, that cooperation in the society did "not imply any sympathy either with slavery or anti-slavery."[205] A fiery exchange followed between proslavery and antislavery preachers. Jeremiah Jeter of Virginia and Fuller firmly denied that slaveholding was necessarily a sin.[206] On the other hand, William Henry Brisbane, a native of South Carolina and a former slaveholding planter, took precisely the opposite view. He also argued that even to hold fellowship with a slaveholder was "to partake of his evil deeds."[207] Once again, however, the coalition held together, and the Fuller amendment was carried by a vote of 123 to 61.[208]

That was the coalition's last victory, and even it was more apparent than real; for already storm clouds warned that a breakup of the Home Mission Society was imminent. Indeed, before the present meeting adjourned a committee of ten was appointed to consider "an amicable dissolution" of the society "or to report such alterations in the Constitution" as would "admit of the co-operation of brethren who cherish conflicting views on the subject of slavery."[209] The committee, of which Heman Lincoln of Boston was chairman, conferred briefly before leaving Philadelphia and agreed to hold its first meeting in April, 1845, two days before the annual session of the Home Mission Society. But in the meantime swiftly moving events rendered its labors useless.

As early as May, 1843, some of the denomination's more aggressive antislavery leaders had already withdrawn from the General Convention and formed the American Baptist Free Mission Society, which limited its membership and missionaries to non-

205. *Ibid.*, 5–6.
206. Foss and Mathews, compilers, *Facts For Baptist Churches*, 90; Putnam, *The Baptists and Slavery*, 39–40.
207. William H. Brisbane, *A Speech Delivered April 30, 1844, Before the Baptist Home Mission Society on the Question of the Propriety of Recognizing Slaveholding Ministers as Proper Missionaries of the Gospel* (n.p., n.d.), 2–6. See also Brisbane, *A Letter to the Baptist Denomination in South Carolina* (Cincinnati, 1840); *Speech of the Rev. W. H. Brisbane, Lately a Slaveholder in South Carolina: Delivered Before the Female Anti-Slavery Society of Cincinnati, February 12, 1840* (Cincinnati, 1840).
208. *Twelfth Report of the American Baptist Home Mission Society, . . . 1844*, 6.
209. *Ibid.*, 6.

slaveholders.[210] Apparently many others were on the verge of leaving the convention after the Philadelphia assembly in 1844, for in the following September the Baptist Anti-Slavery Convention declared "that inasmuch as the Baptist Triennial Convention and its Board, have, in our opinion, manifested an incurable proslavery spirit, and are essentially committed to the fellowship of slaveholders, and the employment of them as missionaries, we do therefore solemnly believe, that the time has come, for a distinct and permanent missionary organization."[211]

This was good news to southern Baptists, for they believed that if the antislavery radicals would withdraw from the General Convention and the other benevolent agencies, a North-South split could be prevented. They wanted to continue relations with their northern antiabolitionist brethren, but they absolutely refused to cooperate with the "fanatics." "The union or separation of our denomination in our General Societies rests, under God, with our Northern brethren, who are not Abolitionists," said William B. Johnson in September, 1844. "If they shall choose to work with the Abolitionists, a separation will take place. But if they shall choose to work with us, the union will continue, and the Abolitionists will go off to themselves, which I think they ought to have done some time ago."[212]

But northern conservative Baptists did not want the rapidly multiplying abolitionists to "go off to themselves," as this would leave the parent body in a precarious plight. If therefore a rupture had to come, they preferred to see the slaveholders go off to themselves. Already conservative northern members of the benevolent boards and societies recognized that the time was drawing near when they would have to take a public stand against employing slaveholders as missionaries, or else run a grave risk of a disastrous division in their regional ranks.

In the fall of 1844 Georgia Baptists apparently heard a rumor that the Home Mission Society was questioning the advisability of continuing its policy of appointing slaveholders as missionaries. To

210. "Constitution and By-Laws of the American Baptist Free Mission Society," in Foss and Mathews, compilers, *Facts For Baptist Churches*, 398.
211. Quoted in Todd, "The Slavery Issue and the Organization of a Southern Baptist Denomination," 255.
212. *Minutes of the Edgefield Baptist Association, ... 1844* (Edgefield, S.C., 1844), 5.

determine whether that was the case, the executive committee of the Georgia Baptist Convention recruited a slaveholding preacher, James Reeve, and requested that he be appointed as a missionary to Georgia Indians. The committee noted in particular that Reeve held slaves. This turned out to be an agonizing case, and the executive board of the society wrestled with it in five three-hour sessions. Finally, by a vote of seven to five, the board rejected the application on the flimsy excuse that the Georgia committee had violated the constitution of the Home Mission Society by injecting the subject of slavery into the Reeve appointment.[213] This rebuff understandably outraged the Georgia brethren.

A similar rumor prompted the Baptist State Convention of Alabama in November, 1844, to present a set of resolutions to Daniel Sharp, president of the board of managers of the General Convention, demanding "the distinct, explicit avowal that slaveholders are eligible, and entitled, equally with non-slaveholders, to all the privileges and immunities of their several unions; and especially to receive any agency, mission, or other appointment, which may fall within the scope of their operations or duties."[214] This inquiry was far from welcome in Boston, but the board replied unequivocally that if "any one should offer himself as a missionary, having slaves, and should insist on retaining them as his property, we could not appoint him. One thing is certain, we can never be a party to any arrangement which would imply approbation of slavery."[215]

Baptist abolitionists rejoiced over the Boston board's decision, but their southern brethren abominated it. The board of the Virginia Foreign Mission Society called it "unconstitutional" and a "violation of the rights of the Southern members of the Convention," and exhorted "aggrieved" southerners to gather in convention at Augusta, Georgia, on May 8, 1845, "to confer on the best means of promoting the Foreign Mission cause, and other interests of the Baptist denomination in the South."[216] Baptist leaders poured

---

213. For the complete reply of the executive board, see Foss and Mathews, compilers, *Facts For Baptist Churches*, 125–26.
214. "The Baptist State Convention of Alabama," *Baptist Missionary Magazine*, XXV (August, 1845), 221.
215. "Reply of the Acting Board, December 17th, 1844," *Baptist Missionary Magazine*, XXV (August, 1845), 222.
216. *Religious Herald* (Richmond), March 13, 1845. This same issue of the *Herald* published the Boston board's reply to the Alabama Baptists.

into Augusta on the appointed day and speedily organized "The Southern Baptist Convention," with William B. Johnson as its first president.[217]

IV

A comparison of the North-South Baptist, Methodist, and Presbyterian debates reveals a common pattern that is worth special reflection. During the antislavery crusade prior to the middle 1840's, virtually all the leading northern clergymen of these three denominations opposed "modern abolitionism" and united with their southern brethren to defeat it. This coalition of northern conservatives and southerners finally came unstuck under the pressure of political events and the growth of antislavery sentiment, but for many years it throttled the abolitionist movement within these three nationwide churches. The main reason usually given by the northern conservative for his antiabolitionist and prosouthern position was that he wanted to prevent a division within his communion. That this was a motivating factor must be acknowledged, because it has been characteristic of the religious conservative to attach greater importance to ecclesiastical unity than to reform. Yet the desire to avoid schism was by no means the only factor in his coalition tactic. In fact, he and his southern brother held positions on slavery that tended to unite them against the abolitionist.

First, the northern conservative disagreed with the abolitionist's fundamental contention that it was sinful, under all circumstances, to hold a fellow being as one's property, and that consequently no slaveholder should be received into the church. He freely acknowledged that slaveholding would be sinful if the master misused his power over the bondsman, but he emphatically denied that the master-slave relation as such was sinful. For him, therefore, a slaveowner had as much right to church membership as the non-slaveholder.

Second, the northern conservative seriously questioned the abolitionist's doctrine of immediate universal emancipation. He considered it a colossal mistake suddenly to turn loose upon the nation

---

217. William B. Barnes, *The Southern Baptist Convention, 1845–1953* (Nashville, 1954), 12–32.

a horde of illiterate, uncouth, and undisciplined blacks. While now and then affirming the desirability of the universal abolition of human bondage, he urged the great necessity of its being accomplished very gradually, and only as fast as the blacks were prepared to make constructive use of their freedom. According to him, the ideal process by which to accomplish emancipation was that of "amelioration." The proper function of the church was thus not to agitate the slavery question at all, but rather to preach the gospel to master and slave alike and to inculcate the duties of each according to the Pauline epistles. Such spiritual teaching, it was believed, would gradually ameliorate the condition of the slave and thus, under the providence of God, eventually result in his freedom with the full consent of his master. It was upon this basis that Charles Hodge of Princeton in 1836 proclaimed that the great duty of the South was "not emancipation," but "improvement" of its slaves.

Third, the northern conservative had little sympathy with the abolitionist's insistence that the Negro, upon liberation, be incorporated into American society on terms of equality with all other racial groups. Prevailingly, he held that the black man could never be granted racial equality without endangering the purity of the white race. The ghost of racial amalgamation always haunted him. Hence he generally supported the American Colonization Society as a means not only of evangelizing Africa, but also of getting rid of the Negro.

In all three respects, then, the northern conservative really had more in common with the southerner than with the abolitionist. When he thus acted in concert with the slaveholding members of his national denominational judicatory, he did so not merely to avoid schism, but also, and perhaps even mainly, because he agreed with much of his southern brother's racial and proslavery philosophy. The abolitionist therefore had considerable ground for maintaining that the northern conservative was an apologist for human bondage.

Chapter III

IN DEFENSE OF BONDAGE

Proslavery sentiment had been steadily growing in the South for at least a full generation before the Baptists and Methodists of that region organized autonomous denominations, but the latter development greatly accelerated that growth. Thereafter Protestant leaders in the slave states redoubled their efforts to frame an apologetic for human bondage that would consolidate southern opinion and also, if possible, undermine abolitionism in the free states.

Ever since the rise of "modern abolitionism," the charge that slaveholding was a sin under all circumstances had deeply agitated the southern churchman's psyche. Inasmuch as southerners considered themselves to be a very religious people, that stricture nettled them more than anything else in the entire abolitionist lexicon. "If slavery be a sin," retorted a Mississippi preacher and slaveowner to the Chillicothe Presbytery in 1836, "then, verily, three fourths of all the Episcopalians, Methodists, Baptists, and Presbyterians, in eleven States of the Union, 'are of the devil.' "[1] Fiercely resenting the stigma, James Smylie and his fellow churchmen published a rash of sermons, articles, and pamphlets to prove that, far from being "of the devil," they were truly Christian.

I

The southern churchman's major argument in defense of human bondage was biblical in nature. He contended relentlessly that the master-slave relation was explicitly sanctioned in both testaments of the Bible, and that consequently to denounce that relation as sinful per se was to impugn God's word. He had already

---

1. James Smylie, *A Review of a Letter from the Presbytery of Chillicothe, to the Presbytery of Mississippi, on the Subject of Slavery* (Woodville, Miss., 1836), 13.

refined this mode of argument in his battle against such internal critics of slavery as David Barrow and George Bourne,[2] and he now employed it to refute the claims of northern abolitionists. Frantically concerned to repel the charge that slaveholding was necessarily a sin, the southern preacher seized upon every crumb of scripture that might possibly support his argument. For our purpose, however, it seems sufficient to draw attention only to those passages of scripture that were regarded as the major bulwarks of slavery. Several of these were in the Old Testament.

As Theodore Weld, a foremost antislavery crusader, remarked in a popular tract, the "prophecy of Noah is the *vade mecum* of slaveholders, and they never venture abroad without it."[3] Upon recovering from a swig of wine, Noah, when informed that his youngest son, Ham—the father of Canaan—had seen him naked, exclaimed: "Cursed be Canaan; a slave of slaves shall he be to his brothers [Shem and Japheth]."[4] This text was employed in two ways. First, it was said to prove that God himself, not man, had inaugurated the institution of human bondage. Despite the fact that Noah was scarcely sober and obviously reacted in a fit of rage, a prominent minister of the Methodist Protestant Church claimed that "he spoke under the impulse and dictation of Heaven. His words were the words of God himself, and by them was slavery ordained. This was an early arrangement of the Almighty, to be perpetuated through all time."[5] Second, Noah's curse allegedly singled out the Negro for perpetual servitude to the white race. "It is gener-

---

2. David Barrow, *Involuntary, Unmerited, Perpetual, Absolute, Hereditary Slavery, Examined; on the Principles of Nature, Reason, Justice, Policy, and Scripture* (Lexington, Ky., 1808), 27–45; George Bourne, *The Book and Slavery Irreconcilable* (Philadelphia, 1816), Chap. 5.

3. *The Bible Against Slavery* (4th ed. enlarged, New York, 1838), 66.

4. Genesis 9:25.

5. Alexander McCaine, *Slavery Defended From Scripture, Against the Attacks of the Abolitionists, in a Speech Delivered Before the General Conference of the Methodist Protestant Church, in Baltimore, 1842* (Baltimore, 1842), 5. See also Frederick Dalcho, *Practical Considerations Founded on the Scriptures, Relative to the Slave Population of South Carolina* (Charleston, S.C., 1823), 8–18; Patrick H. Mell, *Slavery: A Treatise, Showing That Slavery Is Neither A Moral, Political, Nor Social Evil* (Penfield, Ga., 1844), 15; Thornton Stringfellow, *A Brief Examination of Scripture Testimony on the Institution of Slavery* (Richmond, 1841), 6; *Letters of the Late Bishop England to the Hon. John Forsyth, on the Subject of Domestic Slavery* (Baltimore, 1844), 24; James A. Sloan, *The Great Question Answered, or, Is Slavery a Sin in Itself?* (Memphis, 1857), 67–68; John L. Dagg, *The Elements of Moral Science* (New York, 1859), 344.

ally believed," said a South Carolina preacher and slaveholder, "that the Africans or Negroes, are the descendants of Ham; and it is by no means improbable that the very name Ham, which signifies burnt or black, was given to him prophetically, on account of the countries that his posterity were destined to inhabit. The judicial curse of Noah upon the posterity of Ham, seems yet to rest upon them."[6]

This interpretation of Noah's curse was no southern invention; indeed, it had been in circulation long before the discovery of America. Even so, it proved especially useful to white masters of the South, because they had been put on the defensive by the powerful emancipationist movement. Some writers gave this ancient tale a racist twist, as did John Fletcher of Louisiana, a northerner who became one of the South's most faithful defenders of human bondage. In his view, Ham's real sin—and the sin denoted in the judicial curse—was racial amalgamation. The wayward son had contaminated his own race by marrying into the race of Cain, who in consequence of having slain his brother Abel had been smitten with a black skin. On this account, all of Ham's descendants, and not merely those of Canaan, were Africans, or Negroes. On the other hand, Shem and Japheth were blessed with white descendants because they had married within their own race.[7] It was only right therefore that the degenerate black descendants of Ham were doomed to perpetual servitude to the superior white offspring of Shem and Japheth. Thus the white southerner need feel no pangs of conscience in holding property in Negroes. "I am persuaded," wrote David Barrow, "that no passage in the sacred volume of Revelation, has suffered more abuse, than 'Noah's curse or malediction.' "[8] Such concoctions as Fletcher's abundantly supported Barrow's observation.

While proslavery moralists generally cited to their comfort the fact that God's chosen people, such as Abraham, Isaac, and Jacob,

6. Samuel Dunwody, *A Sermon Upon the Subject of Slavery* (Columbia, S.C., 1837), 4. See also Sloan, *The Great Question Answered, or, Is Slavery a Sin in Itself?* 78–81.
7. *Studies on Slavery, in Easy Lessons* (Natchez, Miss., 1852), 435, 437, 442–51, 464–77. Interestingly, Nathan Lord, the proslavery president of Dartmouth College, also ascribed the curse upon Canaan partly to Ham's "forbidden intermarriage with the previously wicked and accursed race of Cain." *A Letter of Inquiry to Ministers of the Gospel of All Denominations on Slavery* (Hanover, N.H., 1860), 5–6.
8. *Involuntary . . . Slavery, Examined*, 28 n.

owned bondsmen, they felt even more confident of their right to hold property in human beings when they could lay their finger upon a "thus saith the Lord." Inevitably, therefore, Leviticus 25:44–46 became the major Old Testament bastion of their biblical argument. The crucial portions of that scripture read: "You may buy male and female slaves from among the nations that are round about you.... You may bequeath them to your sons after you, to inherit as a possession for ever." At the very least, maintained James Smylie, that scripture proved that God "gave a *written permit*, to the Hebrews, then the best people in the world, to *buy, hold, and bequeath, men and women*, to perpetual servitude."[9] In the opinion of Frederick A. Ross, a rigid proslavery new school Presbyterian of Huntsville, Alabama, God did more than merely permit slaveholding. Taking note of the fact that the Authorized, or King James, version used the word "shall" rather than "may," he contended that "God *commanded* them [Israelites] to be slave-holders. He *made it* the law of their social state."[10]

But granting, as most abolitionists did, that slavery in some form existed among the ancient Hebrews, did God intend to continue it forever, or only until the ceremonial rites of his chosen people were abolished? Addressing himself to that question, Smylie acknowledged that certain ceremonial laws may have been instituted for only a limited period. He argued, however, that the Decalogue (Ex. 20:3–17) was intended to be authoritative perpetually, since unlike other laws, it was "*engraven*, not written, on two tables of stone." Inasmuch, then, as both the fourth and the tenth commandments recognized the existence of human bondage, God evidently meant to continue it after the ceremonial regulations had been discontinued. "If God foresaw, or intended, that servitude should expire with the Mosaic ritual, the authority of masters would, probably, not be recognized in a law, intended to be perpetual; nor would there have been, as is the fact, a recognition made of servants, as property."[11]

---

9. *A Review of a Letter From the Presbytery of Chillicothe*, 21. See also *Letters of the Late Bishop England to the Hon. John Forsyth*, 28–29; Stringfellow, *A Brief Examination of Scripture Testimony*, 16; Albert T. Bledsoe, *An Essay on Liberty and Slavery* (Philadelphia, 1856), 145–49.

10. *Slavery Ordained of God* (Philadelphia, 1857), 149.

11. *A Review of a Letter From the Presbytery of Chillicothe*, 22. See also Mell,

The apologist for slavery found his task more difficult when he turned to the New Testament, for it contained no texts which explicitly authorized or sanctioned involuntary servitude. To get around this difficulty he generally claimed that what was explicitly taught in the Old Testament continued to be authoritative in the Christian era unless it was abrogated in the New Testament. A variant of that dubious notion was advanced by Richard Fuller, a South Carolina Baptist clergyman of wide influence in his denomination. "WHAT GOD SANCTIONED IN THE OLD TESTAMENT, AND PERMITTED IN THE NEW," he declared in a dialogue with Francis Wayland, president of Brown University, "CANNOT BE SIN."[12] He considered slavery to be permitted if it was nowhere explicitly condemned in the New Testament. That is to say, silence was tantamount to sanction.

The Fuller theory was especially useful in aligning Jesus on the side of human bondage, since in all four gospels he was entirely silent on the subject. The fact that Jesus in his parables made pedagogical use of the master-slave relation (as in Luke 17:7–10) without ever condemning slavery, signified to Bishop John England of the Diocese of Charleston (Catholic) that he did not regard it as sinful in principle.[13] James Smylie argued that if the relation of master and slave had been inherently sinful, Jesus would have been sure to make that fact clear when he healed the sick bondsman of the Centurion (Luke 7:2–10). Yet, far from reprimanding the Centurion for enslaving his fellowman, he applauded his faith as being greater than that to be found in all Israel. "His High approbation of the Centurion," Smylie said, "was certainly calculated to leave the impression, that slaveholding and Christianity, were not inconsistent with each other."[14] Another staunch apologist for man's ownership of man insisted that if Jesus had considered slavery to be a moral evil, he would not have failed to denounce it when preach-

---

Slavery: A Treatise Showing That Slavery is Neither a Moral, Political, Nor Social Evil, 12; McCaine, *Slavery Defended From Scripture*, 14, 16.

12. *Domestic Slavery Considered as a Scriptural Institution: In a Correspondence Between the Rev. Richard Fuller, of Beaufort, S.C., and the Rev. Francis Wayland, of Providence, R.I.* (New York, 1845), 170.

13. *Letters of the Late Bishop England to the Hon. John Forsyth*, 34. See also William A. Smith, *Lectures on the Philosophy and Practice of Slavery* (Nashville, 1856), 144.

14. *A Review of a Letter From the Presbytery of Chillicothe*, 31.

ing to Jewish congregations in which there were slaveholders.[15]

The abolitionists readily acknowledged that Jesus did not condemn slavery in so many words, but they always insisted that he laid down general principles which could not be reconciled with involuntary servitude. Above all else, they pointed to the law of love (Matt. 22:39) and the golden rule (Matt. 7:12) as subversive of the bondage system.[16] Yet Jesus' law of love to neighbor, replied Thornton Stringfellow, had already been enunciated in the Mosaic code (Lev. 19:18), and since that same code explicitly ordained man's bondage to man, the commandment of love to neighbor was entirely compatible with slavery.[17] The Virginia Baptist implicitly conceded his inability to harmonize slavery with the golden rule on similar grounds, but he urged that if that rule were so construed as to abolish slavery, it would "for the same reason level all human inequalities."[18]

Actually, southern moralists never pretended to apply the golden rule to the bondsman on the supposition that blacks and whites were equal. Just the opposite was the case. A leading theologian and slaveowner, James Henley Thornwell of South Carolina, spoke representatively for his fellow churchmen when he said: "Our Saviour directs us to do unto others what, in their situations, it would be right and reasonable in us to expect from them.... The [golden] rule then simply requires, in the case of slavery, that we should treat our slaves as we should feel that we had a right to be treated if we were slaves ourselves."[19]

Defenders of human bondage felt much more at home in the letters of Paul than they did in the teachings of Jesus, because those documents contained specific instructions on the duties of masters and slaves. In fact, virtually every proslavery tract of any consequence explored the Pauline epistles far more exhaustively than any other portion of the New Testament.[20] The authors of these

15. Smith, *Lectures on the Philosophy and Practice of Slavery*, 143.
16. See, for example, Fuller and Wayland, *Domestic Slavery*, 29–30.
17. *A Brief Examination of Scripture Testimony*, 18.
18. *Ibid.*, 19.
19. "Slavery and the Religious Instruction of the Coloured Population," *Southern Presbyterian Review*, IV (July, 1850), 135. For similar views, see William T. Hamilton, *The Duties of Masters and Slaves Respectively* (Mobile, 1845), 16; Bledsoe, *An Essay on Liberty and Slavery*, 77–79; Smith, *The Philosophy and Practice of Slavery*, 136–38.
20. See, for examples, George A. Baxter, *An Essay on the Abolition of Slavery* (Richmond, 1836), 14–16; Stephen Taylor, *Relations of Master and Servant, as Ex-*

tracts usually claimed to find supporting data in at least six different letters: 1 Corinthians 7:20–21; Ephesians 6:5–9; Colossians 3:22, 4:1; 1 Timothy 6:20–21; and Philemon 10–18. Upon a critical scrutiny of those particular scriptures, they stressed two things. First, Paul again and again admonished masters and slaves to fulfill their respective duties to one another without ever so much as intimating that a man had no right to enslave his fellow being. His silence, urged these writers, at the very least implied the apostle's approval of man's ownership of man. Had Paul perceived the slightest moral taint in human bondage, he never would have been content merely to advise masters to treat their slaves justly and fairly (Col. 4:1); he would certainly have warned them to let the oppressed go free. Besides, if he had really felt that slaveholding was a sin, Paul would not have returned his newly won convert, Onesimus, to his owner, Philemon, without making this fact absolutely clear. Yet far from censuring his "beloved fellow worker," Paul, according to Augustus B. Longstreet, a prominent Methodist preacher of Georgia and a slaveowner, recognized that Philemon's lawful authority over Onesimus was "of a character too sacred to be interfered with."[21]

Second, these proslavery moralists took pains to point out that slaveholders were members of churches founded by Paul and other apostles. This was true, for instance, of Philemon, a resident of Colossae and a member of the church there. To the religious leaders of the South, this fact demonstrated that the early church did not consider slaveholding sinful per se. They were the more certain of this, because applicants for admission to the primitive churches and to the sacraments were subjected to the most rigorous examination with respect to their spiritual qualifications for these privileges. "Before Baptism," noted Richard Fuller, "they [the apostles] required men to repent, that is, to abandon all their sins; yet they

---

hibited in the New Testament (Richmond, 1836), 7–19; George W. Freeman, *The Rights and Duties of Slaveholders* (Raleigh, 1836), 10–11; Smylie, *A Review of a Letter From the Presbytery of Chillicothe*, 36–52; Dunwody, *A Sermon Upon the Subject of Slavery*, 13–16; Fuller and Wayland, *Domestic Slavery*, 188–96; *Letters of the Late Bishop England to the Hon. John Forsyth*, 34–38; Thornton Stringfellow, *Slavery: Its Origin, Nature and History* (Alexandria, Va., 1860), 21–31.

21. *Letters of the Epistle of Paul to Philemon, or the Connection of Apostolical Christianity with Slavery* (Charleston, S.C., 1845), 47. See also Dagg, *Elements of Moral Science*, 349–50.

baptized masters holding slaves. They fenced the Lord's table with the most solemn warnings ... that to eat and drink unworthily was to eat and drink condemnation; yet they admitted to the supper masters holding slaves."[22] In calling attention to this practice of the early church, Fuller of course meant to rebuke those abolitionists who refused to hold fellowship with masters of slaves. He and many other holders of Negro property felt that such antislavery radicals presumed to be more righteous than the early Christians. "He who would debar a slaveholder from the table of the Lord upon the simple and naked ground that he is a slaveholder," declared a stalwart Calvinist, "deserves himself to be excluded for usurping the prerogatives of Christ and introducing terms of communion which cast reproach upon the conduct of Jesus and the Apostles. He violates the very character of the Church—is a traitor to its fundamental law."[23]

Such, then, was the southern churchman's biblical defense of human bondage. Robert L. Dabney, an able Presbyterian theologian of Virginia, contended that if southern clergymen would relentlessly propagate a biblical doctrine of slavery they could convert the bulk of northern Christians to their views and thereby rout the abolitionists. "Here is our policy, then," he said in a letter of 1851 to his brother, "to push the Bible argument continually, drive abolitionism to the wall, to compel it to assume an anti-Christian position. By so doing we compel the whole Christianity of the North to array itself on our side."[24] This, of course, was a pipe dream. Nevertheless, there still were multitudes of conservative churchmen in the free states who loathed abolitionism with a passion and who would have been glad to see it driven to the wall.[25]

22. Fuller and Wayland, *Domestic Slavery*, 196.
23. James H. Thornwell, "Report on Slavery," *Southern Presbyterian Review*, V (January, 1852), 386. This report, written by Thornwell, was originally presented to the Presbyterian Synod of South Carolina.
24. Quoted in Thomas Cary Johnson, *The Life and Letters of Robert Lewis Dabney* (Richmond, 1903), 129.
25. For prominent examples, see John C. Lord, *"The Higher Law," in its Application to the Fugitive Slave Bill. A Sermon on the Duties Men Owe to God and to Government* (New York, 1851); George Junkin, *The Integrity of Our National Union Versus Abolitionism* (Cincinnati, 1843); William Graham, *The Contrast of the Bible and Abolitionism: An Exegetical Argument* (Cincinnati, 1844); Joseph C. Stiles, *Speech on the Slavery Resolutions, Delivered in the General Assembly Which Met in Detroit in May Last* (Washington, 1850); Nathan L. Rice, *A Debate on Slavery* (Cincinnati, 1846); [Anonymous], "The Catholic Church and the Question of Slavery,"

II

While southern churchmen put large stock in their Bible argument for human bondage, they did not fail to make use also of secular modes of reasoning to justify their proslavery views. For one thing, they contended that slavery was inherently right, or nonsinful, because it was a form of government adapted to the Negro's allegedly inferior capacities. Throughout the biblical argument for bondage the idea of Negro inferiority, as implied in Noah's curse, had been present, but that idea had been obscured by the strong stress laid upon the divine decree. But when the abolitionists thrust into the center of debate the Declaration of Independence, religious as well as political spokesmen of the South were prompted to put forward their doctrine of African inferiority. Inevitably therefore the Jeffersonian doctrine of freedom and equality became a subject of intense debate between antislavery and proslavery parties.

In the year 1835, there appeared two northern books that excited widespread critical attention in the slave states, even though both were antagonistic toward abolitionism and were by no means radical in their antislavery sentiments. One of them, entitled *Slavery*, was written by William Ellery Channing, distinguished minister of Federal Street Church (Unitarian) in Boston. The other was Francis Wayland's immensely influential *Elements of Moral Science*. Both authors valued highly the doctrine of freedom and equality as set forth in the Declaration of Independence.

The key contention in Channing's essay was that no man could justly hold a fellow being as his property. "He cannot be property in the sight of God and justice," explained the Boston clergyman, "because he is a Rational, Moral, Immortal Being; because created in God's image, and therefore in the highest sense his child; because created to unfold godlike faculties, and to govern himself by a Divine Law written on his heart, and republished in God's Word."[26]

Inasmuch as ministers in the South likewise believed that man was created in the image of God, they recognized the crucial nature

---

Metropolitan, III (June, 1855), 266, 272–73; John H. Hopkins, *Bible View of Slavery* (n.p., 1861).

26. "Slavery," *Works of William E. Channing, D.D.* (11th ed., 6 vols., Boston, 1849), II, 26. See also Weld, *The Bible Against Slavery*, 8–9.

of Channing's attack upon slavery and felt impelled to undercut his argument. They found this no easy task. In their rejoinder, they usually conceded that it was of course true that man as spirit or immortal being could not be the property of another person. On the other hand, one could, they argued, own another person's service or labor. "When I purchase a slave," remarked a northern-born preacher in New Orleans, "I acquire the right to nothing but his labor during part of his time. None will say that human labor is a thing too sacred to be offered in the market. Man's labor is bought and sold every day, all over the civilized world."[27] Some churchmen claimed that the slave traffic was in fact nothing more than buying and selling human labor. "When we buy and sell them [slaves]," wrote a well-known Presbyterian preacher and slaveowner, "it is not *human flesh and blood* that we buy and sell, but we buy and sell a *right*, established by Providence, and sanctioned by Scripture, to *their labor and service for life*."[28] James H. Thornwell entirely agreed with this reasoning, despite its obvious sophistry. "The property of man in man," he exclaimed impatiently, "is the miserable cant of those who would storm by prejudice what they cannot demolish by argument." No one, he added, ever presumed to own a human being in the sense meant by Channing. "The right which the master has is a right, not to the *man* but to his *labour*.... What he sells is not the man, but the property in his services."[29]

This mode of reasoning may have seemed valid to Thornwell and other slaveholders, but it failed to convince Channing. For the Boston minister clearly recognized that no master ever purchased the right to a slave's labor which did not carry with it legal title to the slave himself. Furthermore, as Francis Wayland reminded Richard Fuller, the master's right to that labor included also the right to prevent the slave from doing anything that might interfere with the exercise of his original right.[30] Since mental enlighten-

27. Theodore Clapp, *Slavery: A Sermon, Delivered in the First Congregational Church in New Orleans, April 15, 1838* (New Orleans, 1838), 38.
28. John B. Adger, *The Christian Doctrine of Human Rights and Slavery* (Columbia, S.C., 1849), 15.
29. "Slavery and the Religious Instruction of the Coloured Population," *Southern Presbyterian Review*, IV, 121–22. For the same type of argument, see Smith, *Lectures on the Philosophy and Practice of Slavery*, 151; Bledsoe, *An Essay on Liberty and Slavery*, 86–92.
30. Fuller and Wayland, *Domestic Slavery*, 23. Fuller admitted the validity of Wayland's contention. *Ibid.*, 139.

ment, for example, made bondsmen discontented with their lot, masters had a legal right to deny them an education. As a matter of fact, the master class exercised this right throughout the South, with the result that the whole slave population was doomed to stark illiteracy. Even though this illiteracy was a woeful handicap in the moral and religious instruction of bondsmen, churchmen accepted the situation with remarkable complacency. Indeed, one of North Carolina's leading rectors in the Protestant Episcopal Church declared in a sermon to masters that it was *"not necessary that they [slaves] should be taught even to read. All the instruction essential to their well-being, both here and hereafter, may be given to them orally—by word of mouth."* [31] The master's right, however, extended far beyond merely refusing his slaves the right to read. For instance, he had the right to say whether or not they might attend public worship, and even to determine what particular preacher they might hear. He also had the right to ignore marriage bonds and sell man and wife apart as the slave market or some other circumstance might dictate. Consequently, Wayland was entirely correct in holding that the master's right to the services of his bondsmen necessarily embraced the exercise of many additional rights of vital importance.

While not discounting Channing's particular mode of argument, Wayland protested human bondage primarily on the ground that it violated the principle of equality. "The relation in which men stand to each other," he wrote, "is essentially the relation of *equality;* not *equality of condition* [endowment], but *equality of right.*" [32] The distinctions made in that statement are important. Wayland recognized that men differ widely in their native mental and physical capacities to use the means of happiness. In this respect, he acknowledged human inequality, or inequality of condition. Yet he urged that inequality of condition by no means diminished one's right to fullest self-expression. In other words, diversity of native gifts did not dictate diversity of right. Or to state the same principle in other terms, superiority in physical or mental capacity conferred no superiority of right. Hence, con-

---

31. George W. Freeman, *The Rights and Duties of Slaveholders,* 36. The Protestant Episcopal Bishop in North Carolina, the Right Rev. L. Silliman Ives, explicitly endorsed Freeman's sentiments.

32. *Elements of Moral Science* (4th ed., Boston, 1848), 190.

cluded Wayland, "all men are created with an equal right to employ their faculties, of body or of mind, in such a manner as will promote their happiness, either here or hereafter."[33]

Without exception, southern moralists rejected Wayland's doctrine of equal rights. Its severest critic was William A. Smith, who had bitterly assailed the antislavery movement ever since the middle 1830's. He assumed the presidency of Randolph Macon College in 1846 and held that office for the next twenty years. In the meantime he, like most other college presidents of this period, taught the course in mental and moral philosophy. The favorite textbook on this subject in southern as well as northern colleges was Wayland's *Elements of Moral Science*. On the whole, Smith valued that work highly and regularly used it as a textbook, but he supplemented it with an extended course of lectures directed against the author's antislavery position. During this period he also delivered the substance of these lectures to numerous audiences in North Carolina and Virginia. He probably did more to generate and consolidate proslavery sentiment in the upper South than any other spokesman of his denomination. Shortly before the outbreak of the Civil War, the Methodist press at Nashville published Smith's proslavery lectures.[34]

According to the Virginian, both Wayland and Thomas Jefferson had reached the conclusion that slavery violated human rights and was therefore sinful only because they were dominated by the natural rights philosophy of the Enlightenment. Jefferson, he complained, introduced this "false" idea into the Declaration of Independence simply because he "had become strongly tinctured with the infidel philosophy of France."[35] The swelling clamor against slavery, said Smith, would surely continue unless the nation purged itself of this subversive philosophy. In his opinion, the first step in doing that was to recognize the true principle of slavery. Drawing substantially upon the political theory of Aristotle, he argued that the abstract principle of slavery, understood as the principle of submission to control by the will of another, formed an indispensable element in all forms or types of government. This was true even in a "democratic republic." To avoid anarchy, the principle of free-

33. *Ibid.*, 204.
34. *Lectures on the Philosophy and Practice of Slavery* (Nashville, 1856).
35. *Ibid.*, 66.

dom had to be counterbalanced by the principle of slavery. In fact, "a government that did not embody the *principle* of slavery would be no government at all."[36] Inasmuch, then, as slavery constituted an essential factor in every form of government, it was nonsense to conclude, with Jefferson and Wayland, that the principle of slavery was wrong. On the contrary, "the great abstract principle of domestic slavery is, per se, RIGHT."[37]

The Methodist educator then laid down a theory of human right whereby he endeavored to justify the enslavement of black people. Once again his argument reflected the influence of Greek thought. The norm of the right, he remarked, is "the good," inasmuch as the good is of the essential nature of God. Since, then, the will of God is but the expression of the good, his will "is a perfect rule of what is right in itself, and proper to be observed by us, as a rule of duty or conduct."[38] Being created in God's image, man, despite his fallen condition, is endowed with the good as an attribute of his being, and he cannot be divested of that good without losing his humanity. "The good as an attribute is in my possession," declared Smith. "I am constituted with it and by it. Hence it is inalienable."[39] The good with which man is thus endowed commands him to do right. In his freedom man, to be sure, has the power to do wrong, but still he has no right to do wrong. He has only the right to do that which is good.[40]

On the other hand, said Smith, it was a fact that man in his fallen condition had failed to live in accordance with the good, and as a result government became necessary to the well-being of society. It was also a fact, he noted, that government had to be adapted to the mental and moral capacities of the governed. In the case of infants, for example, parental government was necessarily absolutist. "This extreme form of despotism, so far from being a curse, is the natural right of infants—the good to which they are entitled by nature."[41] On the same principle, continued Smith, domestic slavery was a necessary form of government for Africans. Unlike many of his fellow southerners, he did not subscribe to the notion that Africans were inferior to whites in their native endowments. Nevertheless, he held that, owing to the primitive conditions under

36. *Ibid.*, 48. See also *ibid.*, 69, 78.
38. *Ibid.*, 92.
40. *Ibid.*, 103, 111, 129.
37. *Ibid.*, 29.
39. *Ibid.*, 97.
41. *Ibid.*, 113.

which they had lived for ages in Africa, they were markedly inferior to whites in their general intellectual and moral development. For this reason, they were unready for freedom. In the words of Smith, "they [the Africans] are not, in point of intellectual and moral development, in the condition for freedom: that is, they are not fitted for that measure of self-government which is necessary to political sovereignty. It cannot, therefore, be justly claimed for them. They have no right to it. It would not be to them an essential good, but an essential evil, a curse."[42]

But granting that the bondsman did not yet have the right to freedom, did he have the right to an equal opportunity to develop his native powers and thus prepare himself for eventual freedom? Specifically, did he have the right to a formal education? It was at this point that the Virginia educator found himself in a crucial dilemma. He had no doubt that the slave was entitled to the benefits of religion and to an opportunity to develop the skills incident to his assigned tasks. But those practical skills did not require formal training; they could be acquired through "the domestic element of the system of slavery." This household method of teaching the slave was not merely "the natural way" to prepare him for his work; it was "the only safe way" to afford the intellectual and moral development of an inferior race dwelling in the midst of a superior race.[43] Smith raised two objections to giving the slave a formal education. For one thing, it would be a waste of time and money, because the black man "is doomed to occupy, so long as he remains in the midst of a white community, the position of an inferior." For another, formal schooling would imbue the bondsman with a spirit of revolt, and this in turn would prompt the master to impose still more rigorous discipline upon him.[44]

But although the Methodist philosopher would deny slaves an equal right to self-development, he frankly conceded that even under the informal experiences of domestic life they were gradually emerging from barbarism, and he predicted that "at some distant day" they would be qualified for freedom and the privileges of citizenship. Upon the dawn of that day, freedom would be their natural right, and it would be despotic to withhold it from them.

42. *Ibid.*, 181–82. 43. *Ibid.*, 237–43.
44. *Ibid.*, 233–36.

However, when that day should arrive, it would "be the duty of the superior race amongst whom the Africans now dwell, to remove them to a land where they can enjoy social equality."[45]

III

In the next place, religious leaders of the South defended domestic bondage on the ground that it both elevated the Negro and served the common good. They consequently fiercely resented the charge of antislavery men that involuntary servitude debased its black subjects. One way in which they tried to mute that criticism was to contrast the condition of the southern slave with that of his brother in Africa. The latter allegedly eked out an existence on the lowest level of barbarism, with no hope of improving his miserable lot. Besides, slavery in its cruelest form existed in that benighted country. Albert Taylor Bledsoe, a former Episcopal clergyman and currently professor of mathematics at the University of Virginia, pointed out in 1856 that forty million of Africa's fifty million inhabitants were reportedly slaves. The native master, he added, held the power of life or death over his bondsmen. "In fact, his slaves were often fed, and killed, and eaten, just as we do with oxen and sheep in this country."[46] The southern slave, on the other hand, was infinitely better off in every respect. "No fact is plainer than that the blacks have been elevated and improved by their servitude in this country. We cannot possibly conceive, indeed, how Divine Providence could have placed them in a better school of correction."[47] Patrick Hues Mell, a young Georgia Baptist destined to become one of his denomination's most distinguished leaders, was equally confident "that, *in* every respect, the condition of the slave, in these United States of America, is better than that occupied by his brethren in any part of the world, now, or during any past age."[48]

Another way often taken to prove that servitude benefited the

---

45. *Ibid.*, 246, 248.
46. *An Essay on Liberty and Slavery*, 293.
47. *Ibid.*, 299. See also Fuller and Wayland, *Domestic Slavery*, 131; W. B. Seabrook, *An Appeal to the People of the North on the Subject of Negro Slavery in South Carolina* (New York, 1834), 14.
48. *Slavery: A Treatise, Showing That Slavery is Neither A Moral, Political, Nor Social Evil*, 37. See also Matthew Estes, *A Defence of Negro Slavery, As It Exists in the United States* (Montgomery, Ala., 1846), Chap. 5.

black man was to amass statistics which purportedly demonstrated the decided inferiority of the free Negro. Resorting to this device, Henry B. Bascom in 1845 claimed that less than two hundred of Virginia's forty thousand free Negroes owned a single foot of land. The Kentucky Methodist also reported that free blacks in the North furnished a vastly disproportionate number of convicts there. In Massachusetts, for example, they supplied one-sixth of all the convicts, even though they constituted only a seventy-fourth of the population. A comparable situation was said to exist in New York, New Jersey, and Pennsylvania.[49]

Some southern churchmen maintained that free Negroes were both physically and mentally inferior to their enslaved brethren. Thornton W. Stringfellow, an ardent proslavery Baptist minister in Virginia, expressed a representative view. Upon comparing the 1850 federal census statistics of the six New England states with those of five South Atlantic states (Maryland to Georgia), he wrote:

> Among the free negroes of New England, one is deaf and dumb for every three thousand and five; while among the slaves of these [five South Atlantic] States there is only one for every six thousand five hundred and fifty-two. In New England one free negro is blind for every eight hundred and seventy; while in these States there is only one blind slave for every two thousand six hundred and forty-five. In New England there is one free negro insane or an idiot for every nine hundred and eighty; while in these States there is but one slave for every three thousand and eighty.[50]

Those statistics, Stringfellow exulted, "show with the most unquestionable certainty, that freedom to this race, in our country, is a curse."[51] Nor had freedom been any less of a curse to this race in

49. *Methodism and Slavery* (Frankfort, Ky., 1845), 57. See also William G. Brownlow, *A Sermon On Slavery; A Vindication of the Methodist Church, South: Her Position Stated* (Knoxville, 1857), 14–16.

50. *Scriptural and Statistical Views in Favor of Slavery* (Richmond, 1856), 128. Deductions of a similar import were drawn from the sixth U.S. census of 1840, notably by John C. Calhoun while Secretary of State. Calhoun to Lord Richard Pakenham, April 18, 1844, in Richard K. Crallé, ed., *Works of John C. Calhoun* (6 vols., New York, 1851–57), V, 337–38. See also Estes, *A Defence of Negro Slavery*, 138–40. That particular census, however, was proven to be factually unreliable with respect to the physical and mental conditions of free Negroes. Leon F. Litwack, *North of Slavery: The Negro in the Free States, 1790–1860* (Chicago, 1961), 40–46.

51. *Scriptural and Statistical Views in Favor of Slavery*, 129.

the West Indies. Generalizing sweepingly, the Virginian even claimed that wherever Negroes were released from slavery they underwent degeneration.[52]

During the decade of the 1850's, many southern churchmen became fantastically extravagant in their praise of the wonder-working power of the bondage system. "In the history of nations," wrote a prominent Presbyterian minister of Virginia, "it would be difficult to find an instance in which people have made more progress upward and onward than the African race has made under the operation of American slavery."[53] Few clergymen held a more romantic view of the elevating influence of human bondage than Iveson L. Brookes of South Carolina. "Next to the gift of his Son to redeem the human race," he proclaimed, "God never displayed in more lofty sublimity his attributes, than in the institution of slavery." Nor "had God's benevolence ever been more marvellously displayed" than when he permitted the Africans to be brought to America, where, as a result of their enlightenment and moral progress under slavery, "thousands will rejoice in redeeming mercy, in every generation, down to the judgment trump."[54]

If, then, the Negro was improving as rapidly as claimed under the influence of servitude, one might logically suppose that he would soon be ready for freedom. Strangely, however, those churchmen who wrote most glowingly of his progress usually doubted that he would ever be qualified for emancipation. Even those who, like William A. Smith, did believe that the black man would eventually be prepared for a life of freedom, placed that time so far into the future that it posed no threat to present vested interests.

Apologists for domestic slavery were confident that it was beneficial to society at large as well as essential to the improvement of the Negro race. According to some southern theorists, human bondage had been the chief means of lifting mankind out of the pit of barbarism. This was the opinion of Edward Brown of South Carolina, who in 1826 maintained that "slavery has ever been the stepping ladder by which civilized countries have passed from bar-

52. *Slavery: Its Origin, Nature and History*, 6–10.
53. George D. Armstrong, *The Christian Doctrine of Slavery* (New York, 1857), 113.
54. *A Defence of the South Against the Reproaches and Encroachments of the North: in Which Slavery is Shown to be an Institution of God Intended to Form the Basis of the Best Social State and the Only Safeguard to the Permanence of a Republican Government* (Hamburg, S.C., 1850), 23.

barism to civilization."[55] In a remarkably influential essay, Thomas Roderick Dew, professor of history, metaphysics, and political law at William and Mary College, expounded in masterly fashion a theory quite similar to Brown's. In the background of his argument lay the terrifying Nat Turner insurrection of August, 1831, in Southampton County, Virginia, and the exciting debate that followed it in the state legislature.[56] Although the legislature in 1831-32 did not, as a persistent legend has claimed, come within one vote of abolishing slavery,[57] it came near enough doing so to frighten conservatives and to elicit from Dew a vigorous counterattack.[58] Probably no other southerner of this period did more to undergird proslavery thought, especially among political spokesmen, than the William and Mary professor.

The most significant part of the *Review* is not Dew's criticism of the proposed schemes of emancipation, but rather his proslavery philosophy of history, an aspect of his thought which has received too little attention.[59] Noting that slavery had been a fact of life ever since ancient times and that philosophers as wise as Aristotle had sanctioned it, Dew argued that human servitude had played a major role in advancing mankind beyond a primitive existence. Slavery had operated, along with private property, to furnish the initial impulse toward social progress. In his words, "domestic slavery seems to be the only means of fixing the wanderer [hunter] to the soil, moderating his savage temper, mitigating the horrors of war, and abolishing the practice of murdering the captives."[60] In particular, slavery had been the means of elevating woman. Having domestics at her command, she ceased to be a beast of burden and became the "animating center of the family," with leisure to cultivate the graceful and charming virtues.[61]

For Dew, this slavery-propelled process of social evolution was

---

55. *Notes on the Origin and Necessity of Slavery* (Charleston, 1826), 6.
56. For an incisive account, see Joseph C. Roberts, *The Road From Monticello: A Study of the Virginia Slavery Debate of 1832* (Durham, N. C., 1941), Chaps. 1-4.
57. *Ibid.*, 34-35.
58. *Review of the Debate in the Virginia Legislature of 1831 and 1832* (Richmond, 1832). This was the first full edition of Dew's essay. The original version, as published in the *American Quarterly Review*, XII (September, 1832), 189-265, was considerably abridged.
59. *Ibid.*, 9-46.
60. *Ibid.*, 13.
61. *Ibid.*, 36.

by no means the outworking of merely naturalistic forces. On the contrary, it was an expression of the benevolent design of the Creator, who had authorized human bondage as a means of accomplishing a useful social purpose in the world. "Let us inquire then," the metaphysician wrote, "what that useful purpose is, and we have no hesitation in affirming, that slavery has been perhaps the principal means for impelling forward the civilization of mankind. Without its agency, society must have remained sunk into that deplorable state of barbarism and wretchedness which characterized the inhabitants of the western world, when first discovered by Columbus."[62]

One of the Virginia professor's most devoted followers was William Harper of South Carolina, the son of a Methodist minister. He was more ultraist than his mentor. Dew went only so far as to view slavery as "the principal means" of civilizing mankind, but Harper boldly remarked, "perhaps nothing can be more evident than that it is the sole cause" of human advancement.[63] A basic aspect of his theory was the contention that primitive man, if left free, would not do any work beyond what was absolutely necessary to maintain a bare existence. Consequently without involuntary servitude there would have been "no accumulation of property, no provision for the future, no taste for comforts or elegancies, which are the characteristics and essentials of civilization."[64] Harper had a ready reply to those who might object to the principle of human bondage. "It is in the order of nature, and of God," he wrote, "that the being of superior faculties and knowledge ... should control and dispose of those who are inferior. It is as much in the order of nature, that men should enslave each other, as that other animals should prey upon each other."[65] He also argued that every man should be left entirely free to exercise his predatory impulses.[66]

Some apologists for the bondage system argued that Negro slavery was a benefit to society in that it generated the consciousness of equality among whites. This was the view of Thomas Roderick

62. *Ibid.*, 28. Dew, like other southerners, contended that slavery was definitely sanctioned in the Bible. *Ibid.*, 9–10, 106–8. On the other hand, strangely, he acknowledged that slavery in fact violated the spirit of Christianity. *Ibid.*, 106.
63. *Memoir on Slavery* (Charleston, S. C., 1838), 4. See also *ibid.*, 19.
64. *Ibid.*, 5.
65. *Ibid.*, 11.
66. *Ibid.*, 6.

Dew. In the celebrated *Review* he noted that since black slaves performed all the menial tasks in the South, they had removed the greatest cause of class distinctions within the white community. "Color alone," he declared, "is here the badge of distinction, the true mark of aristocracy, and all who are white are equal in spite of the variety of occupation."[67]

Some of the more privileged slavocrats held that Negro servitude was a means of advancing the common good, because it freed whites of superior talent to devote themselves to enterprises which were beneficial to society as a whole. Those of this opinion believed that mankind could not advance without the leadership of an elite class, and they glorified "Greek democracy." No one put forward this notion more confidently than Senator James Henry Hammond, former governor of South Carolina and one of that state's largest slaveholders. Though not a church member, he was a diligent student of the Bible and of theology.[68] Militantly antiemancipationist at least as early as 1835, he sharply denounced abolitionism and lauded slavery as a great blessing to mankind. By that time he was also publicly advocating secession and the establishment of a southern slaveholding confederacy.[69]

In 1858, while the Senate was feverishly debating the question of admitting Kansas to the Union, Hammond delivered a fiery speech in favor of a social system resting upon the back of the black race. In all social systems, he argued, there had to be a class "to do the menial duties, to perform the drudgery of life," in order to make possible another class to promote and guide a progressive civilization. Such a class "constitutes the very mud-sill of society and of political government. Fortunately for the South, she found a race adapted to that purpose to her hand. . . . We use them for our purpose, and call them slaves."[70] In the following October he delivered

67. *Review of the Debate in the Virginia Legislature*, 113. However, D. R. Hundley, an Alabama planter, published a book on the eve of the Civil War in which he discussed in great detail the sharp class distinctions prevailing among white southerners. See his *Social Relations in Our Southern States* (New York, 1860), 27–28, 81–93, 193–95, 258–74.
68. Elizabeth Merritt, *James Henry Hammond, 1807–1864* (Baltimore, 1923), 111.
69. *Ibid.*, 32–33, 139.
70. "Speech on the Admission of Kansas, Under the Lecompton Constitution. Delivered in the Senate of the United States, March 4, 1858," in *Selections from Letters and Speeches of the Hon. James Hammond, of South Carolina* (New York, 1866), 318–19.

an address to his fellow South Carolinians, saying: "I believe that God created negroes for no other purpose than to be the 'hewers of wood and drawers of water'—that is, to be the slaves of the white race."[71]

All southern spokesmen agreed that slavery's supreme contribution to the common good was economic in nature. "Cotton *is* king!" Hammond boasted in his speech on Kansas. But he and other planters believed that the reign of king cotton would be short without Negro bondage, and they based their belief upon two assumptions: first, that the climate in the lowlands, where much of the best cotton and rice grew, could be endured only by blacks; and, second, that blacks would not labor productively unless made to do so. As early as 1823, a prominent Episcopal clergyman of South Carolina, Frederick Dalcho, expressed the prevailing sentiment. In his state, he said, "a large portion of our lower country could not be cultivated by white people." Without slavery, therefore, the richest lands would go to waste, and the planters there would be forced to move into the upper part of the state or else to "emigrate to other climes." As for the Negroes, Dalcho was certain that "not one of these people in an hundred would maintain himself by labour" under freedom. Thus on both counts "manumission would produce nothing but evil."[72] Richard H. Rivers, a leading Methodist educator and minister in Alabama, took an equally dim view of the South without slave labor. "Destroy slavery and the supply of cotton would cease," he warned. Then textile mills here and abroad would shut down, with disastrous economic and social consequences.[73] Of the same opinion was the professor of mathematics at the University of Virginia, who predicted that if slavery ceased much of the South's best farmland would soon "be turned into a jungle, with only here and there a forlorn plantation."[74]

According to many political and religious thinkers of the region, slavery was beneficial to society as a whole because it prevented the

---

71. *Ibid.*, 338. See also Hammond, "Two Letters on the Subject of Slavery in the United States, Addressed to Thomas Clarkson, Esq. [1845]," in *Selections From Letters and Speeches*, 124; Brownlow, *A Sermon on Slavery*, 14.
72. *Practical Considerations Founded on the Scriptures, Relative to the Slave Population of South Carolina*, 6–8.
73. *Elements of Moral Philosophy* (Nashville, 1859), 360–61.
74. Bledsoe, *An Essay on Liberty and Slavery*, 287. See also Mell, *Slavery: A Treatise, Showing that Slavery is Neither A Moral, Political, Nor Social Evil*, 20–21.

tensions and disorders which usually occurred in a free labor society. Under the bondage system, for example, a conflict between capital and labor was impossible. In an able proslavery address to the United States Senate in 1837, John C. Calhoun emphasized this point, saying: "Every plantation is a little community, with the master at its head, who concentrates in himself the united interests of capital and labor of which he is the common representative."[75]

During the decade of the 1850's, when North-South tensions were growing increasingly acute, many southerners rhapsodized the slave labor system and disparaged the free labor system. This was strikingly true of William J. Grayson, former collector for the port of Charleston. In a lengthy rhymed poem he aimed his principal barbs at the condition of the serfs of Great Britain. Though free in name, the serf was but a slave "of endless toil" and doomed to a wretched existence:

> In squalid hut—a kennel for the poor,
> Or noisome cellar, stretched upon the floor,
> His clothing rags, of filthy straw his bed,
> with offal from the gutter daily fed.

The black bondsman, on the other hand, was always "guarded from want":

> He never feels what Hireling crowds endure,
> Nor knows, like them, in hopeless want to crave,
> For wife and child, the comforts of the slave.[76]

An equally zealous proslavery theorist was Virginia's George Fitzhugh, who had no use for Thomas Jefferson's equalitarianism and Adam Smith's laissez-faire economics. His two principal works, *Sociology for the South* and *Cannibals All*, received flattering attention in the leading journals of the South. The influential monthly, *De Bow's Review*, carried an amazing number of his essays, most of which preached the gospel of human bondage.[77] For Fitzhugh, free

---

75. Cralle, ed., *Works of John C. Calhoun*, III, 180. See also Fletcher, *Studies on Slavery*, 219.

76. *The Hireling and the Slave* (Charleston, S.C., 1854), 21, 47. Grayson returned to this same subject in his "Mackay's Travels in America: The Dual Form of Labor," *De Bow's Review*, XXVIII (January, 1860), 48–66.

77. Harvey Wish, *George Fitzhugh: Propagandist of the Old South* (Baton Rouge, La., 1943), Chaps. 8, 11–12, 16.

society was a failure, because it set capitalist and laborer against each other, concentrated profits in the hands of the few, and reduced masses of workmen to penury and insecurity. The hirelings were thus "slaves without masters."[78] On the other hand, slave society avoided this cutthroat economic system. Actually, it was "a form of communism," though not of the Marxian type. A southern plantation operated as a kind of "social phalanstery" in which the master contributed the capital and skill and the slaves the labor, with the profits divided, "not according to each one's in-put, but according to each one's wants and necessities." Under this system, the South, unlike the North, was never disturbed by labor unions and strikes, nor was it infested with the radical isms that plagued free society. Besides, it fostered Christian morality.[79]

In one of his most notable discourses, James Henley Thornwell, professor at Columbia Theological Seminary, took much the same position on the slave system as Fitzhugh. In a free labor economy, he observed, there were two causes at work which could only end in revolution and distress. One was the tendency of capital to concentrate in the hands of a few, and the other was the tendency of population to outstrip the demands for employment. In the end, therefore, society would be "divided between princes and beggars." However, the poor and unemployed would "scorn the logic which makes it their duty to perish in the midst of plenty." Given this intolerable situation, the government "must support them, or an agrarian revolution is inevitable." But if the government is not to support them in idleness, it must find a way to employ them, and "the only way in which it can be done, as a permanent arrangement, is by converting the laborer into capital; that is, . . . by slavery." Hence, concluded the theologian, the South had every reason to be thankful for the bondage system, because it served as a safeguard against both pauperism and agrarian revolution.[80]

Yet another general good of domestic bondage, according to some influential ministers, was that it reduced to a minimum white an-

78. *Sociology for the South, or the Failure of Free Society* (Richmond, 1854), 18–28, 38–39, 164–66, 201; *Cannibals All! or, Slaves Without Masters* (Richmond, 1857), 29, 31, 46, 49–52, 108–9.
79. *Sociology for the South*, 48, 69, 200–201.
80. "NATIONAL SINS—*A Fast-Day Sermon, preached in the Presbyterian Church, Columbia, Wednesday, November 21, 1860,*" *Southern Presbyterian Review*, XIII (January, 1861), 680–82.

tipathy toward the black race. This view obviously rested upon the assumption that as long as the Negro remained in servitude, the white man would treat him more kindly than if he were a freeman. In other words, he was better off under a pattern of paternalism. This was clearly the view of Henry B. Bascom, and he maintained it uncompromisingly in his diatribe against his northern brethren after the Methodist division of 1844. "Since the foundation of society," he declared, "the white and black races have never co-existed, under the same government on equal footing, and never can."[81] Thus to free the black man and leave him in America, where he would demand equality, would inevitably subject him to ruthless white hostility, and might even generate a race war that could exterminate him. For, continued the Kentucky slaveowner, "prejudice against the negro increases with the progress of emancipation."[82] This proposition he held to be demonstrated by the animosity visited upon free blacks in the North as well as the South. "Wherever they are found," he declared, "the free negroes of this country . . . are literally suffering a debasement, in everything except the name, worse than slavery."[83]

IV

Finally, many churchmen of the South defended domestic bondage on the ground that it was the divinely designed means of introducing the African race to Christianity. According to their theology of history, American slavery was no merely human contrivance, nor did it result alone from human cupidity. However ruthless may have been the plunderers of the Dark Continent, God was nevertheless so overruling events as to redeem the black race. Contemplating this situation, the moral philosopher at Randolph Macon College drew a parallel between Joseph's sale into Egypt by his jealous brothers and the sale of Africans into America. Just as God sent Joseph into Egypt as a means of preserving the life of his famine-

---

81. *Methodism and Slavery*, 43.
82. *Ibid.*, 45. See also Fitzhugh, *Sociology for the South*, 107, 271.
83. *Methodism and Slavery*, 43. For evidence that Bascom's indictment contained much truth, see Litwack, *North of Slavery*, Chaps. 3–6; John Hope Franklin, *From Slavery to Freedom* (3d ed., New York, 1967), Chap. 14; Eugene H. Berwanger, *The Frontier Against Slavery: Western Anti-Negro Prejudice and the Slavery Extension Controversy* (Urbana, Ill., 1967), Chaps. 1, 2, 6.

stricken kindred in Canaan, explained the philosopher, "so it will be found that he permitted the introduction of the pagan African into this country, that he might be . . . redeemed by the genius of the gospel, and returned to bless his kindred and his country. Thus all Africa shall, sooner or later, share the blessings of civilization and religion."[84] Some theorists assigned the Deity a more direct hand in the rape of Africa than the word "permitted" signified. William J. Grayson, for example, held that the Negro was inducted into American slavery at "God's command."[85] A similar interpretation was offered by Theodore Clapp, a graduate of Yale and a leading minister in New Orleans.[86]

If that proslavery theology of history served to salve the consciences of its proponents, it also placed them under a heavy responsibility to evangelize the slaves as a means of realizing God's redemptive purpose. During the last two decades before the Civil War, there was indeed a growing concern, at least among major church leaders of the region, to discharge this obligation. In the forefront of this movement were the Methodists and Baptists, who constituted the bulk of southern Protestants. According to a report published in 1845, they had a combined Negro membership at that time of 260,000.[87] In numerous churches of both denominations, black communicants outnumbered their white brethren. Although most Negroes attended racially mixed congregations, a growing number of them organized African churches. In Virginia alone, there were at least twenty-one black Baptist churches by 1860.[88]

But along with this increasing white effort to Christianize the Negro was also increasing vigilance to safeguard the institution of domestic bondage. This becomes indisputable if one examines the catechetical manuals that were used during this period to instruct the slave population. The most highly esteemed catechisms were

84. Smith, *Lectures on the Philosophy and Practice of Slavery*, 254. See Fuller and Wayland, *Domestic Slavery*, 132–34.
85. *The Hireling and the Slave*, 36–38.
86. *Slavery: A Sermon*, 55–56.
87. *Proceedings of the Meeting in Charleston, S.C., May 13–15, 1845, on the Religious Instruction of the Negroes Together with the Report of the Committee and the Address to the Public* (Charleston, S.C., 1845), 69–70.
88. W. Harrison Daniel, "Virginia Baptists and the Negro in the Antebellum Era," *Journal of Negro History*, LVI (January, 1971), 4. Yet, as Daniel noted, all these churches were controlled by whites, since their deacons were chosen by whites, their property was held by white trustees, and their pastors were all white men.

those prepared by Charles Colcock Jones of the old school Presbyterian Church, one of Georgia's large slaveholders,[89] and the founder of his denomination's most successful mission to plantation slaves in his state.[90] The following questions and answers in one of his earliest catechetical productions clearly reflect the author's design to employ the resources of religion to strengthen Negro servitude.

> Q. What command has God given to Servants concerning the obedience to their Masters?
>
> A. "Servants be obedient to them that are your Masters, according to the flesh."—Eph. 6:5.
>
> Q. If the Servant professes to be a Christian, ought he not to *set an example* to all the other Servants of love and obedience to his Master?
>
> A. Yes.
>
> Q. And if his Master is a Christian, ought he not especially love and obey him?
>
> A. Yes.—I Tim. 6:1–2.
>
> Q. Is it right for the Servant to run away; or is it right to harbor a *runaway*?
>
> A. No.[91]

Since Jones taught that God instituted the system of black bondage, he was, of course, morally consistent in employing the Christian religion to prevent its abolition.

In the midst of this intensified drive to Christianize black folk and buttress the bondage system, a bomb was dropped by an "American School" of ethnology which threatened to destroy the southern churchman's proslavery theology of history. The explosive aspect of the new ethnology was the contention that the African and Caucasian races did not, as claimed by the Judeo-Christian tradi-

---

89. Rufus Wm. Bailey, *The Issue, Presented in a Series of Letters on Slavery* (New York, 1837), 70–71. Both Bailey and Jones were members of the Presbyterian Synod of South Carolina and Georgia.

90. Ernest Trice Thompson, *Presbyterians in the South*, I: *1607–1861* (Richmond, 1963), 438–41.

91. *A Catechism For Colored Persons* (Charleston, S.C., 1834), 93–94. See also Jones, *A Catechism of Scripture Doctrine and Practice for Families and Sabbath Schools, Designed also for the Oral Instruction of Colored Persons* (3d ed., Savannah, Ga., 1844), 129–30.

tion, stem from common Adamic stock, but instead derived from originally independent creations. When this "heresy" infiltrated the Cotton Kingdom, in the early 1840's, it generated a lively controversy that gave birth to many books and essays. Orthodox clergymen led a vigorous counterattack, contending basically that the new theory of multiple human origins delivered a fatal blow at both the Bible and the worldwide mission of Christianity.

The leading members of the so-called American School were Samuel G. Morton, M.D., of Philadelphia; Swiss-born Louis Agassiz of Harvard; Josiah C. Nott, M.D., of Mobile, Alabama; and George R. Gliddon, sometime United States consul at Cairo.[92] A congenial quartet, they visited in one another's homes and exchanged views frequently. Morton and Agassiz were the two creative thinkers; the other two men were largely salesmen of their ideas. Although Gliddon, after 1840, lectured frequently on Egyptology, probably his greatest contribution was to provide Morton with a considerable collection of Egyptian skulls.

Morton had been a member of Philadelphia's Academy of Natural Sciences since 1820, and at the time of his death, in 1851, he was its president. From 1839 to 1843 he taught anatomy at the College of Philadelphia, and during that period he produced two books in craniology which attracted international attention.[93] In the first, *Crania Americana*, he put forward a theory of the separate origin of the Caucasian and Negro races from which he never deviated. In an introductory essay to that work, "On the Varieties of the Human Species," he said:

> The recent discoveries in Egypt . . . show beyond all question that the Caucasian and Negro races were perfectly distinct in that country upwards of three thousand years ago as they are now: whence it is evident that if the Caucasian was derived from the Negro, or the Negro from the Caucasian, by the ac-

---

92. A useful introduction to this school of thought is William Stanton, *The Leopard's Spots: Scientific Attitudes Toward Race in America, 1815–59* (Chicago, 1960). See also George M. Fredrickson, *The Black Image in the White Mind: The Debate on Afro-American Character and Destiny, 1817–1914* (New York, 1971), Chap. 3.

93. *Crania Americana; or a comparative view of the skulls of various aboriginal nations of North and South America: to which is prefixed an Essay on the Varieties of the Human Species* (Philadelphia, 1839); *Crania Aegyptiaca; or Observations on Egyptian Ethnography—Derived From Anatomy, History, and the Monuments* (Philadelphia, 1844).

tion of external causes, the change must have been effected in at most a thousand years; a theory which the subsequent evidence of thirty centuries proves to be a physical impossibility.[94]

In *Crania Aegyptiaca*, published five years later, Morton developed his pluralistic theory of human origins in much greater detail. He now took the position that the Negroes of ancient Egypt were definitely inferior to the Caucasians of that country. Their social status "was the same that it is now; that of servants or slaves."[95] By the middle 1840's, therefore, the Philadelphia craniologist had arrived at two conclusions: (1) the original diversity of the races of mankind, and (2) the inferiority of the Negro race.

In early October of 1846 Louis Agassiz reached Boston, where in the following December he would deliver a series of lectures under the auspices of the Lowell Institute. Already distinguished for his researches on fossil fishes, he was warmly welcomed by American scientists. Prior to giving the lectures, he visited several men of scientific note, including Benjamin Silliman of Yale, "the patriarch of science in America."[96] It was, however, an extended visit with Samuel George Morton and an inspection of his collection of "six hundred skulls" that most thrilled him.[97] This memorable experience may have been a final factor in inducing him to make public his growing dissatisfaction with the single-pair doctrine of racial origins. At any rate, he did indicate his dissent from the traditional view in the Lowell Lectures, much to the alarm of Boston orthodoxy.[98]

In November, 1847, Agassiz also dismayed orthodox clergymen in Charleston, South Carolina, when he announced before the Literary Society of that city "that he believed in an *indefinite*

---

94. *Crania Americana*, 88 n. Apparently Morton assumed the validity of Archbishop James Ussher's biblical chronology, according to which the world was created in 4004 B.C.

95. Henry S. Patterson, "Memoir of the Life and Scientific Labors of Samuel George Morton," in Josiah C. Nott and George R. Gliddon, *Types of Mankind: or Ethnological Researches, Based Upon the Ancient Monuments, Paintings, Sculptures, and Biblical History* (6th ed., Philadelphia, 1854), xii–xiii.

96. Elizabeth C. Agassiz, *Louis Agassiz: His Life and Correspondence* (9th ed., Boston, 1890), 413; Edward Lurie, *Louis Agassiz: A Life in Science* (Chicago, 1960), 115, 118–19, 123.

97. Agassiz, *Louis Agassiz*, 417.

98. Stanton, *The Leopard's Spots*, 100–4.

number of original and distinctly created races of men."[99] In 1850 he developed this theory at length in the *Christian Examiner*, Unitarianism's leading periodical.[100] The races of mankind, he announced, were originally created in separate geographical centers or provinces, as were the plants and animals. But while the various races did not derive from a common stock, they nevertheless, the naturalist contended, constituted a spiritual community because God had created all of them in his image.[101] In an effort to harmonize his theory with the teaching of Genesis, he argued that Adam and Eve were not the progenitors of all races, but only of the white race.[102]

Like Morton, Agassiz clearly believed the Negro to be inferior to the Caucasian, and he assigned that inferiority to inherent factors rather than to environmental conditions. He maintained that the monuments of Egypt fully documented this conclusion.[103] In his opinion, white Americans ought to keep clearly in mind "the real differences" between themselves and the blacks and refrain from treating them on terms of equality.[104]

The South's most vigilant exponent of the new ethnology was a South Carolinian, Josiah Clark Nott, who practiced medicine for many years in Mobile, Alabama. Though lacking Morton's scientific ability, he excelled him in popularizing the findings of cranial research. In February, 1844, Nott published two lectures on the subject that speedily raised an uproar among orthodox churchmen. He contended (1) that the curse fell upon Canaan, not Ham, and that the former's descendants were Caucasians; (2) that the Negro and Caucasian races sprang from originally distinct creations; (3)

99. Thomas Smyth, *The Unity of the Human Races, Proved to be the Doctrine of Scripture, Reason, and Science* (New York, 1850), 350. See also Lurie, *Louis Agassiz*, 257.
100. "The Diversity of Origin of the Human Races," *Christian Examiner*, XLIX (July, 1850), 110–45. For an introduction to this essay, see Agassiz, "Geographical Distribution of Animals," *Christian Examiner*, XLVIII (March, 1850), 181–204.
101. "The Diversity of Origin of the Human Races," *Christian Examiner*, XLIX, 126–28, 136–39.
102. *Ibid.*, 111 n., 135, 138. See also Agassiz, "Geographical Distribution of Animals," *Christian Examiner*, XLVIII, 184–85.
103. "The Diversity of Origin of the Human Races," *Christian Examiner*, XLIX, 124.
104. *Ibid.*, 144. In later years, Agassiz reiterated his anti-Negro sentiments. Agassiz, *Louis Agassiz*, 594–612.

that the Negro had a smaller skull and brain than the Caucasian, and was both morally and intellectually inferior to the latter; (4) that the mulatto was a hybrid, that a hybrid was shorter-lived, and that hybrid couples were less fertile of progeny than blacks or whites; and (5) that the intermixing of the Negro and Caucasian races resulted in a deterioration of the latter.[105]

Moses Ashley Curtis of North Carolina, an Episcopal minister and a competent botanist, promptly responded in a scathing essay, charging that the Mobile physician was ignorant of both geology and natural history.[106] He challenged Nott's views at two crucial points. First, he held that the doctor was certainly wrong in claiming that the Negro could be differentiated from the Caucasian with respect to such features as size and shape of skull, length of arm, bend of knee, and contour of heel. For all of those so-called distinctive marks of the Negro could be "found more or less in the other races."[107] Second, Curtis vigorously contested Nott's assertion that varieties in the human family were not affected by physical factors, and he gave specific instances of both blacks and whites in which changes in form and color had actually taken place.[108] In two lengthy essays Nott replied to Curtis' attack, relentlessly reaffirming his original contentions.[109] The debate came to a close with a brisk rejoinder from Curtis, who remained as anti-Nott as ever.[110]

By this time Nott had become bitterly antagonistic toward southern clergymen, who all but unanimously repudiated his polygenetic theory as unscriptural.[111] He caustically derided their biblical or-

105. *Two Lectures, on the Natural History of the Caucasian and Negro Races* (Mobile, Ala., 1844), 7, 12–13, 23–24, 28–29, 30, 32, 33, 34, 35, 40, 41. Using the defective U.S. census of 1840, Nott, like Calhoun and other southerners, claimed that the black population in the North contained a much larger percentage of the insane and idiots than did the slave population. *Ibid.*, 29–30.

106. "Unity of the Races," *Southern Quarterly Review*, VII (April, 1845), 372–448.

107. *Ibid.*, 440.

108. *Ibid.*, 430–37.

109. "Dr. Nott's Reply to 'C',"*Southern Quarterly Review*, VIII (July, 1845), 148–90; "Unity of the Human Race: A Letter Addressed to the Editor," *Southern Quarterly Review*, IX (January, 1846), 1–57.

110. "The Unity of the Human Race: Rejoinder to the Reply of Dr. Nott," *Southern Quarterly Review*, IX (April, 1846), 372–91.

111. The Episcopal clergyman, James Warley Miles, who for a time taught Greek philosophy and literature at Charleston College, may have been inclined to favor Nott's theory of racial origins, although he nowhere published an opinion on the subject. Ralph E. Luker, "God, Man and the World of James Warley Miles, Charles-

thodoxy in two lectures, given at the University of Louisiana in December, 1848. Drawing upon the results of German historical criticism, he argued that the Pentateuch and many other portions of the Bible were composite in authorship and unreliable in genealogy and chronology. Genesis, for instance, was "nothing more than an assemblage of very ancient fragments, (or traditions), of unknown origin, put together without order, and consequently of no historical value."[112] Besides, Nott continued, the Genesis account of a race that had stemmed from Adam and Eve was limited to a knowledge of the Israelites living within a few hundred miles of Abraham's birthplace, and did not refer to mankind as a whole.[113] Likewise when Paul proclaimed at Mars Hill that God had made of one blood the people of all nations, he meant only those nations about which he was informed. In short, "the Bible nowhere says that all the races of men now known to us are descended from a single pair, and no one has a right to force such an interpretation upon it."[114]

Two years later, when Nott gave an address before the Southern Rights Association, he told why he had labored so strenuously to prove the validity of the claim that the Caucasian and Negro races had sprung from separate and independent original creations. He had done it with the hope that it would persuade the abolitionists to abandon their crusade against Negro bondage. "As a last appeal," he confessed, "[I] attempted to satisfy them [the abolitionists] that the same God who had permitted Slavery to exist by His *Word*, had stamped the Negro Race with *permanent inferiority*, and that all attempts to elevate it above its proper grade, must eventuate in failure." But alas, they were too much "under the influence of ignorance and fanaticism" to hearken to reason.[115]

Yet even after Josiah Nott had given up all hope of converting the abolitionists to his views, he continued to defend the new

---

ton's Transcendentalist," *Historical Magazine of the Protestant Episcopal Church*, XXXIX (June, 1970), 135–36.

112. *Two Lectures, on the Connection Between the Biblical and Physical History of Man* (New York, 1849), 60. See also *ibid.*, 68–86.

113. *Ibid.*, 58–59.

114. *Ibid.*, 99. See also *ibid.*, 16–17.

115. *An Essay on the Natural History of Mankind, Viewed in Connection with Negro Slavery: Delivered Before the Southern Rights Association, 14th December, 1850* (Mobile, 1851), 4.

ethnology. He particularly insisted that there was an unbridgeable gulf between the black and white races. The Caucasian was "the most perfect work of the Almighty," and "probably the true Adamic race, whose history is so dimly shadowed forth in the Pentateuch."[116] On the other hand, "no Negro Race has ever yet invented an alphabet, however rude, or possessed the semblance of literature." It was thus "a capital error" for zealous churchmen and sentimental philanthropists to think that education, even over a long period, would "expand the defective brains, develop the intellectual faculties of the Negro Races, and thus raise them *by degrees* to the full standard of excellence which belongs to the Caucasian Races."[117] The Mobile doctor even maintained that the Christian religion could "never be comprehended and adopted by African races, as long as their physical type remains unchanged." In fact, all efforts to Christianize the Negroes had done "more harm than good."[118]

Nott's ministerial opponents raised no objection to his theory that the Negro was inferior to the white man, for they agreed with him at that point; but they could not tolerate his critical view of the Bible. They especially frowned upon the two lectures that he presented at the University of Louisiana in 1848. A foremost professor at Columbia Theological Seminary, George Howe, devoted more than sixty pages to a review of those lectures.[119] He denounced as absolutely unfounded the lecturer's notion that the scriptures were a history merely of the white race. Nor did he put any more confidence in Nott's contention that other varieties of human beings antedated Adam's creation. On the contrary, "the early chapters of Genesis represent the whole Antediluvian world as descended from him."[120] The reviewer was astonished that Nott should have been so reckless as to seek to undermine the biblical doctrine of the unity of the human race. Two reasons probably led to his irreverent act. One was that he did not want to believe that he and the African sprang from the same human pair. The other was "a desire to find

---

116. *Two Lectures, on the Connection Between the Biblical and Physical History of Man*, 22.

117. *An Essay on the Natural History of Mankind*, 15.

118. *Two Lectures, on the Connection Between the Biblical and Physical History of Man*, 17–18.

119. "Nott's Lectures [of 1848]," *Southern Presbyterian Review*, III (January, 1850), 427–90.

120. *Ibid.*, 428.

a new basis for slavery." As to the second reason, Howe warned that any defense of slavery which involved a denial of the authenticity of the Bible would inevitably seal the doom of the South's institution of Negro servitude.[121]

Two other Protestant guardians of biblical orthodoxy lambasted not only Nott, but also Louis Agassiz. The Presbyterian minister, Thomas Smyth of Charleston, charged that both ethnologists were clearly unfaithful to the word of God in affirming a diversity of origin of the human races. He further charged them with biblical unfaithfulness by teaching that Adam was the progenitor of only one branch of the human family, the Caucasian race.[122] William T. Hamilton of Mobile, Alabama, devoted a large volume to a detailed analysis of the Pentateuch, in which he, too, assailed Nott and Agassiz on essentially the same grounds.[123] Both clergymen accused the two critics of having struck a blow at the universal saviorhood of Christ. "If the Bible history has respect to one race only," Hamilton wrote, "then Christ lived, and suffered, and died for that one race only."[124]

Among southern clergymen, the most acute critic of the new ethnology was John Bachman. Born into a slaveholding family at Rhinebeck, New York, in 1790, he became pastor of St. John's Lutheran Church of Charleston, South Carolina, in 1815, and held that position for more than sixty years. During most of that time he was the recognized spokesman of his communion in the South.[125] As a result of Bachman's authoritative work on American quadrupeds, he held the respect of scientists, including Morton.[126] From the outset he had rejected the doctrine of plurality in the human species, but not until 1850 did he publish a comprehensive criticism of it.[127]

121. *Ibid.*, 489–90.
122. *The Unity of the Human Races*, xv, 352–54.
123. *The 'Friend of Moses'; or, A Defence of the Pentateuch as the Production of Moses and an Inspired Document, Against the Objections of Modern Skepticism* (New York, 1852), 411.
124. *Ibid.*, 453. See also Smyth, *The Unity of the Human Races*, xix, 45, 374.
125. For an excellent account of Bachman's life and work, see Raymond M. Bost, "The Reverend John Bachman and the Development of Southern Lutheranism" (typed Ph.D. dissertation, Yale University, 1963).
126. Stanton, *The Leopard's Spots*, 123–25.
127. *The Doctrine of the Unity of the Human Race Examined on the Principles of Science* (Charleston, 1850).

According to Bachman, the debate between himself and the pluralists finally narrowed down to a single question: "What constitutes a true species, and what are varieties?"[128] In answering that question, he appealed to the results of his personal experiments in crossing various species of plants, birds, and quadrupeds. Although he had produced numerous hybrids, he found that all of them proved sterile except that of the China and English goose, and even it eventually proved to be only partially and temporarily fertile.[129] From these experimental data, the Lutheran scientist drew the conclusion "that two distinct species of animals are incapable by their organization of producing an intermediate prolific race." Ever afterwards he thus maintained that the fertility or sterility of hybrids constituted a valid test of affiliation. Specifically, if the union of two distinct animals should produce a fertile hybrid offspring, that fact would certify that they belonged to the same species. The same rule, Bachman urged, held in the case of the races of mankind. Inasmuch, then, as the union of Caucasians and Africans did actually produce mulattoes of prolific fertility, one could assume that those two races were only varieties of one and the same species.[130] He therefore regarded Morton's plurality doctrine as untenable.

Yet if all men were of the same species, what specifically had caused the racial varieties of mankind? To this question Bachman gave much thought, but confessed that no satisfying answer had ever

128. *Ibid.*, 33.
129. *Ibid.*, 15.
130. *Ibid.*, 115–16. For a sharp challenge to the claim that hybridity could be depended upon to determine the relationship of two distinct species of animals, see Samuel G. Morton, "Hybridity in Animals, considered in reference to the question of the Unity of the Human Species," *American Journal of Science and Arts*, 2d ser., III (1847), 39–50, 203–12. A lively debate ensued, for which see Bachman, "An Investigation of the Cases of Hybridity in Animals on Record, considered in reference to the Unity of the Human Species," *Charleston Medical Journal and Review*, V (January, 1850), 168–97; Morton, "Letter to the Rev. John Bachman, D.D., on the question of Hybridity in Animals considered in reference to the Unity of the Human Species," *ibid.*, V (May, 1850), 328–44; Bachman, "A Reply to the Letter of Samuel George Morton, M.D., on the question of Hybridity in Animals, considered in reference to the Unity of the Human Species," *ibid.*, V (July, 1850), 466–508; Bachman, "Second Letter to Samuel G. Morton, M.D., on the Question of Hybridity in Animals, considered in reference to the Unity of the Human Species," *ibid.*, V (September, 1850), 621–60; Morton, "Additional Observations on Hybridity in Animals, and on some collateral subjects; being a Reply to the Objections of the Rev. John Bachman, D.D.," *ibid.*, V (November, 1850), 755–805.

dawned upon him. In the final analysis he could only say that the Creator had so formed the human constitution as to render it capable of producing racial varieties adapted to every clime and country.[131] As he well knew, this was no scientific explanation. A scientific solution, however, lay near at hand, for in 1859 Charles Darwin published his epoch-making volume, *On the Origin of Species.*

Still another problem left the Charleston churchman in the dark. Morton, among others, had argued that if all mankind did actually stem from a single pair, the biblical chronology as established by Archbishop Ussher did not allow sufficient time in which to produce such marked racial varieties as existed. He pointed to recent discoveries in Egypt as evidence "that the Caucasian and Negro races were as perfectly distinct in that country upwards of three thousand years ago as they are now."[132] Assuming, then, the validity of Ussherian chronology, all the racial types must have been produced within the first millennium of the world's existence. Only a miracle, mused Morton, could do that! Bachman replied that it was "neither unreasonable or unscientific" to suppose "that in those early times before the races had become permanent, they were more susceptible of producing varieties than at a later period."[133] Once again, the Lutheran naturalist had substituted farfetched speculation for a scientific solution to a tantalizing problem. Even so, he doggedly stuck to the theory that all the racial varieties of the human family were the result of man's geographical dispersion and adaptation to environment. As William Stanton has observed, "Bachman formulated a theory of his own that approached evolution."[134] If he had been able to cut loose from Ussher's timetable, he might have run Darwin a close race.

Although Bachman rejected the theory of plural creations, he made it perfectly clear that he was no less opposed to abolitionism and to Negro equality than were the advocates of that theory. As early as 1835 he had heartily supported the action taken by the South Carolina Synod of the Lutheran Church in condemning

---

131. *The Doctrine of the Unity of the Human Race,* 205.
132. *Crania Americana,* 80 n.
133. *The Doctrine of the Unity of the Human Race,* 202.
134. *The Leopard's Spots,* 133.

abolitionists as a threat to the cause of morals and religion.[135] A slaveholder himself, Bachman held that the institution of human bondage had been initiated by God in the Noachian decree.[136] He became deeply aroused in 1857, when the Middle Conference of the Pittsburgh Synod of his denomination adopted a report, saying: "We hold that slavery . . . wars not only against the principles of the word of God, but against some of its express and plain declarations, and is therefore sinful."[137] To this report he replied in a lengthy paper, in which he argued that slavery was entirely biblical, and therefore "not, per se, sinful." He furthermore insisted that wherever blacks had been liberated from slavery, as in Santo Domingo, they had "degenerated into idleness and vice" and were "fast returning to barbarism."[138] Like Nott and other proponents of the new ethnology, he urged that nature had "stamped on the African race the permanent marks of inferiority."[139] The Negro's intellect was so "greatly inferior to that of the Caucasian" that he was "incapable of self-government" and had to be protected by the white man.[140]

In many respects, the theory of plural racial creations offered a plausible basis upon which to defend Negro bondage. Some of the South's political, medical, and literary leaders did seem to favor it, at least privately.[141] On the other hand, the clergy strenuously fought it from first to last. Their objections were chiefly two. First, they urged that the new doctrine was rank heresy from the standpoint of the Bible, according to which all mankind sprang from a single pair, Adam and Eve. Second, they warned that it denied Christ's universal saviorhood. No one presented the issue more decisively than did James H. Thornwell, who declared:

135. The resolutions are reprinted in Bost, "The Reverend John Bachman," 406–407. Bachman was a member of the committee that drew up the resolutions.
136. *The Doctrine of the Unity of the Human Race*, 291–92.
137. The full report is in *The Missionary* (Pittsburgh), October 1, 1857.
138. The paper is published in *The Missionary*, December 10, 1857.
139. *The Doctrine of the Unity of the Human Race*, 8.
140. "Nott and Gliddon on *Types of Mankind*," *Charleston Medical Journal and Review*, IX (September, 1854), 657.
141. William S. Jenkins, *Pro-Slavery Thought in the Old South* (Chapel Hill, N.C., 1935), 248–49, 253, 262. However, the South's foremost anatomist, James L. Cabell of the University of Virginia, vigorously defended "the specific and common origin of all the varieties of man." *The Testimony of Modern Science to the Unity of Mankind* (New York, 1859).

No Christian man . . . can give any countenance to speculations which trace the negro to any other parent than Adam. If he is not descended from Adam, he has not the same flesh and blood with Jesus, and is therefore excluded from the possibility of salvation. Those who defend slavery upon the plea that the African is not of the same stock with ourselves, are aiming a fatal blow at the institution, by bringing it into conflict with the dearest doctrines of the Gospel.[142]

That sentiment was echoed throughout southern orthodoxy. The preachers rightly perceived that if they yielded to the new ethnology, they would undermine their doctrine of inerrant scripture and torpedo their theory of God's plan for the redemption of the Negro race.

---

142. "NATIONAL SINS—*A Fast-Day Sermon, . . . November 21, 1860,*" *Southern Presbyterian Review*, XIII, 682–83.

Chapter IV

TO THE BITTER END

From the Wilmot Proviso controversy until the presidential election of 1860, the Union was increasingly imperiled by intersectional strife over an extension of slavery. When it became evident that the United States would acquire new territory as a result of its war with Mexico, David Wilmot of Pennsylvania offered an amendment to an appropriation bill in the House (known as the "two million bill") in August, 1846, to the effect that neither slavery nor involuntary servitude would ever be permitted in any part of said territory. This proposal dramatically revived an old issue that had been more or less dormant since the Missouri Compromise. The most ominous speech on the southern side was made by John C. Calhoun of the Senate. He presented a set of resolutions which, together with his "remarks," maintained that all territories were "the property of the States united; held jointly for their common use," and that consequently Congress had no constitutional right to make any law that would prohibit slaveholders from taking their property into such territories. Referring to the fact that he was "a cotton planter" and "a slaveholder," Calhoun said: "I would rather meet any extremity on earth than give up one inch of our equality—one inch of what belongs to us as members of this great republic!"[1] The Wilmot Proviso did not pass, but that was not the end of the matter. The fact that every northern state legislature except one adopted resolutions approving the Wilmot measure gave notice that the people in the free states were determined to confine slavery to its present limits. Since, however, the South was equally determined not to be bottled up, the issue was destined to be settled by the sword.

1. "Remarks . . . made in the Senate, February 19th, 1847," in Richard K. Crallé, ed., *The Works of John C. Calhoun* (6 vols., New York, 1851–57), IV, 344–45, 348.

I

When Wilmot and his fellow free-soilers tried to block the further spread of slavery, they outraged southern ministers of the gospel as well as the politicians. In many instances the clergy excelled the politicians in whipping up proslavery sentiment. This was certainly true of Augustus B. Longstreet of Georgia, one of southern Methodism's most respected spokesmen. While the Wilmot Proviso was under debate, he published a stinging indictment of abolitionism, charging that it was "one of the most frightful, disgusting monsters, that ever reared its head among a Christian people," and he accused Massachusetts of being "the mother" of that monster.[2] The Wilmot Proviso was merely abolitionism's latest political device to rob the South of its equal territorial rights, and the inevitable result of such discriminatory action would be a dissolution of the Union "unless God interpose to arrest its progress."[3] Longstreet evidently did not expect God to arrest the course of abolitionism, for he advised the southern states to leave the Union in a body as soon as all three divisions of the federal government came under its control. Assuming that war would swiftly follow disunion, he told his fellow southerners that they should begin at once to prepare for the conflict. "We should have a military school in every State, and . . . tactics should be a part of the study and training of every College. . . . Each State should have complete equipments for twenty thousand soldiers at least, always on hand and in good order."[4]

During 1850, intersectional passions rose to unprecedented heights as northern and southern partisans debated Henry Clay's proposed formula for a restoration of harmony. The final legislative result, known as the Compromise of 1850, contained four principal measures: (1) the admission of California as a free state; (2) the organization of New Mexico and Utah as territories without reference to slavery; (3) a stringent fugitive slave law; and (4)

---

2. *A Voice From the South: Comprising Letters From Georgia to Massachusetts, and to the Southern States* (Baltimore, 1847), 27. Only two of the eleven letters were addressed to the South.
3. *Ibid.*, 22.
4. *Ibid.*, 57–58.

abolition of the domestic slave trade in the District of Columbia. The compromise left nobody happy, least of all the lower South. Mercurial South Carolina, the stronghold of firebrands, teetered on the brink of secession. Governor Whitemarsh B. Seabrook actually recommended that the state "interpose" its "sovereignty" to avert "the doom which impends over the civil institutions of the South." Holding that "the enactments of the last Congress of the United States have destroyed the equal rights of the Southern States," the General Assembly recommended that South Carolinians gather in church on December 6 for a day of "fasting," and that the clergy unite with their flocks in beseeching God to "direct and aid" the assembly's efforts to devise means by which to meet the crisis. This body also invited Whitefoord Smith, a prominent Methodist, to deliver a sermon to the General Assembly on the same occasion.

The Methodist leader responded with a moving discourse. After paying homage to the late Calhoun as "our Moses," he plunged into the burning issue of the hour, the menace of abolitionism. The abolitionists, he charged, had forsaken the Bible for "A HIGHER LAW." Under "the affectation of Christianity," they were spreading "the doctrines of devils."[5] There was a time, said Smith, when many churchmen in the South viewed slavery "with an evil eye," but a wise and gracious God had led them to change their minds. Missionary efforts to convert the Negro race "turned the attention of Christians" to a "correct appreciation of slavery." They had thus come to see that bondage was sanctioned by divine revelation. When therefore "the battle-cry of fanaticism was raised in its first serious attack upon the slave institution, its first bold repulse was from the Christian church, whose adamantine fortification was the Word of God!"[6] Being then sure that those "who make slavery a cause of offense, fight not against us, but against God," Christians may be depended upon "to plant themselves in the breach, and defend with their lives this institution of God."[7] The legislators were so enthralled by the "eloquent" sermon that they unanimously re-

5. *God, the Refuge of His People. A Sermon, Delivered Before the General Assembly of South Carolina, on Friday, December 6, 1850, Being a Day of Fasting, Humiliation and Prayer* (Columbia, S.C., 1850), 14.
6. *Ibid.*, 16.
7. *Ibid.*, 13, 16–17.

quested its publication, and ordered the printing of two thousand copies for general distribution. It was a forceful propaganda instrument, even though the preacher stopped short of calling for secession.[8]

Despite the political tumult, James H. Thornwell strongly cautioned South Carolina not to rush into secession prematurely, or alone. A dissolution of the Union should be a "last desperate remedy for the disorders of the government." As for "single-handed secession," it boded nothing "but defeat and disaster—insecurity to slavery—oppression to ourselves—ruin to the State."[9] At the same time, Thornwell warned the North that the southern states had almost exhausted their patience, and that unless their equal territorial rights were respected they would "set up for themselves."[10] The Constitution, he said, made no distinction between slaveholding and non-slaveholding states, and therefore Congress had no right to say whether new territories should or should not exclude slavery when they were ready for admission into the Union. At the same time, he contended that such territories "should be kept open to any emigrants from any section of the Confederacy." Thornwell took note of the fact that many northern people were so deeply convinced of the evil of bondage that they could no longer consent to its extension into the territories. In that case, he argued, it was the duty of the northern states "to dissolve the Union" rather than to pervert the Constitution.[11]

While Thornwell wanted to save the Union, he did not want to save it badly enough to liberate the black man. "The Southern States," he asserted, "will not abandon their institutions. This is certain as fate."[12] Upon that premise, the intersectional struggle was bound to grow more acute with each passing year, for the free states would neither dissolve the Union nor abate their drive to remove from it the blot of human bondage.

Recognizing that their "peculiar institution" was being fatefully encircled, the leaders of southern Protestantism lashed out

8. Iveson L. Brookes, a Baptist preacher of South Carolina, took a more hawkish stand. *A Defence of the South Against the Reproaches and Incroachments of the North* (Hamburg, S.C., 1850), 47–48, and *passim*.
9. "Critical Notices," *Southern Presbyterian Review*, IV (January, 1851), 449, 452.
10. *Ibid.*, 450.
11. *Ibid.*, 445–46.
12. *Ibid.*, 450.

fiercely at their antislavery foes. Once again Longstreet played a leading role, when he gave the baccalaureate address to the graduating class of 1859 at South Carolina College, of which he was president. All signs, said the veteran churchman, indicated that the Union was "upon the eve of a lamentable revolution," the sole fomenters of which were the infatuated abolitionists. Future generations would be astonished and indignant that "the most Heaven-favored people" on earth should "have put at hazard their all for the sake of an abject race of negroes, who never knew freedom and never can maintain it."[13] Such, however, was the way with fanaticism.

Like other state rights extremists, Longstreet argued that the federal government's only role in relation to slavery was "to protect it," and that therefore all appeals to that government to interfere with slavery constituted "a direct attack upon the fundamental laws of the Confederacy."[14] Yet antislavery men had repeatedly violated that law in their ruthless course to destroy the system of domestic bondage. Thus if the slave states should finally withdraw from the Union, the blame would not rest upon them, but upon the subverters of the Constitution.

If the slave states were to secede from the Union, would not war follow? Although conceding that the usual answer was "yes," Longstreet himself boldly took issue with that opinion, declaring that there "will be no war if the Southern States move off in a body. I would stake everything I am worth upon this position."[15] Supposing, however, that war would result from secession, the South need not fear the enemy, because it could "put 200,000 men in the field, and more if need be, and support them there longer than any nation on the globe of the same white population. . . . Away then with this notion of whipping us into the Union, or whipping us at all."[16]

The militant preacher was obviously itching for a fight, for he announced that if other slave states were willing to sacrifice their

---

13. "Baccalaureate Address Delivered at the University of South Carolina to the Graduating Class of 1859," in O. P. Fitzgerald, *Judge Longstreet: A Sketch* (Nashville, 1891), 97–98.
14. *Ibid.*, 98.   15. *Ibid.*, 104.
16. *Ibid.*, 104–5.

rights still further to save the Union, South Carolina should "put her cause in the hands of God and take her stand alone."[17] Such fire-eaters as the state's Robert Barnwell Rhett doubtless rejoiced over that summons to the colors.

II

Although antislavery doings of the 1850's had offended the southern clergy, it was Abraham Lincoln's election to the presidency in 1860 that transformed them into ardent secessionists. "Black Republican" was the mildest epithet they ever applied to Lincoln and his followers. Once again, preachers in the lower South led their profession in generating disunion sentiment.

When South Carolina, a hotbed of clerical secessionists, appointed November 21, 1860, as a day of "fasting, humiliation, and prayer," there was an outburst of political preaching all across that state. In Charleston alone, at least three patriotic sermons were delivered and immediately published. One of them was by William C. Dana, minister of Central Presbyterian Church. The whole question before South Carolinians, he said, was whether they would "permit a *foreign and hostile government* to bear rule over them."[18] Accusing the impending Lincoln government of being an instrument of a movement that violated both God's word and the Constitution with respect to domestic slavery, Dana declared flatly that the southern states owed "no fealty" whatever to that government. "*The South alone should govern the South*," he exclaimed. The truculent churchman exhorted his fellow southerners to emulate their revolutionary ancestors and "shake off" their allegiance to an alien power.[19]

The second Charleston sermon was delivered by William O. Prentiss, rector of St. Peter's Episcopal Church. Abolitionism, he charged, was the heretical offspring of latter-day New England Puritanism, which had substituted the authority of a "higher law"

17. *Ibid.*, 106.
18. *A Sermon Delivered in the Central Presbyterian Church, Charleston, S.C., Nov. 21st, 1860, Being the Day Appointed by State Authority for Fasting, Humiliation and Prayer* (Charleston, 1860), 6.
19. *Ibid.*, 6–7.

for that of divine revelation.[20] Owing to this rejection of God's word, New Englanders had become so corrupt that it would be impossible for the South to "coalesce" with those people without suffering corruption and thus bringing down upon itself "the awful doom which awaits them." The rector therefore called for a speedy secession of the slave states. "Draw back now," he warned, "and dishonor awaits you."[21] Those who executed their "heaven appointed work" with success, he prophesied, would make "the name Carolinian more famous than ever was that of Roman." Besides, their glorious victory would assure the future South of an "empire" that would extend into "the tropics" and wax powerful on the labor of the African, whose normal condition was "that of subjection to the white man."[22] Not surprisingly, this discourse awakened so much enthusiasm that Prentiss was prompted to repeat it at St. Peter's four days later and then preach it before the state legislature.

The third of Charleston's fast-day discourses was preached by Thomas Smyth, minister of the Second Presbyterian Church. He passionately attacked the Declaration of Independence as a godless document. "God is introduced to give dignity and emphasis, . . . and then He is banished," said the clergyman.[23] It was this very atheistic Declaration which had inspired the "higher law" doctrine of the radical antislavery men. If the mischievous abolitionists had only followed the Bible instead of the godless Declaration, they would have been bound to acknowledge that human bondage was divinely ordained. The mission of southerners was therefore clear; they must defend the word of God against abolitionist infidelity. "Upon this rock [the Bible] let the South build her house, and the gates of hell shall not prevail against it," proclaimed the spirited proslavery apologist.[24]

---

20. *A Sermon Preached at St. Peter's Church, Charleston, Wednesday, November 21, 1860, Being a Day of Public Fasting, Humiliation, and Prayer* (Charleston, 1860), 6–8. Prentiss claimed that the seeds of the revolt against biblical authority were to be found in John Robinson's theory of church government, which allegedly ascribed "infallibility" to the local congregation. *Ibid.*, 9. The patriarch of Plymouth Colony never advanced any such idea.

21. *Ibid.*, 17, 18.

22. *Ibid.*, 18–20.

23. *The Sin and the Curse; or the Union, the Source of Disunion, and Our Duty in the Present Crisis. A Discourse Preached on the Occasion of the Day of Humiliation and Prayer . . . on November 21, 1860* (Charleston, S.C., 1860), 13.

24. *Ibid.*, 18.

During this same November, 1860, leading preachers in other cities of South Carolina advocated secession no less boldly than Dana, Prentiss, and Smyth of Charleston. This was notably true of James Clement Furman of Greenville, president of Furman University. Like his distinguished father, Richard Furman, he owned a farm and slaves. Following Lincoln's election, he stumped the Greenville district on behalf of immediate disunion, and won a seat in the state secession convention.[25] Speaking at a mass meeting in Greenville on November 22, he complained that by failing to obey the fugitive slave law the North was robbing the South of "hundreds of thousands of dollars" every year. By excluding slavery from the western territories the North was also guilty of violating the Constitution. Consequently, said Furman, "the sooner we renounce" the Constitution, "the better." After all, South Carolina "has the right to do as she pleases," and if the state should decide to withdraw from the Union, "the General Government has no more right to say nay than she has to veto an act of the British Parliament."[26] John C. Calhoun was never more extreme in his state rights doctrine than the president of Furman. The Baptist "lion of the hour" received "a liberal share of the votes" cast for permanent president of the secession convention.[27]

On Thanksgiving Day, 1860, two able clergymen of New Orleans preached highly inflammatory sermons in favor of secession before a single state had left the Union. W. T. Leacock, rector of Christ Church, assured "northern adversaries" that he and other southerners held their slaves on Christian principle, and that consequently they had no fear of abolitionists. Nevertheless, Leacock charged that "our enemies" had not only defamed the character of southerners, but had denied their constitutional rights and stolen their slave property. In fact, "nothing has been left untried which the deepest malice could invent for our injury or destruction."[28]

---

25. Harvey T. Cook, *The Life Work of James Clement Furman* (Greenville, 1926), 201. Two prominent Baptist leaders in the state, John A. Broadus and James Petigru Boyce, professors at Southern Baptist Theological Seminary (Greenville), opposed Furman's secessionist doctrine. *Ibid.*, 194–95.

26. *Ibid.*, 197–200.

27. *Ibid.*, 201.

28. "Thanksgiving Sermon, . . . at Christ Church, in New Orleans [November 29, 1860]," in B. M. Palmer and W. T. Leacock, *The Rights of the South Defended in the Pulpits* (Mobile, 1860), 15.

What, then, should be the course of the South? "I give it as my firm and unhesitating belief," said Leacock, "that nothing is left to us but secession.... To advance is to secure our rights; to recede, is to lay our fortunes, our honor, our liberty, under the feet of our enemies.... I am willing, at the call of my honor and my liberty to die a freeman; but I'll never, no, never, live a slave; and the alternative now presented by our enemies is secession or slavery. Let it be liberty or death!"[29]

Equally militant was the Thanksgiving discourse of Benjamin Morgan Palmer, minister of the First Presbyterian Church. A native of South Carolina, he was perhaps the most eloquent preacher in southern Presbyterianism.[30] Palmer fully recognized that human bondage was at stake in the imminent bloody conflict, and he boldly announced that the South was providentially invested with the duty *"to conserve and to perpetuate the institution of domestic slavery as now existing,"* and to extend it *"wherever Providence and nature may carry it."*[31] This duty, Palmer urged, had to be performed by the South not only to save itself from economic disaster, but also to safeguard its bondsmen, since "freedom would be their doom." But above all, the South owed it to God to follow this course of action, because "the abolition spirit is undeniably atheistic."[32] The South would, the New Orleans churchman prophesied, fulfill its divinely appointed mission in the face of every peril. Should the madness of the hour result in war, "we will not shrink even from the baptism of fire." Indeed, "not till the last man has fallen behind the last rampart" will the sword "drop from our hands."[33]

Feeling certain that Lincoln's victory had placed slavery in jeopardy, Palmer exhorted political leaders of the South to gather in convention as soon as possible and reclaim the powers their states had delegated to the Union. "Let them further take all the necessary

---

29. *Ibid.*, 16. When, in April, 1862, New Orleans surrendered to General Benjamin F. Butler, Leacock refused to take the oath of allegiance to the Union and was banished from the city.

30. For the best account of Palmer's ecclesiastical contributions, see Doralyn J. Hickey, "Benjamin Morgan Palmer: Churchman of the Old South" (typed Ph.D. dissertation, Duke University, 1962).

31. *The South: Her Peril, and Her Duty. A Discourse, Delivered in the First Presbyterian Church, New Orleans, on Thursday, November 29, 1860* (New Orleans, 1860), 6, 11.

32. *Ibid.*, 7–10.

33. *Ibid.*, 11.

steps looking toward separate and independent existence; and initiate measures for framing a new and homogeneous confederacy. Thus, prepared for every emergency, let the crisis come." By rising up as one man the South could "roll back for all time" the abolitionist "curse." If southerners failed to meet the crisis, human bondage would be overthrown and the South would become a wasteland.[34]

This dramatic sermon catapulted Palmer into South-wide fame overnight. The New Orleans *Daily Delta,* a zealous advocate of secession, published the entire discourse three times within a period of four days, and many other papers throughout the South published all or large portions of it. It was distributed by the thousands in pamphlet form.[35] As a generator of disunion sentiment, it excelled every other pulpit deliverance of the southern clergy.

Ecclesiastical secessionists were busy in other states of the deep South. In Alabama, few men did more to prod that state into withdrawing from the Union than Basil Manly, former president of the University of Alabama and eminent Baptist preacher. Owner of much land and many bondsmen, he contended that God had expressly ordained slavery.[36] After Lincoln's victory of 1860, he campaigned diligently to win a seat in the state secession convention, and his failure to achieve this objective was a great disappointment. On the other hand, he was elated by his selection as chaplain at the inauguration of Jefferson Davis. "I rode in a coach drawn by six gray horses, in company with the President and Vice President," he pridefully recorded in his diary.[37]

In Florida, two high-ranking churchmen instilled anti-Union sentiments. One was Francis H. Rutledge, bishop of the Protestant Episcopal Church. During the deliberations of the Florida secession convention, he mingled freely with delegates and observers, exerting his influence in behalf of southern independence.[38] When

34. *Ibid.,* 16.
35. Wayne C. Eubank, "Benjamin Morgan Palmer's Thanksgiving Sermon, 1860," in Jeffery Auer, ed., *Antislavery and Disunion, 1858–1861* (New York, 1963), 115–17; Haskell Monroe, Jr., "Bishop [sic] Palmer's Thanksgiving Address," *Louisiana History,* IV (Spring, 1963), 115–17.
36. Harold Wilson, "Basil Manly, Apologist For Slavocracy," *Alabama Review,* XV (January, 1962), 38–53.
37. W. Stanley Hoole, ed., "The Diary of Dr. Basil Manly, 1858–1867," *Alabama Review,* IV (April, 1951), 147.
38. The Virginia fire-eater, Edmund Ruffin, who was on hand as an observer, was

President Buchanan proclaimed January 4, 1861, as a day of humiliation and prayer, the bishop refused to attend the service held at St. John's Church of Tallahassee on this occasion on the ground that the proclamation was a tacit rebuke to disunionists. Rutledge was so eager to see Florida cut its national ties that he promised $500 toward the new government's expenses just as soon as an ordinance of secession was passed.[39]

The other prominent churchman was Augustin Verot, Vicar Apostolic of the Roman Catholic Church in Florida. Unlike Rutledge, he observed President Buchanan's proclamation with an able sermon, preached at the Church of St. Augustine. However, he aligned himself firmly with the South, and he argued that the imminent national disaster had stemmed from a controversy over slavery, and especially from the machinations of radical abolitionists. "The true source of the misfortunes which weigh already upon the land, and bid fair to increase a hundred fold, lies in the misrepresentation of ignorant and fanatical zealots, who desecrate and pollute the Divine word, speaking in the name of God, although they gainsay all the teachings of God."[40] As dogmatically as Benjamin Palmer, the bishop argued that human bondage had the explicit sanction of Holy Writ. In a further defense of slavery, he appealed to the law of nature and to the canon law of Roman Catholicism.[41]

Verot's discourse met with mixed reactions among his fellow Catholics. Napoleon Joseph Perché, editor of *Le Propagateur Catholique* (New Orleans), hailed it enthusiastically. On the other hand, Francis Patrick Kenrick, archbishop of Baltimore, was so convinced that it would have a divisive effect upon American Catholicism that he strongly urged Verot to suppress the tract.[42] The prelate's proslavery argument seems to have raised some ques-

---

greatly impressed with Rutledge's "ardent & active patriotic sentiments." Dorothy Dodd, "Edmund Ruffin's Account of the Florida Secession Convention, 1861," *Florida Historical Society Quarterly*, XII (October, 1933), 69–70.

39. Dorothy Dodd, "The Secession Movement in Florida, 1850–1861," *Florida Historical Society Quarterly*, XII (October, 1933), 60.

40. *A Tract For the Times. Slavery and Abolitionism, Being the Substance of a Sermon Preached in the Church of St. Augustine, Florida, on the 4th Day of January, 1861, Day of Public Humiliation, Fasting and Prayer* (new ed., New Orleans, 1861), 13.

41. *Ibid.*, 5–11.

42. Michael V. Gannon, *Rebel Bishop: The Life and Era of Augustin Verot* (Milwaukee, 1964), 49–51.

tion also at the Vatican, for a copy of his sermon in the archives of the Sacred Congregation of Propaganda bears a note by the secretary of that body, saying: "It would seem that one cannot accept everything which is affirmed in this argument."[43] The "rebel" bishop's argument for slavery may have been too extreme for Rome, but southerners welcomed it as the essence of truth.

Before Mississippi broke away from the Union, clerical patriots in that state were also preaching the gospel of secession. A major crusader was Thomas W. Caskey, pastor of a church of the Disciples of Christ at Jackson from 1855 to 1861. At the request of his fellow churchmen, Caskey, a slaveholder and farmer, lectured throughout the state in 1860 on behalf of the presidential candidacy of John C. Breckinridge, whose extreme state rights platform demanded the protection of slavery in the territories. His campaigning, it is said, contributed significantly to Breckinridge's sweeping victory.[44] Many Mississippians apparently believed that secession would not lead to war, for during the public discussion of this proposed step Caskey allegedly heard Lucius Q. C. Lamar, one of the best informed politicians in the state, say: "*I will pledge myself to drink every drop of blood that is shed by this act of secession.*"[45]

The advocacy of secession was not confined to a few distinguished clergymen; religious journals and church bodies also heartily promoted political disunion. In this respect, too, the lower South led the way. The church papers of South Carolina were ardently secessionist in spirit. In a long editorial, the *Southern Episcopalian* of Charleston, a monthly periodical, castigated "Northern fanatics" for their antislavery conduct. The election of Lincoln, said the editors, "has satisfied the South that *disunion* is the only escape from destruction."[46] The *Southern Presbyterian* of Columbia was second to none in anti-Union sentiment. "We say it is the duty of the South to resist now," wrote the editor shortly after the "Black

---

43. Quoted in James J. Pillar, O.M.I., *The Catholic Church in Mississippi, 1837-65* (New Orleans, 1964), 176.
44. B. F. Manire, ed., *Caskey's Last Book, Containing an Autobiographical Sketch of His Ministerial Life* (Nashville, 1896), 26-29. Caskey served as confidential adviser to Governor John J. Pettus during the secession crisis. *Ibid.*, 27.
45. *Ibid.*, 28.
46. "South Carolina and the Union," *Southern Episcopalian*, VIII (December, 1860), 489.

Republicans" were victorious.[47] A day before South Carolina voted to withdraw from the Union, the *United States Catholic Miscellany* of Charleston announced the removal of "United States" from its name, remarking that those words were "obnoxious" to a journal professing to serve as an organ of truth.[48]

The religious press in the gulf states likewise promoted the secessionist cause. In the vanguard was Napoleon Perché's *Le Propagateur Catholique*. A native of France, Perché came to America in 1837. Along with his editorial duties, he served as chaplain at the Ursuline convent in New Orleans. Even after the war came and that city was occupied by Union forces, Perché remained so pro-Confederate that the publication of his paper was suspended and he himself was placed under house arrest.[49] Soon after Lincoln's election to the presidency, the *South Western Baptist* of Tuskegee, Alabama, urged that "the only remedy" for the South's grievances was abandonment of the Union. Far from deploring this hazardous course, the editor wrote: "We see in it peace, happiness and unbounded prosperity."[50] In January, 1861, the *Texas Baptist* of Anderson castigated "Black Republicans," and declared that the South could no longer postpone its decision to secede from the Union without a disgraceful submission to them. Like numerous other proslavery churchmen, the editor said: "We are sure that God has given us the right to buy and own slaves as a perpetual inheritance, and to transmit them to our children."[51]

Meanwhile, leading church bodies in the lower South were taking actions in support of secession. In November, 1860, the Presbyterian Synod of South Carolina expressed the belief that South Carolinians "are now solemnly called on to imitate their revolu-

---

47. *Southern Presbyterian*, November 17, 1860, quoted in Haskell Monroe, Jr., "The Presbyterian Church in the Confederate States of America" (typed Ph.D. dissertation, Rice University, 1961), 55.

48. Madeline H. Rice, *American Catholic Opinion in the Slavery Controversy* (New York, 1944), 145.

49. Roger Baudier, *The Catholic Church in Louisiana* (New Orleans, 1939), 426. For Perché's pro-Confederate views, see *Le Propagateur Catholique* (New Orleans), January 26, February 2, 16, June 15, July 13, 1861. Perché's political opposite was his New Orleans friend, Adrien-Emmanuel Rouquette, a devoted Unionist and a sharp critic of secessionists. Dagmar Renshaw Leberton, *Chahta-Ima: The Life of Adrien-Emmanuel Rouquette* (Baton Rouge, 1947), 89, 219–22.

50. *South Western Baptist*, November 29, 1860. See also *ibid.*, January 24, 1861.

51. *Texas Baptist*, January 3, 1861.

tionary fathers, and stand up for their rights."[52] On December 18, 1860—two days before South Carolina adopted an ordinance of secession—the South Carolina Conference of the Methodist Episcopal Church, South, announced: "We feel bound, by honor and duty, to move in harmony with the South in resisting Northern domination."[53] The missionary society of this conference held that separation of the state from the Union would facilitate its effort to Christianize blacks. "The secession of South Carolina will settle forever the question of slavery," said the board of managers of the society. "The vague dreams of abolition-redemption will soon fade away from the mind of the slave, and leave him happy and contented."[54]

Alabama Baptists and Methodists were no less eager for disunion than their brethren of South Carolina. At their state convention, held at Tuskegee in November, 1860, the Baptists voted unanimously that they could "no longer hope for justice, protection [of their 'peculiar property'], or safety" within the Union, and that they therefore stood ready to defend Alabama's independence.[55] Early in December, 1860, Methodists of the Alabama Conference, which included portions of Mississippi and Florida, declared unanimously that they felt "bound by honor and duty to move in harmony with the South in resisting Northern domination."[56]

The same spirit of political rebellion permeated organized religion in Florida. When, for instance, Baptists gathered in their state convention during late November, 1860, they were ready for a revolt against the Union. Noting that current national events would of "necessity affect to an incalculable extent the Christian, as well as the political welfare of our whole population, and more especially of our slaves," they expressed their "hearty approbation

---

52. Quoted in Ernest Trice Thompson, *Presbyterians in the South*, I: *1607–1861* (Richmond, 1963), 558.

53. *Charleston Daily Courier*, December 20, 1860. This action is not recorded in the published minutes of the South Carolina Conference.

54. *Minutes of the . . . South Carolina Conference of the Methodist Episcopal Church . . . 1860* (Charleston, S.C., 1861), 26. According to the report of the board of managers, southern Methodism was in 1860 supporting 210 missions for "colored people," and 26 were in South Carolina.

55. *Minutes of the Alabama Baptist State Convention, . . . 1860* (Tuskegee, 1860), 11.

56. *Minutes of the Alabama Conference of the Methodist Episcopal Church, South . . . 1860* (Nashville, 1861), 41.

of those who were determined to maintain the integrity of our Southern States, even by a disruption of all existing political ties."[57]

This extended sampling of evidence clearly indicates that the deep South churches were in the forefront of the secessionist movement. There were indeed a few prominent clergymen in that section who opposed this movement, such as Adrien-Emmanuel Rouquette of Louisiana, James A. Lyon of Mississippi, William A. Baker of Texas, and James Petigru Boyce of South Carolina, but they were of no avail against the die-hard disunionists. The clerical secessionists often paid lip service to the traditional theory that preachers should not deal with political questions in the pulpit, but they in fact freely promoted the southern cause from their pulpits.[58]

III

Religious leaders in the lower South, like their political counterparts, recognized the tactical advantage of forming an independent confederacy before Lincoln could assume the office of president. This was notably true of James Henley Thornwell, a keen observer of political events. The moment Lincoln was elected, he abandoned all hope of saving the Union. On November 24 he wrote a letter to Robert L. Dabney of Virginia, saying: "I wish the people of Virginia could see their way to hoist the standard of Southern rights, and to lead us in this most necessary revolution."[59]

Virginians, including Dabney, were not yet ready to risk such a perilous course of action, and it therefore fell to Thornwell's native state to hoist the revolutionary standard. Dauntlessly, South Carolina unanimously adopted an ordinance of secession on December 20, 1860. Twelve of the 169 delegates participating in that fateful decision were ministers, and all except one led the convention in prayer at least once.[60] One hundred and fifty-three delegates,

---

57. *Minutes of the ... Baptist Convention of Florida, ... 1860,* 7.

58. For a prime example, see James H. Thornwell, "NATIONAL SINS—*A Fast-Day Sermon, preached in the Presbyterian Church, Columbia, Wednesday, November 21, 1860,*" *Southern Presbyterian Review,* XIII (January, 1861), 650–54.

59. Thomas Cary Johnson, *Life and Letters of Robert Lewis Dabney* (Richmond, 1903), 224. Only three days earlier, Thornwell had preached a powerful sermon, laying down in detail the sins of the North. "NATIONAL SINS—*A Fast-Day Sermon, ... November 21, 1860,*" *Southern Presbyterian Review,* XIII, 664–73.

60. John A. May and Joan R. Faunt, *South Carolina Secedes* (Columbia, S.C.,

or 90.5 per cent, owned slaves. Seventy of that number, or 41.4 per cent, owned fifty or more each, while twenty-seven, or 16 per cent, owned a hundred or more per person.[61] As the clerical delegates generally belonged to the more affluent class of their profession, a majority of them probably held blacks. At any rate, one of the twelve owned sixty-two slaves, and another, one hundred or more.[62]

Since 90 per cent of the convention delegates held property in Negroes, it is no surprise that, in specifying the causes which had prompted South Carolina to quit the Union, they should have assigned the major cause to the North's opposition to human bondage. The people of the free states, the convention charged, had failed to suppress the subversive abolition societies; they had denounced slaveholding as sinful; they had induced thousands of Negroes to flee from their masters; and they had finally placed in power a sectional political party committed to excluding slavery from the territories. Consequently South Carolina was forced into secession in order to protect the institution of domestic slavery.[63]

Thornwell rejoiced in South Carolina's withdrawal from the Union, and he immediately composed an able article urging all other slave states to do the same as speedily as possible. "The triumph of the principles which Mr. Lincoln is pledged to carry out," he wrote, "is the death-knell of slavery."[64] Even though acknowledging that the president-elect had pledged not to interfere with slavery where it was already established, he contended that the spirit of abolitionism would never rest until it had eradicated the bondage system throughout the nation. Consequently the slave states could only escape their impending doom by forming an independent confederacy. The sooner that could be done the better. Such a con-

---

1960), 109, 132–33, 139–40, 141–42, 146–47, 152, 159–60, 172–73, 177–78, 202–4, 219–20, 221–22. Ralph A. Wooster, *The Secession Conventions of the South* (Princeton, 1962), 18, listed only five of the delegates as ministers, but he followed the classification of the 1860 census, which categorized as ministers only those who were serving local pastorates. For the texts of the prayers offered by the clerical delegates, see the *Charleston Daily Courier*, December 19–22, 24, 25, 27, 29, 31, 1860; January 3–5, 7, 1861.

61. Wooster, *The Secession Conventions of the South*, 19.
62. May and Faunt, *South Carolina Secedes*, 142, 222.
63. "Declaration of the Immediate Causes Which Induce and Justify the Secession of South Carolina from the Federal Union," in May and Faunt, *South Carolina Secedes*, 80–81.
64. "The State of the Country," *Southern Presbyterian Review*, XIII (January, 1861), 881.

federacy "will be a center of unity, and, once combined, we are safe. . . . Conquered we can never be. It would be madness to attempt it."[65]

Thornwell had every reason for gratification, because by February 1, 1861, six other states had followed South Carolina's example, in the following order: Mississippi, Florida, Alabama, Georgia, Louisiana, and Texas. The secession conventions of those six states included fifteen clergymen, seven of whom were members of the Georgia delegation. Louisiana alone had no clerical delegate. The proportion of slaveholding delegates ranged from 70 per cent in Florida to 85 per cent in Mississippi.[66] In seeking to justify separation from the Union, all six of these conventions, like that of South Carolina, traced their major grievances to northern opposition to black bondage.

Representatives of these great cotton-growing states met at Montgomery, Alabama, on February 4 with the determination to constitute "a center of unity" as quickly as possible. Within a fortnight they had agreed upon a constitution, formed a provisional government of the Confederate States of America, and inducted into office Jefferson Davis of Mississippi as president, and Alexander Stephens of Georgia as vice president.

The Constitution of the Confederate States duplicated most of the provisions of the Federal Constitution, but it departed significantly from the latter with respect to slavery.[67] Section 9 of article I declared: "No bill of attainder, ex post facto law, or law denying or impairing the right of property in Negro slaves shall be passed." Furthermore, section 3 of article IV stipulated that in any subsequently acquired territory "the institution of Negro slavery, as it now exists in the Confederate States, shall be recognized and protected by Congress and by the Territorial Government." In thus prohibiting state and territorial governments from outlawing slavery, the Confederate Constitution plainly compromised the South's traditional theory of state rights. This fact alone

---

65. *Ibid.*, 887, 888.
66. Wooster, *The Secession Conventions of the South*, 32, 54, 70, 87, 107, 127.
67. The complete text of the Confederate Constitution is reprinted in Edward McPherson, *The Political History of the United States of America During the Great Rebellion* (Washington, 1864), 91–100.

revealed the new confederacy's determination to perpetuate Negro servitude.

Indispensable to an understanding of the Negro's status in the Confederate States is a remarkable address which Vice President Stephens gave at Savannah, Georgia, on March 21, 1861. Acknowledging that slavery "was the immediate cause of the late rupture [of the Union] and present revolution,"[68] he told his audience that the Confederate Constitution had laid that issue to rest forever. The Federal Constitution, he said, had been framed at a time when Jefferson and many other leading statesmen believed that the enslavement of the black man violated the laws of nature. In their view, slavery was politically, socially, and morally unjust. They saw no immediate solution to the problem, but at the same time they believed that, under the providence of God, human servitude would eventually pass away. Their ideas, Stephens contended, "were fundamentally wrong. They rested upon the assumption of the equality of races. This was an error." This sandy foundation could not sustain a government, and when the political storm came it fell. "Our new government," on the other hand, "is founded upon exactly the opposite idea; its foundations are laid, its corner-stone rests, upon the great truth, that the negro is not equal to the white man; that slavery—subordination to the superior race—is his natural and normal condition."[69]

The Georgian boasted that the Confederate government was the first government in history to be "instituted upon principles in strict conformity to nature, and the ordination of Providence." Many governments, it was true, had been based upon class principles involving the same race; but all of them had violated the laws of nature. "Our system," Stephens argued, "commits no such violation of nature's laws. With us, all of the white race, however high or low, rich or poor, are equal in the eye of the law. Not so with the

---

68. After the war, however, Stephens downgraded slavery as a cause of the southern revolt, and claimed that the fundamental cause of the revolt grew out of divergent theories of government. "It was a strife," he wrote, "between the principles of Federation, on the one side, and Centralism, or Consolidation, on the other." *A Constitutional View of the Late War Between the States* (2 vols., Philadelphia, 1868–70), II, 10.

69. Henry Cleveland, *Alexander H. Stephens, in Public and Private, with Letters and Speeches* (Philadelphia, 1866), 721.

negro. Subordination is his place. . . . It is, indeed, in conformity with the ordinance of the Creator."[70]

The *New Orleans Christian Advocate* applauded the Savannah address, and predicted that the racial theory advanced by Stephens was "sure to win its way" everywhere among "the friends of truth." The editor held that "all anti-slaveryism logically leads to negro equality, amalgamation, and ultimate servile war."[71] Perhaps few church papers in the Confederacy were as virulently anti-Negro as the New Orleans journal, but no evidence has come to light that any of them ever challenged the "corner-stone" dogma of the vice president. Nor is there anything to indicate that a single one of them took issue with the principle of Negro inferiority as reflected in the Confederate Constitution. Indeed, representative church papers across the South published that document as a whole or in part with at least tacit approval.[72]

IV

While the cotton-state Confederates faced the future with courage, they nevertheless courted diligently the states immediately north of them: Virginia, North Carolina, Tennessee, and Arkansas. But in those states unionist sentiment was strong, especially in western Virginia, western North Carolina, eastern Tennessee, and northwest Arkansas. In the presidential election of 1860, John Bell, the Constitutional Union candidate, had carried Virginia and Tennessee, and had run John C. Breckinridge a close race in North Carolina. Even though Breckinridge took Arkansas, unionist sentiment in that state was far from weak.[73] On the whole, the people in these four states regarded the Compromise of 1850 as more or less satisfactory, all things considered. Nor did their most responsible political spokesmen believe that the election of Lincoln as such was a sufficient cause for secession. They therefore deplored the precipitate action of the cotton states and urged that still further effort be

70. *Ibid.*, 722–23.
71. Quoted in the *Richmond Christian Advocate*, May 2, 1861.
72. See, for example, *South Western Baptist*, February 21, 1861; Nashville *Christian Advocate*, February 21, 1861; Richmond *Religious Herald*, May 9, 1861; *Texas Baptist*, April 4 and 11, 1861.
73. Wooster, *The Secession Conventions of the South*, 155–56.

made to find a way to save the Union and at the same time to protect the rights of the South.[74]

The church leaders of the upper South generally agreed with the sentiments of their political brethren. This was notably true of Robert Lewis Dabney, a dominant force in Virginia Presbyterianism. Ever since the middle 1850's he had been increasingly alarmed by the drift toward disunion, and had pleaded with the spokesmen of both sections to restrain their angry passions before it was too late.[75] He was harshly critical of South Carolina's hot-headed action. "I regard the conduct of South Carolina," he wrote a close Richmond friend, "as unjustifiable towards the United States at large, and towards her Southern sisters, as treacherous, wicked, insolent, and mischievous."[76] About the same time Dabney circulated "A Pacific Appeal to Christians," entreating his "dear brethren of the South" to give concerned leaders in the North "one more opportunity to achieve our rights and peace for us by the weapons of argument."[77] His sentiment was shared not only by other leaders of Virginia Presbyterianism, but also by prominent Baptist and Methodist ministers in the Old Dominion.[78]

During the fall and winter of 1860–61, dominant clerical sentiment in North Carolina agreed substantially with that in Virginia. The state's four leading Protestant papers—*Biblical Recorder* (Baptist), *North Carolina Christian Advocate* (Methodist), *Church Intelligencer* (Episcopalian), and *North Carolina Presbyterian*—were all critical of the lower South's impulsive rush into independence.[79]

74. For a brief account of the efforts made to adjust sectional differences, see Dwight L. Dumond, *The Secession Movement, 1860–1861* (New York, 1931), Chaps. 8, 11–12.

75. See, for example, Dabney, "Christians Pray For Your Country," in C. R. Vaughan, ed., *Discussions by Robert L. Dabney, D.D., LL.D.*, II: *Evangelical* (Richmond, 1891), 393–400. This article first appeared in the *Central Presbyterian* (Richmond), March 29, 1856.

76. Dabney to Moses Drury Hoge, January 4, 1861, in Johnson, *The Life and Letters of Robert Lewis Dabney*, 222. Writing to his mother on December 28, 1860, Dabney charged that South Carolina was "as great a pest as the Abolitionists." *Ibid.*, 215.

77. *Ibid.*, 216. The "Appeal," which bore the signatures of eighteen prominent preachers and educators of at least three Protestant denominations in Virginia, was published in the *Central Presbyterian* in March, 1861.

78. W. Harrison Daniel, "Virginia Baptists, 1861–1865," *Virginia Magazine of History and Biography*, LXXII (January, 1964), 94–95; *Richmond Christian Advocate*, February 14, 1861.

79. W. Harrison Daniel, "Southern Protestantism and Secession," *The Historian*, XXIX (May, 1967), 397–98.

According to the *North Carolina Presbyterian* of November 24, 1860, a "very large majority" of the people in the state were strongly opposed to secession.[80] When South Carolina seceded from the Union, the *North Carolina Advocate* called that step immoderately hasty. The *Advocate* also criticized South Carolina Methodists for passing resolutions in support of it.[81]

Church leaders in Tennessee likewise generally decried secessionism. "I implore my brothers not to lend their influence to weaken the ligament that binds together the States of this Union," said J. M. Pendleton, co-editor of the *Tennessee Baptist*. He deplored the premature attack upon Lincoln, who was "elected in accordance with the provision of the Constitution." He also cautioned that disunion, far from rendering slavery more secure, would likely lead to its "utter extirpation."[82] During this same period, James Hervey Otey, veteran bishop of the Episcopal Church in Tennessee, denounced the course of South Carolina "as infamous." He blamed President Buchanan "for neglecting to enforce the laws. Had he done his duty . . . and throttled nullification all this fuss had been ended long ago."[83] Perhaps the sharpest Tennessee critic of the anti-Union movement was William G. Brownlow, Methodist preacher and editor of the *Knoxville Whig*. Although a fervent defender of slavery, he lost no opportunity to denounce secessionists.[84]

Yet despite a desire of these upper-South states to remain in the Union, they were determined to hold on to chattel slavery. This fact linked them closely with their Confederate neighbors. They were also linked with them in the contention that a state had the constitutional right to secede from the Union. They were thus

80. Haskell Monroe, Jr., "Southern Presbyterians and the Secession Crisis," *Civil War History*, VI (December, 1960), 357.

81. W. Harrison Daniel, "A Brief Account of the Methodist Episcopal Church, South in the Confederacy," *Methodist History*, VI (January, 1968), 28. The resolutions as adopted by South Carolina Methodists are in the *Charleston Daily Courier*, December 20, 1860.

82. *Tennessee Baptist* (Nashville), November 24, 1860. See also *ibid.*, December 1, 1860, for an even stronger editorial against secessionists.

83. Otey to Edward C. Burks [Bedford, Virginia], November 23, 1860, in James E. Walmsley, ed., "[Letters:] The Change of Secession Sentiment in Virginia in 1861," *American Historical Review*, XXXI (October, 1925), 98.

84. E. Merton Coulter, *William G. Brownlow, Fighting Parson of the Southern Highlands* (Chapel Hill, N.C., 1937), Chap. 6.

greatly shaken when Lincoln, in his inaugural address of March 4, 1861, proclaimed that the Union was perpetual, and that no state could get out of it "upon its own mere motion." In effect the president had served clear notice that he intended to save the Union even at the cost of war. His declaration speedily turned upper-South men into secessionists. It was, however, Lincoln's call for 75,000 volunteers in answer to the Confederate attack upon Fort Sumter (April 12) that prompted four more states to join the Confederacy. Virginia, the largest and wealthiest of the southern states, officially seceded from the Union on April 17, and was followed by Arkansas on May 6, by Tennessee on May 7, and by North Carolina on May 20. The secession conventions of all four of these states, like those in the lower South, were dominated by slaveholders, most of whom were ardent disunionists.[85]

The ecclesiastical spokesmen in these four states gave their full support to the southern cause. Only three days after Virginia passed an ordinance of secession, Robert Lewis Dabney submitted an open letter to the *New York Observer*, a conservative Presbyterian journal, arguing that the bombardment of Fort Sumter was "an act of *strict self-defence*," and accusing Washington of unconstitutionally coercing free and sovereign states. Angrily, he vowed that Virginia and the other members of the Confederacy would resist the aggressor "to the death."[86] Three weeks before North Carolina bolted the Union, the *North Carolina Christian Advocate* urged that state to meet force with force. The war upon the South, the editor wrote, was motivated by "the demon spirit of Abolitionism." Southern Methodists had "tested it fully, and found it to be heartless, inhuman and Christless."[87] Confessing that he had "undergone a great change" since Lincoln's appeal for troops, Bishop James H. Otey in July, 1861, said that it was the duty of southerners "to repel

---

85. According to the federal census of 1860, 76.6 per cent of Virginia's delegates held slaves. For Arkansas, the percentage was 61.1; for Tennessee, 66.6; and for North Carolina, 80.2. Wooster, *The Secession Conventions of the South*, 145, 161, 177, 197.

86. Johnson, *The Life and Letters of Robert Lewis Dabney*, 225-31. The *Observer* rejected the letter, but Dabney published it in pamphlet form for general distribution.

87. Quoted in the *Richmond Christian Advocate*, May 2, 1861. The *Advocate* in this same issue also quoted the *Memphis Christian Advocate* as saying, "Abolitionism intends to use the sacred name of *law* to justify a relentless war against the institution of slavery." See also the *Biblical Recorder* (Raleigh), April 24, 1861.

force by force, and to make every sacrifice rather than to submit to an administration that tramples down every barrier raised by our Forefathers for the protection of personal, social and public rights."[88] An unusually hawkish preacher and slaveholder was Holland N. McTyeire, editor of the Nashville *Christian Advocate*, general organ of the Methodist Episcopal Church, South. Unlike most religious leaders of his region, he had never been critical of the cotton-state radical disunionists.[89] On the other hand, he had often denounced abolitionism and had contended that slaveholding was not necessarily a sin.[90] Twelve days before Tennessee withdrew from the Union, he published a fiery editorial on "Civil War—Our Duty," warning that northern soldiers, "in the service of the Black Republican party," were preparing "to overrun and subjugate the South." Saying that "fanatic legions are moving down upon our borders and coasts," McTyeire summoned Confederates to arms. "As the North is one, so let the South be," he exclaimed. "We must meet the issue now and quit ourselves like men, or be slaves hereafter. We must fight for our altars and firesides—*fight*, that is the word."[91]

Such, then, was the prevailing sentiment of churchmen in the upper South by the end of April, 1861. They had closed ranks with their clerical brethren in the lower South and were ready, as Dabney said, to wage war "to the death."

v

In the period of warfare, as in that of the secession crisis, clergymen were second to no other professional class in buttressing the struggle for southern independence.[92] They not only cared for parishes and served as chaplains or missionaries to the troops, but

---

88. Otey to Edward C. Burks, July 17, 1861, in Walmsley, ed., "[Letters:] The Change of Secession Sentiment in Virginia in 1861," *American Historical Review*, XXXI, 100.

89. See, for example, his "Editorial Letters," reporting his observations during a month's visit in the lower South. *Christian Advocate*, January 3 and 10, 1861. See also *ibid.*, January 17, 1861.

90. *Ibid.*, March 24, 1859; May 3 and November 29, 1860.

91. *Ibid.*, April 25, 1861.

92. Robert L. Stanton, *The Church and the Rebellion* (New York, 1864), 154, 467; James W. Silver, *Confederate Morale and Church Propaganda* (Tuscaloosa, Ala., 1957), 23-24, 93, 101.

enlisted by the hundreds in the fighting ranks. Reportedly, a single Arkansas regiment contained forty-two ordained preachers.[93] In May, 1861, the *New Orleans Christian Advocate* said, "Nearly every clergyman we know is a member of a military company."[94] Almost 20 per cent of the Methodist ministers in the Tennessee Conference were on military duty in the fall of 1862. In many instances, a minister would organize a company and become its captain.[95] A few clergymen held prominent military positions. Leonidas Polk, bishop of the Protestant Episcopal Church in Louisiana and a large planter, became a major general and was killed in action near the close of the war. William N. Pendleton, Robert E. Lee's chief artillery officer, held the rank of brigadier general. Robert L. Dabney served briefly as Thomas J. ("Stonewall") Jackson's chief of staff. Numerous ministers held the rank of captain, major, or colonel.

With few exceptions—notably the Society of Friends—religious bodies within Confederate territory officially supported the southern cause. A few dissenters were to be found in practically every denomination,[96] but they were of no avail in determining the policy of their respective communions. As a result, those churchmen who had not already cut official ties with their northern brethren before the war began, did so before it ended. Old school Presbyterians organized a separate general judicatory in December, 1861; Episcopalians did the same in September, 1862; and Lutherans followed suit in May, 1863.[97] Methodist Protestants had been estranged from their northern co-religionists over the slavery question since the late 1850's, but they did not establish a southern general conference. Even so, they were left with the equivalent of one in 1862,

93. Charles F. Pitts, *Chaplains in Gray* (Nashville, 1957), 28.
94. Quoted in the *Christian Advocate* (Nashville), May 9, 1861.
95. For examples, see Fred T. Wooten, Jr., "Religious Activities in Civil War Memphis," *Tennessee Historical Quarterly*, III (June, 1944), 137, 140; T. Conn Bryan, "The Churches in Georgia During the Civil War," *Georgia Historical Quarterly*, XXXIII (December, 1949), 288–89; Willard E. Wight, "The Churches and the Confederate Cause," *Civil War History*, VI (December, 1960), 370.
96. W. Harrison Daniel, "Protestant Clergy and the Union Sentiment in the Confederacy," *Tennessee Historical Quarterly*, XXIII (September, 1964), 284–90.
97. *Minutes of the General Assembly of the Presbyterian Church in the Confederate States of America . . . Vol. I, A.D., 1861* (Augusta, Ga., 1861), 7; William A. Clebsch, ed., *Journals of the Protestant Episcopal Church in the Confederate States of America* (Austin, Texas, 1962), Journal III, 8–9; Richard C. Wolf, *Documents of Lutheran Unity in America* (Philadelphia, 1966), Document 51.

when the northern and western members of their church organized a competing general conference.[98] Cumberland Presbyterianism, with a large constituency in Tennessee and Kentucky, managed to avoid organic rupture; nevertheless, its communicants within the Confederacy were proslavery in sentiment and overwhelmingly supported the movement for southern independence.[99] Roman Catholics in the South also remained in communion with their northern co-religionists, yet all their bishops except James Whelan of the Nashville diocese were loyal to the Confederate cause.[100]

Although, as already noted, many ministers served the Confederacy as soldiers, most of them remained in the parish and devoted their energy to generating morale and sustaining faith in the southern cause. Like leaders in the other professions, they frequently justified the life-and-death struggle on political grounds, but their distinctive apologetic was religious in nature. Predominantly that apologetic was twofold. First, God had assigned to the South the high duty of perpetuating domestic bondage as his appointed means of redeeming the slave and of communicating the gospel to continental Africa. Second, northern abolitionism had replaced the authority of the word of God with that of a "higher law," and had thus become a rationalistic and atheistic movement perilous to Christian faith. Only a Confederate victory would assure the fulfillment of God's design for the Negro and preserve true Christianity in America. Unquestionably, then, God was on the side of the South.[101] This conviction dominated "God Save the South," a popular song much used in General Lee's Army of Northern Virginia. The following verse reveals its general sentiment:

98. Ancel H. Bassett, *A Concise History of the Methodist Protestant Church, from its Origin* (3d ed., Pittsburgh, 1887), 234–37; Edward J. Drinkhouse, *History of Methodist Reform Synodical of General Methodism 1703 to 1898 with Special and Comprehensive Reference to Its Most Salient Exhibition in the History of the Methodist Protestant Church* (2 vols., Baltimore, 1899), II, 446.

99. Lewis G. Vander Velde, *The Presbyterian Churches and the Federal Union, 1861–1869* (Cambridge, Mass., 1932), 406–14.

100. Benjamin J. Blied, *Catholics and the Civil War* (Milwaukee, 1945), Chap. 4; James J. Pillar, *The Catholic Church in Mississippi, 1837–65*, 166.

101. The unionists, and especially the Christian abolitionists, likewise maintained that God was on their side, as was clearly reflected in the stirring "Battle Hymn of the Republic." For an account of the clerical morale builder in the North, see Stuart W. Chapman, "The Protestant Campaign for the Union" (typed Ph.D. dissertation, Yale University, 1939), Chaps. 3–4.

> God made the right
> Stronger than might.
> Millions would trample us
> Down in their pride.
> Lay *Thou* their legions low,
> Roll back the ruthless foe,
> Let the proud spoiler know
> God's on our side.[102]

The initial victories of Confederate arms were viewed as sure signs of divine favor, and the clergy made full use of officially proclaimed fast days to stress this point. When President Davis proclaimed June 13, 1861, as a day of fasting, humiliation, and prayer, this was the keynote of a rash of sermons. From his Charleston pulpit Thomas Smyth jubilantly declared that the fall of Fort Sumter "was a signal gun from the battlements of heaven, announcing from God to every Southern State, 'This cause is mine.' "[103] That almost miraculous event, he added, "sealed the declaration of Southern independence; . . . created a new empire on the earth; . . . and arrested . . . the fanatical, unholy, and atheistic crusade against God's Word and . . . the vital institutions of the South."[104] Equally sure that God was on the side of the South, the president of South Carolina College exclaimed: "Gallant sons of a gallant State, away to the battle field, with the Bible in your arms and its precepts in your hearts. If you fall, the shot which sends you from earth, translates you to Heaven."[105]

The clergyman who most persistently linked God with the Confederate movement was Stephen Elliott, bishop of the Georgia diocese of the Protestant Episcopal Church and former professor at South Carolina College. This theme appeared in most of his eight or more published wartime sermons. In his fast-day sermon

---

102. *The Army Songster. Dedicated to the Army of Northern Virginia* (Richmond, 1864), 65.
103. "The Battle of Fort Sumter: Its Mystery and Miracle—God's Mastery and Mercy," *Southern Presbyterian Review*, XIV (October, 1861), 392.
104. *Ibid.*, 380.
105. Augustus B. Longstreet, *Fast-Day Sermon: Delivered in the Washington Street Methodist Episcopal Church, Columbia, S.C., June 13, 1861* (Columbia, S.C., 1861), 9–10.

of June 13, 1861, the bishop maintained at length that it was God himself who had finally rescued the South from the clutches of an oppressive North. Reviewing past history, he said that God had permitted the people of the South "to be humiliated" over many years. They had been "systematically slandered and traduced" merely because they, like Abraham and Philemon, were slaveholders. Southern Christians had been excluded from the Lord's Supper by their northern brethren, and their ministers had been denied "brotherly interchange of services."[106] All this treatment, though galling, the South had endured without overt resistance. But the "fanatics" did not stop with a mere war of words; they virtually disfranchised the southern people, even while retaining the forms of constitutional liberty and keeping up the appearance of equality. "This scheme," continued Elliott, "was devised by a far-seeing statesman [Lincoln], now occupying a position of commanding influence, who laid his plans with consummate skill and had pursued them, for twenty years." He advanced from stage to stage "with the steady pace of inevitable destiny, drawing his lines closer and closer around his fluttering yet unresisting victim." Lincoln perceived that only a dissolution of the Union could possibly thwart his plans, but he declared that to be an impossible step.[107] However, just when the schemer believed the southerners to be deserted and doomed, God's overruling presence enabled them to pass through the perilous crisis of secession and to organize an independent government.[108] Because of these unusual "tokens of God's presence," the Confederates need have no fear whatever of the invaders, despite their numerical superiority. Summarizing the "great principles" and "sacred objects" for which the South was fighting, the bishop said:

> We are fighting to prevent ourselves from being transferred from American republicanism to French democracy. We are fighting to protect and preserve a race who form a part of our household, and stand with us next to our children. We are

106. *God's Presence with the Confederate States. A Sermon Preached in Christ Church, Savannah, on Thursday, the 13th June, Being the Day Appointed at the Request of Congress, by the President of the Confederate States, As A Day of Humiliation, Fasting and Prayer* (Savannah, Ga., 1861), 4.
107. *Ibid.*, 5–6.
108. *Ibid.*, 7–18.

fighting to drive away from our sanctuaries the infidel and rationalistic principles which are sweeping over the land and substituting a gospel of the stars and stripes for the gospel of Jesus Christ.[109]

For the Georgia churchman, God's protective care of the Confederacy manifested itself in a very special manner at Bull Run (Manassas Junction) on July 21, 1861, when the Union forces were scattered in confusion. A week after that debacle, he preached a stirring sermon at Christ Church (Savannah) in commemoration of the triumph of southern arms, proclaiming the victory as "God's victory," the "crowning token of his love—the most wonderful of all the manifestations of his divine presence with us." Long before that remarkable battle, he continued, "we truly believed that our cause was his cause; that we were defending a condition of society [Negro slavery] which He had established," but God displayed himself so marvellously at Bull Run "that the pillar of cloud by day and of the fire by night was not more plain to the children of Israel."[110]

Yet, however signally God may have revealed his presence on the side of the South in all previous engagements with the enemy, he came to the aid of Confederates even more wonderfully during the series of brilliant victories which culminated in the crushing defeat of General John Pope's army at the Second Battle of Bull Run on August 29-30, 1862.[111] This spectacular accomplishment, which may well have saved Richmond from invasion, was so thrilling to Stephen Elliott that he devoted an entire sermon to a religious interpretation of Lee's sweeping triumph. The discourse elaborated a proslavery theology of the Confederate revolution. According to the bishop, God had "caused the African race to be planted here" in order to prepare the way for Africa's redemption. The church of

109. *Ibid.*, 21.
110. *God's Presence with our Army at Manassas! A Sermon, Preached in Christ Church, Savannah, on Sunday, July 28th, Being the Day Recommended by the Congress of the Confederate States, To Be Observed as a Day of Thanksgiving, in Commemoration of the Victory at Manassas Junction, on Sunday, the 21st of July, 1861* (2d ed., Savannah, Ga., 1861), 6, 8.
111. The Bull Run victory in 1862, wrote Samuel Eliot Morison, "was the neatest, cleanest piece of work that Lee and Jackson ever performed. Their combination of audacious strategy and perfect tactics had undone the Union gains of an entire year in the Virginia theater of the war." *The Oxford History of the American People* (New York, 1965), 650.

the future "will see and confess that as Egypt was the land of refuge and the school of nurture for the race of Israel, so were these Southern States first the home and then the nursing mother of those who were to go forth and regenerate the dark recesses of a benighted Continent."[112] If therefore the people of the South remained faithful in fulfilling their duties to their bondsmen, God would never allow them to be defeated.

Elliott documented his thesis by recalling past evidences of God's providential presence in preserving the southern system of human bondage. There was a time, for instance, when the scanty profits from rice and indigo had imperiled the future of Negro servitude, but God "permitted a new staple [cotton] to be introduced." At another time, when a "false philanthropy of Europe was making many converts to its views," even in the South, God "permitted" the West Indies to experiment with an emancipation scheme which demonstrated the folly of abolitionism. At yet another time, "when the deeply-laid conspiracy of Black Republicanism threatened to undermine this divinely-guarded institution, God produced" an overwhelming southern sentiment in favor of human bondage.[113] In view of such clear manifestations of God's design to perpetuate Negro slavery, the people of the South were surely being directed by him. "This noble cause," concluded the bishop, "has made him [God] our guide and overruling governor, and we are moving forward . . . as truly under his direction, as did the people of Israel when he led them with a pillar of cloud by day and of fire by night."[114]

Elliott apparently feared that the war might come to an end before it had destroyed abolitionism root and branch. He urged its continuance "until England shall be convinced that slavery . . . is essential to the welfare of the world, until the North shall find that her fanaticism was a madness and a delusion, until . . . all shall acknowledge, with one consent, that it is a divinely guarded system, planted by God [and] protected by God." In particular, the war

112. *Our Cause in Harmony with the Purposes of God in Christ Jesus. A Sermon Preached in Christ Church, Savannah, on Thursday, September 18th, 1862, Being the Day Set Forth by the President of the Confederate States of America as a Day of Prayer and Thanksgiving* (Savannah, Ga., 1862), 11.
113. *Ibid.*, 12–13.
114. *Ibid.*, 15.

"will not have finished its work until punishment shall have been rolled back upon that fountain of evil," the Northeast, and especially Boston, where "every accursed heresy [has] been spued out of the mouths of men who called themselves the ministers of God."[115] In concluding this remarkable discourse, the militant Confederate cautioned the congregation at Christ Church against "any improper exultation," lest it "turn away God's wrath from our enemies, and especially from these wretched infidels."[116]

Although General Lee suffered a setback at bloody Antietam on September 17, 1862, he scored a notable victory at Fredericksburg the following December, and still another at Chancellorsville in May, 1863.[117] As a result, southern clergymen continued to preach that God was surely in charge of the Confederate hosts. A typical fast-day sermon during this period was preached to the Georgia legislature by George Foster Pierce, a leading bishop of southern Methodism.[118] Reviewing the last two years of southern warfare, he said: "My hope is buoyant .... It is the Lord's doing, and it is marvellous in our eyes." His "cheerful assurance" of Confederate independence rested upon the "single fact" that southerners had "never corrupted the gospel of Christ." They had never substituted a "higher law" for divine revelation. With them the Bible had "been a mount that burned with fire, which no man dared to touch."[119] Their northern adversaries, on the other hand, had erected "their reason into a counsellor of the Almighty." Wise above God's written word, they had "inverted the order of heaven and taught that the social status of the negro was more vital to him and to them than his religious privileges or moral destiny, and to establish his theoretic political equality, they have dissolved the Union and drenched the land in blood." Furthermore, these "loud-mouthed champions" of Negro freedom had "seduced or stolen as

---

115. *Ibid.*, 21–22.
116. *Ibid.*, 23.
117. According to a distinguished historian of the Civil War, "The famous high-water mark of the Confederate cause came in the fall of 1862 rather than at Gettysburg. . . . Confederate victories that fall might well have won the war." Bruce Catton, "Glory Road Began in the West," *Civil War History*, VI (September, 1960), 233.
118. *Sermons of Bishop Pierce and Rev. B. M. Palmer, D.D., Delivered Before the General Assembly at Milledgeville, Ga., on Fast Day, March 27, 1863* (Milledgeville, Ga., 1863), 3–17.
119. *Ibid.*, 4, 5.

yet uncounted slaves, and left them to starve and freeze and die." Surely "the doom of Uzzah will be their epitaph."[120]

VI

Throughout the long and bitter conflict, religious leaders of the South remained absolutely adamant in their claim that human bondage had been divinely instituted, and that consequently it was not a sin per se to hold property in black folk. This view was vigorously asserted by the newly organized General Assembly of the Presbyterian Church in the Confederate States of America. At Augusta, Georgia, in December, 1861, that assembly unanimously adopted an Address, directed "to all the churches of Jesus Christ throughout the earth," in which it declared: "God sanctions it [slavery] in the first table of the Decalogue, and Moses treats it as an institution to be regulated, not abolished; legitimated and not condemned. We come down to the age of the New Testament, and we find it again in the Churches founded by the Apostles under the plenary inspiration of the Holy Ghost. . . . Shall we [then] be branded with the stigma of reproach, because we cannot consent to corrupt the word of God to suit the intuitions of an infidel philosophy?"[121] The assembly included in that Address two significant claims with respect to black people. One was that without the maintenance of domestic bondage, the Negro race could "never be elevated in the scale of being." The other was that as long as that race remained in "comparative degradation" and lived side by side with the white race, bondage was "its normal condition."[122]

When the General Council of the Protestant Episcopal Church in the Confederate States of America met at Augusta, Georgia, in November, 1862, the bishops, of whom Stephen Elliott was a dominant figure, sent forth a Pastoral Letter, urging, among other things, that both clergy and laity bestir themselves to furnish religious

---

120. *Ibid.*, 6. For the fate of Uzzah, see 2 Sam. 6:6–7.

121. *Minutes of the General Assembly of the Presbyterian Church in the Confederate States of America . . . . Vol. I, A.D., 1861*, 56, 57. James H. Thornwell was the author of the Address, which was personally signed by all ninety-three commissioners of the General Assembly. Paul L. Garber, "A Centennial Appraisal of James Henley Thornwell," in Stuart C. Henry, ed., *A Miscellany of American Christianity: Essays in Honor of H. Shelton Smith* (Durham, N.C., 1963), 100.

122. *Ibid.*, 58.

instruction to the black people. The clergy, they added, "must strip themselves of pride and fastidiousness and indolence, and rush, with the zeal of martyrs, to this labor of love." The bishops acknowledged the need to remove from domestic bondage its "unchristian features," such as separating husbands and wives, but they tacitly approved without a whisper of criticism "the system [of Negro servitude] upon which we are about to plant our national life." On the other hand, they branded abolitionism as "that hateful infidel pestilence."[123]

In its annual report of December, 1862, the board of managers of the missionary society of South Carolina Methodism once again enunciated its long-standing apology for Negro bondage. "Slavery has been appointed by the Great Head of the Church as the means to liberate him [the African] from the dominion of Satan and the curse of sin," declared the managers. "With a low type of intellect and a transmitted degradation from debased progenitors, freedom degrades and corrupts him, and slavery elevates and improves him." The board added another reason for not liberating the black man. "When free, the white man is his rival and enemy, with whom he has neither energy nor sagacity to compete; in slavery, the white man is his friend and guardian."[124] In other words, racial harmony was contingent upon the Negro's subjection to the white man. This is the root out of which stemmed the postwar doctrine of white supremacy.

The most significant proslavery document to be issued by Confederate Protestantism was "An Address to Christians Throughout the World," first published in the *Central Presbyterian* of Richmond in late April, 1863.[125] Drawn up by a committee of five ministers from five communions, the Address, as first published, bore the signatures of ninety-six religious leaders from eleven denomina-

---

123. Clebsch, ed., *Journals of the Protestant Episcopal Church in the Confederate States of America*, III, 227.
124. *Minutes of the . . . South Carolina Conference of the Methodist Episcopal Church, South, . . . 1862* (Charleston, S.C., 1863), 16.
125. *Central Presbyterian*, April 23, 1863. The Address was widely circulated through the southern religious press. It was also quickly issued in pamphlet form at Philadelphia for general distribution. According to the New York *Independent* of September 3, 1863, Moses Drury Hoge, a prominent Presbyterian minister of Richmond, Virginia, took a copy of the Address to England, where it was "widely circulated by most of the religious magazines." Reportedly, a copy of it was found on the Chancellorsville battlefield. *Independent*, June 18, 1863.

tions—predominantly Baptist, Methodist, Presbyterian—and from every Confederate state except Arkansas.[126] It was evidently prompted by Lincoln's Emancipation Proclamation, which announced that, as of January 1, 1863, all slaves within rebel-ruled territory were forever free. Even though issued as a strictly military measure, the Proclamation elevated the Union cause to the level of a moral crusade for freedom, and it generated enormous enthusiasm among abolitionists at home and abroad.[127] Within the Confederacy, however, it aroused anger and contempt.[128]

The Address sharply denounced the Proclamation, charging that it was "a ruthless persecution, a cruel and shameful device, adding severity and bitterness to a wicked and reckless war." The measure was "in no proper sense an act of mercy to the slave, but of malice toward the master." Even supposing that its "diabolical" design could be carried out on Confederate soil, it "would inevitably lead to the slaughter of tens of thousands of poor deluded insurrectionists!" Far from conceding that slavery was an inherently evil institution, these ninety-six churchmen testified "in the sight of God, that the relation of master and slave among us . . . is not incompatible with our holy Christianity." They were confident that slavery was the biblical and providential plan whereby the Negro was to be introduced to the good news of the gospel. In fact, the South had "done more than any people on earth for the christianization of the African race."[129] They, on the other hand, charged that abolitionism was "an interference with the plans of Divine Providence" for elevating the black people. "Instead of blessing, it has brought forth cursing; instead of love, hatred; instead of life, death."

Roman Catholic leaders in the South were generally more moderate in expressing their proslavery sentiments than their Protestant neighbors; nevertheless, most of them steadfastly supported the in-

---

126. The ninety-six churchmen included three bishops, nine editors of church papers, eleven college and university presidents, eleven professors in theological seminaries, and many eminent parish ministers.

127. James M. McPherson, *The Struggle For Equality: Abolitionists and the Negro in the Civil War and Reconstruction* (Princeton, N. J., 1964), 121-22.

128. For the reaction of southern politicians and journalists, see John Hope Franklin, *The Emancipation Proclamation* (Anchor Books, New York, 1965), 117-20.

129. A footnote to the Address reported that "the number of *colored communicants* is about *five hundred thousand*."

stitution of Negro servitude throughout the war. This was certainly true of French-born Augustin Verot, who became bishop of Savannah in July, 1861. In his sermon of January 4, 1861, as already observed, he heartily sanctioned human bondage. Like Protestant churchmen, he traced the origin of secession and the war to abolitionism.[130] In his peace pastoral of November 22, 1863, he justified the rebellion on the ground that the North had broken the federal compact with respect to slavery, despite the fact that slavery accorded with both the law of nature and the law of the gospel.[131] Verot's fellow prelate, Auguste Martin, bishop of the Diocese of Natchitoches (Louisiana), was equally proslavery in sentiment. In a pastoral letter, issued on August 21, 1863, he affirmed that slavery, "far from being an evil ... is an arrangement eminently Christian by which millions pass from intellectual darkness to the sweet brilliance of the Gospel."[132]

One of the severest Catholic critics of abolitionism was Courtney Jenkins, editor of the Baltimore *Catholic Mirror*, official organ of the archbishop of Baltimore and of the bishops of Richmond and Wheeling. The *Mirror* was the only southern newspaper of its communion to survive the Civil War, and it circulated widely in the upper slave states. Jenkins, a southerner who had been brought up amid masters and slaves, contended all through the bloody conflict that while general emancipation would be unfortunate for whites, it would deal a fatal blow to blacks. "Abolition, in the hands of the party now fostering it, must be *fatal* to the negro race in the South," he predicted in May, 1862. The freedmen, he explained, "must become the most wretched of pariahs," for "they cannot live upon any terms of equality among their recent masters," and the free states "will be closed against them."[133] Jenkins rejected

---

130. Patrick N. Lynch, bishop of Charleston, likewise traced the root of secession and the war to abolitionism. See his letter of August 4, 1861, to Archbishop John Hughes of New York, in the *Catholic Mirror* (Baltimore), September 6, 1861.

131. Vincent de Paul McMurry, "The Catholic Church During Reconstruction, 1865–1877" (typed M.A. essay, Catholic University, 1950), 23–24. See also Willard E. Wight, "Bishop Verot and the Civil War," *Catholic Historical Review*, XLVII (July, 1961), 153–54.

132. Quoted in Blied, *Catholics and the Civil War*, 65. In the main, Martin agreed with Verot's views on slavery as put forward in the latter's discourse of January 4, 1861. Benjamin J. Blied, "Bishop Verot of Savannah," *Georgia Review*, V (Summer, 1951), 165.

133. *Catholic Mirror*, May 10, 1862. See also *ibid.*, February 8, 1862.

the abolitionist's charge that southern slavery had degraded the bondsmen. On the contrary, it was "as clear as daylight, that they have been elevated, vastly elevated." Moreover, until the war came, "there was not a happier people on earth than the slaves" of the South.[134] While the editor occasionally denied that he was an advocate of slavery, he nonetheless definitely held that it did not violate divine law. "It is fanaticism, or hypocrisy," he declared in 1863, "to condemn slavery as in itself criminal, or opposed to the laws of God."[135]

In the course of the war a few Confederate churchmen tried to bring about some minor reforms in the slave code.[136] Their concern did not arise, however, from a belief that the institution of slavery was inherently evil. Rather, they felt that by making it more tolerable to bondsmen and less vulnerable to outside criticism it would be placed upon a more secure foundation. One of the earliest advocates of slavery reform was Bishop Verot. In his sermon of January 4, 1861—published shortly after the Confederacy was formed—he earnestly entreated the leaders of southern society to remove from Negro bondage its blighting abuses. He was deeply outraged by a report that some people were wanting to see the African slave trade revived. If that "worst of piracies" were to be renewed, he warned, the Confederacy would surely suffer a "speedy downfall." Three other evils upon which he vented his wrath were, first, the practice of re-enslaving or else banishing free Negroes; second, the widespread habit of the white man of subjecting black women to his lustful passions; and, third, the general disregard of the matrimonial rights of slaves. Pressing for prompt reform, the bishop said: "I propose . . . that a servile code be drawn up and adopted by the Confederacy, defining clearly the rights and duties of masters, and the rights and duties of slaves. This will be the means of proving to the world that the South is on the side of justice, morality, reason and religion."[137]

Bishop George F. Pierce told the Georgia legislature in 1863 that slavery was "a great missionary institution," but he charged that it

---

134. *Ibid.*, February 28, 1863.
135. *Ibid.*, December 5, 1863.
136. Bell I. Wiley, "The Movement to Humanize the Institution of Slavery During the Confederacy," *Emory University Quarterly*, V (December, 1949), 207–20.
137. *A Tract For the Times. Slavery and Abolitionism*, 16–20, 22.

was encumbered with two evils which should be removed. One was a Georgia statute forbidding any one to teach bondsmen to read. That law, said the Methodist bishop, invaded the rights of the master and the privileges of the slave. Furthermore, it interfered with the Negro's immortal welfare. "The negro is an immortal being and it is his right by the law of creation and the purchase of redemption to read for himself the epistles of his Redeemer's love. If the institution of slavery cannot be maintained except at the expense of the black man's immortal interests, in the name of Heaven I say —*let it perish.*" However, the preacher at once assured his fellow masters that a Bible in the cabin would in no way endanger their property interests, because the literate slave would discover for himself that his servitude had been ordained by God. The other thing that troubled Pierce was the general disregard of slave marriage rights. As a result, husbands and wives were "subject to all the contingencies of time and circumstances—of gain and avarice—of passion and caprice." This immoral situation cast a dark shadow over southern Christianity and exposed domestic bondage to criticism. "Let us," exhorted Pierce, "put slavery upon its scriptural basis ... [and thus prove] to the world that it is ... really consistent with the highest development and the greatest happiness of the negro race."[138]

By the end of 1863, when military defeat began to seem likely, some prominent churchmen explained that God was using the enemy as a rod of iron to punish the Confederacy for its sins, and that reverses on the battlefield would continue unless those sins were acknowledged and forsaken. Among those taking this position was Calvin H. Wiley, a Presbyterian minister and superintendent of common schools in North Carolina from 1852 to 1865. Although himself a slaveholder, he felt that the Confederacy's afflictions were caused in large measure by its failure to develop a more humane institution of servitude. "It is extremely probable," he wrote in a widely read book, "that God is now chastening the country for its sins in connection with slavery."[139] According to Wiley, the church

138. *Sermons of Bishop Pierce and Rev. B. M. Palmer*, 14–15.
139. *Scriptural Views of National Trials: Or the True Road to Independence and Peace of the Confederate States of America* (Greensboro, N.C., 1863), 191. See also *ibid.*, 98, 115. This work evidently aroused great interest, for by May, 1864, more than four thousand copies of it had been sold in North Carolina alone. Paul M. Ford,

had been especially slow to press for reforms in the slave code, although practically all thoughtful observers admitted that it was not what it should be. Church leaders, he charged, had been so concerned to show that slavery was biblical that they had neglected to emphasize the duties of masters and slaves as required by the Bible. They had been entirely too indifferent to the cruelties of masters toward their slaves. They had also done little to safeguard the marriage rights of the slaves, or to provide the slaves with anything like a comprehensive program of religious instruction. In short, the church, as a whole, was "not as ripe for improvements in our slave code as the State."[140] The crisis called for courageous action, not for self-congratulation over past performances. "Let us," exhorted Wiley, "crown our deeds ... BY DARING TO DO WHAT IS RIGHT, and our triumph will be certain and our history glorious!"[141]

The most drastic condemnation of the existing slave code was made by James A. Lyon, pastor of the First Presbyterian Church at Columbus, Mississippi. His views were contained in a paper, which he presented to the General Assembly of his communion in 1863.[142] He prefaced his proposals for reform with a lengthy defense of slavery, contending that it was "a Bible institution, and consistent with the highest type of piety and practical godliness." He also argued that the black man belonged to "an inferior variety" of the human species, and that consequently his "most favorable condition" was "that of servitude." Yet if slavery was to "redound to the honor and glory of God," the southern people would have to "correct its abuses, remove its evils, and bring it up to the Bible standard."[143]

First of all, the master was obligated by "the law of God"—both natural and revealed—to cultivate the slave's mental and moral ca-

---

"Calvin H. Wiley's View of the Negro," *North Carolina Historical Review*, XLI (January, 1964), 13.
140. *Scriptural Views of National Trials*, 189–96.
141. *Ibid.*, 200.
142. "Slavery, and the Duties Growing Out of the Relation," *Southern Presbyterian Review*, XVI (July, 1863), 1–37. In 1861 the General Assembly appointed a committee, with Lyon as chairman, and instructed it to submit to the next assembly a report on the religious instruction of Negroes. No report was made to the assembly in 1862, but Lyon read the present paper to the General Assembly in 1863.
143. *Ibid.*, 7, 10, 13. 16.

pacities "to a degree consonant with his condition as a slave." A cultivated slave was not only more valuable than an ignorant one, but he would be less likely to commit crime or to engage in insurrectionary activity. Although the reformer admonished masters to encourage the intellectual and spiritual growth of their bondsmen, he did not advise them to send the blacks to schools. Yet he wanted to see the slaves able to read the Bible, and therefore he urged that all laws prohibiting the teaching of them to read be repealed. A second need, according to Lyon, was to restore to slavery the patriarchal character which it enjoyed in biblical times. He deplored the fact that the owners of large plantations were moving to the towns and leaving their Negroes in the hands of hired overseers, most of whom felt no personal interest in their welfare. An institution thus operated was "not Bible slavery." To measure up to biblical demands, the master would have to live in the midst of his slaves, so as to hear their complaints and share their sorrows.[144] A third need was to curb the cruelty of overseers. Under absentee ownership, their conduct had become increasingly harsh. The poor slaves were virtually helpless, since they were legally barred from defending themselves against the assaults of a white man. Even if they testified against a white oppressor, their testimony was invalid in court. A malicious overseer could therefore kill an innocent slave and yet escape punishment if the only witness to his crime was a black man. In order to mitigate this evil, Lyon proposed that legislators permit the testimony of slaves in murder cases to count as "*circumstantial evidence.*"[145] A fourth overdue reform was appropriate legislation to protect the marriage and domestic relations of slaves. "The laws of the land ... wholly ignore the marriage relation as existing among slaves," said Lyon. "There is nothing in our legislation ... that prohibits fornication, adultery, bigamy, incest, or even rape amongst them."[146] Such conditions rendered it impossible to civilize and Christianize the black race. Indeed, the whole gospel could "not be preached" to that race under existing circumstances. A fifth requisite was a more adequate religious ministry to bondsmen. A slave had a natural right to the benefit of the gospel, and if masters

---

144. *Ibid.*, 21–22. 145. *Ibid.*, 23–24.
146. *Ibid.*, 26.

failed to make it available to their slaves, they would be held accountable "at the inexorable bar of a just and holy God."[147]

In his advocacy of slavery reform, Lyon was motivated not merely by humanitarian considerations but also by a keen desire to allay abolitionist criticism. Appealing to his fellow churchmen, he said: "Let us correct these abuses... and elevate slavery to the Gospel standard, and the prejudice now arrayed against it... will subside."[148] He was of course quite wrong in thinking that such reforms as he proposed would shut the mouths of antislavery critics. Yet even if he had been right, those reforms had little chance of being favorably acted upon in either state legislatures or general church judicatories. One reason for this was that Confederate leaders were preoccupied with pressing military problems, but a more fundamental reason was opposition or apathy on the part of slaveholders, including ministers of Christ. Not even Lyon's own denomination ever enacted his program of reform. The General Assembly of 1863 assigned his proposed reforms to a partially new committee, and thereafter they remained in the hands of some committee until they finally perished in the assembly of 1865, just when the Confederacy was falling to pieces.[149]

Doubtless there was a prevailing feeling among southern masters that any basic reform of the bondage system would tend to curb their authority over their Negroes. If, as Lyon advised, the slaves had been equipped with even the rudiments of education, there is little reason to believe that they would have been more contented with their lot, or that they would have been less inclined to take steps to escape from bondage. Or again, if slave marriages had been legalized, masters and slave traders would have found it more difficult to sell apart husbands and wives. At the very time that Lyon and other reformers were pleading for the legalization of marriage among slaves, an unsigned article appeared in the *Southern Presbyterian Review* vigorously opposing any such measure. It would, the writer argued, invade the prerogative of the master, who alone

147. *Ibid.*, 35.
148. *Ibid.*, 36.
149. *Minutes of the General Assembly of the Presbyterian Church in the Confederate States of America,* ... I, *A.D., 1863* (Columbia, S.C., 1863), 126–27; *Minutes* I, *A.D.,* 1864 (Columbia, S.C., 1864), 283, 293; *Minutes,* I, *A.D.,* 1865 (Augusta, Ga., 1865), 350–51.

was the slave's lawgiver. He further contended that such a law would acknowledge the right of a slave to enter into a civil contract and that this "would amount to a revolution in the status of the slave." In short, it would destroy the distinctive principle of slavery and "let in as a flood many of the evils of a virtual emancipation."[150] Probably most masters felt the same way.

The plain truth is that the white ruling class in the Confederate South was bent upon maintaining Negro servitude, even though the slave code fell short of "the Gospel standard." By and large, the Confederacy's religious leaders were equally determined to perpetuate it. We have a striking exhibition of this determination in the "Narrative on the State of Religion," which was adopted by the General Assembly of the Presbyterian Church in the Confederate States at Charlotte, North Carolina, in the spring of 1864. Said the Narrative: "The long-continued agitations of our adversaries have wrought within us a deeper conviction of the divine appointment of domestic servitude, and have led to a clearer comprehension of the duties we owe to the African race. We hesitate not to affirm that it is the peculiar mission of the Southern Church to conserve the institution of slavery, and to make it a blessing both to master and slave."[151]

That the South's most highly respected clergymen proclaimed the divine ordination of Negro slavery to the bitter end is representatively documented in two moving discourses, delivered within the last fifteen months of the war. Both were preached on fast-day occasions and under heartbreaking circumstances. Benjamin Morgan Palmer delivered one of them before the General Assembly of South Carolina in December, 1863. The disaster at Gettysburg and the surrender at Vicksburg in the preceding July had deeply shaken the valiant Confederate, and he read with anxiety the signs of the times. "The nations of the earth have no pity for our distress, no tear of sympathy for our wrongs," lamented the lonely churchman.

150. "A Slave Marriage Law," *Southern Presbyterian Review*, XVI (October, 1863), 146, 147.
151. *Minutes of the General Assembly of the Presbyterian Church in the Confederate States of America, . . .* I, *A.D., 1864* (Columbia, S.C., 1864), 293. This statement prompted a great outcry among northern Presbyterians and caused no little embarrassment to Moses Drury Hoge, a member of the 1864 General Assembly. His letter to the Philadelphia *Presbyterian* is reprinted in the *Central Presbyterian* (Richmond), September 14, 1865.

Yet even though "all alone," the embattled southerners would continue the struggle.[152]

But why spill any more blood in a virtually lost cause? Palmer's answer was mainly twofold. First, the people of the South felt "a commission from the God of Heaven" to defend "republicanism" —government controlled by "the superior and ruling class"—against the "unlicensed democracy" of the old Union. Second, the southern people were convinced of "a solemn duty . . . to protect the slave . . . from the schemes of a false philosophy which threaten his early and inevitable extermination."[153] According to the eminent preacher, the Negro had to be protected because he was inferior to the white man, and the only way he could be protected and elevated was by being held to servitude. "All history," he argued, "attests the impossibility of two unequal races living side by side with mutual advantage. The inferior gives way before the energy and resources of the superior." The black man's divinely "allotted destiny" was consequently to remain a slave. Contrary to the overwhelming sentiment of Christendom, Palmer once again, as often before, affirmed that human bondage was "clearly ordained of God." He also told the South Carolina legislators that he himself had "no compunction of conscience in the holding of slaves."[154]

The other sermon was preached by Stephen Elliott, the ablest bishop in his communion. He delivered it at Christ Church in Savannah, Georgia, on September 15, 1864, in observance of the fast day appointed by the governor. The people of Savannah were terrified over the prospect that General William T. Sherman, then already occupying Atlanta, would soon be marching toward their city with sixty thousand troops. The intrepid bishop must have been burdened with anxiety, yet he told the shuddering congregation that the South would never be conquered, because it was God's design to overthrow abolitionism in order to save black people from a freedom that would result in their annihilation. The war was "God's war," and he would terminate it in his own way upon the

---

152. *A Discourse Before the General Assembly of South Carolina, on December 10, 1863, Appointed by the Legislature as a Day of Fasting, Humiliation and Prayer* (Columbia, S.C., 1864), 6.
153. *Ibid.*, 10, 11, 12.
154. *Ibid.*, 14–15.

achievement of his purposes.[155] However, Elliott presumed to sketch the strategy whereby God would rescue the embattled Confederates. The re-election of Lincoln, he explained, would be necessary for their deliverance. "We need his folly and his fanaticism for another term.... His re-election will give him fresh courage and additional madness. He will drive all sound and rational men from his side; he will gather around him the radical and the fanatic." In due course, when the sober people of the Union can no longer endure the madman's misrule, they will rise up against him; and "then will come the conflict which shall deliver us." Even "the fall of Atlanta, the victories at Mobile, our reverses of whatever kind, are so many links ... in the chain of our deliverance."[156]

Doubtless few members of Christ Church took seriously Elliott's solution of their desperate situation. Nevertheless, the fantastic illusion clearly demonstrates that he maintained to the very last that God had appointed the black man to perpetual servitude to the white man. In this respect he and Palmer reflected the overwhelming clerical sentiment in the Confederacy right down to the surrender at Appomattox.

---

155. *A Sermon Preached in Christ Church, Savannah, on Thursday, September 15, 1864, Being the Day of Fasting, Humiliation, and Prayer, Appointed by the Governor of the State of Georgia* (Macon, Ga., 1864), 9–10.

156. *Ibid.*, 19.

Chapter V

NEW PATTERNS ON OLD PREMISES

The fall of the Confederacy plunged many southern ministers into the valley of despair. Writing to his sister soon after Lee surrendered, Moses Drury Hoge of Richmond said:

> I forget my humiliation for a while in sleep, but the memory of every bereavement comes back heavily, like a sullen sea surge, on awaking, flooding and submerging my soul with anguish. The idolized expectation of a separate nationality, of a social life and literature and civilization of our own, together with a gospel guarded against the contamination of New England infidelity, all this has perished, and I feel like seaweed on a desert shore. . . . God's dark providence enwraps me like a pall.[1]

That was doubtless the dominant mood of virtually all of the South's church leaders in the immediate wake of the lost cause. It is no wonder that God's providence seemed so "dark" to them, for they had confidently predicted again and again that God would never permit Black Republicans to triumph over a people whom he had chosen to serve as guardians of Negro bondage.

I

Yet however baffled these churchmen may have been over God's providential dealings with them, they held fast to two wartime contentions: first, that human bondage was a divinely sanctioned institution, and, second, that the slave states had a legal and moral right to secede from the Union.

When the General Assembly of the Presbyterian Church in the

---

1. Peyton H. Hoge, *Moses Drury Hoge: Life and Letters* (Richmond, 1899), 235.

Confederate States met at Macon, Georgia, in December, 1865, it gave special attention in its pastoral letter to the nature of slavery, even though the bondage system had been swept away by the war. Referring to the assembly's Address of 1861, which took a strong proslavery position, the Macon assembly said: "We here reaffirm its whole doctrine [of slavery] to be that of Scripture and reason." The pastoral letter went so far as to say that "the dogma" of the inherent sinfulness of slavery was "one of the most pernicious heresies of modern times," and that its countenance by any church was "a just cause of separating from it."[2] That sentiment was fully shared by John B. Adger, professor of church history at Columbia Theological Seminary, who lost thirty slaves in the South's defeat. "As for ourselves," he wrote in 1866, "we retain all our former opinions respecting slavery. . . . It was a good institution, although some abuses were connected with it which demanded reformation, and would have been reformed had the South been let alone of her persecutors." He accused northern Presbyterians of taking "a rationalistic and practically infidel attitude" toward black bondage, and he gave this as one reason why southern Presbyterians could not reunite with them.[3] Returning to the same subject in 1871, Adger said: "Slavery is a form of government which the Bible does not condemn. The Southern [Presbyterian] Church did not therefore condemn it. She does not condemn it now. . . . Any man or any church who says it is a sin takes some other rule of faith, and is so far infidel." It was "not supposable," he added, that southern Presbyterians would ever change their minds on this question.[4]

One of the most relentless Presbyterian defenders of slavery in the postwar era was Robert L. Dabney of Union Theological Seminary. He published far more on slavery after it was abolished than he did during its existence. "Men ask," he wrote in *A Defence of Virginia*, "'Is not the slavery question dead? Why discuss it longer?' I reply: Would God it were dead!" Far from being dead, said he, it was still alive because abolitionism lived on in the church

---

2. *Minutes of the General Assembly of the Presbyterian Church in the Confederate States of America, . . . I, A.D., 1865* (Augusta, Ga., 1865), 385. For the General Assembly's Address of 1861, see *ibid.*, 51–60.

3. "Northern and Southern Views of the Province of the Church," *Southern Presbyterian Review*, XVI (March, 1866), 409, 411.

4. "The Presbyterian Union, North," *Southern Presbyterian Review*, XXII (July, 1871), 398, 399.

"as infidelity," and had become "more rampant and mischievous than ever."[5] Dabney insisted that the Christian world would eventually acknowledge that the South had held the true view of human bondage. "Meantime," he retorted, "let the arrogant and successful wrongdoers flout our defence with disdain: we will meet them with it again, when it will be heard."[6]

Contrary to Bishop Stephen Elliott's numerous predictions, the Confederacy lost the war. Nevertheless, he remained unshaken in his conviction that slavery had exerted an elevating influence upon "an inferior race." The non-violent behavior of the slaves during the war, despite fanatics urging them to strike for their rights, was "the sublimest vindication of the institution of slavery, as it existed among us."[7] In the bishop's opinion, the abolition of servitude was "the greatest calamity which could have befallen" black people. He saw "no future" for them in this country. "Avarice and cupidity and interest will do for their extinction what they have always done for an unprotected inferior race."[8]

Of the same sentiment was Jeremiah Bell Jeter, senior editor of the Richmond *Religious Herald,* the leading newspaper of Southern Baptists. In a lengthy editorial of January, 1866, Jeter reaffirmed his belief that domestic bondage was a righteous institution, and that it had served to humanize and elevate the Negro race. At the same time he freely admitted that he did not want abolition not only because slavery had been beneficial to blacks, but also because whites and blacks were so different that if they were to live together "they should sustain to each other the relation of master and slave."[9]

---

5. *A Defence of Virginia (and Through Her, of the South), in Recent and Pending Contests Against the Sectional Party* (New York, 1867), 6. The *Defence* was highly commended in a review published in the *Southern Presbyterian Review*, XVIII (November, 1867), 589–94. "The necessary working of events," declared the reviewer, "must result in one way or another in the vindication of slavery." *Ibid.,* 591.

6. *A Defence of Virginia,* 356. Charging that the Yankees had "killed that which made the South the South," Dabney tried to induce some former Confederates to unite with him in planting a colony in some other country as "the only chance to save any of the true Christianity of the South." Thomas Cary Johnson, *The Life and Letters of Robert Lewis Dabney* (Richmond, 1903), 303–10. After some four years of fruitless effort, he reluctantly abandoned the idea.

7. "Address," *Journal of the Fourth Annual Council of the Protestant Episcopal Church in the Diocese of Georgia, . . . 1866* (Savannah, Ga., 1866), 26.

8. *Ibid.,* 29.

9. *Religious Herald,* January 25, 1866.

In the fall of 1871, J. L. Reynolds told South Carolina Baptists that the Southern Baptist Convention had "never receded" from its views on slavery, and that it had "no confession to make" and "no repentance to offer" for those views. "This Convention may not have done its whole duty to the slave; but, in its recognition of him as a bondsman, it holds itself to have been in accord with the teachings of the New Testament, and therefore guiltless in the sight of God." The northern Baptists, on the other hand, were "victims of a moral malaria, which poisoned the Christian world, and jaundiced the vision of even wise and good men."[10]

Leaders of southern Methodism were equally indisposed to renounce their proslavery views. This fact is forcefully revealed on the annual conference level in the case of John H. Caldwell, pastor of the Methodist church at Newnan, Georgia. Although a loyal Confederate throughout the war, he "received new light" under the shock of the South's defeat, and in June, 1865, delivered two sermons to his congregation, explaining his new insights. It suddenly dawned upon him that God had wiped out slavery "all *because we would not give that which was just and equal unto our servants.*"[11] Caldwell still acknowledged that God sanctioned slavery, but actually the preacher had become an abolitionist. He and other southerners, he charged, had been "strangely inconsistent"; they "fought professedly for liberty," but in reality "it was to perpetuate the chains of slavery." "We reproached our enemies for fighting against the God of heaven, and we defended our institution as one existing by Divine right.... Thus [we] hastened blindly to our ruin."[12]

But why had the people of the South failed to recognize the monstrous evils connected with slavery? Because, replied Caldwell, the "slave power"—numbering "about *four hundred thousand persons*"—held sway over the press, the teachers, the politicians, and the preachers. "All preferment in Church or state was confined to

---

10. "Historical Discourse, Delivered at the Semi-Centennial Anniversary of the State Convention of the Baptist Denomination in South Carolina, . . . November 23, 1871," in *Minutes of the Fifty-First Session of the Baptist State Convention. . . . 1871* (Charleston, S.C., 1871), Appendix, 36. See Rufus B. Spain, *At Ease in Zion: Social History of Southern Baptists, 1865–1900* (Nashville, 1967), 18.

11. *Slavery and Southern Methodism: Two Sermons Preached in the Methodist Church in Newnan, Georgia [on June 11 and 18, 1865]* (New York, 1865), 29.

12. *Ibid.*, 29–31.

those who in one way or another preached the gospel of *proslavery!*" It was the slave power that split Methodism in 1844. At long last, though, that imperial power dug its own grave by bringing on secession and the war. "It fell before the majesty of that awful truth, which it had the sophistry to pronounce a lie: *all men are created equal."* [13]

Before Caldwell had finished his first sermon, at least a third of his congregation had left the church in explosive indignation. Nevertheless, he resumed the subject on the following Sunday and devoted most of his sermon to showing wherein the Methodist Episcopal Church, South, had capitulated to the slave power. In response to the angry reaction, the presiding elder of the district relieved Caldwell of his Newnan charge and assigned him to an isolated missionary station, where any expression of his antislavery views would have endangered his life. When, however, he declined the appointment, his presiding elder preferred charges against him at the Georgia Conference in the following November. After much discussion the charges were withdrawn, but the two offending sermons were condemned.[14] Finding himself rejected by his ministerial brethren, Caldwell reluctantly withdrew from the conference. Soon afterwards he joined the Methodist Episcopal Church and became a leading minister to the Georgia freedmen.[15] In the meantime he also served in the Georgia legislature, and played a significant role in political reconstruction. Referring to this aspect of his work, he said: "I labored . . . heart and soul, for what I called a NEW SOUTH, and was the first, I believe, to give it that name."[16]

Few southern Methodists underwent John Caldwell's postwar conversion. The vast majority remained wedded to the proslavery sentiments of the General Conference of 1874, as expressed in its report on fraternal relations with the Methodist Episcopal Church. The report acknowledged that slavery was a major factor in causing

---

13. *Ibid.*, 31, 35, 39–40.
14. Caldwell to Bishop E. S. James, New York, November 24, 1865 (MS letter in Special Collection, Interdenominational Theological Center Library, Atlanta, Ga.).
15. John H. Caldwell, *Reminiscences of the Reconstruction of Church and State in Georgia* (Wilmington, Del., 1895), 8–9.
16. *Ibid.*, 11. In the early 1870's, Caldwell, feeling that he had finished his work in the South, moved to Delaware. Joining the Wilmington Conference of his denomination, he served several important churches in that state. He also served briefly as president of Delaware College. *Ibid.*, 18.

the rupture of Methodism in 1844, and it maintained that the position which the southern delegates took in the debate over slavery was entirely biblical. "Our positions have undergone no change," said the report.[17]

For the next quarter century, key spokesmen of Methodism, South, reiterated the traditional view. In 1875 Thomas O. Summers, editor of the Nashville *Christian Advocate*, vigorously attacked the old abolitionist contention that slavery was an inherently sinful institution. In an effort to sustain his position he appealed to Abraham, the Ten Commandments, Jesus, Paul, and church history, just as he and other proslavery preachers had done prior to and during the Civil War.[18] The editor of the *New Orleans Christian Advocate*, Linus Parker, as late as 1880 still argued that the overall good of slavery "greatly exceeded" whatever evils may have been connected with its maintenance. "The hand of God was in it," because it was the instrumentality whereby multitudes of African savages "were brought in contact with the very best type of Anglo-Saxon character, and with the purest form of the gospel as preached by the Southern Methodists and others." Among other good results, "the salvation of the African continent is likely to grow out of American slavery."[19] In his *The Gospel Among the Slaves*, William P. Harrison, book editor of the Methodist Episcopal Church, South, paid domestic bondage numerous compliments, but blistered "New England fanatics" who crusaded for Negro freedom. "The abolitionists of forty years ago," he said, "renounced St. Paul, the Bible, and the God of heaven, because it was impossible to defend their insane denunciations of Southern slaveholders by the pages of Holy Writ."[20]

In the postwar period, southern churchmen were equally unrepentant over secession. While the Confederacy lasted, large numbers of clergymen argued that its constituent states had a full con-

---

17. *Formal Fraternity. Proceedings of the General Conferences of the Methodist Episcopal Church and the Methodist Episcopal Church, South, in 1872, 1874, and 1876, and of the Joint Commission of the Two Churches on Fraternal Relations, at Cape May, New Jersey, August 16–23, 1876* (New York, 1876), 38.
18. *Christian Advocate*, August 13, 1875.
19. *New Orleans Christian Advocate*, July 1, 1880. For similar commendations of slavery by various correspondents, see especially the issues for November 19, 1874; January 20, 1876; and October 30, 1879.
20. *The Gospel Among the Slaves* (Nashville, 1893), 15.

stitutional right to withdraw from the Union. Fiery Thomas Smyth of Charleston even claimed that the South had "the divine right of secession."[21] However, after the Confederacy collapsed, most ministers left this question to the politicians. Yet those who did discuss it usually reaffirmed their wartime views. Three of the most persistent postwar defenders of secession were Albert Taylor Bledsoe, Robert L. Dabney, and John William Jones.

Bledsoe, a native of Kentucky, was teaching mathematics at the University of Virginia when the war began. After serving briefly as a colonel in the Confederate army, he became assistant secretary of war. Some years after the war he entered the Methodist ministry.[22] Although he preached occasionally, he devoted his time chiefly to editing the *Southern Review*, which he founded in 1867 and dedicated to the "despised" and "downtrodden" people of the South.

Just before launching the *Review*, Bledsoe published a lively tract against the notion that secession was unconstitutional. Like all Confederates who followed in the footsteps of Calhoun, he argued that in view of the reserved powers contained in the tenth amendment to the Constitution, a state could legally secede from the Union.[23] He furthermore argued at great length that the slave states were driven into secession by the selfish aggression of the North. In framing the compact of 1787, the fathers tried, he said, to establish a balance of power between the rival sections, but in fact failed to do so. Consequently from the outset the South did not enjoy political equality in either House or Senate. The fathers assumed that in view of population trends, the South would eventually gain control of the House, but this did not happen, and thus

21. "The War of the South Vindicated," *Southern Presbyterian Review*, XV (April, 1863), 499.

22. Bledsoe graduated from West Point in 1830, but remained in military service only two years. He devoted the rest of his life mainly to teaching mathematics, practicing law, and journalism. Early in his civilian career, he entered the priesthood of the Protestant Episcopal Church and served briefly as rector of a church at Hamilton, Ohio. He soon resigned from the priesthood, however, because he could not accept the doctrine of baptismal regeneration as taught in the Prayer Book. Bledsoe, "How and Why I became a Methodist," *Southern Review*, IX (January, 1874), 105–23. The Kentuckian was a born polemicist. John B. Bennett, "Albert Taylor Bledsoe: Social and Religious Controversialist of the Old South" (typed Ph.D. dissertation, Duke University, 1942).

23. *Is Davis a Traitor; or Was Secession a Constitutional Right Previous to the War of 1861?* (Baltimore, 1866), Chap. 16.

the South remained a minority section.[24] That spelled the ruin of the South, since "all majorities are, in fact, unjust, despotic and oppressive." The breaking point was reached when Lincoln came to power, for he had vowed to exclude slavery from the territories, despite the Constitution. Unwaveringly, Bledsoe repeated this argument in issue after issue of the *Review*.[25]

In his book on Thomas J. Jackson, Robert L. Dabney devoted a fifty-page chapter to a defense of the South's constitutional right to secede from the Union.[26] Like Bledsoe, he also insisted that the South was driven into secession by "a long course of treachery and oppression" on the part of the northern states. The North's "chief sectional outrage," Dabney charged, was perpetrated against slavery. From 1820 onward, it was the design of the free states to monopolize the western territory, and they knew that in order to do so it would be necessary to exclude slavery from that region. Their selfish maneuver culminated in Lincoln's election. The victors tried to calm the South's fears by promising not to interfere with slavery where it was already established, but realistic southerners knew that the North would soon push through an amendment to the Constitution abolishing human bondage everywhere. The slave states were therefore justified in bolting the Union.[27]

Probably no preacher of his generation did as much to keep alive the old Confederate spirit as John William Jones, a Virginia Baptist who served in Lee's army first as a combatant and then as a chaplain. He is perhaps best known today as the author of *Christ in the Camp*, which presents a vivid account of the great religious revival that occurred in the Army of Northern Virginia during the last two winters of the war,[28] but most of his writing was in defense of the lost cause. In one of his bulky volumes he cast Jefferson Davis

---

24. *Ibid.*, 224–25, 230–38.
25. "Origin of the Late War," *Southern Review*, I (April, 1867), 257–73; "The North and the South," *ibid.*, II (July, 1867), 122–46; "Causes of Sectional Discontent," *ibid.*, II (July, 1867), 200–230; "The Missouri Compromise of 1820," *ibid.*, III (April, 1868), 346–86; "Alexander H. Stephens on the War," *ibid.*, IV (October, 1868), 249–300.
26. *The Life and Campaigns of Lieut. Gen. Thomas J. Jackson* (New York, 1866), Chap. 5.
27. *Ibid.*, 138–47, 169.
28. *Christ in the Camp; or Religion in Lee's Army* (Richmond, 1887). The troops built "forty chapels"—crude log huts—along the Rapidan in the winter of 1863–64, and "over sixty" more the next winter behind the Richmond and Petersburg entrenchments. *Ibid.*, 261.

in the role of a "stainless gentleman," a noble exponent of secession as a constitutional right.[29] Near the end of the century, Jones set forth his definitive views of the Confederacy in a book designed for use in southern schools and colleges. While professing to be "fair to all sections" of the country, he was actually highly partisan, especially in his account of the southern revolt against the Union. Like Bledsoe and Dabney, he defended secession as a constitutional right, but he also said that it was the only way in which the South could protect Negro servitude against abolitionism.[30]

The Virginia churchman hotly denied that Confederates fired the first gun of the Civil War. Instead, "the 'first gun' was really fired by John Brown at Harper's Ferry," and "the second gun was fired by Major Anderson [at Sumter]." Thus the bombardment of Sumter by the Confederates was "as pure an act of self-defense . . . as is to be found in history." In reality, then, "the war was begun by the Federal Government, and that government alone is responsible for all the horrors which ensued."[31] Jones deeply resented the Emancipation Proclamation. It was not only unconstitutional, but was "as bold a piece of wholesale robbery as ever the conqueror inflicted upon the conquered."[32]

II

The emphatic refusal of rebel churchmen to abandon or compromise their conviction that slavery had been ordained by God and that secession was a constitutional right, clearly warned northern missionaries to expect a cool reception in the postwar South. A cool reception became all the more certain when some prominent religious leaders in the North charged that southern churchmen were morally unfit to serve as Christian reconstructionists in their region. "The great territorial churches of the South," said Henry M. Dexter, editor of the *Congregationalist* (Boston), "have been so corrupted with the spirit of slavery and are still so tainted with sympathy for the rebellion that they are utterly unfitted for the moral

---

29. *The Davis Memorial; or Our Dead President, Jefferson Davis* (Richmond, 1890), Chaps. 12–13.
30. *School History of the United States* (Baltimore, 1896), 233–41.
31. *Ibid.*, 231.
32. *Ibid.*, 293.

work of reconstruction."[33] Following a visit to Tennessee in the spring of 1865, Lyman Abbott told an anniversary gathering of the American Missionary Society that "the Northern Missionary must undo all that the Southern clergy had been doing for half a century." According to him, the southern soldier was more trustworthy than the minister. "We can not trust the cause of Christ to the Judas who has betrayed it," exclaimed Abbott. "We can not intrust the Gospel of liberty and humanity to Dr. [Moses Drury] Hoge in Virginia, or Dr. [Benjamin Morgan] Palmer in New Orleans."[34]

In a scorching article, Theodore Tilton, editor of the New York *Independent*, charged that while Grant had crushed the military power of the Confederacy, the spirit of rebellion was "still potent and insolent in its civic and religious forms," and that the task of eradicating it imposed upon the northern people a twofold duty. First, they must wage a ceaseless war against any recognition of the rebel states until they had become fully democratic, including provision for Negro suffrage. Second, the northern churches "must work entirely independent" of the "unregenerate and apostate" religious bodies of the South; they "must plant their missions in every center," and free from all racial discrimination; and "they must organize schools [and colleges] where no barrier of color shall cast its hideous shadow." This racially inclusive movement, Tilton acknowledged, would make the regional denominations all the more determined to maintain their autonomy. "The Presbyterian, Methodist, and Baptist, will not soon resign their independent form for Northern fraternity. They will indulge their rancor and pride in the safe walls of their ecclesiastical fold."[35]

Such criticisms, even though containing a measure of truth, were a psychological liability, because they widened the gulf of communication between victors and vanquished and thus rendered the northern missionary's work in the South all the more difficult. Nevertheless, the northern mission to freedmen marks one of the finest chapters in the history of American Protestant benevolence.

That mission was initiated only a few months after the war started. It began with the Negro refugees—"contrabands"—at For-

33. *Congregationalist*, February 24, 1865.
34. "The Ministry For the South," *Home Missionary*, XXXVIII (November, 1865), 159, 160.
35. *Independent*, August 10, 1865.

tress Monroe, Virginia, on September 3, 1861, when Lewis C. Lockwood arrived there as an agent of the American Missionary Association (A.M.A.), a body organized in 1846 by a small band of aggressive Congregational abolitionists.[36] True to the Association's evangelical concern, Lockwood first of all provided church facilities for the refugees. Within a fortnight, however, he had also started a day school for them, with Mrs. Mary Peake, a free mulatto, as teacher.[37] Thereafter the Association's mission to freedmen grew as the Union forces penetrated the Confederacy, and when the war ended it had three hundred and twenty workers in the field, deployed in an area extending from Virginia to Mississippi.[38] Within the next two years, the number increased to five hundred and twenty-eight. For the fiscal year 1866–67, the A.M.A. spent over $280,000 in its educational and religious ministry to the freedmen.[39]

Since the American Missionary Association was already in business before the war broke out, it was able to lead off in the freedmen's aid movement. But special agencies were soon formed to meet the growing needs. Three of the most effective voluntary societies were set afoot early in 1862: the New England Freedmen's Aid Society, the National Freedmen's Relief Association of New York, and the Philadelphia Port Royal Relief Committee (later renamed the Pennsylvania Freedmen's Aid Commission).[40] Their initial field of service was Port Royal and the other sea islands of South Carolina, territory which had been captured by a federal

36. From the outset, the A.M.A. was non-sectarian, even though financed chiefly by Congregationalists. Prior to the Civil War it had supported some 440 missionaries (some of whom had labored in the border slave states) and had been the means of establishing about 400 churches. These churches were founded upon abolitionist principles and were open to blacks. Clifton H. Johnson, "The American Missionary Association, 1846–1861: A Study in Christian Abolitionism" (typed Ph.D. dissertation, University of North Carolina at Chapel Hill, 1958). See also Bertram Wyatt-Brown, *Lewis Tappan and the Evangelical War Against Slavery* (Cleveland, 1969), Chap. 15.

37. Richard B. Drake, "The American Missionary Association and the Southern Negro, 1861–1888" (typed Ph.D. dissertation, Emory University, 1957), 7–10; A.M.A., *History of the American Missionary Association* (New York, 1874), 11–12; Augustus F. Beard, *A Crusade of Brotherhood: A History of the American Missionary Association* (Boston, 1909), 121–23.

38. A.M.A., *History of the American Missionary Association*, 18.

39. Julius H. Parmelee, "Freedmen's Aid Societies, 1861–1871," *Negro Education: A Study of the Private and Higher Schools For Colored People in the United States* (U.S. Bureau of Education Bulletin, 1916, No. 38) (2 vols., Washington, 1917), I, 275; Drake, "The American Missionary Association," 278 (Table 3).

40. Parmelee, "Freedmen's Aid Societies, 1861–1871," *Negro Education*, I, 272–75, 276–77.

fleet on November 7, 1861. By the following spring more than fifty teachers and farm superintendents—self-styled "Gideonites"—were at work on these islands, seeking, under the guidance of Edward L. Pierce of Boston, to develop a pilot project for freedmen which might serve as a pattern for general postwar reconstruction.[41]

Meanwhile, western churchmen were making plans to meet the needs of bondsmen who had fled to Union forces in Tennessee and adjacent territory. Out of their efforts grew the Western Freedmen's Aid Commission, which was organized in 1863. Levi Coffin, a native of North Carolina and a dedicated Quaker abolitionist, became its administrative officer. Within a short time so many freedmen's aid organizations sprang up all across the free states that it became necessary to federate them in more inclusive bodies in order to avoid duplication of effort and sheer anarchy. The most inclusive of these federations, the American Freedmen's Union Commission, was formed in 1865. By 1867, its ten branches embraced almost all of the distinctly freedmen's aid organizations.[42]

The freedmen's aid movement was greatly strengthened when, on March 3, 1865, Congress established the Bureau of Refugees, Freedmen, and Abandoned Lands, and authorized the appointment of a commissioner and up to ten assistant commissioners.[43] The commissioner, General Oliver Otis Howard, a Congregational layman, employed the resources of the Bureau not only to feed the hungry and clothe the naked but also to banish illiteracy. The Bureau's educational superintendent, John W. Alvord, an Oberlin graduate and long-time abolitionist, gave his hearty support to the various freedmen's aid societies, especially the American Missionary

41. Willie Lee Rose, *Rehearsal For Reconstruction: The Port Royal Experiment* (Indianapolis, 1964), Chap. 2; James M. McPherson, *The Struggle For Equality: Abolitionists and the Negro in the Civil War and Reconstruction* (Princeton, N.J., 1964), 158–69; Edward L. Pierce, "The Freedmen at Port Royal," *Atlantic Monthly*, XII (September, 1863), 302–15.

42. Parmelee, "Freedmen's Aid Societies, 1861–1871," *Negro Education*, I, 271. This merger, however, soon fell apart over an argument as to whether teachers should refrain from propagating religion in the freedmen's schools. The Garrisonians or secularists preferred neutrality with respect to religion, but the evangelicals, such as the A.M.A. teachers, insisted that the schools inculcate vital Christianity. McPherson, *The Struggle For Equality*, 401–2; Drake, "The American Missionary Association and the Southern Negro," 16–24.

43. George R. Bentley, *A History of the Freedmen's Bureau* (Philadelphia, 1955), 49. From the outset of the war abolitionists had urged the formation of an agency of this kind, and the Bureau was largely the result of their efforts. McPherson, *The Struggle For Equality*, Chap. 8.

Association. The Bureau made available to them, rent free, numerous government buildings to be used as schoolhouses. For a time it also furnished subsistence and transportation to the teachers employed by the benevolent societies.[44] The Congress looked with favor upon this cooperative effort and appropriated funds for the promotion of freedmen's schools. Thus from 1865 to 1871 the Freedmen's Bureau contributed more than five million dollars toward Negro education in the South. Through the combined effort of the Bureau and the benevolent societies, 3,300 teachers were engaged in instructing 149,581 black pupils in 1870.[45]

At first most of the northern Protestant denominations funneled their freedmen's aid contributions through the non-sectarian benevolent societies, but they soon began sending them through their own mission boards or through specially created agencies. This naturally weakened the non-sectarian societies, and most of them speedily went out of business for lack of support. The New England Freedmen's Aid Society lasted longest, but it also disbanded in 1874. Meanwhile the denominational agencies increased in strength and influence. Besides, whereas the non-sectarian societies had confined their southern activities to relieving poverty and operating common schools, the denominational boards or societies not only continued those types of service but also planted churches and gave special attention to higher education.

For many years the American Missionary Association was the service agency of both the benevolent societies and such smaller denominations as the Free Will Baptists and the Wesleyan Methodists, but after 1870 it became mainly the freedmen's aid agency of Congregationalism.[46] During its early postwar work in the South, the A.M.A. concentrated its efforts upon establishing schools and colleges and gave little attention to organizing churches.[47] Between 1866 and 1877 the Association, in addition to maintaining a host of

44. Bentley, *A History of the Freedmen's Bureau*, 171. For a critical re-evaluation of the work of the Freedmen's Bureau, see William S. McFeely, *Yankee Stepfather: General O. O. Howard and the Freedmen* (New Haven, 1968), 73, 85, 90, 126, 140–44, 146, 273, 287.

45. Parmelee, "Freedmen's Aid Societies, 1861–1871," *Negro Education*, I, 289. These statistics excluded all Sunday schools and also many private and night schools.

46. Drake, "The American Missionary Association and the Southern Negro," 26–28, 121.

47. After 1870, Congregational leaders put forth more effort to establish churches in the South. *Ibid.*, Chap. 4.

elementary and secondary schools, founded seven higher institutions which are still in operation: Atlanta University, Fisk University (Tennessee), Hampton Institute (Virginia), Talladega College (Alabama), Tougaloo College (Mississippi), Tillotson College (Texas), and Straight University (Louisiana).[48]

In August, 1866, eleven Methodist ministers and laymen met at Cincinnati, Ohio, and organized the Freedmen's Aid Society of the Methodist Episcopal Church, with Richard S. Rust as field superintendent (later named corresponding secretary). During its third year of operation, the Society collected over $93,000 and supported one hundred and five teachers in nine southern states.[49] Like the A.M.A., the Society found it necessary to provide schools of higher learning in which to train a native black leadership, and by 1873 it was furnishing financial aid to fifteen such institutions, including Central Tennessee College, Claflin University and Baker Institute (South Carolina), Clark University and Clark Theological Seminary (Georgia), New Orleans University and Thomson Biblical Institute, and Wiley University (Texas).[50] "Of the three thousand pupils in these schools," noted Richard Rust in 1874, "more than one thousand of them are preparing to assist in the elevation of their race by teaching school or by preaching the Gospel."[51]

By May, 1865, the Home Mission Society of the American Baptist Convention had sixty-eight missionaries at work with freedmen in twelve southern states.[52] They promoted evangelism, organized black churches, and taught elementary schools for the masses. In order to equip a Negro leadership, the Society by 1870 was maintaining several normal schools or institutes, as at Richmond, Virginia; Raleigh, North Carolina; Columbia, South Carolina; Augusta, Georgia; and New Orleans, Louisiana.[53] Out of these schools eventually sprang important colleges and theological seminaries.

48. *Ibid.*, 163–72 (Appendix B). The A.M.A. also aided in the founding, in 1866, of Berea College (Kentucky), the forerunner of which was a one-room school begun by John G. Fee in 1855.
49. *Third Annual Report of the Freedmen's Aid Society of the Methodist Episcopal Church* (Cincinnati, 1869), 11.
50. *Sixth Annual Report of the Freedmen's Aid Society of the Methodist Episcopal Church* (Cincinnati, 1873), 14.
51. *Seventh Annual Report of the Freedmen's Aid Society of the Methodist Episcopal Church* (Cincinnati, 1874), 19.
52. Charles L. White, *A Century of Faith* (Philadelphia, 1932), 104.
53. *Ibid.*, 300–301.

Of the Society's early missionary-educators, two men were notably influential: Canada-born Charles Corey and Henry M. Tupper of Massachusetts. Both graduated from Newton Theological Institution (now Andover Newton Theological School) and both ministered to freedmen for more than twenty-five years. From the fall of 1865 until the spring of 1867, Corey traveled widely in South Carolina, organizing Negro churches.[54] In the fall of 1867 he became president of Augusta Institute in Georgia, but in the following July entered upon his greatest work as president of Richmond Institute (chartered as Richmond Theological Seminary in 1886), where he remained until his retirement in 1894. By the time he retired, this school had trained five hundred and thirty Negro ministers.[55]

Shortly before Henry Tupper was discharged from the Union army, he received a commission from the American Home Mission Society to go South as a missionary to the freedmen and was told to select his own field. He chose Raleigh, North Carolina, and in December, 1865, established Raleigh Institute, the forerunner of Shaw University.[56] In 1890 Shaw had five brick buildings, some four hundred students, and twenty-seven faculty members, thirteen of whom were black. During its first twenty-five years, it sent into service about four thousand teachers and hundreds of ministers. Some of its finest alumni became missionaries to Africa.[57]

Of the several branches of northern Presbyterianism, the old school Presbyterian Church in the U.S.A. led in the work with freedmen. In 1869 the new school Presbyterians united with their old school brethren, but neither before that event nor afterwards did they distinguish themselves in service to the ex-bondsmen.[58] The old school churchmen greatly surpassed them. Their General Assembly of 1864 appointed two regional committees to direct a

---

54. Charles H. Corey, *A History of Richmond Theological Seminary, with Reminiscences of Thirty Years' Work Among the Colored People of the South* (Richmond, 1895), 36–38.

55. *Ibid.*, 136. The Richmond Institute was founded in July, 1867, by Nathaniel Colver, one of the earliest Baptist abolitionists. As quarters for the Institute, he leased Lumpkin's Old Slave Jail. *Ibid.*, 54.

56. Henry L. Morehouse, *H. M. Tupper, D.D.: A Narrative of Twenty-five Years' Work in the South* (New York, 1890), 8–9.

57. *Ibid.*, 15–17.

58. Lewis G. Vander Velde, *The Presbyterian Churches and the Federal Union, 1861–1869* (Cambridge, Mass., 1932), 446–53.

ministry to freedmen, but the next year's assembly created a single Committee on Freedmen and empowered it to gather and disburse funds, commission missionaries, and supervise the whole enterprise.[59] The churches responded with remarkable enthusiasm. In its fourth year of operation, the committee collected more than $75,000 and sustained one hundred and seventy-nine missionaries, one hundred and twenty-six of whom were Negroes. As of May, 1869, the missionaries (twenty-six of them were ordained ministers) were servicing seventy-two churches, with over 5,600 communicant members. In the past year they had completed sixteen church buildings and had started on nine new ones.[60] With an eye to preparing Negro leaders as preachers and teachers, the Committee on Freedmen in 1867 established at Charlotte, North Carolina, Biddle Memorial Institute, out of which sprang Johnson C. Smith University.

In 1865 the Protestant Episcopal Church projected a similar mission to the former slaves, and appointed the Freedmen's Commission to solicit funds and administer the enterprise. During its first year, the Commission raised $26,000 and financed ten schools for blacks. By the end of a three-year period, it had collected a total of nearly $100,000, and was then supporting a force of sixty-five missionary-teachers. The Commission took a strategic step in 1867 toward training a native Negro leadership by helping to found St. Augustine's Normal School in Raleigh, North Carolina, the forerunner of St. Augustine College.[61]

One of the most remarkable missions to freedmen was conducted by two northern-born Negro denominations: the African Methodist Episcopal Church (1816), and the African Methodist Episcopal Zion Church (1820). Prior to the Civil War both had been barred from virtually all territory below Washington, D. C.

Two ministers of the African M.E. Church, James Lynch of the Baltimore Conference and James D. S. Hall of the New York Conference, began a mission at Hilton Head, South Carolina, in May,

59. *Minutes of the General Assembly of the Presbyterian Church in the United States of America, ... 1865,* XVII (Philadelphia, 1865), 544–45.
60. *Minutes of the General Assembly of the Presbyterian Church in the United States of America, ... 1869,* XVIII (Philadelphia, 1869), 988–89.
61. Raymond W. Albright, *A History of the Protestant Episcopal Church* (New York, 1964), 258–59. See also H. Peers Brewer, "The Protestant Episcopal Freedmen's Commission, 1865–1878," *Historical Magazine of the Protestant Episcopal Church,* XXVI (December, 1957), 361–85.

1863. They also entered Charleston and Savannah, Georgia, just as soon as Union troops opened the way. Fellow missionaries about the same time penetrated the coastal region of North Carolina. Within a two-year period, there were flourishing African Methodist Episcopal churches in Georgia and the Carolinas, with nearly three thousand communicants. Thus in May, 1865, Bishop Daniel A. Payne organized the South Carolina Conference to give direction to the work in those three states.[62] This body established missions in Florida during the next year, and reaped a bountiful harvest. By its third annual session, it reported a total church membership of over fifty thousand. At this time action was taken to organize a separate conference for Georgia and Florida.[63]

In the meantime, African M.E. missionaries had fanned out into many other sections of the South, and as a result of their labors the Louisiana Conference was organized in November, 1865, thus affording administrative guidance to churches in Alabama, Louisiana, Mississippi, Texas, and Arkansas. By the end of 1865, African Methodism had established a permanent foothold in nine former Confederate states. Among its pioneer missionaries were three men of unusual ability: Henry M. Turner, James Lynch, and Hiram R. Revels. In addition to preaching the gospel, they fought doggedly to secure equal political and civil rights for the former slaves. During the trying years of reconstruction they held important political offices at one time or another. Revels, for example, became a U.S. senator from Mississippi in 1870.[64]

The African M.E. Zion Church launched a dynamic mission to freedmen at New Bern, North Carolina, when James W. Hood, a son of Pennsylvania, arrived there in January, 1864. On finding a Negro church already in existence in that town and another at

---

62. *Minutes of the South Carolina Annual Conference of the African M.E. Church, 1865, 1866, 1867* (Charleston, 1867), 5. Thirty years earlier Daniel Payne had been forced out of his native city of Charleston because his private school for blacks was put out of business as a result of an act passed by South Carolina's General Assembly, forbidding any person to teach either free Negroes or slaves to read or write. Daniel A. Payne, *Recollections of Seventy Years* (1888; New York, 1968), 27–28.

63. *Minutes of the South Carolina Annual Conference of the African M.E. Church, 1865, 1866, 1867*, 16.

64. John Hope Franklin, *Reconstruction: After the Civil War* (Chicago, 1961), 88; Vernon L. Wharton, *The Negro in Mississippi, 1865–1890* (Harper Torchbooks ed., New York, 1965), 154–55, 159.

Beaufort, he persuaded both to unite with his denomination. The field was evidently white unto harvest, because before the year closed he had brought into the Zion Church some three thousand black people. Consequently Bishop Joseph J. Clinton had the pleasure of organizing the North Carolina Conference of the communion in December, 1864.[65] As soon as the war ended, Hood and his fellow preachers moved swiftly across the state and into the northwestern section of South Carolina. Meanwhile zealous missionaries swept through other states of the old Confederacy, gathering thousands of freedmen into the church. By 1869, the Zion branch of African Methodism was maintaining annual conferences in seven states, covering a territory from Virginia to Florida. North Carolina, however, comprised the heartland of the Zion Church. In that state the Central Conference alone had one hundred preachers in 1882 and served a communicant membership of twenty thousand.[66] Hood was the pre-eminent leader of his denomination in North Carolina. Although carrying a heavy load as a minister, he served as assistant state superintendent of public instruction for several years during the reconstruction period. Understandably, by 1872 he was elected a bishop of the African M.E. Zion Church.

Still other northern Protestants shared in this service to freedmen, including Friends, Free Will Baptists, Wesleyan Methodists, and Unitarians. Viewed as a whole, the mission made two outstanding contributions. First, it generated an unprecedented religious awakening among blacks who had been unresponsive to the indigenous denominations, and drew tens of thousands of them into the missionary churches, especially those of the two African communions. Second, the mission secondary schools and colleges trained a black leadership that was indispensable to the freedman's advancement.[67]

The teachers in the missionary institutions, wrote William E. B. Du Bois in 1903, "came not to keep the Negroes in their place, but

65. James W. Hood, *One Hundred Years of the African Methodist Episcopal Zion Church* (New York, 1895), 289–94.
66. *Ibid.*, 299.
67. "The freedmen's aid societies of Northern Protestant churches established more than a hundred institutions of college and secondary education for Negroes after the Civil War." James M. McPherson, "White Liberals and Black Power in Negro Education, 1865–1915," *American Historical Review*, LXXV (June, 1970), 1357.

to raise them out of the defilement of the places where slavery had wallowed them."[68] Inasmuch as many of them were abolitionists or the offspring of abolitionists,[69] and endeavored to erase the traditional color line, they were widely held in suspicion by white southerners, including clergymen. "Every person imported from abroad to instruct these [black] people," warned Bishop Stephen Elliott, "is an influence . . . widening the breach between the races."[70] In view of the fact that the native white denominations were in the forefront of the postwar movement to establish new patterns of racial segregation, the bishop had good reason to be wistful.

III

According to a report presented to the Southern Baptist Convention in May, 1859, "not less than 150,000" Negroes were communicant members of churches affiliated with the convention.[71] Upon the fall of the Confederacy and the liquidation of slavery, white and black Baptists were faced with the question of their future ecclesiastical relationship. Did either race really want to continue the pattern of biracial churches? There is little evidence that whites had any burning desire to do so.[72] Although by 1866 Negroes were pouring out of Baptist churches, the Southern Baptist Convention of that year expressed no desire to stop the outflow. Furthermore, when the convention met in 1867, the Board of Domestic and Indian Missions reported that blacks were "usually withdrawing from the white churches and organizing churches of their own, and this course is approved by the [white] brethren."[73]

An examination of resolutions adopted by state conventions on the subject fails to show that white Baptists were eager to continue racially mixed churches. In so far as biracialism was favored it generally sprang from paternalistic impulses or from a desire to coun-

68. *The Souls of Black Folk* (Chicago, 1903), 100.
69. Henry Lee Swint, *The Northern Teacher in the South, 1862–1870* (Nashville, 1941), Chap. 3; McPherson, *The Struggle for Equality*, 386–88.
70. "Address," *Journal of the Fourth Annual Council of the Protestant Episcopal Church in the Diocese of Georgia, . . . 1866*, 28.
71. *Proceedings of the Southern Baptist Convention, . . . 1859* (Richmond, 1859), 60.
72. An able Baptist historian thinks that Baptist sentiment in 1865 "was decidedly in favor of maintaining a biracial membership," but even he admits that this sentiment rapidly declined. Rufus B. Spain, *At Ease in Zion*, 49.
73. *Proceedings of the Southern Baptist Convention, . . . 1867* (Baltimore, 1867), 49.

teract the "pernicious" influence of Yankee missionaries. At their state convention of 1865, Alabama Baptists acknowledged the right of their black brethren to establish their own churches, but they added: "We... believe that their highest good will be subserved by their maintaining their present relation to those who know them, who love them, and who will labor for the promotion of their welfare."[74]

Before the end of 1865, black Baptists by the thousands had abandoned their former masters' churches in Virginia. In that same year seven all-black churches in Richmond, Petersburg, and Manchester organized Shiloh Baptist Association, one of the earliest Negro associations to be formed in the South. Only a year later that association contained twenty-five churches with a total membership of more than fourteen thousand.[75] This trend was not at all displeasing to white Virginia Baptists. On the contrary, the Baptist General Association of Virginia voted in 1866 to encourage black Baptists to form their own churches and associations.[76]

As early as 1866, white Baptists of South Carolina were hopeful that all blacks in their churches would "of their own accord seek separation and a distinct organization." They agreed, however, to permit those wishing to remain in local churches with whites to do so, "provided they studiously avoid occasions of irritation and offence." At the same time, they passed an amendment to their state convention's constitution providing that every convention delegate "shall be a white member of some Baptist Church in this State or vicinity."[77]

White Baptists in North Carolina were less restrained in voicing their sentiments. "Whenever the numbers and abilities are sufficient," declared the state convention in May, 1866, "the colored members in our churches should be encouraged and assisted to organize separate and independent churches and Associations."[78]

74. *Minutes of the ... Alabama Baptist State Convention, ... 1865* (Atlanta, 1866), 10.
75. *Religious Herald* (Richmond), June 6, 1867.
76. *Minutes of the Baptist General Association of Virginia, ... 1866* (Richmond, 1866), 26.
77. *Minutes of the ... State Convention of the Baptist Denomination in South Carolina, 1865 and 1866* (Greenville, S.C., 1866), 234, 239.
78. *Proceedings of the ... Baptist State Convention of North Carolina, ... 1866* (Raleigh, 1866), 19.

A year later a committee recommended to the convention that churches and associations be permitted to receive or reject black applicants on the merits of each particular case. The proposal was vehemently opposed by James Dunn Hufham, editor of the Raleigh *Biblical Recorder,* who contended that such latitude was "not to be thought of," because it implied "that persons of both races ought to be received promiscuously, with equal privileges, into our Churches, Associations and Conventions." He therefore moved an amendment "that our colored brethren be encouraged to form separate Churches and Associations." The convention adopted this amendment and thus in effect reaffirmed its action of the previous year.[79] Black Baptists were doubtless well aware of the attitude of their white brethren, for they had already abandoned most of their churches. In 1865 they had organized the Roanoke Association. Only two years later they formed a state-wide organization, which in 1882 reported eight hundred churches, four hundred and fifty ministers, and 95,000 members.[80]

White Baptist spokesmen generally explained the black exodus on the ground that the freedmen really preferred churches of their own. Undoubtedly they did prefer a separate existence, but why was this the case? At least three factors prompted their withdrawal from the white ecclesiastical establishment. For one thing, they probably felt impelled to leave their late master's church as a symbolic expression of their new freedom. For another, they wanted to demonstrate their ability to establish and maintain their own churches. For yet another thing, they deeply resented being denied equal rights and privileges in the house of God. To escape these humiliating and degrading experiences, they fled the white man's church. White racism was probably the greatest single factor in moving black people to establish churches of their own.

Leading Baptist clergymen of the period openly proclaimed the dogma of Negro inferiority and advocated racial segregation in organized religion as a means of avoiding racial amalgamation. A distinguished representative of this position was Jeremiah Jeter, who vigorously promoted his ideas through the widely read *Re-*

[79]. *Proceedings of the . . . Baptist State Convention of North Carolina, . . . 1867* (Raleigh, 1867), 24–27.

[80]. John L. Bell, Jr., "Baptists and the Negro in North Carolina During Reconstruction," *North Carolina Historical Review,* XLII (October, 1965), 408.

ligious Herald (Richmond), of which he was chief editor. In June, 1866, he argued that God had implanted in man an instinct which set apart blacks and whites, and that social mingling between them violated the divine plan, since such mingling would result in miscegenation, and thus "degrade our noble saxon race . . . to a race of degenerate mongrels."[81] During the next decade, the venerable Baptist repeated this opinion many times. "Social intercourse and intimacy between the races," he wrote in 1873, "must lead to the blunting, if not the extermination, of the instincts divinely implanted, and to the encouragement of intermarriages between the races and their ultimate amalgamation."[82] It was upon this premise that he relentlessly argued that black Baptists "should be organized into separate and independent churches."[83]

True to his logic, Jeter also objected to interracial Baptist associations. This issue arose when Pamunkey church—comprising Indians and Negroes—applied for membership in the Dover Baptist Association of Virginia. A committee was appointed, with Jeter as chairman, to recommend appropriate action. The report, which was drafted by the chairman, emphatically opposed admission of the Pamunkey brethren on purely racial grounds. "This mingling of the races," said the report, "must lead, more or less rapidly, to amalgamation, and to the obliteration of their distinctive marks. . . . Who can contemplate the *mongrelization* of our noble Anglo-Saxon race without emotions of profoundest horror?"[84]

IV

In 1860 Methodism, South, had a black membership of 171,857, but it dropped to 78,857 by 1866. The decline is reflected dramatically in the annual conferences during that six-year period. In Virginia the black membership fell from 7,567 to 1,212; in South

---

81. *Religious Herald*, June 28, 1866.
82. *Ibid.*, December 25, 1873. See also *ibid.*, March 19, 1868; August 19, 1869; January 14, 1875.
83. *Ibid.*, March 19, 1868.
84. *Ibid.*, August 19, 1869. The full report was published in this issue of the *Herald*, with a prefatory note saying that the report was not presented to the Dover Association, because the committee, although concurring in its conclusion, "were not agreed as to the reasoning by which it was supported." Nevertheless, the report clearly reflects the author's antipathy toward the Negro.

Carolina, from 49,774 to 16,390; in Georgia, from 27,385 to 14,993; and in Mississippi, from 17,529 to 5,417.[85]

This massive loss in Negro communicants apparently caused relatively little agonizing concern on the part of most white Methodist leaders. It is true that they sometimes told the vanishing blacks that they would be better off spiritually if they remained in the old household. Yet those same leaders showed no inclination to accept the freedmen as equals if they continued their present connections. On the contrary, their black brethren were given the distinct impression that they would still be treated as second-class Methodists.

In reality, it appears very doubtful that the major leaders of southern Methodism either seriously expected or genuinely wanted the freedmen to continue ecclesiastical fellowship with them. This is evident, for example, in sentiments expressed by an influential Virginian, David S. Doggett—elected bishop in 1866—editor of the newly established *Episcopal Methodist*. Only a few months after the war closed he devoted a two-part editorial to a discussion of his denomination's future relations to its black members. He severely criticized "the negrophilists of the North," accusing them of rushing into the defeated Confederacy "to gather under their wings the sable Christians of the South, as if to rescue them from the clutches of their direst foes." Their ministry, said the editor, was "fraught with mischief."[86] The new situation, he urged, laid upon Methodism, South, the immediate duty, first, to organize its black members into "independent congregations, in precisely the same manner that distinguishes the white [Methodist] population"; and, second, to supply their pulpits "with judicious white ministers" until native ministers of their own race could be secured. The second duty, added Doggett, was especially imperative because the black and white ministers from the North "would inflict incurable damage upon these nascent churches."[87]

85. *Minutes of the Annual Conferences of the Methodist Episcopal Church, South, For the Year 1860* (Nashville, 1861), 293; *Minutes of the Annual Conferences of the Methodist Episcopal Church, South, For the Year 1866* (Nashville, 1870), 94. The Negro membership of southern Methodism in 1860 has been generally reported as 207,766, but that figure included 35,909 "probationers," who, according to the official classification, were not actually "members." See *Minutes of the Annual Conferences, . . . 1860*, 293.

86. *Episcopal Methodist* (Richmond), July 26, 1865.

87. *Ibid.*, August 2, 1865.

The editorial articulated what was evidently a growing sentiment. Holland McTyeire, also destined to become a bishop in 1866, contributed to the *Episcopal Methodist* a "Letter from Montgomery, Ala[bama]," dated September 14, endorsing in the main Doggett's proposed racial policy for southern Methodism.[88] At their annual conference of November, 1865, Virginia Methodists voted in favor of virtually the same policy. Specifically, they recommended to the General Conference (1) that all-Negro churches be organized, and that "pastors be sent to them as soon as it can be done with propriety"; (2) that the General Conference make provision for licensing and ordaining suitable black preachers; and (3) that the General Conference "establish, as soon as circumstances justify, one or more Annual Conferences of colored preachers, under the superintendence of our own Bishops."[89]

Plainly, a movement was rapidly gathering momentum as early as the summer of 1865 to draw the color line in the Methodist Episcopal Church, South. By the spring of 1866, when the General Conference convened at New Orleans, the inauguration of a new racial pattern had become a certainty. In their address to the delegates, the bishops said, "If the colored people do not remain under our pastoral care, their departure . . . is necessitated by no indifference on our part."[90] They already knew the mind of the delegates, and they appeared chiefly concerned at this stage to insinuate that blacks, not whites, were responsible for the action about to be taken. Not surprisingly, the General Conference voted unanimously to form an all-black church modeled upon the organizational pattern of the parent body and founded upon the same system of doctrine.[91] Upon the completion of its structure from local church to general conference in 1870, the new communion took as its official name "The Colored Methodist Episcopal Church in America."

The new racial policy was joyfully welcomed by white southern Methodism. In the opinion of J. M. Burke, editor of the *Southern Christian Advocate*, it represented "the greatest and best thing"

88. *Ibid.*, October 11, 1865.
89. *Ibid.*, December 6, 1865.
90. *Journal of the General Conference of the Methodist Episcopal Church, South . . . 1866* (Nashville, 1866), 18.
91. *Ibid.*, 58–59.

that the General Conference had ever done. "We stand before the world," he declared, "with a Church constitution that accords blacks and whites equal Church privileges, while by a happy and prudent separation, it pays due respect to those mysterious antipathies which seem to be the indications of Heaven with regard to the two races."[92] The writer tacitly admitted that racism had prompted the "prudent separation." Another churchman, J. E. Evans, who also applauded the General Conference's racial decision, spoke more plainly. He frankly conceded that the freedmen would withdraw from any religious body that did not accept them on terms of equality, but at the same time he added: "Public opinion and the social relations of the two races at the South, preclude the idea of such equality in a common organization with whites."[93]

The commitment of Methodism, South, to an all-white membership spelled stubborn resistance to those northern Methodist missionaries who were seeking to establish interracial churches and schools in the former Confederacy. Leaders of southern Methodism deeply resented the efforts of their northern brethren to organize even white churches in their territory, to say nothing of racially inclusive churches. The result was bitter strife between the two Methodisms for many years.[94]

Unfortunately for the missionaries, their northern fellow churchmen also generally favored a policy of racial separatism. In 1864 the General Conference of the Methodist Episcopal Church specifically declared "that it is the duty of our church to encourage *colored pastorates for colored people* where practicable." Accordingly this body immediately authorized the bishops to organize "mission conferences" wherever "in their godly judgment the exigencies of the work may demand it."[95] Within a few months the bishops did actually organize two all-Negro mission conferences: the Washington and the Delaware conferences. Almost one hundred preachers held membership in them.

92. *Southern Christian Advocate*, May 4, 1866.
93. *Ibid.*, June 15, 1866.
94. Ralph E. Morrow, *Northern Methodism and Reconstruction* (East Lansing, Mich., 1956), Chap. 7.
95. *Journal of the General Conference of the Methodist Episcopal Church, . . . 1864* (New York, 1864), 252. It should be noted that "mission conferences" were not entitled to representation in the General Conference.

This exhibition of white racism drew forth a scorching and protracted protest from Gilbert Haven, pastor of North Russell Street Church in Boston and Methodism's foremost apostle of racial equalitarianism.[96] A radical abolitionist, he had often observed that the destruction of slavery was but the first and easier accomplishment. The real and more exacting task was to demolish racial caste, the root of all forms of injustice to black people. "Many abolitionists . . . have fancied their sole work was to liberate the slaves," he noted in an address at Boston's Tremont Temple in 1863. "It is their least work. We are to be made one family."[97] It was thus a bitter pill when his own branch of Methodism, yielding to the caste spirit, set up the Delaware and Washington bodies. He was all the more distressed because he feared that they were merely the beginning of a racial pattern that his denomination would follow in its mission to the post-bellum South. But to go South on that basis would only strengthen the "Satanism of caste" already deeply rooted there. "The only right and successful way," wrote Haven in the New York *Christian Advocate and Journal* in May, 1865, "is *to entirely ignore the idea of color in the organization of our Churches and conferences.*"[98] A color-blind mission, he argued in the next issue of the *Advocate*, would be the means of regenerating the North as well as the South. In Haven's opinion, churchmen of the North were as guilty of the sin of racial caste as those of the South. "We have cast them [Negroes] out of our congregations, or into the back corners of them, as if infamous lepers." Both sections therefore were sorely in need of a moral cleansing.[99]

Despite his irrepressible outcry against racial caste, Gilbert Haven—the Amos of northern Methodism—did not succeed in converting the leaders of his church to a color-blind ecclesiastical policy. "We do not take share in the zeal for an immediate inauguration of a Church without regard to distinction of races," declared

---

96. William B. Gravely, "Gilbert Haven, Racial Equalitarian: A Study of His Career in Racial Reform, 1850–1880" (typed Ph.D. dissertation, Duke University, 1969), 156–77.

97. Gilbert Haven, *National Sermons: Sermons, Speeches and Letters on Slavery and Its War* (Boston, 1869), 367. See also *ibid.*, 349–51, 593, 598, 600, 608.

98. *Christian Advocate and Journal*, May 25, 1865.

99. *Ibid.*, June 1, 1865. For a full account of Haven's "crusade against caste," see Gravely, "Gilbert Haven, Racial Equalitarian," Chap. 4.

Daniel D. Whedon, editor of the *Methodist Quarterly Review*.[100] In substantial agreement with Whedon was Daniel Curry, editor of the *Christian Advocate and Journal,* northern Methodism's leading newspaper. It was at "the expressed wishes of the colored ministers themselves," he argued, that "the colored mission conferences" were organized. On the other hand, he tacitly conceded that if the black ministers' demand for "social and official equality" were met, they might well prefer membership in interracial conferences. But "everybody must know," he added, that any such concession on the part of white Methodists "is impossible." The editor acknowledged that racial equality in Methodism was "an *ideal* to be aimed at and labored for," but he held that it was unrealistic to expect its immediate achievement.[101] Whedon and Curry doubtless expressed the predominant sentiment of the spokesmen of their church.

Gilbert Haven, however, was not a man to ask what was realistic, but rather what was the law of Christ. He therefore continued to plead with the missionary board of his communion to inaugurate an integrationist racial policy in the South. This policy, he urged, would not only result in the moral regeneration of northern Methodism; it would "give Congress the key-note it hesitates to strike;— the key-note it must yet strike—the political equality of all citizens."[102] The board rejected Haven's appeal.

Nevertheless, Haven's robust equalitarianism encouraged such missionaries as T. Willard Lewis and Alonzo Webster of South Carolina to persevere in their efforts to maintain racially inclusive schools and churches. Actually, all nine of the annual conferences that were organized in the South between June 5, 1865, and October 17, 1867, began as racially integrated bodies, although relatively few whites belonged to most of them.[103] Yet from the very beginning, the missionaries found it extremely difficult to erase the color line in a white-dominated society which for centuries had propa-

---

100. In a review of a "Report of the New England Annual Conference for 1865 on Church Reconstruction," *Methodist Quarterly Review,* XLVII (July, 1865), 482. Gilbert Haven drafted this report, which was also approved by both the Maine and New Hampshire Methodist conferences.

101. *Christian Advocate and Journal,* May 25, 1865.

102. *Northwestern Christian Advocate* (Chicago), November 7, 1866.

103. See editorial in the Atlanta *Methodist Advocate,* as reproduced in the New York *Christian Advocate and Journal,* August 4, 1870.

gated the dogma of Negro inferiority. Two other local factors augmented their difficulties. One was the fact that white southerners disagreed with the missionaries' contention that black people were entitled to equal political and civil rights. The other was the fact that the pattern of racial separatism was spreading in all the territorial denominations. To overcome these obstacles required a moral and intellectual stamina that probably few missionaries possessed. Add to this the racially compromising attitude of the major architects of Methodist missionary policy and the outcome was predictable.

The General Conference of 1868 reflected the fateful trend in three decisions. First, it tabled Gilbert Haven's motion to dissolve the Washington and Delaware all-Negro conferences.[104] Second, the bishops were authorized to organize the black ministers within the bounds of the Kentucky Conference into a separate conference "if said ministers request it, and if, in the judgment of the Bishops, the interest of the work requires it."[105] Third, the conference passed a blanket resolution authorizing the bishops "to divide Conferences which are already formed in the South, provided that two thirds of the members of such Conference or Conferences shall concur in such division."[106] Nothing in the resolution specified that the authorized division would be according to color, but this fact was well understood by all delegates.

Inasmuch as the great racial equalitarian, Gilbert Haven, was elected bishop by the General Conference of 1872, it might appear that his racial sentiments were becoming more acceptable to his fellow Methodists; but this was not the case either in the northern churches or on the southern mission field. No new legislation on the subject was enacted by the General Conference of 1872, but the question of mixed conferences received much attention, and the discussion revealed sharp differences of opinion. For example, Erasmus Q. Fuller, editor of the Atlanta *Methodist Advocate* and a stalwart opponent of integrated church organizations, presented various papers and memorials from Georgia Methodists urging the

104. *Journal of the General Conference of the Methodist Episcopal Church, . . . 1868* (New York, 1868), 308.
105. *Ibid.*, 307.
106. *Ibid.*, 308.

formation of a separate black conference in their territory.[107] On the other hand, more than three hundred Methodists (predominantly Negroes) in South Carolina, Louisiana, and Mississippi submitted petitions against the organization of separate black conferences.[108] The situation was so confusing that the conference evidently decided to await further developments before taking decisive action.

When the General Conference met at Baltimore in 1876, racial separatists were present in great strength. Once again, the Negro-controlled Louisiana and Mississippi conferences pleaded for the maintenance of integrated conferences, but they were no match for Erasmus Fuller and other white segregationists. In the final crunch, the conference by a lopsided vote of 226 to 66 declared that whenever "a majority" of the members of each race of any annual conference requested a division of said conference, "such division should be made." In that case, said the conference, "the presiding Bishop is hereby authorized to organize the new Conference or Conferences."[109]

As a contemporary observed, that action by Gilbert Haven's own church "was as gravel to his teeth."[110] Even so, it probably did not surprise him in view of his firsthand southern experiences during the preceding quadrennium. Upon his election to the episcopacy in 1872, he had been assigned to supervise his church's missionary work in the former Confederacy, with headquarters in Atlanta. From the outset, his black constituents greeted him warmly, but the whites, with few exceptions, received him frigidly. In some instances, as he made the rounds of the annual conferences, his white brethren openly balked at taking part in interracial sacramental and ordination services.[111] Furthermore, white antagonism toward color-blind conferences, instead of subsiding, rose with each passing year of Haven's administration. There is indeed good reason

107. *Journal of the General Conference of the Methodist Episcopal Church, . . . 1872* (New York, 1872), 92–94.
108. *Ibid.*, 115, 116, 120.
109. *Journal of the General Conference of the Methodist Episcopal Church, . . . 1876* (New York, 1876), 328, 331.
110. W. H. Daniels, ed., *Memorials of Gilbert Haven, Bishop of the Methodist Episcopal Church* (Boston, 1882), 91.
111. George Prentice, *The Life of Gilbert Haven, Bishop of the Methodist Episcopal Church* (New York, 1884), 413–28.

to believe that racial separatism was virtually victorious over integrationism before it received the blessing of the General Conference in 1876.[112]

With the exception of Gilbert Haven, the bishops accepted the failure of integrationism with remarkable complacency. Most of them probably shared the sentiment of Bishop Jesse T. Peck, who, shortly after presiding over the division of the North Carolina Conference, commented: "It seems to be ordained in the providence of God that white Churches should have white preachers, and colored Churches colored pastors."[113]

After their northern brethren capitulated to the spirit of racial caste, southern Methodists became much more inclined to fraternize with them. It was thus no mere coincidence that only a few months after the General Conference of 1876 signed the death warrant of integrationism, the two Methodisms formally buried the hatchet at Cape May, New Jersey.[114]

V

Upon the Confederacy's military defeat, the Presbyterian Church in the United States was so slow in establishing a postwar racial policy that it lost most of its black communicants, who may have numbered as many as ten thousand in 1861.[115] The General Assembly of 1865 issued a pastoral letter to its member churches, saying: "Do all you can for their [the freedmen's] best welfare, and do it quickly, for they already begin to pass rapidly away [from us]."[116] A committee was appointed, with John L. Girardeau as chairman, to study the ecclesiastical relations of the two races and to report its conclusions to the next assembly. In the meantime, in response to

112. Morrow, *Northern Methodism and Reconstruction*, 190–200.
113. *Zion's Herald* (Boston), February 20, 1879.
114. *Formal Fraternity. Proceedings of the General Conference of the Methodist Episcopal Church and the Methodist Episcopal Church, South, in 1872, 1874 and 1876, and the Joint Commission of the Two Churches on Fraternal Relations at Cape May, New Jersey, August 16–23, 1876*, 59–84.
115. B. W. Moseley, "Evangelization of the Colored People," *Southern Presbyterian Review*, XXV (April, 1874), 238.
116. *Minutes of the General Assembly of the Presbyterian Church in the United States, . . . 1865*, A.D., I (Augusta, Ga., 1865), 386. (The *Minutes* for this session of the General Assembly were also printed under the name of the Presbyterian Church in the Confederate States of America, which was the name of the denomination from 1861 to 1865.)

an overture, the General Assembly adopted a resolution saying that it saw no reason to abandon its ante-bellum policy of racially mixed churches. At the same time the assembly said that if the black communicants should "think it best to separate from us, and organize themselves into distinct organizations, . . . this Church will do all in its power to encourage, foster and assist them."[117]

Girardeau found it impossible to secure a meeting of his committee, but he solicited ideas from its members by mail. The replies revealed such a diversity of views that he was unable to frame a report that would embody the sentiments of a majority. He did not attend the next General Assembly, which met at Memphis, Tennessee, in 1866, but he prepared a paper and sent it to those members of his committee who were at that gathering, expressing the hope that they would accept it as their report. They did not do so, but the assembly permitted the paper to be read and published.[118] While the paper was not formally adopted, the positions taken at the Memphis meeting reflected much of Girardeau's thinking. The Assembly did not favor a division of the denomination along racial lines, and urged that "every warrantable effort" be made to prevent it. It nevertheless said that if its black members should "decline this fellowship of ordinances, and desire a separate organization, then our sessions are authorized to organize them into branch congregations." As branch congregations, they should be permitted to elect black superintendents or watchmen as overseers of their operations. The assembly recommended that sessions or presbyteries license qualified blacks as exhorters among their own race. The supreme judicatory, however, explicity advised against the ordination of Negroes as ministers, explaining that if this were done it would present difficulties on account of "the general structure of society, and from providential causes."[119] These difficulties were not specified, but the commissioners (delegates) needed no explanation.

Some southern Presbyterians regretted the assembly's refusal to sanction the ordination of black men to the ministry. This was especially the case in Virginia. Thus when the Synod of Virginia

---

117. *Ibid.*, 370–71.
118. Girardeau, "Our Ecclesiastical Relations to Freedmen," *Southern Presbyterian Review*, XVIII (July, 1867), 1–17.
119. *Minutes of the General Assembly of the Presbyterian Church in the United States, . . . 1866* (Columbia, S.C., 1866), 35–36.

convened in November, 1867, it overtured the General Assembly "to declare . . . that ordination to the work of the Gospel Ministry is to be given to all those called of God to, and qualified for, that work, without respect to persons [race]."[120]

It so happened that Robert L. Dabney was temporarily absent from the church when that measure was adopted, and when he returned and discovered what had taken place he was furious. After his friends managed to secure a reconsideration of the overture, he attacked it with every forensic weapon at his command.[121] Although opposing the overture on several grounds, Dabney found fault with it mainly because of its racial implications. There had, he charged, "broken out among many a sort of morbid craving to ordain negroes; to get their hands on their heads." The impulse stemmed from "moral and mental *malaria*," a pernicious disease that had infected a large portion of mankind.[122] He would not, he said, entrust the destinies of his church "in any degree whatever, to black rulers, because that race is not trustworthy for such position." The Negro's "temperament, idiosyncrasy, and social relation" disqualified him for exercising ecclesiastical power. Besides, the black folk had "deserted their true friends, and natural allies, and native land, to follow the beck of the most unmasked and unprincipled demagogues on earth [the Yankees], to the most atrocious ends."[123]

In an effort to excite revulsion against the overture, Dabney portrayed in lurid rhetoric what could happen to white Presbyterians if a Negro were ordained to the gospel ministry. There were still some churches of the denomination, he observed, with predominantly black memberships. If they were to call a Negro preacher, social equality could not be denied him. "Do you tell me," inquired the frenzied theologian, "that after you have admitted this negro thus to your . . . pulpits, your sick and dying beds, your weddings and funerals, you will still exclude him from your parlours and

---

120. *Minutes of the Synod of Virginia, . . . November, 1867* (Lynchburg, Va., 1867), 37.
121. An observer said Dabney's "voice trembled with emotion, his frame shook, his eyes snapped fire, and his arms flew vigorously in all directions." Quoted in Johnson, *The Life and Letters of Robert Lewis Dabney*, 321.
122. *Ecclesiastical Relation of Negroes: Speech . . . in the Synod of Virginia, Nov. 9, 1867; Against the Ecclesiastical Equality of Negro Preachers in Our Church, and Their Right to Rule Over White Christians* (Richmond, 1868), 5.
123. *Ibid.*, 6.

tables?" Of course not! But in that case, prepare for the worst. "I tell you, Sir, this doctrine [of Negro equality] . . . means ultimately, *amalgamation.*"[124] In order to prevent "this most repugnant thing," white churchmen must not only deny Negroes ordination to the ministry, but must also bar them from a seat in any of the church's courts, whether session, presbytery, synod, or general assembly. If they refuse to remain in the communion under white rule, said Dabney, "I would assist and encourage them to build up a black Presbyterian Church, ecclesiastically independent of, and separate from ours."[125]

This bitter tirade, consuming three quarters of an hour, had its intended effect. The synod was so overwhelmed by the master polemicist that it not only rescinded the measure to which he objected, but it immediately took action overturing the next General Assembly, which was to meet within a few days, "to revoke the paper adopted by the last General Assembly on the subject of the relation of our church to the colored people, on the ground that the whole subject of licensing and ordaining persons to the Gospel Ministry is by the constitution placed . . . in the power of the Presbyteries."[126]

That overture of the Virginia Synod had a far-reaching effect upon southern Presbyterianism, for the next General Assembly, meeting at Nashville, did in fact revoke its 1866 legislation with respect to the freedmen. It also declined, "on the ground of constitutional incompetency, to make any declaration respecting the future ecclesiastical organizations of such freedmen as may belong to our communion."[127] But two years later, in 1869, the supreme judicatory in effect conceded that it did, after all, possess constitutional power to extend a helping hand to its black communicants. Responding to the recommendations of a special committee, of which John L. Girardeau was chairman, the General Assembly declared "that separate colored churches may be established, the same to be united with adjacent white churches under a common pastorate"; that black men "may be employed," under the direction of

---

124. *Ibid.*, 11.
125. *Ibid.*, 16.
126. *Minutes of the Synod of Virginia,* . . . *1867*, p. 40.
127. *Minutes of the General Assembly of the Presbyterian Church in the United States,* . . . *1867* (Columbia, S.C., 1867), 145.

white ministers, as exhorters among their own people; and that presbyteries "may" license, or even ordain, qualified Negroes for service "in colored churches."[128]

In enacting that legislation in permissive rather than mandatory form, the General Assembly revealed that it was still uncertain as to what its racial policy should be. For the next five years, however, the assembly provided no clearer guidance on the question, and during that time the remaining handful of black communicants were as sheep without a shepherd.

Finally, in 1874, widespread pressure from the lower judicatories prompted the General Assembly to take more decisive action on the tantalizing subject. When the assembly of that year convened at Columbus, Mississippi, overtures from the Presbytery of East Hanover (Virginia), and from the synods of Memphis (Tennessee), South Carolina, and Mississippi urged the high court to set the freedmen apart in a completely independent African communion.[129] The most impressive overture came from the Synod of Mississippi, in the form of a lengthy paper which had been adopted by that body in November, 1873, upon the recommendation of a committee headed by Benjamin Morgan Palmer.[130] The overture argued that throughout the past eight years southern Presbyterians had "been steadily moving" toward a separate communion for their Negro communicants. The blacks themselves, said the overture, had preferred this racial pattern all along. Their exodus from the predominantly white churches could not properly be assigned to any contingent cause, including the allurements of Yankee missionaries. Instead, their withdrawal had been prompted by "the most controlling sentiment known to the human heart—*the instinct of race.*"[131] There were, continued the overture, definite advantages for the blacks in having their own communion. For one thing, it would accelerate their spiritual development, since they would be

---

128. *Minutes of the General Assembly of the Presbyterian Church in the United States, . . . 1869*, II (Columbia, S.C., 1869), 389.

129. For texts of the overtures, see *Minutes of the General Assembly of the Presbyterian Church in the United States, . . . 1874*, III (Richmond, 1874), 588–96.

130. *Minutes of the Synod of Mississippi: Sessions of 1873 and 1874* (Jackson, 1875), 12. The paper, which bears the marks of Palmer's authorship, was not printed in the minutes, but it was published in the *Southwestern Presbyterian* (New Orleans), November 6, 1873.

131. *Minutes of the General Assembly of the Presbyterian Church in the United States, . . . 1874*, III, 592.

thrown upon their own resources. For another, it would enable them to adapt Presbyterian standards to their particular needs. On the other hand, a separate black denomination would be advantageous to whites. In the first place, it would "quietly" lay on the shelf "all those thorny questions which arise from the commingling of two dissimilar races, and which no amount of diplomatic skill can harmoniously adjust."[132] In the second place, a black body would "eventually draw into itself the entire African element that is disposed to Presbyterianism at all," and thus would remove a source of collision between white Presbyterians, North and South.[133]

The General Assembly responded affirmatively and decisively; it voted unanimously to proceed with the gradual formation of an African Presbyterian Church. As a first step, the assembly recommended that sessions and presbyteries "encourage and aid in the formation of coloured churches . . . with the view to form these churches in due time into Presbyteries, as convenience may dictate."[134] Higher judicatories were to be organized as needed, including a general assembly. White churchmen were urged to give every possible assistance to "these infant organizations while they are struggling toward complete development." With a view to increasing the black communion's membership, the assembly set up a Negro Evangelization Fund, to be administered under the direction of the parent body.[135]

Unlike the black Baptist and Methodist denominations which resulted from emancipation, the African Presbyterian Church began as a very feeble body. It had been claimed that if the Negro Presbyterians were organized as a separate communion, their white brethren would rally to their support. This did not happen. In 1875, for example, contributions to the Negro Evangelization Fund totaled, in round numbers, only $326, as against $6,643 donated for the evangelization of whites. A survey of the field in that same year re-

132. It should be noted that almost two years before this overture was presented to the General Assembly, Palmer had explicitly congratulated Dabney for his opposition to Negro equality in the Presbyterian Church, U.S. See his letter to Dabney of December 30, 1872, as quoted in Johnson, *The Life and Letters of Robert Lewis Dabney*, 321.

133. *Minutes of the General Assembly of the Presbyterian Church in the United States*, . . . *1874*, III, 594.

134. The Mississippi overture noted that there were already in existence six Negro churches: two in Alabama, and four in Charleston, South Carolina. *Ibid.*, 595.

135. *Ibid.*, 517-18.

vealed that over half of the presbyteries were doing nothing at all for the religious welfare of the black people in their midst. Of the remainder, only one was providing anything approaching a systematic ministry to Negroes. Reportedly, there were eight or ten black Presbyterian ministerial candidates, but they were receiving no formal theological education.[136] In 1876, however, the General Assembly did establish an institute for "colored ministers," with C. A. Stillman in charge of it. The institute was located at Tuscaloosa, Alabama, and its entire "plant" consisted of one room, which was rented for two dollars per month. Six students were enrolled during the first academic year, but only two of them were Presbyterians.[137] Yet it was "no easy matter" to finance even this meager enterprise.[138]

The outlook for the new African denomination was thus far from bright; and, indeed, it never did really flourish. In retrospect, it seems lamentable that the black Presbyterians did not remain in the old household. They might very well have been happy to do so on terms of equality with their white brethren, but the dogma of Negro inferiority and the ghost of racial amalgamation prevented this pattern of Christian fellowship.

Northern missionaries of the Presbyterian Church, U.S.A., fully capitalized on the failure of the southern church to grant its black communicants ecclesiastical equality. By May, 1868, they had formed, in the Carolinas and Georgia, three presbyteries—Catawba, Atlantic, Knox—and sixty churches, with a total of 4,603 communicant members. In that same year Biddle Memorial Institute was instructing forty-three students, twenty of whom were ministerial candidates. In 1869 the Synod of Atlantic was organized, embracing the communion's missionary work on the Atlantic seaboard from North Carolina to Florida.[139]

Precisely how many of these black people were formerly con-

---

136. *Minutes of the General Assembly of the Presbyterian Church in the United States, . . . 1875*, IV (Richmond, 1875), 53–54, 57.

137. *Minutes of the General Assembly of the Presbyterian Church in the United States, . . . 1877*, VI (Wilmington, N.C., 1877), 438–39, 451–53.

138. John B. Adger, "The General Assembly at New Orleans [1877]," *Southern Presbyterian Review*, XXVIII (July, 1877), 586.

139. "Abstract of Third Annual Report of the Assembly's Committee on Freedmen," *Minutes of the General Assembly of the Presbyterian Church in the United States of America [Old School], . . . 1868*, XVII (Philadelphia, 1868), 732, 734–37.

nected with the Presbyterian Church, U.S., is unknown, but the number is generally believed to have been rather large, especially in western North Carolina, where several ministers in the southern church defected to the northern communion and served as missionaries to Negroes in that section of the state.[140] This exodus into the northern church prompted many leaders of southern Presbyterianism to accuse the missionaries of ecclesiastical sheep stealing. While this may have been true in some instances, the main reason for making a change was the black man's desire to unite with a communion in which he would be less exposed to racial discrimination.

VI

The other religious bodies which had supported the Confederate cause apparently had less difficulty in forming their postwar racial patterns than did the Baptists, Methodists, and Presbyterians. At any rate, they soon drew the color line in one form or another. This was true, for example, of southern Lutherans, who, following the war, continued their ecclesiastical identity under the name of the Evangelical Lutheran General Synod in North America.[141]

In 1859, there were nine hundred and sixty-nine Negro Lutherans in South Carolina, and one hundred and ninety-five of them were members of St. John's Church (Charleston), of which the eminent John Bachman was pastor.[142] Despite the postwar status of the former slaves, the South Carolina Synod declined to change its racial policy. That is to say, blacks and whites were to continue as members of the same congregations, but blacks would have no voice in determining basic congregational policy, and they would sit in pews which signified their inferiority. Not surprisingly, the congregations lost all their Negro communicants within a few

140. Andrew E. Murray, *Presbyterians and the Negro—A History* (Philadelphia, 1966), 141–47, 177–79; John L. Bell, Jr., "The Presbyterian Church and the Negro in North Carolina During Reconstruction," *North Carolina Historical Review*, XL (January, 1963), 15–36.
141. Hugh George Anderson, *Lutheranism in the Southeastern States, 1860–1886: A Social History* (The Hague, 1969), 208.
142. *Ibid.*, 39; Raymond M. Bost, "The Reverend John Bachman and the Development of Southern Lutheranism" (typed Ph.D. dissertation, Yale University, 1963), 125.

years. The membership roll of St. John's, for instance, listed only twenty in 1867, and none at all after that year.[143]

The Synod of Tennessee, on the other hand, favored a racially separatist policy from the beginning. In 1866 this body declared that "owing to the plainly marked distinctions which God has made between us and them [Negroes] . . . there ought to be separate places of worship, and, also, separate ecclesiastical organizations, so that every one could worship God with the least possible embarrassment." The synod authorized the licensing of qualified black Lutherans "to preach to, catechise, baptize, and celebrate the rites of matrimony among those of" their "own race." Such licensing, the synod stressed, "does not authorize them to preach in our [white] churches, or take part in our ecclesiastical meetings."[144] Members of the synod promised to assist Negro Lutherans in organizing their own churches, but nothing came of the gesture. As in South Carolina, therefore, the blacks simply abandoned Lutheranism.

Of all the southern synods, the Synod of North Carolina was the only one that revealed more than incidental interest in Negro evangelization, and its interest soon waned. In 1868 this body formally adopted the Tennessee pattern of racial separatism,[145] and by 1876 it had licensed three black men as missionaries to their own race in western North Carolina. These black pastors were excluded from synodical meetings. The leading Negro missionary, D. J. Koontz, was ordained in 1880. Not even his labors, however, produced much of a harvest; in fact, by 1885 he had gathered only forty communicants into four feeble congregations. A year later the synod virtually washed its hands of the whole Negro mission.[146] The mission would have perished altogether had it not been for the perseverance of the black leaders, who in 1889 organized an independent body under the name of the Alpha Synod of the Evangelical Lu-

143. Bost, "The Reverend John Bachman and the Development of Southern Lutheranism," 126.
144. *Minutes of the Evangelical Lutheran Tennessee Synod, . . . 1866* (Statesville, N.C., 1866), 16–17. In compliance with this action, the clerical members of a committee were appointed to examine candidate Thomas Fry, a freedman. Apparently he was never licensed.
145. *Minutes of the Evangelical Lutheran Synod and Ministerium of North Carolina, . . . 1868* (Concord, N.C., 1868), 24–25.
146. *Minutes of the . . . Evangelical Lutheran Synod and Ministerium of North Carolina, . . . 1886* (New Market, Va., 1886), 9–10.

theran Church of Freedmen in America. Upon their request in 1891, what is known today as the Lutheran Church–Missouri Synod came to their rescue, supplying both money and supervisory assistance.[147]

Like other communions in slave territory, the Protestant Episcopal Church soon lost most of its black members when the Confederacy broke down. As a rule, the dioceses endeavored to continue a ministry to them by establishing separate Negro churches. Thus by 1867 the Diocese of Virginia had formed such churches in Richmond, Norfolk, and Petersburg.[148] There were similar achievements in other dioceses. Some black churches were members of the diocesan conventions, as in Virginia, North Carolina, and Florida. This relationship, however, became a bone of contention in several dioceses. By far the most bitter controversy over this question occurred in the Diocese of South Carolina.[149]

The issue arose in 1875, when St. Mark's Church of Charleston, a well-to-do black congregation, applied for admission to the diocesan convention. The application was referred to a commission for study and appropriate recommendation. At the next convention that commission reported a split decision. Three members were against admission, contending (1) that the applicant would be unable to send qualified delegates to the convention; (2) that the admission of St. Mark's would open the door to other Negro churches; (3) that to admit the Charleston church would tend to encourage "miscegenation," since it comprised predominantly mulattoes; and (4) that some white churches might withdraw from the convention if Negroes secured membership in it.[150] Two members heartily urged the admission of St. Mark's, arguing that a refusal would violate the fundamental principle of the unity of the church as the Body of Christ. William B. W. Howe, bishop of the diocese, read a penetrating paper in which he said that if the convention closed the door to St. Mark's, it "would do a most uncatholic act, and register

---

147. Anderson, *Lutheranism in the Southeastern States*, 217.
148. *Journal of the Seventy-Second Annual Council of the Protestant Episcopal Church in Virginia, . . . 1867* (Richmond, 1867), 58–59.
149. George B. Tindall, *South Carolina Negroes, 1877–1900* (paperback ed., Baton Rouge, 1966), 194–200; George Freeman Bragg, Jr., *History of the Afro-American Group of the Episcopal Church* (Baltimore, 1922), 157–58.
150. *Journal of the . . . Convention of the Protestant Episcopal Church in the Diocese of South Carolina, . . . 1876* (Charleston, S.C., 1876), 25–40.

the Church in this Diocese as the Church of a caste."[151] Yet in the end the motion to admit St. Mark's failed to pass because of the non-concurrence of orders. The clergy voted in favor of admission by 17 to 9, but the laity voted against it by 17 to 12.[152] It was a stunning blow to the bishop and most of the clergy.

For several years thereafter, the issue remained dormant; but it re-emerged in the middle 1880's over whether a black clergyman was entitled to a seat in the convention. On allegedly constitutional grounds, a party comprising mostly laymen attempted in 1885 to deny seats to two Negro ministers, H. G. Bishop and Thomas G. Harper. Upon their defeat, they entered a vigorous protest against the convention's decision.[153] Two years later the dissidents resorted to a pressure strategy. After failing to unseat J. H. M. Pollard, black minister of St. Mark's Church, a considerable number of delegates, including many from the more influential churches, withdrew from the convention.[154] They argued in a published pamphlet that it was "not only unconstitutional but in itself dangerous in the extreme" to seat Negro clergymen in the diocesan convention. According to them, the policy was dangerous because it would encourage whites to recognize blacks as their equals, and any such recognition would ultimately result in contaminating the Caucasian race. The dissidents frankly conceded that they were fighting to prevent Negro equality from being forced upon them.[155]

The anti-Negro churchmen had hoped that the withdrawal strategy would accomplish their purpose, and they were not disappointed. For in May, 1888, the diocesan convention declared that it had become "essential" to effect an "entire and complete" ecclesiastical separation of black and white Episcopalians. Accordingly a committee of seven, with Bishop Howe as chairman, was autho-

---

151. *Ibid.*, 43–63.
152. *Ibid.*, 63.
153. *Journal of the ... Convention of the Protestant Episcopal Church in the Diocese of South Carolina, ... 1885* (Columbia, S.C., 1885), 19, 29–32, 38–40.
154. *Journal of the ... Convention of the Protestant Episcopal Church in the Diocese of South Carolina, ... 1887* (Charleston, S.C., 1887), 22–23.
155. C. G. Memminger, et al., *Statement of the Causes Which Led to the Withdrawal of the Deputies from the Late Diocesan Convention of South Carolina* (Charleston, S.C., 1887), 36, 39. For an able reply to the proponents of an all-white convention, see E. M. Seabrook, *The Law and the Gospel as Applied to the Questions Before the Diocesan Convention of the Episcopal Church of the Diocese of South Carolina, 1887* (Charleston, S.C., 1887). For a defense of an all-white convention, see John S. Fairly, *The Negro in His Relations to the Church* (Charleston, S.C., 1889).

rized to consult with the vestries of the four black churches in the diocese and "to effect the complete separation into two complete organizations, under the Bishop of the Diocese."[156] Pursuant to its task, the committee drafted Canon XIII, hoping that the black churchmen would consent to the division. In fact, the clergymen and vestries of all four Negro churches rejected the Canon practically unanimously.[157] Not to be outdone, the convention of 1889 so amended its constitution as to bring about the same result. In the end, therefore, the white racists won a decisive victory, despite the opposition of Bishop Howe and a large majority of his clergy.

The leaders of American Roman Catholicism also had the task of determining a feasible racial policy with respect to blacks in the post-Confederate South. In a pastoral letter, issued by the Second Plenary Council, meeting at Baltimore in October, 1866, the bishops exhorted both clergy and laity to employ every available means to minister to the religious needs of the freedmen.[158] While the council agreed to leave each bishop free to determine racial policy in his own diocese, it nevertheless recommended that, wherever possible, separate churches be built for Negro Catholics.[159] Significantly, the president of the council, Martin J. Spalding, archbishop of Baltimore, already had an all-black church within his jurisdiction—St. Francis Xavier Church, established in 1864.[160] Spalding evidently favored separate churches for blacks, because he told his clergy in a pastoral letter of May 1, 1867, that he would "be highly gratified to find the number of churches for colored people multiplied."[161]

The Archbishop opened a wide door to the Negro's religious

156. *Journal of the . . . Convention of the Protestant Episcopal Church in the Diocese of South Carolina, . . . 1888* (Charleston,, S.C., 1888), 19.

157. *Journal of the . . . Convention of the Protestant Episcopal Church in the Diocese of South Carolina, . . . 1889* (Charleston, S.C., 1889), 16–20.

158. Peter Guilday, *The National Pastorals of the American Hierarchy, 1792–1919* (Washington, 1923), 221.

159. John T. Gillard, S.S.J., *Colored Catholics in the United States* (Baltimore, 1941), 121. "This recommendation," said Gillard, "was urged again by the Third Plenary Council [1884] and several Provincial Councils of Baltimore." *Ibid.*, 121–22.

160. Vincent de Paul McMurry, S.S., "The Catholic Church During Reconstruction, 1865–1877" (typed M.A. thesis, Catholic University of America, 1950), 220. "It was the first church building exclusively for colored Catholics in the United States," said McMurry. *Ibid.*, 220.

161. Quoted in John C. Murphy, *An Analysis of the Attitudes of American Catholics toward the Immigrant and the Negro, 1825–1925* (Washington, 1940), 58.

advancement when, in December, 1871, he welcomed to Baltimore four Josephite priests, recent graduates of St. Joseph's College (Mill Hill, England), an institution founded in 1866 by Father Herbert Vaughan—future bishop and cardinal—to provide special training for prospective missionaries. Vaughan had accompanied the missionaries to America. Spalding provided the Josephites with a house and sixty acres of land.[162] Thus began a dedicated ministry to black Americans that was destined to spread throughout American Catholicism.

After seeing his charges settled in their new home, Vaughan traveled extensively in the South and visited many cities, including Charleston, Savannah, Memphis, Mobile, Natchez, and New Orleans.[163] Everywhere he went, he recorded in his diary, white racism prevailed. Even the priests took little interest in black folk. In Memphis, for instance, they regarded them "as so many dogs." "What perplexed him [Vaughan] more than anything else," wrote his biographer, "was the inequality before the Blessed Sacrament." While in New Orleans, Vaughan was especially outraged by the treatment of a wealthy Negro Catholic who was married to a white woman. The husband, he confided to his diary, "pays for a pew at the Cathedral—his wife sits in it, but he is obliged to go behind the altar."[164]

Like their fellow Protestant policy-makers, Catholic bishops in the former Confederacy generally capitulated to the racial mores. This was true of the most racially liberal Augustin Verot, bishop of Savannah and administrator apostolic of Florida.[165] More than any other prelate in the region, he labored to provide the blacks with schools. Shortly after the Confederacy fell, he made a trip to his native France to solicit funds and recruit teachers for this purpose.[166] His mission bore fruit; by late August, 1866, eight sisters of St. Joseph had arrived at St. Augustine. Within the next two

162. John G. Snead-Cox, *The Life of Cardinal Vaughan* (2 vols., London, 1910), I, 167–68.
163. *Ibid.*, 169–79. Interestingly, Vaughan interviewed Jefferson Davis, who still contended that men were "warring against God" when they freed the Negro. *Ibid.*, 174.
164. *Ibid.*, 170–71.
165. After Florida became a separate diocese, in 1870, Verot was placed in charge of it, and he held that post until his death in 1876.
166. Michael V. Gannon, *Rebel Bishop: The Life and Era of Augustin Verot* (Milwaukee, 1964), 131–32.

years, other sisters joined them. Just before the first teachers came, Verot wrote a pastoral letter (August 1, 1866) to the clergy and laity of his jurisdiction in which he urged the importance of maintaining schools for the freedmen. In the hope of smoothing the path of his sisters, he wrote: "We exhort all to put away all prejudice, all dislike, all antipathy, all bitterness against their former servants. The golden rule, *love thy neighbor as thyself*, must not admit of any exception."[167] Verot himself very likely preferred racially inclusive schools, but he operated none of this type, not even in such leading cities as Savannah and St. Augustine.[168] The bishop seems not to have established any separate black churches, yet he permitted the practice of segregating blacks in the regular parish churches. Furthermore, he himself once led a financial campaign "to enlarge the colored gallery in the parish church" at St. Augustine.[169]

When William H. Gross became bishop of Savannah, he went well beyond Verot in drawing the color line. "I believe in the principle of having churches just for the negroes," he wrote his fellow bishop of Natchez, William H. Elder, in December of 1877. "Consequently I have erected a church in Savannah for them exclusively. . . . So soon as my means allow it, I shall erect similar churches in Augusta, Atlanta, Macon, and the other large cities of the diocese."[170] The bishop of Charleston, Patrick N. Lynch, who had served as Jefferson Davis's agent at the Vatican during the war, likewise believed that black Catholics should be set apart in institutions of their own. In a lengthy letter, addressed to the central boards of the Association of the Propagation of the Faith on June 17, 1867, Lynch reported that he was already maintaining a school in Charleston for Negro children, and that he hoped soon "to establish a convent for colored nuns." He also reported that he had bought a building in Charleston for a Negro church, which was to "be inaugurated before Christmas." In the following January, he dedicated St. Peter's Church, the first all-black Catholic church in the lower South. "We look forward to a time," said the bishop, "when the negroes will have a clergy, schools, orphanages, and re-

---

167. *Catholic Mirror* (Baltimore), September 1, 1866.
168. Gannon, *Rebel Bishop*, 136 n.
169. *Ibid.*, 126.
170. Quoted in McMurry, "The Catholic Church During Reconstruction," 214.

ligious communities of their own."[171] Wherever other Catholic bishops of the postwar South founded freedmen's institutions, they implemented a racial policy similar to that of Lynch and Gross.

In Roman Catholicism, the pattern of racial segregation spread more slowly than it did in Protestantism. In New Orleans, the stronghold of the Roman Church in the South, there was not a single all-black Catholic church until 1895, when St. Catherine's was established.[172] Not another was organized in that city until the opening of the next century. During the administration of Archbishop James H. Blenk (1906–17), however, seven Negro churches were organized there. His successor, Archbishop John W. Shaw (1918–34), was instrumental in founding twelve more.[173] By this time, the forming of black churches for black people had become the prevailing policy of Catholic leadership throughout the nation, and especially in the South. By 1928, said a Catholic historian, "there were 120,271 colored Catholics worshipping in their own churches."[174]

VII

Meanwhile, ex-Confederate churchmen also stoutly opposed the postwar movement to accord black people political and civil equality. They were the more adamant because this movement was being supported not only by political radicals in Congress, but by northern Protestant denominations which had furnished most of the abolitionist missionaries. The Congregationalists, sustainers of the American Missionary Association's enterprises in the South, were a prime example. At their notable National Council, held at Boston in June, 1865, they proclaimed that justice and honor alike demanded that black Americans be granted "the rights of the elective franchise, and all the privilege[s] of freemen."[175] In May of the

---

171. "Letter of the Right Rev. P. N. Lynch, Bishop of Charleston, . . . June 17th, 1867," *Annals of the Society For the Propagation of the Faith*, XXIX (January, 1868), 58.

172. Roger Baudier, *The Catholic Church in Louisiana* (New Orleans, 1939), 489.

173. *Ibid.*, 509, 524. This remarkable growth in black churches was a result, in large measure, of the energetic ministry of Josephite missionaries.

174. Gillard, *Colored Catholics in the United States*, 139.

175. *Congregational Quarterly*, VII (July and October, 1865), 362. The National Council numbered 492 delegates and represented Congregational churches in twenty-four states, plus several foreign countries, including England and France. *Ibid.*, 242.

same year the American Baptist Home Mission Society resolved that it was "indispensable" to national peace and prosperity that the freedmen "be invested with the elective franchise, and with all the privileges of whatever kind that belong to American citizenship."[176] During 1865 and 1866, five New England annual conferences of the Methodist Episcopal Church voted in favor of Negro suffrage.[177] Members of the Maine Annual Conference went so far as to say that the rebel states should never be restored to the Union "until they ... secure to all their people equal civil and political rights." They warmly commended Congress "for triumphantly passing the 'Civil Rights Bill' [1866] over the veto" of President Andrew Johnson.[178]

This drive of radical politicians and abolitionist preachers to enfranchise blacks and to grant them equal political privileges deeply enraged religious leaders of the white South. "Nothing could induce me to enter our [state] Capitol," wrote Moses Drury Hoge of Richmond, Virginia, to his sister in January, 1868. "Others have gone in from curiosity, but I wish to escape the spectacle of beastly baboons sitting where sages and patriots once sat."[179] As that remark clearly implies, the white southerner objected to Negroes in politics not so much because he feared they might dominate legislative decisions—something virtually impossible even in the heyday of Congressional Reconstruction—[180] but because this was not the proper role of "beastly baboons."

During the entire reconstruction era, white spokesmen of south-

---

176. *Thirty-Third Annual Report of the American Baptist Home Mission Society, May 18-23, 1865* (New York, 1865), 44.

177. *Minutes of the New England Conference, ... 1865* (Boston, 1865), 25; *Minutes of the New Hampshire Annual Conference, ... 1865* (Boston, 1865), 21; *Minutes of the Maine Annual Conference, ... 1866* (Boston, 1866), 25; *Minutes of the East Maine Annual Conference, ... 1866* (Boston, 1866), 24; *Minutes of the Vermont Annual Conference, ... 1866* (Montpelier, Vt., 1866), 40.

178. *Minutes of the Maine Annual Conference, ... 1866*, 25. The Civil Rights Bill, conferring citizenship upon Negroes and invalidating such legislation as the Black Codes, was originally passed by Congress on March 13, 1866. It was vetoed by President Andrew Johnson on March 27, and passed over his veto on April 9. For text of the Civil Rights Act, see Henry S. Commager, ed., *Documents of American History* (two volumes in one, 7th ed., New York, 1963), Document No. 252. With respect to the Black Codes, see Theodore B. Wilson, *The Black Codes of the South* (Tuscaloosa, Ala., 1966).

179. Hoge, *Moses Drury Hoge*, 239.

180. Franklin, *Reconstruction: After the Civil War*, 133-36; Kenneth M. Stampp, *The Era of Reconstruction, 1865-1877* (New York, 1965), 167.

ern Christianity inveighed against so-called "Negro rule." Jeremiah Jeter of Richmond implored the North not to impose Negro suffrage upon the South, arguing that it "would lead to an inevitable conflict between the white and colored races."[181] Passage by Congress of the Fifteenth Amendment, said Father Abram J. Ryan, editor of the *Banner of the South*, Roman Catholic organ of the Diocese of Savannah, was infamous because it forced the people "to give Negroes not only the right to vote, but to hold offices of honor [and] trust."[182] Recurring to the same subject a few months later, the celebrated poet of the fallen Confederacy proclaimed: "This is a 'white man's Government,' and upon this doctrine future political contests must be fought until the question is finally and irrevocably settled."[183] In 1874, Albert Taylor Bledsoe devoted much of a lengthy essay to contending that the black man could never hope to share rulership with the white man in America. "It would bring ruin to [the Negro] *himself, and to his people, and to his cause*, as well as to others, were he to have the reins of government in his hands."[184] In the same year Edwin T. Winkler, editor of the *Alabama Baptist* and a leading spokesman of Southern Baptists, sketched an extremely dismal image of black people. "There is no merchant who deals with the South, in New York or Liverpool, whom our Negro legislatures have not mulcted," he charged. Moreover, as a juror the Negro had been "a failure," and as a witness he had demonstrated "no sense of the sanctity of an oath." In short, "the thin varnish of civilization" could "not conceal the barbarism of the race."[185] Year after year, Linus Parker—destined to become a bishop in the Methodist Episcopal Church, South—employed the official newspaper of the Alabama, Mississippi, and Louisiana conferences to denounce "negro domination" in the Louisiana legislature. "Any State that is Africanized is bound to go down," he editorialized on "The New South" in 1874. In a later

---

181. *Religious Herald*, November 14, 1867.
182. *Banner of the South* (Augusta), March 20, 1869.
183. *Ibid.*, September 25, 1869. For Father Ryan's best known poems on the Confederacy, see John Tracy Ellis, ed., *Documents of American Catholic History* (Milwaukee, 1956), 395–400.
184. "The African in the United States," *Southern Review*, XIV (January, 1874), 152.
185. "The Negroes in the Gulf States," *International Review*, I (September, 1874), 581, 582, 583.

editorial on "Political Principles," he argued that "no sensible man, not blinded by political prejudice and religious fanaticism, will deny that the political control of the Southern States should be in the hands of the white people."[186]

If white churchmen of the South wanted no Negro equality in politics, they wanted it even less in the more sensitive area of social relations, where their supreme taboo of "social equality" was more subject to infringement. While slavery lasted, the South had little need to draw the color line by law; for masters could regulate the conduct of their bondsmen, and the social folkways were usually sufficient to determine the free Negro's public behavior.[187] With the abolition of slavery, however, Jim Crow laws spread rapidly in the former Confederacy. Legalized segregation had long existed in the free states, but by the end of the Civil War that system had begun to be dismantled in some places.[188] In the South, on the other hand, Jim Crow steadily expanded his realm. By November, 1865, Mississippi had enacted a law forbidding railroads to allow blacks to ride in first class cars reserved for white passengers.[189] "Even before the Radicals came into power in South Carolina in 1868," noted Joel Williamson, "native whites had already defined a color line in government-supported institutions, on common carriers, in places of public accommodation and amusement, and, of course, in private organizations."[190] A similar racial pattern was emerging in all other former slave states.[191]

Yet just when that racial pattern was getting well established,

186. *New Orleans Christian Advocate*, April 16, 1874; July 20, 1876. For similar anti-Negro sentiments, see *ibid.*, February 18, 1875; October 25, 1877; October 30, 1879.
187. In a few urban centers of the ante-bellum South, free blacks were segregated by law. Richard C. Wade, *Slavery in the Cities: The South 1820–1860* (New York, 1964), 266–71.
188. James M. McPherson, "Abolitionists and the Civil Rights Act of 1875," *Journal of American History*, LII (December, 1965), 495, 498.
189. Vernon L. Wharton, *The Negro in Mississippi, 1865–1890* (Harper Torchbooks ed., New York, 1965), 230.
190. *After Slavery: The Negro in South Carolina During Reconstruction, 1861–1877* (Chapel Hill, N.C., 1965), 280.
191. Ever since C. Vann Woodward first published *The Strange Career of Jim Crow* (1955), historians have been debating the question as to the origin and spread of racial segregation, *de facto* and *de jure*, in the South. For a review of the argument up to 1968, see Joel Williamson, ed., *The Origins of Segregation* (New York, 1968). The latest reflections on the controversy are in Woodward, *American Counterpoint: Slavery and Racism in the North-South Dialogue* (Boston, 1971), 243–60.

Charles Sumner on May 13, 1870, introduced a bill in the Senate (S. 916) designed to deal it a deadly blow. The bill prohibited racial discrimination by common carriers, licensed theaters, hotels, restaurants, juries, public schools, church institutions, and cemetery associations legally incorporated.[192] The enactment of this measure, its author believed, would be the crowning work of reconstruction.[193] During the next three and a half years the valiant crusader for racial equality employed every resource at his command to secure the passage of his bill, but he was outmaneuvered by his opponents, including Republicans as well as Democrats.[194] Sumner died on March 11, 1874, but with virtually his last breath he pleaded for the enactment of "my bill, the civil-rights bill."[195] In February of the next year, Congress finally passed the late Senator's bill, but not until its heart, the school clause, had been removed. Signed by President Grant, the Civil Rights Act of 1875 thus became law on March 1.

During the long controversy over the Sumner bill, key clergymen in the South passionately assailed its provisions, especially that prohibiting segregated public schools. For years they had criticized abolitionist missionaries for trying to mix blacks and whites in schools and churches, and they were absolutely bent upon preventing this pattern in the emerging system of public schools. Typically, Jeremiah Jeter vigorously attacked racially mixed schools on the ground that they would result in "mongrelizing" the races. If there was no way to prevent such schools, he favored no schools at all. "Greatly as we would dread barbarism," he wrote, "we prefer it infinitely to *mongrelization*." Although confessing his antipathy toward mixed schools, the Virginian denied that it was prompted by prejudice. Instead, it was the expression of "an instinct, divinely implanted" to maintain a gulf between blacks and whites. "God has made the difference, and human governments should not ig-

---

192. *Congressional Globe*, 41st Cong., 2d sess., 3434.
193. David Donald, *Charles Sumner and the Rights of Man* (New York, 1970), 531.
194. Alfred H. Kelly, "The Congressional Controversy Over School Segregation, 1867–1875," *American Historical Review*, LXIV (April, 1959), 546–51; McPherson, "Abolitionists and the Civil Rights Act of 1875," *Journal of American History*, LII, 500–506.
195. Donald, *Charles Sumner and the Rights of Man*, 586.

nore it."[196] Linus Parker of New Orleans agreed essentially with Jeter. The fact that his own city was operating mixed schools filled him with rage. "The purpose to Africanize our schools, and to insult and degrade the white people, is evident," he growled. Noting that J. C. Hartzell, a northern Methodist missionary and editor of the *Southwestern Christian Advocate* (New Orleans), was a member of the city school board, Parker commented: "He and Bishop [Gilbert] Haven are the champions of miscegenation and negro social equality."[197] Even the Atlanta *Methodist Advocate*, a journal of northern Methodism, joined white southerners in combating the proposed civil rights bill. The editor, Erasmus Q. Fuller, conceded that blacks had "not been treated justly in multitudes of cases," but at the same time he in effect told them to be content with their own separate schools, at least for the present. Yielding to the phobia of "mongrelization," he, like Jeter, declared that "it would be better for every public school in the South to be discontinued forever than that the children of both races should be . . . thrown promiscuously together through all the land at this time."[198]

Southern whites, including ministers and educators, were virtually unanimous in their contention that the people of the former slave states would abolish the public schools before they would maintain them on a racially mixed basis. "An Act of Congress requiring the South poles of all magnets to attract each other, would not be a whit more absurd than one requiring education to be conducted on a race-mixture in the late slave states," said William H. Ruffner, superintendent of public instruction in Virginia. Were Congress to enact a civil rights bill requiring mixed schools, the South's young public school system "would inevitably be destroyed." All that blacks "may justly claim," argued Ruffner, is that their own schools "shall *be equal* in all respects to those provided for the whites." He therefore hoped that "profound thinkers may yet rebuke the vulgar spirit of miscegenation in all its forms"

196. *Religious Herald*, January 8, 1874. See also *ibid.*, October 8, 1874; January 7, 1875. Jeter's anti-Negro sentiments were widely shared in Virginia. Charles E. Wynes, *Race Relations in Virginia, 1870–1902* (Charlottesville, Va., 1961), 123–25.
197. *New Orleans Christian Advocate*, September 23, 1875.
198. *Methodist Advocate*, July 3, 1874. It should be noted that the other southern newspaper of northern Methodism, the *Southwestern Christian Advocate*, unwaveringly backed the civil rights bill and staunchly advocated interracial public schools. See *ibid.*, April 20, May 7, and June 18, 1874.

and evolve a system of public schools by which to preserve "the separate races of man in their purity."[199] John Q. Eaton, Jr., United States commissioner of education and former chaplain in the Union army, also doubted that the white South would tolerate nonsegregated schools.[200] Even more convinced of this fact was the distinguished Baptist clergyman, Barnas Sears, former president of Brown University and currently general agent of the Peabody Education Fund, a trust established in 1867 by George Peabody, a native of Massachusetts, for the benefit of southern education. From the outset he had opposed efforts to mix blacks and whites in the South's public schools. In 1870, for instance, he wrote Robert C. Winthrop, chairman of the Peabody board of trustees, saying: "South Carolina, like Louisiana, is afflicted with the curse of trying to have mixed schools."[201] During the later stages of the congressional debate over the civil rights bill, he spent much time in Washington, seeking to persuade key sponsors of that bill to delete altogether, or at least soften, its mandatory mixed-school clause. Nor did he fail to solicit the help of President Grant, the most prestigious trustee of the Peabody Fund.[202]

These multiple pressures—southern and extra-southern—produced a compliant response in Congress; the Civil Rights Act of 1875, as already observed, omitted all reference to public schools. It thus indirectly gave aid and comfort to the already vocal advocates of the "separate but equal" doctrine. As for the emasculated Act, it was stillborn; and even at that was soon to be pronounced unconstitutional by the Supreme Court. In the meantime, Jeremiah Jeter doubtless reflected the dominant sentiment of the white South when he said that it was "a measure with little meaning, little worth."[203]

199. "The Co-Education of the White and Colored Races," *Scribner's Monthly*, VIII (May, 1874), 86, 89, 90. The *Methodist Advocate* (Atlanta) of April 29, 1874, reprinted this essay with full approval of Ruffner's argument for segregated public schools.
200. Walter J. Fraser, "John Eaton, Jr., Radical Republican," *Tennessee Historical Quarterly*, XXV (Fall, 1966), 239–60. Prior to becoming U.S. commissioner of education, Eaton had established a system of public schools in Tennessee.
201. Quoted in Jabez L. M. Curry, *A Brief Sketch of George Peabody, and a History of the Peabody Education Fund Through Thirty Years* (Cambridge, Mass.; 1898), 62.
202. *Ibid.*, 64–65.
203. *Religious Herald*, March 11, 1875.

Chapter VI

THE TRIUMPH OF RACIAL ORTHODOXY

By 1875 the Democrats—the self-styled "redeemers"—were in control of every former Confederate state except Florida, Louisiana, and South Carolina. In the elections of 1876 they claimed victory in those three states, but the Republicans—a combination of carpetbaggers, scalawags, and blacks—disputed that claim. Under the famous Compromise of 1877, however, President Rutherford B. Hayes withdrew the remaining federal troops from South Carolina and Louisiana, and the Democrats swiftly "redeemed" the rest of the old Confederacy.[1] This marked the end of reconstruction and the beginning of a policy of conciliation toward the white South. The Hayes policy was especially significant in two respects: first, it accepted the principle of "home rule," for which state rights southerners had been clamoring; second, it entrusted the freedman's future to his former master. This "new departure" gladdened the heart of every old rebel. "Fervently do I pray . . . for the success of that policy of pacification so wisely begun by our noble President," wrote Jabez L. M. Curry, Southern Baptist preacher-educator and former Confederate congressman.[2] So prayed all other white southern churchmen.

While Hayes felt it imperative to pacify southern whites, he hoped that his friendly gesture would induce their political leaders to uphold the freedman's rights in terms of the Fourteenth and Fifteenth Amendments of the Constitution. He was encouraged in this hope by the fact that the redeemer governors of South Carolina and Louisiana, Wade Hampton and Francis T. Nicholls, had promised him, prior to his removal of federal troops, that they would

---

1. For an authoritative account of the Compromise of 1877, see C. Vann Woodward, *Reunion and Reaction: The Compromise of 1877 and the End of Reconstruction* (rev. ed., New York, 1956).

2. *Independent* (New York), January 3, 1878. See also *ibid.*, April 4, 1878.

enforce the constitutional rights of blacks. Pledges of support on the part of some leading Negroes gave him additional confidence in his policy. Among them were two bishops of the African Methodist Episcopal Church, with jurisdictional responsibilities in seven southern states.[3] In September, 1877, the President, with a party which included Wade Hampton, took a nineteen-day tour through Kentucky, Tennessee, Georgia, and Virginia that reinforced his faith in the correctness of his southern strategy. "Received everywhere heartily," he recorded in his diary. "The country is again one and united! I am very happy to be able to feel that the course taken has turned out so well."[4]

Yet by the fall of 1878, as the elections proved, that policy had been shattered upon the rock of political events. The redeemer Democrats had not only ousted numerous Republican officeholders but had flagrantly violated the constitutional rights of blacks. That was notoriously true in South Carolina and Louisiana, the very states expressly pledged to protect Negro rights. Hayes himself acknowledged in his diary on November 12 that in those two states, "and perhaps in some of the other cotton States," fraud, intimidation, and "violence of the most atrocious character" had been the means of depriving black citizens of their suffrage rights.[5]

This miscarriage of justice came as no surprise to Laura Towne, a Philadelphia Quaker who had taught freedmen on St. Helena Island, South Carolina, since 1862, and who conducted Penn School there until her death in 1901.[6] From the first she distrusted the Hayes policy. "I have been in raging indignation at Hayes," she wrote in her diary on April 15, 1877. "I hope we have not another Buchanan in the President's chair, but I fear we have. He is too easy and ready to think well of everybody."[7] Nor did the fraud and violence perpetrated in the election of 1878 in the least surprise Bishop Gilbert Haven of Atlanta. Almost a month before election day

3. *Ibid.*, March 29, 1877. See also Vincent P. De Santis, *Republicans Face the Southern Question: The New Departure Years, 1877–1897* (Baltimore, 1959), 127–31.
4. Charles R. Williams, ed., *The Diary and Letters of Rutherford B. Hayes*, III (Columbus, Ohio, 1924), 443.
5. *Ibid.*, 510. See also Stanley P. Hirshson, *Farewell to the Bloody Shirt: Northern Republicans & the Southern Negro, 1877–1893* (Bloomington, Ind., 1962), 47–49, 52–53.
6. Willie Lee Rose, *Rehearsal For Reconstruction: The Port Royal Experiment* (Indianapolis, 1964), 76–78, 233, 373, 405.
7. Rupert S. Holland, ed., *Letters and Diary of Laura Towne. Written From the Sea Islands of South Carolina, 1862–1884* (Cambridge, Mass., 1912), 61.

he anticipated the outcome, and charged it up to growing northern indifference toward the freedmen. The southern states, he complained, had for years been increasingly "given up to the shot-gun by the cowardice of the North." He viewed the Hayes policy as an expression of the northern retreat. The President began his administration by putting "a secessionist" (David M. Key) in his cabinet and "surrendering" South Carolina and Louisiana "into the hands of their enemies." Not long thereafter "he calls the chief of these rebels [Wade Hampton] to go with him through the South." The vote on election day was thus predictable.[8]

Hayes was clearly unrealistic in believing that his compromising policy would persuade the new Democratic leaders to grant equal suffrage to a race that for two and a half centuries had been proclaimed inferior to the white race. Besides, by then those leaders viewed the policy of pacification less as a gesture of fraternity than as a sign of the North's waning interest in the freedmen. They correctly surmised that they would run no serious risk of arousing punitive action against themselves by robbing the black man of his ballot. While in his annual message to Congress Hayes did denounce the late election irregularities, neither he nor Congress took effectual action to prevent their recurrence.[9] Hayes's successors in the White House during the rest of the century did no better. There was, it is true, an occasional outburst of bloody shirt rhetoric, but blacks were not its beneficiaries. The white South meanwhile moved apace to deprive the minority race of its civil and political rights. And just as they had done during slavery and the reconstruction era, clerical spokesmen gave aid and comfort to this anti-Negro movement. Their most distinctive contribution was to articulate a racial creed as a bulwark of white supremacy. Once that creed won the status of sacrosanct orthodoxy, woe to that man, black or white, who willfully violated it.

I

Before giving attention to the growth of racial orthodoxy, it must be made clear that there were important extra-southern factors

---

8. *Independent,* October 10, 1878.
9. Hirshson, *Farewell to the Bloody Shirt,* 50–51, 53–54.

which helped to generate a social climate favorable to this version of anti-Negro thought.

For one thing, many influential northerners had come to doubt the value of Negro suffrage. This was true of Washington Gladden, one of America's leading apostles of social Christianity. "The ballot was given to the Negro," he wrote in 1876, "in the expectation that it would protect him, educate him, and make him an element of strength, rather than of weakness, in the state. Neither of these results has been realized." While not opposed to Negro suffrage in principle, he held that "a very large share" of the enfranchised blacks were no better qualified to cast a ballot than was a two-year-old child to use an open jackknife. As a result, "they have placed in office rascals who have robbed the state."[10] Henry C. Bowen, editor of the New York *Independent*, shared Gladden's sentiment. "Four millions of ignorant and imbruted serfs," he declared, "cannot be made into voters and officeholders by an edict, without grave abuses of the political franchise."[11] After personally investigating the Mississippi election of 1875, James Redpath, a former abolitionist crusader, wrote a devastating criticism of Republican operations in that state. "We [Republicans] ought never to have given the Negro a vote," he confessed, "or we ought to have forced him to learn to read and built a school for him in every township. He has shown that he is not fit to rule in Mississippi. . . . Fellow Republicans, it is idle to denounce the South. We are to blame."[12] According to Redpath, "sentimental abolitionists" were as responsible for the sad condition of Mississippi as the "fiendish Negro-haters." "The blacks were ruined as good citizens by the chronic prattle about their rights, and they were never roused to a noble manhood by instruction as to their duties."[13] William Graham Sumner, professor of social science at Yale and a former clergyman in the Protes-

10. *Independent*, September 7, 1876. See also Gladden, "Safeguards of the Suffrage," *Century*, XXXVII (February, 1889), 621–22; Gladden, *Recollections* (Boston, 1909), 179.
11. *Independent*, February 4, 1875.
12. *Ibid.*, August 3, 1876.
13. *Ibid.*, August 31, 1876. Democratic papers in the South were jubilant over Redpath's two articles in the *Independent* and made effective use of them in discrediting Republicanism with respect to Negro suffrage. To offset their influence, he published a documented report on "The Mississippi Plan" in which he showed that in the election of 1875 the Mississippi Democrats practiced fraud and violence on an appalling scale. *Ibid.*, September 28, 1876.

tant Episcopal Church, branded southern reconstruction as a *"reductio ad absurdum"* from the standpoint of classical Democratic principles. "The demands which are now made on the South," he charged, "really amount to asking that civilization shall be voluntarily subjected to barbarism."[14]

Another factor tending to increase white racism in the South was a burgeoning pride in Anglo-Saxonism among Americans in general. The influx of non-English stocks following the war undoubtedly encouraged its expression. In May, 1882, Congress passed an act excluding from America all Chinese laborers, both skilled and unskilled, for the next decade. The same act provided "that hereafter no State court or court of the United States shall admit Chinese to citizenship."[15] Anglo-Saxon racism surfaced stridently in the wake of the Spanish-American War over the question of whether the multiracial peoples of the insular territory ceded to the United States were to be granted the full rights of citizenship with white Americans. Even liberal journals, such as the *Nation*, were unwilling to admit these "inferior races" to political equality.

During the last two decades of the century, some prominent clergymen caught the Anglo-Saxon fever. One of the most vocal of this group was Congregationalist Josiah Strong, general secretary of the American division of the Evangelical Alliance from 1886 to 1898. Like Washington Gladden, he preached what in his time was called the "social gospel."[16] In his *Our Country* (1885), of which one hundred and thirty thousand copies were sold within a five-year period, he devoted an entire chapter to glorifying the virtues and predicting the manifest destiny of the Anglo-Saxon race. He even argued that the American type of Anglo-Saxon man was decidedly superior to that in England.[17] The American breed, he prophesied, would eventually enter upon a world-conquering mission that would not end until it had "Anglo-Saxonized mankind." While

14. "The History and Practice of Elections," *Princeton Review*, 4th ser., VI (July, 1880), 29. Sumner was a member of a special committee of the Republican National Committee that investigated the disputed election in Louisiana in 1876.

15. Henry S. Commager, ed., *Documents of American History* (two volumes in one, 7th ed., New York, 1963), Document No. 307.

16. Dorothea R. Muller, "The Social Philosophy of Josiah Strong: Social Christianity and American Progressivism," *Church History*, XXVIII (June, 1959), 183–201.

17. *Our Country: Its Possible Future and its Present Crisis* (rev. ed., New York, 1891), 216–17, 219–20.

Strong did not hold that the "inferior races" to be encountered in this mission should be liquidated, he nevertheless was confident that they could not survive the resulting competitive struggle.[18] According to him, America's imperial thrust into the islands of the Caribbean and Pacific waters was surely a fulfillment of Anglo-Saxonism's divinely appointed destiny.[19]

Much of *Our Country* was serialized in southern newspapers and journals. Although Strong scarcely mentioned the black American, southerners were well aware of the implications of his Anglo-Saxon dogma. Reviewing the book in a leading theological journal of the South, Robert A. Webb, a Presbyterian minister, expressed the wish that it "were in the hands of every American."[20]

A third factor that facilitated the subjugation of blacks to the white South was a series of United States Supreme Court decisions.[21] Three of those decisions were especially significant in reflecting a waning concern to achieve racial equality. In 1883 the court invalidated the Civil Rights Act of 1875, contending, among other things, "that no countenance of authority" for its passage could be found "in either the Thirteenth or Fourteenth Amendment of the Constitution."[22] This decision elated southern whites, even though they had treated the Act as a dead letter from the first. Negro spokesmen, on the other hand, bitterly attacked the court's decision. Henry M. Turner, a bishop of the African Methodist Episcopal Church, called it "far more abominable . . . than the Dred Scott decision."[23] The Supreme Court, in *Plessy v. Ferguson* (1896), denied "that the enforced separation of the two races stamps the colored race with a badge of inferiority." On the other hand, it contended that legislation was "powerless to eradicate racial in-

---

18. *Ibid.*, 222-23, 225. See also Josiah Strong, *The New Era or the Coming Kingdom* (New York, 1893), 79-80.

19. Josiah Strong, *Expansion Under New World Conditions* (New York, 1900), 208-9, 212-13, 301-2. See Dorothea R. Muller, "Josiah Strong and American Nationalism: A Reevaluation," *Journal of American History*, LIII (December, 1966), 487-503.

20. *Presbyterian Quarterly*, I (October, 1887), 390.

21. Robert J. Harris, *The Quest For Equality: The Constitution, Congress and the Supreme Court* (Baton Rouge, 1960), Chap. 4.

22. Commager, *Documents of American History*, Document No. 292.

23. *Christian Recorder* (Philadelphia), January 17, 1884. See also Henry Turner, *Civil Rights: The Outrage of the Supreme Court of the United States upon the Black Man* (Philadelphia, 1889); August Meier, *Negro Thought in America, 1880-1915* (Ann Arbor, Mich., 1966), 71.

stincts or to abolish distinctions based upon physical differences." By thus sanctioning the doctrine of "separate but equal," the court encouraged the South to universalize the pattern of racial segregation.[24] The third decision was rendered with respect to the so-called Mississippi Plan. In 1890 Mississippi adopted a new constitution with several built-in devices, including a poll tax, a literacy test, and an "understanding" clause, all of which were designed to reduce the number of Negro voters without ostensibly violating the Fifteenth Amendment of the Constitution.[25] Eight years later the Supreme Court, in *Williams v. Mississippi* (1898), passed favorably upon this astutely framed plan, and thereby opened the way for the wholesale disfranchisement of blacks and not a few poor whites throughout the old Confederacy.[26]

In sum, then, at least three factors—northern disenchantment with Negro suffrage, waxing Anglo-Saxonism, and restrictive judicial interpretations of the Fourteenth and Fifteenth Amendments of the Constitution—fostered a southern climate favorable to the triumph of the dogma of Negro inferiority.

II

During this period, white religious leaders in the South seemed increasingly desirous of being soundly orthodox in their racial faith. Evidently racial heresy was becoming more damaging to clerical reputations than theological heterodoxy. Sensitivity in this respect was clearly reflected in a significant editorial published in the *Christian Index* in March, 1883, under the caption, "Are We Orthodox on the Race Question?" Its author, Henry Holcombe Tucker, was a highly distinguished minister-educator of the Southern Baptist denomination, and he had formerly served as president of Mercer University and of the University of Georgia. The editorial may have been prompted by a rumor that Tucker was not "safe" on the Negro question. At any rate, he articulated with care

24. Commager, *Documents of American History*, Document No. 343. In *Brown v. Board of Education of Topeka* (1954), the Supreme Court reversed the Plessy ruling. *Ibid.*, Document No. 617.
25. These disfranchising devices are critically analyzed in V. O. Key, *Southern Politics in State and Nation* (Caravelle ed., New York, 1949), 537–38.
26. C. Vann Woodward, *Origins of the New South* (Baton Rouge, 1951), Chap. 12; John Hope Franklin, *From Slavery to Freedom: A History of Negro Americans* (3d ed., New York, 1967), 338–41.

what he styled his "Confession of Faith." After having predicated "the original unity of the human race," he went on to say:

> We do not believe that "all men are created equal," as the Declaration of Independence declares them to be; nor that they will ever become equal in this world. . . . We think that our own race is incomparably superior to any other. . . . As to the Negro, we do not know where to place him; perhaps not at the bottom of the list, but certainly not near the top. We believe that fusion of two or more of these races would be an injury to all, and a still greater injury to posterity. We think that the race-line is providential, and that . . . any . . . great intermingling [of races] must have its origin in sin.[27]

"We think that we are orthodox," concluded the editor. "If we are not so, we should be glad for some one to point out the heresy."

No one seems to have questioned that statement of Tucker's racial faith. Indeed, there was no ground upon which to do so, because he had articulated virtually every white southerner's belief. The key tenets of the Georgian's *confessio fidei* may be framed in four affirmations: (1) human races are unequal, and will remain unequal to the end of history; (2) the Negro is far inferior to the Caucasian; (3) the racial fusion or amalgamation of black and white peoples is injurious to both races; (4) free social intermingling of blacks and whites "must have its origin in sin." That creed undergirded the South's expanding system of racial segregation.

Henry Tucker's racial creed bore essential continuity with that of the ante-bellum white southerner. But after slavery was abolished, it became more imperative, because the white man could no longer employ the power of ownership to keep freedmen in "their place," and thus had to provide social sanctions (buttressed by laws) to produce the same result. In order to make the social sanctions do the work of the old slavemaster, white dissent had to be held to a minimum regardless of the cost to society in terms of freedom of thought and action. This explains in large measure why post-bellum whites became such zealous defenders of racial orthodoxy.

Racial orthodoxy, as herein understood, includes both a mod-

27. *Christian Index* (Atlanta), March 22, 1883. Tucker's racial creed was that of virtually all his fellow Southern Baptists. Rufus B. Spain, *At Ease in Zion: Social History of Southern Baptists, 1865–1900* (Nashville, 1967), 113–19.

erate and a rigid or hard-line type of belief. Both types subscribed to the dogma of Negro inferiority—the cardinal doctrine of orthodoxy—but beyond that they varied considerably. The moderate, for example, had more faith in the growth potentiality of the black race than did the hard-line believer. Some moderates tended to concede, as against their more rigid brethren, that the black man might, in the far distant future, be able to narrow the intellectual gulf between himself and the white man. They were therefore more concerned to provide the Negro with educational facilities than was the hard-liner. Other variations will appear in the course of our discussion. The leading adherents of racial orthodoxy were far too numerous to be considered as a whole, but those selected for attention are representative of their particular wing of racial doctrine.

One of the boldest advocates of hard-line racial orthodoxy was Robert Lewis Dabney of Virginia. Following a thirty-year professorship at Union Theological Seminary (1853–83), he taught mental and moral philosophy at the University of Texas for eleven years. To the very end of his life, the old school Calvinist argued that the Negro was an inferior member of the human race whom God had appointed to play a subservient role in a white-ruled church and state. As observed in our last chapter, he flatly refused to sanction the ecclesiastical equality of black Presbyterians on the claim that they were an inferior type of man, even though created in the image of God. When, in 1882, the General Assembly of his own denomination voted to establish fraternal relations with the Presbyterian Church in the U.S.A., Dabney bitterly assailed that action on racial as well as doctrinal grounds. Fraternal relations, he warned, could well lead to ultimate "fusion with Northern Presbyterians," with the result that white southern Presbyterians would once again be involved "in the ecclesiastical amalgamation with negroes." This would then mean "accepting negro presbyters to rule white churches and judge white ladies; a step which would seal the moral and doctrinal corruption of our church in the South, and be a direct step towards that final perdition of Southern society, domestic amalgamation."[28]

---

28. "The Atlanta Assembly and Fraternal Relations," in C. R. Vaughan, ed., *Discussions By Robert L. Dabney, D.D., LL.D.*, II (Richmond, 1891), 524. This article

Dabney was extremely hostile to granting blacks political equality. Negro suffrage, he wrote in 1876, was a "fatal innovation," which, if allowed to continue, would "destroy both American liberty and civilization."[29] Recurring to the same subject in an address given at Hampden-Sydney College in 1883 on "The New South," he denounced black suffrage as the "last extreme of political madness."[30] One of his major objections to the political equality of Negroes was that this "would prepare the way for social equality," and thus open the door to racial amalgamation. "It is only our pride which hides the danger from our eyes," he contended.[31] The true remedy for the situation in Virginia, said Dabney, would be an immediate repeal of that part of the Underwood Constitution—ratified in 1869—which provided for Negro suffrage. Conceding, however, that this was practically impossible, he urged white citizens to write into the Underwood document such property and literacy qualifications for voting as "would exclude the great multitude of Negroes."[32]

True to his theory of Negro inferiority, Dabney sharply opposed Virginia's system of public schools for blacks. Educated Negroes, he argued, would not be content to continue as manual laborers, and thus white people would be forced into drudgery. "I do not see any humanity in taking the Negro out of the place for which nature has fitted him, at the cost of thrusting my own kindred down into it." But the professor opposed Negro schools on social as well as economic grounds. He argued that if these schools should result in elevating the black race socially, they would be a menace to the white race, because they would "only prepare the way for that abhorred fate, *amalgamation*."[33]

---

was originally published in the *South-Western Presbyterian* (New Orleans), August 3, 1882.

29. "The Negro and the Common School," *Southern Planter and Farmer*, XXXVII (April, 1876), 253.

30. *The New South* (Raleigh, 1883), 8.

31. "The Negro and the Common School," *Southern Planter and Farmer*, XXXVII, 258–59.

32. *Ibid.*, 259. In 1876 Virginia did actually ratify several amendments to the Underwood Constitution whereby black voting was drastically reduced. Charles E. Wynes, *Race Relations in Virginia, 1870–1902* (Charlottesville, Va., 1961), 13–14.

33. "The Negro and the Common School," *Southern Planter and Farmer*, XXXVII, 258.

Similarly rigid in his racial faith was R. N. Sledd of Virginia, who served many leading southern Methodist churches in the Old Dominion. From 1878 to 1898, he was a delegate to every General Conference of his communion. At the zenith of his professional career he outlined his racial theory in a notably candid essay.[34] "Through all the ages," Sledd unabashedly claimed, "the Caucasian has held the highest place, and the negro the lowest in the racial scale."[35] Whereas the former had "ever held the mastery of the world," the latter had "achieved nothing" in any department of human enterprise that entitled him "to a single chapter in the world's history." The Virginia Methodist held out no hope that the black man would ever rise to the mental and moral level of Caucasian man. On the other hand, the white man would never descend to the level of the black man. "He will suffer extinction with infinitely better grace than he will consent to be accounted no better than a negro."[36]

In Sledd's opinion, legislation had done nothing toward creating a spirit of racial harmony; on the contrary, it had "deepened the distrust and intensified the antipathy" between blacks and whites. The race problem itself was largely a product of misguided or partisan legislation, especially with respect to Negro suffrage. It was well enough to grant freedom to the Negro, but when to that was immediately added his right to vote, both races were injured.[37]

While Sledd did not, like Dabney, decry Negro education, he doubted that blacks were capable of a high degree of intellectual development. Nor was he hopeful that the public school would ever fit them for the duties of citizenship. So far at least, the common school had failed either to instill in them right moral principles or to eradicate their many vicious traits and criminal tendencies. But even if it should finally be demonstrated that Negroes were capable of a high degree of learning, the white man would still feel himself superior to them. "So far from bringing them into each other's embrace as equals, the tendency of such a condition of

---

34. "A Southern View of the Race Question," *Quarterly Review of the Methodist Episcopal Church, South*, XXXI (July, 1890), 327-44.
35. *Ibid.*, 327.
36. *Ibid.*, 332.
37. *Ibid.*, 333-36.

things would be, without some powerful counteracting influence, to deepen and widen the breach and precipitate a conflict for racial supremacy." [38]

An even more dismal hard-line view of the Negro was taken by Sledd's fellow Methodist, William M. Leftwich, then a member of the Tennessee Annual Conference.[39] He resented "the insane clamor for negro equality," and argued that neither constitutional amendments nor any other type of legislation could overcome "race instincts" and bring blacks and whites together upon a basis of social and political equality. No matter how well qualified the Negro might be for the higher professions, his color would deny his entrance upon them among whites, and "would forever keep him not only at the lowest place in the social scale, but in marked inferiority to his white brethren." [40]

The Tennessee preacher took keen delight in recalling the failure of the northern Methodist missionaries to maintain racially mixed churches and conferences in the postwar South. They had pleaded earnestly for racial equality, but in the end "race instincts proved to be stronger than the visionary theory of equality," and that theory "went to the wall." Leftwich rejoiced over the failure of the experiment, for he held that it was impossible to practice equality without racial amalgamation.[41]

Leftwich did not believe that blacks and whites could ever dwell together in peace with equality of civil and political rights, and he advocated colonizing the "inferior" race in Africa. He noted with great joy that Bishop Henry M. Turner of the African Methodist Episcopal Church also favored this solution of the racial problem. So the Tennessee churchman urged the federal government to use the treasury's surplus funds to establish a line of steamers between this country and Africa, and offer incentives to educated Negroes to go there. Within a few years, he prophesied, a tide of emigration would set in that would not only bless the Dark Continent but also

---

38. *Ibid.*, 338. Sledd never explained what he meant by "some powerful counteracting influence."
39. "The Race Problem in the South," *Quarterly Review of the Methodist Episcopal Church, South,* XXX (April, 1889), 86–96.
40. *Ibid.*, 86–87.
41. *Ibid.*, 92–94.

relieve America of its burning domestic problem. "God speed the day!" exclaimed the colonizationist.[42]

One of the foremost southern Methodist exponents of a rigid type of racial orhodoxy was Richard H. Rivers, who, when the Civil War broke out, was serving as professor of moral philosophy at Wesleyan College in Florence, Alabama. His *Elements of Moral Philosophy*, first published in 1859, was his communion's standard work in ethics. Revised in 1871, its widespread denominational use is indicated by the fact that between 1887 and 1890 it was reprinted at least three times.[43]

Inasmuch as slavery had been abolished, the revised edition replaced the chapter on human bondage with one designed to indicate the white man's proper attitude toward freedmen. The duties of whites to blacks, explained the author, "are no longer the duties of masters to slaves. They are, however, the duties of superiors to inferiors."[44] The ante-bellum tradition of racial caste was thus perpetuated under new terminology.

Like many other clergymen of his generation, Rivers maintained that the Caucasian race was superior to all other races of mankind, and that it would remain superior "until the ages shall cease." With equal assurance he asserted that the inferiority of the Negro was "so marked" and had "continued so long" that there was "no more prospect of its being removed than of the Ethiopian's changing his skin."[45] He also said that when separated from whites, blacks tended to revert to the barbarism of Africa. It was the duty of whites, Rivers added, to endeavor to prevent this reversion. Yet that duty did "not include social equality," for social equality "implies intermarriage, and must bring with it all the horrible consequences of miscegenation."[46] It was the churchman's fear of social equality that prompted his opposition to racially inclusive schools. Far from uplifting

---

42. *Ibid.*, 94–96. For a good account of Bishop Henry M. Turner as a colonizationist, see Edwin S. Redkey, *Black Exodus: Black Nationalist and Back-to-Africa Movements, 1890–1910* (New Haven, 1969), Chaps. 2, 8.

43. The *Elements* served not only as a college textbook in Methodist institutions, but it also became a regular part of the annual conference course of study for ministerial candidates by action of the General Conference of the Methodist Episcopal Church, South. *The Doctrine and Discipline of the Methodist Episcopal Church, South* (Nashville, 1882), 348.

44. *Elements of Moral Philosophy* (2d ed., Nashville, 1887), 330.

45. *Ibid.*, 330–31.

46. *Ibid.*, 333–34.

the "inferior race," mixed schools "would serve to degrade the superior."[47]

Richard Rivers lived until 1894, but he held fast to the dogma of Negro inferiority. In 1889, as editor of the Louisville *Central Methodist*, he reaffirmed his traditional view, saying that as long as the two races lived together on American soil the black man "must occupy the position of inferiority," that "Ham must be subservient to Japheth." If peace and harmony could not be preserved on this basis, then the editor was for colonizing Negroes in some section of the nation's unoccupied territory, just as had been done with the Indians.[48]

By the dawn of the new century, the two races were more deeply estranged from each other than they had been at any time since the reconstruction era. An aggressive white South had drawn a color line straight through society, consigning the Negro to an inferior caste. The ballot was fast becoming exclusively a white man's privilege. Racial equality in the dual system of public education was a myth.[49] Lynching remained a commonplace, and the victims were sometimes burned alive.[50] Since the late 1890's race riots had become more frequent; and, as John Hope Franklin observed, they proved more widely terrifying than individual lynchings, for they exposed entire Negro communities to bloodshed.[51] Rabid racism had become highly profitable to political opportunists such as Ben Tillman of South Carolina and James K. Vardaman of Mississippi.

As might be expected, this emotion-laden racial climate emboldened apostles of hard-line orthodoxy. Such was true of John W. Stagg, who served prominent Presbyterian churches in Tennessee, North Carolina, and Alabama. During his ministry at Charlotte, North Carolina, he addressed the Unity Club of New Bedford,

---

47. *Ibid.*, 337.
48. *Central Methodist*, January 19, 1889.
49. Louis R. Harlan, *Separate and Unequal. Public School Campaigns and Racism in the Southern Seaboard States, 1901–1915* (Chapel Hill, N.C., 1958), 11–18 and *passim*.
50. Arthur F. Raper, *The Tragedy of Lynching* (Chapel Hill, N.C., 1933), 25–27, 480–83; Ray Stannard Baker, *Following the Color Line* (1908; Harper Torchbooks ed., New York, 1964), Chap. 9; NAACP, *Thirty Years of Lynching in the United States, 1889–1918* (New York, 1919).
51. *From Slavery to Freedom*, 440–44. See also Rayford W. Logan, *The Betrayal of the Negro: From Rutherford B. Hayes to Woodrow Wilson* (New York, 1965), 349–52. (Originally published in 1954 as *The Negro in American Life and Thought: The Nadir, 1877–1901*.)

Massachusetts, on the "Race Problem in the South," and presented a brutal view of black Americans.[52] The "best friend" of Negroes, he announced at the outset, was he who recognized that they were "not equal" to the whites. No power of man could ever make the two races equal for the reason that "a negro is a negro and a white man a white man."[53]

Stagg directed much of his anti-Negro tirade against the Fifteenth Amendment, charging that its enactment was "the most egregious wrong ever perpetrated in the history of the Republic." That amendment, by enfranchising the freedmen, had "destroyed the white man's authority" over the Negro, because it led the latter to think that he was equal to his former master. As a result, the Negro's attitude toward the white man changed from kindness to hate, from respect to contempt, from reverence to insult. "In a word, the Negro was brutalized."[54] For the black race's own good, the lecturer urged, the nation should repeal the Fifteenth Amendment. Implicitly conceding, however, that this was unlikely, he heartily favored the massive disfranchisement of Negro southerners.[55]

The clergyman boasted that in his own city and county whites alone were the rulers and determiners of racial justice. The Negro "does not sit on the jury, and members of his race . . . are tried by a jury of the white race; and, if the property rights of any colored man are in jeopardy, men of the white race exclusively determine what his rights are." The white rulers were "not only merciful and kind to the black man," but were "absolutely just towards him."[56]

John Stagg's idea of justice and mercy was, as he frankly admitted, dictated by his doctrine of Negro inferiority. "We in the South will do anything to help negroes as negroes, but if they arrogate to themselves equality of race, that moment life is in jeopardy. There is a boundary beyond which he cannot pass."[57] For the Charlotte preacher of the gospel, that boundary could not even be passed in the house of God. It would seem, he confessed, that a white southerner would worship with his black brother "as an equal in every respect; but it is a fact that he will not." He "knows that in God's sight a

52. "Race Problem in the South," *Presbyterian Quarterly*, XIV (July, 1900), 317–48.
53. Ibid., 317.
54. Ibid., 326, 330.
55. Ibid., 332–34.
56. Ibid., 345, 346.
57. Ibid., 342.

negro's soul is as good as his," but he also knows that "it is not a violation of any New Testament principle for him to recognize, in worship, those distinctions of race, which God has made." The segregationist prophesied that there "will never be a church, in the South, of any denomination, that will allow negroes in its courts or within its walls as equals so long as the race question is involved."[58]

During this period of growing racial friction, it was a common complaint that Negroes of the younger generation were deteriorating morally; that they were generally more inclined to criminal conduct than their parents. "The South is to-day overrun with a shiftless, vagabond, ignorant, vicious to the last degree, type of savage," declared the president of Wofford College in 1904.[59] He traced the major blame for this "wholly new kind of negro" to visionary federal legislation and to a type of education that did not equip blacks to work on the farm and in the shop. Another educator said bluntly, "The negro does not need high schools and academies at public expense."[60]

John Roach Straton, professor at Mercer University, challenged the notion that it was within the power of any kind of education to cure the criminal propensities of blacks.[61] He made the startling claim that, according to U.S. census returns, criminality among blacks had steadily risen with their educational advancement. Their illiteracy declined by 10 per cent between 1870 and 1880, but at the same time they became 25 per cent more criminal. During the next decade, they grew more criminal by 33⅓ per cent, despite the fact that their illiteracy decreased by over 18 per cent.[62] Northern Negroes were "almost three times as criminal as those of the South," even though they were "about three times as well educated." Within the South alone, the Negro "is most criminal in the states where he is best educated."[63]

From those findings Straton concluded that black people were

---

58. *Ibid.*, 343, 344.
59. Henry N. Snyder, "Lawlessness in the South: An Analysis of Conditions," *Methodist Quarterly Review, South*, LIII (January, 1904), 91.
60. Charles P. Curd, "Preparatory Education From a Southern Stand-Point: The Negro," *Quarterly Review of the Methodist Episcopal Church, South*, XXXII (January, 1891), 378.
61. "Will Education Solve the Race Problem?" *North American Review*, CLXX (June, 1900), 785-801.
62. *Ibid.*, 786.
63. *Ibid.*, 789.

either receiving the wrong kind of education, or that something within themselves was counteracting its normal ethical benefits. Booker T. Washington's system of industrial education seemed more suitable for Negroes, but Straton doubted whether even it would check their moral degeneration. He ventured the thesis that blacks were in process of ethical decay because the educator was suddenly thrusting them into high Anglo-Saxon civilization before they were ready for it. Reflecting the influence of Charles Darwin and Josiah Strong, he asked: "Does not the history of races show that the effort on the part of a superior people to lift up inferiors at a single stroke not only fails but establishes conditions which lead to the actual destruction of the weaker race?"[64] As examples of this, he cited the Tasmanians and the American Indians, alleging that both races suffered moral degeneracy from contact with whites. The "tearing-down process" in the Negro race, said Straton, doubtless was taking place during slavery, but sudden universal emancipation had greatly hastened it.[65]

While the Baptist educator acknowledged that his theory was still in the speculative stage, he took it seriously enough to spell out its implications. In short, if Negro Americans were to escape destruction as a race, they must be put beyond Anglo-Saxon contact. Straton conceded that wholesale colonization would be impracticable, but he believed that under proper incentives, enough blacks would emigrate "to ease the present strain in this country" and "to assure them a racial future."[66]

The South's most rabid anti-Negro propagandist of the early 1900's was Thomas Dixon, Jr., who achieved notoriety overnight by the smashing success of *The Leopard's Spots* (1902).[67] The son of a Baptist preacher and slaveowner, he was born near Shelby, North Carolina, in January, 1864, and grew up amid the storms of reconstruction. Upon graduation from Wake Forest College, in 1883, with highest scholastic honors and a string of medals, he entered Johns Hopkins University, where he studied history and political science for a few months under two great teachers, Herbert

64. *Ibid.*, 794.
65. *Ibid.*, 795-99.
66. *Ibid.*, 801.
67. Maxwell Bloomfield, "Dixon's The Leopard's Spots: A Study in Popular Racism," *American Quarterly*, XVI (Fall, 1964), 387-401.

B. Adams and Richard T. Ely. Restless in spirit and striving for the spectacular, he went to New York in the following January with the dream of becoming an actor. That dream, however, was quickly blasted, and he returned to Shelby to get his bearings. Soon afterwards he won a seat in the North Carolina legislature, but after serving in one session of that body he gave up a promising political career, studied law, and was admitted to the bar. But finding the life of a lawyer also less than dazzling, he finally, in the summer of 1886, entered the Baptist ministry. A spellbinding orator, he quickly became a pulpit wonder. By November, 1887, he had completed brief pastorates at Goldsboro and Raleigh and was in Boston as minister of Dudley Street Church. Still greater things beckoned, and within less than a year he was called to the Twenty-Third Street Church in New York City. To accommodate the crowds, it soon became necessary to hold services in Association Hall. In the spring of 1895 he gave up that pulpit and launched a non-denominational Church of the People, with services in the Academy of Music. Once again he drew overflowing crowds. He often preached on political and social questions, and he carried on a running battle with Tammany Hall. Finally, in 1899, he gave up the parish ministry to devote his full time to lecturing.[68]

Seeds of *The Leopard's Spots* were likely planted in Dixon's mind during the reconstruction era, for as a boy he witnessed hooded clansmen parading in his neighborhood and listened to blood-curdling stories of rape and lynching.[69] In any case, they were rapidly germinating during his college years. In an article on "The Coming Question," published in the *Wake Forest Student* in 1882, he complained that the Civil War had resulted in exalting "millions of base and ignorant Africans" to the plane of voters, and he called for an educational qualification for suffrage in order to prevent "this low and wretched race," and also ignorant immigrants, from debauching democracy.[70] During his Boston ministry, Dixon addressed the Oil and Paint Club on "The Southern Question," charging that "the enfranchisement of the negro turned loose too

---

68. Raymond A. Cook, *Fire From the Flint: The Amazing Careers of Thomas Dixon* (Winston-Salem, N.C., 1968), Chap. 4.
69. J. Zebulon Wright, "Thomas Dixon: The Mind of a Southern Apologist" (typed Ph.D. dissertation, George Peabody College for Teachers, 1966), 38–46.
70. "The Coming Question," *Wake Forest Student*, I (July, 1882), 297.

much power." According to him, some forty counties in North Carolina had been "hopelessly wrecked" by black men "under the leadership of adventurers and villains."[71]

Two events seem to have been especially potent in convincing Dixon that the time was ripe to publish the *Spots*. One was America's victory over Spain in 1898, raising a question of whether to grant political equality to the darker peoples of the Caribbean islands who had come under American control. The other—and far more personal—event was the sweeping gubernatorial victory of Charles B. Aycock of North Carolina in 1900 on a platform of white supremacy. This achievement, together with similar victories in other southern states, must have transformed Thomas Dixon into a flaming apostle of Anglo-Saxonism.

Appropriately, the scene of *The Leopard's Spots* is laid in North Carolina, with Charles Gaston (Charles Aycock) as the hero. Next in importance is Gaston's pastor, John Durham, a former slaveholder who declined an invitation to a wealthy northern church in order "to maintain the racial absolutism of the Anglo-Saxon in the South." To Durham fell the role of foster father to young Gaston, who had lost his own father in the Civil War. A belligerent racist, the preacher seized every opportunity to exhort his foster son to take up "the white man's burden" and deliver his state from "the black death." As Gaston recalled in later years, "the Preacher" said to him "a thousand times": "*My boy, the future American must be an Anglo-Saxon or a Mulatto! We are now deciding which it shall be.... The South must fight this battle to a finish.*"[72]

Durham's admonition was not in vain; long before Gaston raised the banner of white supremacy as candidate for governor, he was convinced that "the beginning of Negro equality as a vital fact is the beginning of the end of this nation's life."[73] Thus when the day arrived to deliver the address that resulted in his unanimous choice as a candidate for the governorship, he trembled with anti-Negro ferocity. "If we attempt to move forward we are literally chained to the body of a festering Black Death!" he exclaimed. In a climactic oratorical outburst, Charles Gaston proclaimed: "This is a white

71. *Living Problems in Religion and Social Science* (New York, 1889), 251–53.
72. *The Leopard's Spots: A Romance of the White Man's Burden, 1865–1900* (New York, 1902), 198.
73. *Ibid.*, 242.

man's government, conceived by white men, and maintained by white men through every year of its history—and by the God of our Fathers it shall be ruled by white men until the Archangel shall call the end of time!"[74] No wonder "two thousand [white] men went mad" as the "redeemer" took his seat.

In the course of developing his "romance of the white man's burden," Dixon wove in every cardinal tenet of hard-line orthodoxy. Thanks to the vaulting spirit of Anglo-Saxonism, the *Spots* sold by the truckload. Its nationwide enthusiastic reception sealed the author's decision to devote the rest of his life to preaching against "the black ape." Within the next five years he completed his projected trilogy with *The Clansman* (1905) and *The Traitor* (1907), both of which also enjoyed massive sales. However, neither they nor any of his subsequently published works added anything essentially new to the creed of *The Leopard's Spots*. By the time of Dixon's death in 1946, southern racism had begun to decline; nevertheless, his last book, *The Flaming Sword* (1939), reflected not the slightest abatement of his traditional sentiments. Happily for America, it was generally ignored.

III

Fortunately for black Americans, a significant minority of white churchmen in the postwar South held to a moderate type of racial orthodoxy. A leading member of this group was Atticus G. Haygood, a Georgia Methodist clergyman and former chaplain in the Confederate army. In 1880, while serving as president of Emory College, he preached a remarkable sermon in defense of the "New South." He pleaded with his fellow Georgians to stop re-threshing "dead issues," since the South's golden age lay in the future. The common man was already better off than he had ever been in antebellum times. Furthermore, a larger cotton crop had been grown in 1879 than was ever produced in a single year by slave labor.[75] The Emory president thanked God that slavery had been abolished, for it had been a millstone around the South's neck. "Our provincialism, our want of literature, our lack of educational facilities, and

74. *Ibid.,* 442.
75. *The New South: Gratitude, Amendment, Hope: A Thanksgiving Sermon for November 25, 1880* (Oxford, Ga., 1880), 7–9.

our manufactures, like our lack of population, is all explained by one fact and one word—slavery."[76]

Soon afterwards Haygood published *Our Brother in Black*, in which he moved to the left of the Dabneys and Dixons. He dismissed the various colonization schemes as "utter nonsense." The Negro was here to stay, and he urged his fellow whites to help their black brethren to become productive members of society.[77] One of the best ways to help them was to lift them out of the pit of illiteracy. Haygood lamented the fact that so few southern whites were willing to teach black children. He also regretted that the northern missionaries had not been properly appreciated.

During the closing weeks of 1881, the Georgia Methodist visited New England, where he delivered sixteen addresses in a further expression of his relatively liberal social and racial views.[78] Everywhere he pleaded for the burial of sectionalism in the interest of overcoming as rapidly as possible the bitter legacies of the late war.[79]

Owing largely to sentiments expressed in *Our Brother in Black*, Haygood was soon given a great opportunity to advance the cause of Negro education. In 1882 John F. Slater of Norwich, Connecticut, a textile manufacturer, established a million dollar trust for the purpose of "uplifting the lately emancipated population of the Southern States, and their posterity, by conferring on them the blessings of Christian education."[80] The Georgia churchman was appointed as general agent of the Slater Fund.[81] Resigning from the presidency of Emory College, he spent the rest of the decade in

---

76. *Ibid.*, 14. For the same position taken earlier by another Georgian, see John C. Reed, *The Old and New South* (New York, 1876), 11.

77. *Our Brother in Black: His Freedom and His Future* (Nashville, 1881), 17-23.

78. Haygood, *Sermons and Speeches* (Nashville, 1883), 340-72.

79. John E. Fisher, "Atticus Haygood and National Unity," *Georgia Historical Quarterly*, L (June, 1966), 113-25.

80. "Letter of the Founder [March 2, 1882]," in *Documents Relating to the Origin and Work of the Slater Trustees, 1882 to 1894* (Baltimore, 1894), 7. Slater designated Rutherford B. Hayes as the first president of the corporation. Three of the ten trustees were from southern or border states: Daniel C. Gilman (Maryland), James C. Boyce (Kentucky), and Alfred H. Colquitt (Georgia).

81. Harold W. Mann, *Atticus Greene Haygood: Methodist Bishop, Editor, and Educator* (Athens, Ga., 1966), 144-49. While on a speaking tour in New England, Haygood was probably told about the plan to establish the Slater Fund, and may well have been asked whether he would be interested in becoming its general agent. Haygood to Leonard W. Bacon, January 25, 1882, in Louis D. Rubin, Jr., ed., *Teach the Freemen: The Correspondence of Rutherford B. Hayes and the Slater Fund for Negro Education, 1881-1887* (2 vols., Baton Rouge, 1959), I, 67-70.

dedicated service to Negro advancement in the South. During the school year of 1883-84, for example, he made Slater grants to seventy-three institutions, including Hampton Institute, Tuskegee Normal School, Talladega College, and Claflin, Shaw, and Fisk universities.[82]

The Slater agent meanwhile pleaded with his fellow southern Methodists to do more for their own ecclesiastical offspring, the Colored Methodist Episcopal Church. That body, he charged, had become "Our Hagar in the Wilderness" (Gen. 21:9-14). Besides turning over to their black brethren the buildings which they had used while in slavery, and which the whites "did not want," the white Methodists had done very little except talk for the past thirteen years. While the General Conference of 1882 had voted to establish Paine Institute for black Methodists, the financial response of white Methodism had been exceedingly discouraging. "If we send 'Hagar' into the wilderness, we must not complain if God sends an angel to take her up. But it will be a shame forever to Abraham and all his house."[83] That critical comment sparked a heated controversy, touched off by Charles W. Miller of Lexington, Kentucky, who accused Haygood of greatly exaggerating the extent to which the General Conference had ever promised to assist Negro Methodism. At the root of Miller's reaction was his utter distaste for what he called Haygood's "mania for the Negro." "Our church does not desire any Gilbert Havenism on this Negro question thrust upon her," he retorted. "That ill-starred Bishop carried about with him the ghastly corpse of this Negro question, and thrust it forward on all occasions."[84]

Yet in all his efforts to educate the freedmen, Haygood, like his more rigid brethren, operated on the premise of Negro inferiority. This fact he clearly reflected in his contention that "only lunatics and visionaries" would want to educate blacks and whites in the same school. "Southern white children, as a class, won't sit at the

---

82. Haygood, *The Case of the Negro As to Education in the Southern States; A Report to the Board of Trustees [of the Slater Fund]* (Atlanta, 1885), 36. By April, 1894, the Slater trust had contributed a total of $439,981.78 toward Negro education in the South. J. L. M. Curry, *Education of the Negroes Since 1860. The Trustees of the John F. Slater Fund: Occasional Papers No. 3* (Baltimore, 1894), 32.

83. *Christian Advocate* (Nashville), August 18, 1883.

84. *Ibid.*, September 8, 1883. For other responses in the *Christian Advocate*, see especially the issues for September 22, 29; October 6, 13, 20, 1883.

same desks with negro children, and southern black children, as a class, don't want to sit at the same desks with white children."[85] To compel whites and blacks to attend the same school, said the Slater agent, would result in psychologically damaging both races. Precisely what the nature of that damage might be was not specified. Haygood was no less opposed to racially inclusive churches. He held that black churchmen had been prompted by a fundamental race instinct to leave the white churches, and that any repression of that divinely implanted instinct could well "mar their evolution."[86] When some northern Methodists protested the enforcement of a Jim Crow pattern at an Epworth League convention in Chattanooga, Tennessee, Haygood called their complaint "simply ridiculous" and dismissed the matter as merely a "tempest in a teapot."[87]

On becoming a bishop of the Methodist Episcopal Church, South, in 1890, Haygood resigned the Slater agency. His interest in the "brother in black" did not cease; nevertheless, he tended to move to the right on the race question. During the closing decade of the century, when black citizens were being widely deprived of the ballot, he raised not the slightest objection. On the contrary, in a surprising essay on "The Black Shadow in the South," he charged that the general enfranchisement of Negroes had been a deadly "crime against republican government and civilization."[88] He was critical of the younger generation of blacks, who were said to manifest "a spirit of insubordination to the social order," and he held that "the older negroes, as a class," were "the best citizens as well as the best laborers" of his day.[89] He expressed horror at the current practice of burning Negroes alive, but he implicitly condoned the savagery by saying, "Sane men who are just will consider the provocation."[90]

When Haygood gave up the Slater agency, he was succeeded by Jabez L. M. Curry, who, since 1881, had served as general agent of

85. *Our Brother in Black,* 145. See also Haygood, "The South and the School Problem," *Harper's New Monthly Magazine,* LXXIX (July, 1889), 226.
86. *Our Brother in Black,* 235. See also Haygood, *Pleas For Progress* (Nashville, 1889), 39–40.
87. *Christian Advocate,* July 25, 1895.
88. "The Black Shadow in the South," *Forum,* XVI (October, 1893), 170. For an editorial endorsement of the article, see Nashville *Christian Advocate,* October 12, 1893.
89. "The Black Shadow in the South," *Forum,* XVI, 173, 174.
90. *Ibid.,* 168.

the Peabody Education Fund. Shortly after the Civil War, Curry abandoned his long-time political career and devoted the rest of his life to the cause of religion and education. Although becoming an ordained Baptist minister in 1866, he declined invitations to settle down as a local pastor. After serving briefly as president of Howard College (now Samford University), he accepted a professorship at Richmond College, where he remained until called to the Peabody agency. His supreme passion from 1881 onward was to popularize public education in the South, and during the last two decades of the century he again and again pleaded the cause of public schools before every state legislature of the former Confederacy.[91]

Prior to 1865, Curry had unwaveringly defended the institution of slavery, but not long after the war he freely confessed that slavery had both degraded the Negro and throttled southern economic progress. By the summer of 1865 he was urging Alabamians to establish schools for blacks. As president of the Alabama Baptist State Convention, he also prodded his fellow churchmen to take more vigorous steps to provide religious instruction for the freedmen.[92] Upon taking up the Slater agency, he redoubled his efforts on behalf of Negro education. One of his main immediate concerns was to improve the quality of instruction in black schools, and thus he selected a few of the stronger institutions and gave them extra-large grants from the Slater Fund. Meanwhile he sharply disputed the claim of such men as John Roach Straton that education had not improved the mind and moral character of blacks. Likewise he strenuously opposed attempts, as in North Carolina, to finance Negro public schools exclusively from taxes paid by the black population. Any such form of racial discrimination, he warned legislators, "would be dangerous."[93]

Like the first Slater Fund agent, however, Jabez Curry promoted black schools on the premise of Negro inferiority. He left no doubt about this in an address to Georgia legislators in 1888, and he told them in no uncertain language that the only way the South could

91. Edwin A. Alderman and Armistead C. Gordon, *J. L. M. Curry: A Biography* (New York, 1911), 456–57.
92. Jessie Pearl Rice, *J. L. M. Curry: Southerner, Statesman and Educator* (New York, 1949), 55, 194.
93. *Speech . . . Delivered Before the North Carolina Legislature, January 21, 1891* (Raleigh, N.C., 1891), 4. See Frenise A. Logan, *The Negro in North Carolina, 1876–1894* (Chapel Hill, N.C., 1964), 155–63.

continue to maintain a white man's government was by developing a more efficient system of white schools. "He who thinks the negro problem has been solved is a fanatic or a fool," declared Curry. "It casts its black baleful shadow over the immediate and the later future. . . . To be *Africanized* will be a depth of degradation and despair from which all the potencies of Christian civilization will not rescue you."[94] In an address before the legislature of Alabama shortly thereafter, Curry sounded the same alarm in even stronger terms. After charging that reconstructionists a generation ago had deliberately tried "to degrade the white man and give supremacy to the Negro," he claimed that renewed efforts were afoot "to subject several of the Southern States entirely, and all partially, to the dominance of the negroes."[95]

In 1899, the Baptist educator published a surprisingly critical essay on "The Negro Question."[96] Even though still contending that emancipation was "a triumph of the inalienable rights of man," he nevertheless claimed that the younger generation of blacks had undergone serious moral deterioration. Far from favoring the political equality of Negroes, he branded the black ballot "a farce, a burlesque on elections, and only evil," and he expressly endorsed the disfranchising movement then in progress.[97] He held out no hope whatever that blacks and whites could ever form a truly harmonious and unified society. "The negro is no nearer common fellowship, equality of association, than he was in 1865." The approximation of equality, even if possible, would be dangerous, since the two races "are unassimilable and immiscible without rapid degeneracy."[98]

Falling within the racial perspectives of Haygood and Curry were the views of Charles Betts Galloway, a native of Mississippi

94. *Address, Delivered [Before the Georgia Legislature] December 13th, 1888* (Atlanta, 1889), 11.

95. *Address, Delivered to the Alabama Legislature, February 1, 1889* (Montgomery, 1889), 9–10, 12. Curry evidently referred to the so-called "Force Bill" that Henry Cabot Lodge introduced into the House on June 26, 1890, providing for the federal supervision of federal elections. It barely passed in the House and failed in the Senate. Logan, *The Betrayal of the Negro*, 70–74, 76–81.

96. "The Negro Question," *Popular Science Monthly*, LV (June, 1899), 177–85.

97. *Ibid.*, 181, 182. Curry expressed the sentiments of most Southern Baptist spokesmen. Spain, *At Ease in Zion*, 83–84.

98. *Ibid.*, 179, 182.

and one of southern Methodism's most influential leaders.[99] In 1886, following a four-year editorship of the *New Orleans Christian Advocate*, he was elected a bishop of his church. From then until his death in 1909 he was the most progressive member of the episcopacy. His mature racial thought is contained in an address on "The South and the Negro," delivered at the Seventh Annual Conference for Education in the South, held at Birmingham, Alabama, in 1904. From the outset Galloway maintained that the black man was entitled to "equal opportunity" with all other Americans "to fulfil in himself the highest purposes of an all-wise and benevolent Providence."[100] This was said to include, among other things, equal educational opportunity. Taking to task such men as John Roach Straton, the bishop vigorously disputed the current claim that illiterate Negroes were less criminal than were the educated members of their race. He cited U.S. census data as proof that illiterate blacks, as a class, committed forty per cent more crimes than did the educated class of Negroes.[101]

Nevertheless, when Bishop Galloway elaborated his racial theory in concrete terms, he revealed his firm adherence to the dogma of Negro inferiority. There were four things, he declared, which had been "definitely and finally settled" by the white South: first, that "there will never be any social mingling of the races"; second, that blacks "will worship in separate churches and be educated in separate schools"; third, that political rule "will remain in present [white] hands"; and fourth, that "the great majority of the negroes" will stay in the South.[102]

Galloway's young fellow Methodist, Andrew Sledd, professor at Emory College in Georgia since 1898, subscribed to the central tenet of racial orthodoxy, but tried to narrow the gap between northern and southern views of the black man. The country as a whole, he urged, had to recognize two fundamental facts. One of them was that *"the negro belongs to an inferior race."*[103] This in-

---

99. William L. Duren, *Charles Betts Galloway* (Atlanta, 1932), Chap. 13. See also an editorial by Galloway in the *New Orleans Christian Advocate*, March 29, 1883.
100. *The South and the Negro* (New York, 1904), 6.
101. *Ibid.*, 14.
102. *Ibid.*, 8.
103. "The Negro: Another View," *Atlantic Monthly*, XC (July, 1902), 66.

feriority had not resulted from slavery, nor from poverty, ignorance, or degradation; instead, it was grounded in the fact that the black man was "lower in the scale of development than the white man." This being the case, "emancipation could not eradicate the essential inferiority of the negro." If the negrophilists of the North would recognize this fact and cease their sentimental talk about racial equality, intersectional friction would be less acute.[104] But it was equally necessary, continued Sledd, to recognize that "*the negro has inalienable rights.*"[105] While the North had erred in seeking to solve the vexing problem on the "unsound postulate" of Negro equality, the South had erred far more grievously in carrying the idea of the Negro's inferiority almost to the point of his dehumanization. Even the well-educated and "God-fearing" Negroes were subjected to galling treatment. They tipped their hats to prominent men, but their salutations were never returned. When traveling, they were denied association with whites in railroad cars, and refused admission to white restaurants and hotels. Should they attend a white church, they were "bidden to call upon God . . . from a place apart." All these prohibitions were but ways of reminding the black man that he belonged to an inferior caste. Even lynching, although often claimed to be an expression of indignation over the violation of the law, was but the white brute's barbarous method of teaching the Negro "the lesson of abject and eternal servility." In the final analysis, then, "the radical difficulty is not with the negro, but with the white man!"[106]

The professor stirred up a hornet's nest, for even though he paid homage to the South's cherished dogma of Negro inferiority, he assailed racial patterns which, to Georgians at least, followed logically from that dogma. Mrs. William H. Felton, well-known in the state as a keen politician, a vigorous suffragette, and a fierce hater of blacks,[107] opened the onslaught with a caustic letter to the Atlanta *Constitution*, dubbing Sledd's essay an "outrageous indictment of southern manhood," and accusing the "sniveling inkslinger" of

104. *Ibid.*, 66–67.
105. *Ibid.*, 67.
106. *Ibid.*, 68–71.
107. John E. Talmadge, *Rebecca Latimer Felton: Nine Stormy Decades* (Athens, Ga., 1960), Chaps. 5, 12, 13.

vomiting "rot" into the *Atlantic Monthly* just "because he was paid for it!" The indignant woman not only called upon white Georgians to kick him out of their state, but she warned him that he would be lucky to make his exit without a coat of tar and feathers.[108] Angry protests poured in upon the president and trustees of Emory, forcing Sledd's speedy resignation. As making partial amends, the college provided him with a thousand dollar fellowship for graduate study at Yale.

The South's leading exponent of a moderate version of racial orthodoxy at the opening of the twentieth century was Edgar Gardner Murphy. Although a native of Arkansas, he grew up in San Antonio, Texas. In 1889 he graduated from the University of the South, where he was deeply influenced by William Porcher DuBose, an outstanding theologian of the Protestant Episcopal Church.[109] Ordained a priest of the Episcopal Church in 1893, Murphy in rapid succession served parishes in Texas, Ohio, New York, and Alabama. His most prominent church was St. John's in Montgomery, Alabama, where he began as rector in December, 1898. There, as elsewhere, he became deeply interested in the pressing social and political problems of the city. In reality, Murphy was a preacher of what was then called the social gospel. He battled for clean city government at Chillicothe, Ohio, and he crusaded against child labor in Alabama's cotton mills.[110]

Unlike most advocates of the social gospel, however, Murphy made the racial problem one of his primary concerns. During his ministry at Christ Church in Laredo, Texas, whites burned a Negro to death there in 1893, and he organized a public protest against it. Shortly after going to Montgomery, he took the lead in organizing a "Southern Society for the Promotion of the Study of Race Conditions and Problems in the South." Under its auspices a South-wide conference was held at Montgomery in May, 1900, and prominent white leaders, mostly from the region, presented papers

---

108. *Constitution*, Sunday, August 3, 1902. For a good account of the response to the Felton letter, see Henry Y. Warnock, "Andrew Sledd, Southern Methodists, and the Negro," *Journal of Southern History*, XXXI (August, 1965), 251–71.
109. Hugh C. Bailey, *Edgar Gardner Murphy: Gentle Progressive* (Coral Gables, Fla., 1968), 3–4.
110. *Ibid.*, 11–12, 64–84, 102–6.

on black-white relations in the contexts of politics, education, and religion.[111] Virtually all the papers were framed upon the postulate of Negro inferiority, and those presented by Mayor Alfred M. Waddell of Wilmington, North Carolina, John Roach Straton of Mercer University, Paul B. Barringer of the University of Virginia, and John Temple Graves, editor of the Atlanta *News*, were particularly offensive to black leaders.[112]

A second conference was announced, but it never met; even the society itself quickly expired. The rector of St. John's, however, soon received a call to undertake a mission dear to his heart. In the fall of 1901 a small group of northern philanthropists and southern educators organized the Southern Education Board as a means of awakening the South to the need for more and better schools for both races. The dynamo of the board was its chairman, Robert C. Ogden, manager of John Wanamaker's New York store, but other key board members included George Foster Peabody, New York banker; William H. Baldwin, Jr., president of the Long Island Railroad; Charles D. McIver, president of Greensboro Normal School for Women; Charles W. Dabney, president of the University of Tennessee; and Edwin A. Alderman, president of Tulane University and former president of the University of North Carolina.[113] Ogden asked his young friend of Montgomery to become the executive secretary of the board. Resigning from his beloved parish, Murphy became a vibrant educational evangelist to his native region during the next seven years. Meanwhile, he led the board in conducting one or more public school campaigns in most of the southern states. The campaigners, however, touched lightly, if at all, upon the delicate question of Negro schools, fearing a white

---

111. *Race Problems of the South: Report of the Proceedings of the First Annual Conference Held Under the Auspices of the Southern Society . . . at Montgomery, Alabama, May 8, 9, 10, A.D. 1900* (Richmond, 1900).

112. George Allen Mebane, *"The Negro Problem" As Seen and Discussed by Southern White Men in Conference at Montgomery, Alabama* (New York, 1900), *passim*. Booker T. Washington of Tuskegee Institute regarded Paul Barringer's address as "the most discouraging" that he had ever heard. Washington, "The Montgomery Race Conference," *Century*, LX (August, 1900), 631.

113. The board was not a funding agency, but it worked closely with John D. Rockefeller's General Education Board (established in 1902), which contributed many millions to southern schools. For good accounts of the Southern Board's activities, see Harlan, *Separate and Unequal*, Chap. 3, and Bailey, *Edgar Gardner Murphy*, Chap. 5.

backlash. Makers of board policy, including Murphy, wanted to improve Negro education, but they proceeded on the unrealistic theory that if whites became better educated, they would then push for equal educational facilities for blacks. This of course proved entirely fallacious.[114]

During the opening decade of the century, Murphy often wrote on the race question, and even after failing health forced him to give up the secretaryship of the Southern Education Board, in January, 1909, he published his longest work on it, *The Basis of Ascendancy*. From first to last his racial policy was determined by his belief that the black man was inferior to the white man, a belief reflected in the curious remark, "the negro is a negro."[115]

This explains Murphy's excessive fear of "racial fusion" and his frequent stress upon "racial integrity" as "the fundamental dogma" of white southerners.[116] This fear generated his advocacy of racial segregation. In an address at Philadelphia in 1900, he held that "racial antipathy" was a "public good" in that it prevented a union of the races.[117] Speaking to the students and faculty of Washington and Lee University, Murphy not only declared that blacks and whites "must live apart," but he contended that "the whole world has accepted the dogma of separation and segregation which the South proclaims."[118] As late as 1909, he argued that this dogma "trenches upon no legal right or social right. . . . It is a dogma not of repression but of self-protection and self-development."[119]

Loyalty to the dogma of Negro inferiority led Murphy to give his unwavering support to the South's dual system of public education. This pattern, he declared in 1904, was "inevitable and unchangeable."[120] On the other hand, he conceded that such a pattern "often

---

114. Harlan, *Separate and Unequal*, 92–97; Bailey, *Edgar Gardner Murphy*, 175–77. By 1907 Murphy confessed, "The proposal to take from the negro public schools all revenues save the negro's meagre contribution in direct taxes is everywhere in the air." "The Task of the Leader," *Sewanee Review*, XV (January, 1907), 22.
115. *The Basis of Ascendancy* (New York, 1909), xv, xxii.
116. *Problems of the Present South* (New York, 1904), 34.
117. *The White Man and the Negro at the South* (n.p., n.d.), 19. This address was delivered at Philadelphia on March 8, 1900, under the auspices of the American Academy of Political and Social Science, the American Society for the Extension of University Teaching, and the Civic Club of Philadelphia.
118. *The Task of the South: An Address Before the Faculty and Students of Washington and Lee University, Dec. 10, 1902* (Montgomery, Ala., n.d.), 10.
119. *The Basis of Ascendancy*, 233.
120. *Problems of the Present South*, 37.

made the negro schools inferior to the white schools."[121] The Southern Education Board was caught in this quandary throughout its entire fourteen-year existence. Murphy and many members of the board—especially Robert C. Ogden—sincerely desired to see the black child enjoy an equal educational opportunity, yet they helped to delay the realization of that laudable goal by lending their sanction to a dual system of schools. Ironically, the greater their success in stimulating a southern educational revival, the wider grew the gulf between the two systems.[122]

Like other racial moderates, Murphy regarded universal Negro suffrage as a menace to good government. He advised the use of a literacy and property test to limit the black vote, but at the same time he urged that the same test be applied to whites.[123] He sharply criticized an Alabama scheme to disfranchise illiterate blacks without also disfranchising illiterate whites.[124] He likewise assailed the Mississippi Plan of 1890 because it contained "subterfuges of legislation" that enabled local officials to deprive the minority race of its suffrage rights.[125] Yet, surprisingly, Murphy argued that the only way to assure Negroes of political equity was to modify the Fifteenth Amendment in such a manner as to make the state the sole determiner of the franchise. "Make the franchise a local issue, and you have opened to him [the Negro] the only possibility of ultimate justice before the law," he proclaimed with incredible unrealism.[126]

While Murphy theoretically sanctioned the principle of equality of suffrage, he in fact compromised it in favor of the white man. In his Philadelphia address of 1900 he explicitly stated that no illiterate Confederate veteran should be deprived of the ballot.[127] This exception alone extended the franchise to a considerable body of white illiterates. By 1905 he seems to have broadened his compromise to include some illiterate whites who had not served in the

---

121. *Ibid.*, 34.
122. Harlan, *Separate and Unequal*, 254–56, 268–69.
123. *The White Man and the Negro at the South*, 28.
124. *An Open Letter on Suffrage Restriction, and Against Certain Proposals of the Platform of the State Convention* (4th ed., Montgomery, Ala., 1901), 9, 14, 19.
125. *The White Man and the Negro at the South*, 29. See also Murphy, "The Task of the Leader," *Sewanee Review*, XV, 26.
126. *The White Man and the Negro at the South*, 33.
127. *Ibid.*, 29.

Confederate forces. In justification, he argued that the illiterate white man "excels the negro voter by the genius of his race, by inherited capacity and by a political training which has formed part of the tradition of his class."[128]

The Episcopal clergyman had little to say about black-white relations within his own communion. Yet the fact that during his ministry he established a separate Negro Episcopal church in Chillicothe, Ohio, and another in Montgomery, Alabama, is sufficient evidence that he sanctioned racial segregation at least on the parish level.[129] On the other hand, in 1907 he strongly attacked a proposed Negro episcopate, saying that it would "not help the negro nor strengthen the episcopate." The result would be a second-class bishop and a largely disfranchised body of black communicants. "Imagine S. Paul as a 'suffragan' or as a modern 'missionary bishop,' holding his jurisdiction at the discretion and under the limitations enacted by another race, and representing a vague dependent constituency of the ecclesiastically disfranchised!"[130]

IV

Since racial orthodoxy was the dominating creed of the postreconstruction South, it required uncommon independence for any white southerner to become a dissenter. Nevertheless, a small remnant of heretics challenged the ruling faith. A foremost dissenter was a Presbyterian layman, George Washington Cable, who achieved special literary fame for his short stories on the Creoles of old New Orleans.[131] The son and grandson of slaveholders, he was born in New Orleans in 1844. As the racial heretic recalled in

128. Murphy, "Shall the Fourteenth Amendment Be Enforced?" *North American Review*, CLXXX (January, 1905), 125, 126.
129. Bailey, *Edgar Gardner Murphy*, 12, 24.
130. *The Churchman*, September 21, 1907. Nevertheless, in 1907 the General Convention of the Protestant Episcopal Church enacted a law providing for a suffragan bishop to supervise the Negro work of the communion. *Journal of the General Convention of the Protestant Episcopal Church, 1907* (New York, 1907), 157, 160–61. See also David M. Reimers, *White Protestantism and the Negro* (New York, 1965), 66–71.
131. A standard account of Cable's career is Arlin Turner, *George W. Cable: A Biography* (Durham, N.C., 1956; paperback ed., Baton Rouge, 1966). See also Lucy L. C. Bikle, *George W. Cable: His Life and Letters* (New York, 1928).

later years, he was "reeking with patriotism of the strongest proslavery type" when Lincoln was elected president.[132] When the war broke out, the young patriot was not old enough for military service, but he later enlisted in the Confederate cavalry in Mississippi. Upon the cessation of hostilities, he returned to his native city and took a clerkship in a prominent countinghouse. Except for a short time as a reporter for the New Orleans *Picayune*, he held that position until the end of 1879, when he became a full-time writer and public reader of his short stories.

During the reconstruction era, Cable slowly awakened to the evil of slavery and the folly of secession. Though initially hostile to mixing the races in the New Orleans public schools, he finally became a convert to the innovation. In a letter of September 26, 1875, addressed to the editor of the New Orleans *Bulletin*, Paul M. Baker, he deplored the furor over mixed schools, and argued that the proposal to establish racially separate schools rested upon an "odious" distinction. "If the [black] race is inferior [to the white race], we can the better afford to give them an even start," he maintained.[133] Baker published the letter, but sharply criticized its sentiments, saying that he hoped "never to see white boys and girls of America forgetful of the fact that Negroes are their inferiors."[134]

Almost ten years were to pass before Cable publicly revived the sensitive question, but this did not mean that it troubled him any the less. A dedicated Christian, he became increasingly aware of the radical contradiction between the teaching of Jesus and racial discrimination. This fact he drove home in an address given at a meeting of the New Orleans Sunday School Association in April, 1881. Using as a text the parable of the Good Samaritan, he reminded the gathering that the Samaritans were "a mongrel" race of people whom the Jews viewed "as emphatically their inferiors." New Orleans, he observed, had its Samaritans, among whom was the black man. "Do we love *this neighbor* as ourselves?" he asked.

---

132. "My Politics," in Arlin Turner, ed., *The Negro Question: A Selection of Writings on Civil Rights in the South by George W. Cable* (Garden City, N.Y., 1958), 2.

133. "Letter to the Editor, New Orleans *Bulletin*, September 26, 1875," in Turner, ed., *The Negro Question*, 29.

134. Quoted in Turner, ed., *The Negro Question*, 30. Cable replied in a letter, but Baker refused to publish it. The *Picayune* also declined to publish the letter.

"Do we run great risks both with and for him? Do we give him our seat in God's house? Or do we tell him to go to the gallery? When he makes his peace with God, does he take the blessed cup and bread with us or after us?"[135]

By 1885, no longer able to hold his peace, Cable published a withering indictment of southern racial policy.[136] All across the South, he charged, the freedman's civil rights were being flagrantly abridged, thanks partly to an apathetic North and to the action of the Supreme Court in voiding the Civil Rights Act of 1875. The ruling regime, taking advantage of a golden opportunity, was boldly "flourishing the hot branding-iron of ignominious distinctions" at the entrance "to every public privilege and place—steamer landing, railway platform, theater, . . . public library, court-house, church, everything." The white southerner "forbids the freedman to go into the water until *he* is satisfied that he knows how to swim, and for fear he should learn hangs mill-stones about his neck."[137]

It was imperative, said Cable, for white leaders of the South to identify and critically evaluate the sentiments which prompted them to deprive the black man of his constitutional rights. For the novelist, those sentiments were predominantly two. The first and foremost was the rigidly held idea that the African was "of necessity an alien," and that he would never be otherwise despite the civilizing influence of the majority race. Come what might, he would "be and remain a kind of connecting link between man and the beasts of burden." The other primal sentiment was the notion or belief "that there was, by nature, a disqualifying moral taint in every drop of negro blood." For this reason the black man was by nature degenerate, fit only for menial service. Even his testimony was legally invalid if given against a white man. These two deeply rooted sentiments nurtured and perpetuated Negro servitude; they

---

135. "The Good Samaritan," in Turner, ed., *The Negro Question*, 36. In both New Orleans and Northampton, Mass., Cable was a devoted Sunday School worker. As a Bible teacher, he was rarely excelled. For a time his Northampton class numbered nearly 700. For fifteen months he conducted a class on Bible study at Tremont Temple in Boston which had an average weekly attendance of 2,000. Bikle, *George W. Cable*, 194–202.

136. "The Freedman's Case in Equity," *Century*, XXIX (January, 1885), 409–18. In September of the previous year Cable had read this paper at the annual meeting of the American Social Science Association, held at Saratoga, New York.

137. *Ibid.*, 414.

at the same time welded the master class into a solid mass and fixed an impassable gulf between the ruling and the serving race.[138]

Then suddenly, as if by a stroke of lightning, the tree of slavery was snapped off at the ground by the war, leaving untouched the sentiments of white superiority and black inferiority in which it was rooted.[139] Surviving the war, those sentiments denied civil and political equality to the freedman during reconstruction, and they had been doing the very same thing ever since that time. "The South stands on her honor before the clean equities of the issue," declared the Louisiana humanitarian. "It is no longer whether constitutional amendments, but whether the eternal principles of justice, are violated. And the answer must—it shall—come from the South."[140]

The answer did indeed come from the South, but it was far from what Cable wanted to hear. A flood of angry letters overwhelmed the *Century*. Instead of printing any of them, the management asked the editor of the Atlanta *Constitution*, Henry Woodfin Grady, to respond to the novelist on behalf of the South. He did so with characteristic alacrity.[141] The Georgian conceded that one might find here and there a "dreaming" southerner who would subscribe to Cable's theory of race mixing, but he said that "the thoughtful men of the South" universally opposed it, and that they could "never be driven into accepting it." Like white southerners in general, he assured his readers that "neither race wants it."[142] The editor contended that resistance to the intermingling of blacks and whites was prompted by natural instinct, not prejudice; and in defense of his claim he appealed to an experiment by Bishop Gilbert Haven, who in the early 1870's endeavored to mix the races in Atlanta's one northern Methodist church. By the end of a month "his church was decimated"; blacks and whites alike "left it in squads." The New Englander "contended with prayer and argument and threat against the inevitable, but finally succumbed. Two churches were established, and each race worshiped to itself. . . . Each race

138. *Ibid.*, 410–11.
139. *Ibid.*, 411.
140. *Ibid.*, 418.
141. "In Plain Black and White," *Century*, XXIX (April, 1885), 909–17.
142. *Ibid.*, 910.

simply obeyed its instinct." The same experiment was tried by the northern Methodists when they established annual conferences in the South after the war. All the conferences began on an integrated basis, but all of them soon divided into black and white bodies. "Underneath all this was a race instinct, obeying which, silently, they drifted swiftly apart."[143]

Henry Grady nowhere disputed Cable's charge that the South had already drawn the color line at every vital point in its social and institutional system; on the contrary, he freely admitted it, and attributed the segregated pattern to the operation of an "ineradicable" instinct.[144] But what if, as the novelist held, there was no such thing as a race instinct? If the South, rejoined the editor, had any reasonable doubt of its existence, "it would, by every means in its power, so strengthen the race prejudice that it would do the work and hold the stubbornness and strength of instinct."[145] Underneath Grady's tenacious faith in race instinct was the traditional fear that, if blacks and whites were permitted to intermingle on terms of equality, the white race would be contaminated through miscegenation.

A few months later Cable replied to his critic, saying that the Georgian had evaded the question of civil rights by "miscalling it 'social intermingling,'" and then had argued that neither race wanted it.[146] To be sure, blacks did not want social mingling as such, but they eagerly desired equal civil and political privileges. As evidence of this, said the novelist, they had sent him expressions of approval in abundance. Not one of the eighty Negro newspapers had disagreed with "The Freedman's Case in Equity."[147]

Cable emphatically disputed Grady's claim that black southerners were receiving equal accommodations with whites in public facilities. In some places, as in the mountainous parts of Kentucky, there was "but one colored school district in a *county*." The railroad cars assigned to Negroes were generally inferior in equipment and all too often utterly filthy. Restaurants and places of refresh-

143. *Ibid.*, 911.
144. *Ibid.*, 914–16.
145. *Ibid.*, 912.
146. "The Silent South," *Century*, XXX (September, 1885), 677.
147. *Ibid.*, 679–80.

ment along the railways were rarely open to black passengers. As for public libraries, not even the one in Grady's Atlanta would allow a Negro to draw out a book for his personal use.[148] These and other inequities, reiterated the Louisiana dissenter, were the tragic legacy of a caste system born and bred of slavery. "The problem before us is the green, rank stump of that felled Institution," he rightly asserted. Even though chattel slavery was no more, out of its surviving green stump had sprouted "the slavery of *civil caste*," in consequence of which the rights of black men were merely *"racial civil rights."*[149]

Despite the apathy or antagonism of his white fellow southerners, George Cable for several more years wrote and spoke fervently in the cause of Negro civil and political rights;[150] nevertheless, the movement of racial orthodoxy steadily gathered momentum. From the beginning, in fact, he had been mistaken in thinking that there was a considerable "Silent South" in favor of his doctrine. On this point, Henry Grady was correct in estimating that white southerners of Cable's views were few and far between.

Another fearless foe of racial orthodoxy was Lewis Harvie Blair, a Confederate veteran and a leading businessman of Richmond, Virginia. Although stemming from generations of orthodox Presbyterians, including distinguished clergymen, he was a free-thinker in religion and rejected much of traditional theology. Nevertheless, his racial sentiments reflected the spirit of Jesus to a remarkable degree. In the summer of 1887 he published a series of five articles in the New York *Independent* on "The Prosperity of the South" which broke sharply with traditional notions of the Negro.[151] By the time the second article appeared, he was forced to resign as treasurer of the Richmond Democratic Committee.[152] The furor, however, did not silence him; eighteen months later he published

148. *Ibid.*, 684–86.
149. *Ibid.*, 679, 690.
150. See especially the following contributions: "The Negro Question in the United States," *Contemporary Review*, LIII (March, 1888), 443–68; "A Simpler Southern Question," *Forum*, VI (December, 1888), 392–403; "Congregational Unity in Georgia," *Congregationalist* (Boston), September 26, 1889; *The Southern Struggle For Pure Government* (Boston, 1890).
151. *Independent*, June 16, 23, 30; July 14, 28, 1887.
152. Charles E. Wynes, "Lewis Harvie Blair, Virginia Reformer: The Uplift of the Negro and Southern Prosperity," *Virginia Magazine of History and Biography*, LXXII (January, 1964), 8.

a book reaffirming and expanding all the basic positions taken in the *Independent*.[153]

Contrary to the New South optimists, Lewis Blair argued that the eleven states of the former Confederacy had made very little economic progress since the Civil War, except in a few industrial areas. Not a single important bank had been established in twenty-two years, and capital savings were meager. Even the urban centers were almost static. During the decade of 1870–80, thirty of the South's principal cities had a combined growth of only 142,259.[154] What was the cause of this economic stagnancy? According to the Virginian, it was primarily the result of a failure to elevate the black man. White southerners "can keep the Negro in his present degraded position, but they cannot do so without at the same time laying the axe at the root of their own welfare."[155]

In order to elevate the Negro, the South, said Blair, "must cease to look upon him as inferior fundamentally."[156] He, like George Cable, loathed racial caste, and believed it to be the white southerner's most crippling social malady.[157] Appealing to the Declaration of Independence, he declared: "If these truths are 'self-evident, that all men are created equal; that they are endowed with certain inalienable rights'; . . . then we have no defense for that caste upon which Southern society is built."[158]

From his anticaste perspective, Blair bluntly attacked the South's policy of racial segregation. He particularly condemned the dual public school system, not merely because a poverty-stricken region could not provide quality education for either race on this basis, but because it necessarily implanted in the minds of children the poisonous germs of racial caste. From their very first grade, he lamented, children would be "taught two dogmas—first, that white children are and shall *forever* be fundamentally superior to black children; and second, that black children are and *forever* shall be

---

153. *The Prosperity of the South Dependent Upon the Elevation of the Negro* (Richmond, 1889).
154. *Ibid.*, Chaps. 3-4; *Independent*, June 16, 1887.
155. *The Prosperity of the South*, 45.
156. *Independent*, June 23, 1887.
157. *The Prosperity of the South*, 134. This affliction was not confined to the South. "Caste pursues and cripples the Negro in the North as it does in the South." *Ibid.*, 145.
158. *Ibid.*, 135.

fundamentally inferior to white children."[159] On the same ground, the Richmond dissenter repeatedly denounced the "caste sentiment" that refused black people free and equal admission to hotels, restaurants, centers of entertainment, and other public facilities. It was no valid excuse to deny blacks such privileges on the ground that these places were private property; for, although privately owned, they were public with respect to their functions.[160]

When white southerners, including clergymen, were widely decrying Negro suffrage, Lewis Blair urged that it was an "absolute necessity," and that it was in fact the "most valuable of all" the freedman's rights.[161] He thus sharply criticized North Carolina's county government act of 1876 and South Carolina's eight-box ballot law of 1882, because both were enacted with the definite design to decrease the political power of black citizens.[162] Whites could not deprive Negroes of their suffrage rights, said Blair, and escape moral decay. "Ruin must follow communities that persistently degrade any large portion of its citizens. Tyranny . . . degrades not only those imposed upon, but it also demoralizes the doers of the wrong."[163]

Despite the dominance of racial caste, the Virginia heretic predicted that it would finally "fall before the assaults of the world."[164] Already he professed to see signs that the caste system was crumbling. This optimistic note is surprising, for the caste structure was actually becoming more firmly rooted throughout the South. However, Blair's optimism soon waned. In a paper on "The Southern Problem and Its Solution," prepared for delivery at the African Congress, which was held in connection with the Chicago World's Fair of 1893, he once again analyzed the racial situation in the South, but gave no indication that it was improving. On the contrary, he left the impression that any fundamental solution of the problem lay far ahead, and even hinted that it might never be

159. *Ibid.*, 108. See also *Independent*, July 14, 1887.
160. *The Prosperity of the South*, 60, 62.
161. *Ibid.*, 84–85.
162. *Ibid.*, 113, 119–20. See Frenise A. Logan, *The Negro in North Carolina, 1876–1894*, 48–63; George B. Tindall, *South Carolina Negroes, 1877–1900* (Baton Rouge, 1966), 68–70.
163. *The Prosperity of the South*, 84–85.
164. *Ibid.*, 136.

achieved.[165] Alas, sometime after 1898 the reformer himself forsook his equalitarian faith and embraced a rigid type of racial orthodoxy.[166]

A more steadfast critic of racial orthodoxy was John Spencer Bassett, a native of North Carolina and a loyal Methodist layman. After graduating from Trinity College (now Duke University) in 1888, he specialized in history under Herbert Baxter Adams at Johns Hopkins University, receiving his Ph.D. degree in 1894. From 1893 to 1906 he taught at Trinity, and speedily became the recognized leader in southern historical scholarship.[167]

From the first, young Bassett was deeply interested in slavery and antislavery leaders, and published three monographs in this general area within four years.[168] Meanwhile he had also projected a comprehensive history of black Americans.[169] That he had more than an academic interest in the Negro is clear from a paper which he published in 1900, entitled "North Carolina Methodism and Slavery." While he commended his communion for its ante-bellum ministry to the bondsmen, he charged that since the Civil War it had virtually abandoned the freedmen. "The black man is our brother and will remain so," he wrote. "To him our church has a duty. Does it perform it by letting him alone?"[170] In that same year Bassett further disclosed interest in black people when he addressed the graduating class of Slater Industrial and State Normal School, a Negro institution at Winston-Salem, North Carolina. He urged black youth of ability to aspire to a higher form of vocational activity than that of menial labor. Negroes, he said, had made "very creditable progress" since the abolition of slavery, and he predicted

165. "The Southern Problem and Its Solution," *Our Day*, XII (November, 1893), 376. See also *ibid.*, 362, 364. Pressing business affairs detained Blair in Richmond, but his paper was read to the African Congress.
166. Wynes, "Lewis Harvie Blair," *Virginia Magazine of History and Biography*, LXXII, 15–16.
167. Wendell H. Stephenson, "John Spencer Bassett as a Historian of the South," *North Carolina Historical Review*, XXV (July, 1948), 289–317.
168. *Slavery and Servitude in the Colony of North Carolina* (1896); *Anti-Slavery Leaders of North Carolina* (1898); *Slavery in the State of North Carolina* (1899).
169. Wendell H. Stephenson, "The Negro in the Thinking and Writing of John Spencer Bassett," *North Carolina Historical Review*, XXV (October, 1948), 428–30.
170. "North Carolina Methodism and Slavery," *An Annual Publication of Historical Papers, Published by the Historical Society of Trinity College*, Ser. 4 (Durham, N.C., 1900), 11.

that when given an adequate education they could qualify for every occupation available to whites.[171]

In the hope of stimulating fresh and unfettered thought on current problems, the energetic historian founded the *South Atlantic Quarterly* in 1902 and served as its editor until January 1, 1905.[172] As the Negro question was then being widely discussed, he published seven articles on various aspects of that question during his editorship, three of them being his own. The editor's most memorable article, entitled "Stirring Up the Fires of Race Antipathy," appeared in October, 1903, and immediately touched off a stormy controversy.[173]

That historic essay was largely provoked by Bassett's growing displeasure over the fact that North Carolina Democrats had been exploiting the race issue, especially since 1898, to advance their political interests. After the election of 1898, in which the Democrats defeated the Fusionists (a coalition of Populists and Republicans) and regained control of the state legislature,[174] he wrote Herbert B. Adams of Hopkins that the campaign had been a shocking affair. It "ended in a riot at Wilmington [killing eleven blacks]—justifiable at no point—a riot directly due to the 'white man's campaign.'" In his opinion, "the white man will continue to run over the negro until the negro learns how to defend himself." If there had been "about 25 white men" dead as a result of the Wilmington riot, "the whites would be a little more careful of how they go into a riot there again." Bassett added, "I do not have the honor to agree with most of my fellow Anglo Saxons on the negro question."[175]

---

171. "The Position of the Negro in Southern Life," in *Some of the Commencement Addresses of the Slater Industrial and State Normal School, Winston-Salem, N.C., May 1900* (n.p., n.d.), 5, 10, 16.

172. For a collection of the leading articles published in the *Quarterly* during a half century, see William H. Hamilton, ed., *Fifty Years of the South Atlantic Quarterly* (Durham, N.C., 1952). Professor Hamilton's introductory essay is exceptionally illuminating.

173. "Stirring Up the Fires of Race Antipathy," *South Atlantic Quarterly*, II (October, 1903), 297–305.

174. For a graphic account of the election of 1898, see Josephus Daniels, *Editor in Politics* (Chapel Hill, N.C., 1941), Chap. 26. "The militant voice of White Supremacy" in that campaign was the Raleigh *News and Observer*, of which Daniels was the editor. See also Helen G. Edmonds, *The Negro and Fusion Politics in North Carolina, 1894–1901* (Chapel Hill, N.C., 1951), Chap. 10; Robert F. Durden, *The Climax of Populism: The Election of 1896* (Lexington, Ky., 1965), 165–68.

175. Bassett to Adams, November 15, 1898, in William Stull Holt, ed., *Historical Scholarship in the United States, 1876–1901: As Revealed in the Correspondence of*

Three months later the Trinity historian informed his Hopkins friend that the North Carolina "white man's government" was "in full blast." The legislators were, he reported, in process of passing a Jim Crow railroad-car law; and they were also planning a suffrage amendment which would disfranchise blacks and not disfranchise ignorant whites. The projected amendment was at best "an enamelled lie," since it would teach the people "that it is right to lie, to steal, & to defy all honesty in order to keep a certain party in power."[176]

When, in 1900, Charles B. Aycock ran for governor, he and his fellow Democrats did campaign zealously to secure the ratification of an amendment to the constitution requiring voters to pass a literacy test. Bands of militant whites, clad in red shirts and armed with shotguns, staged "white supremacy jubilees" as a means of frightening Negroes away from the polling places.[177] Aycock won overwhelmingly, and the amendment carried substantially. The aftermath was a wave of violence, resulting in eight Negro lynchings during the first half of the governor's four-year term.

In August, 1903, yet another anti-Negro outburst occurred. A party of thirty-eight prominent black men, including Booker T. Washington, detrained at Hamlet, North Carolina, for a prearranged breakfast, and were seated in the main dining room of the dinner house. When a handful of white passengers, including Senator Augustus B. Bacon of Georgia, also sought breakfast, they were directed to a smaller room. The senator angrily charged that Negroes were being put ahead of whites, and journalists and politicians across the state magnified the incident into a major insult to the white race.

Unable to restrain himself any longer, Bassett hastily drafted the celebrated editorial. In addition to warning against exploiting the Negro question for political gain, he directly attacked the white man's racial creed. His democratic spirit rebelled against the tra-

---

Herbert Baxter Adams (Baltimore, 1938), 257-59. Unlike Bassett, southern Methodism's leading newspaper, the Nashville *Christian Advocate*, December 1, 1898, defended the Wilmington uprising. For an inside account by a local black Baptist preacher, see J. Allen Kirk, *A Statement of Facts Concerning the Bloody Riot in Wilmington, N.C.*, (n.p., n.d.).

176. Bassett to Adams, February 18, 1899, in Holt, ed., *Historical Scholarship in the United States*, 265.

177. Oliver H. Orr, Jr., *Charles Brantley Aycock* (Chapel Hill, N.C., 1961), 174-77.

ditional notion that a black person was to be arbitrarily assigned a "place" in human society. "The 'place' of every man in our American life is such one as his virtues and his capacities may enable him to take," he asserted. "Not even a black skin and a flat nose can justify caste in this country."[178] In opposition to those hard-line conservatives who wanted either to expatriate or to subjugate Negroes, he urged that the only right solution was to incorporate the latter fully into American society.[179] He furthermore predicted that, despite the prevalent antipathy toward black people, "they will win equality at some time."[180] In deliberate defiance of the traditional dogma of Negro inferiority, he called Booker T. Washington "all in all the greatest man, save General Lee, born in the South in a hundred years."[181]

This spirited attack upon race mongering aroused a witch hunt, led by Josephus Daniels of the Raleigh *News and Observer*, which almost cost Bassett his professorship.[182] Bassett tendered his resignation, but the trustees declined to accept it by a vote of eighteen to seven. They nevertheless made it clear that their action was taken solely in defense of academic freedom, not in support of the historian's racial views. They not only explicitly disavowed his racial opinions, but disclaimed all responsibility for them on the ground that the *Quarterly*, in which they had been expressed, "was in no sense an organ of the college."[183] In a memorial to the trustees, all members of the faculty except one, who was then "out of town," had likewise declared that they did "not assent to the views of our colleague," although they solidly urged the board of trustees to retain the services of Bassett on the principle of academic freedom.[184]

178. "Stirring Up the Fires of Race Antipathy," *South Atlantic Quarterly*, II, 301.
179. Bassett had already caustically reviewed Thomas Dixon's *The Leopard's Spots*, dismissing its proposed solution of the Negro problem as an "impossible piece of social quackery." *South Atlantic Quarterly*, I (April, 1902), 189.
180. "Stirring Up the Fires of Race Antipathy," *South Atlantic Quarterly*, II, 304.
181. Since Bassett's previous articles in the *Quarterly* had been ignored by the southern papers, he injected the Lee-Washington remark "to make them take notice" of his writings. Bassett to Edwin Mims of Trinity College, January 1, 1909 (Bassett Papers, in the possession of Mr. Richard H. Bassett, Milton, Mass.).
182. Earl W. Porter, *Trinity and Duke, 1892-1924: Foundations of Duke University* (Durham, N.C., 1964), Chap. 4; Daniels, *Editor in Politics*, Chap. 37.
183. "The Statement of the Trustees," *South Atlantic Quarterly*, III (January, 1904), 62-64.
184. "Memorial From the Faculty to the Trustees," *ibid.*, 65-68.

It was the sentiment of the student body, said an editorial in the *Archive*, that Bassett, in publishing views "so radical from a Southern point of view," had "made a grave but not unpardonable blunder." Loving and respecting him as a man, they "forgave him his mistake."[185]

Two years after the controversy, Bassett told Oswald Garrison Villard, editor of the New York *Evening Post*, that it had "long been" his hope to "say something which would put the white people of the South in a way to realize their line of duty" toward the black man. "One little attempt that I made ended as you know. I am not discouraged; some time I shall have another opportunity and I shall speak again."[186] Although Bassett held his Trinity professorship until 1906, when he accepted a position at Smith College in Massachusetts, he did not "speak again" on the sensitive subject while serving his alma mater. This is understandable, for even though he had been granted academic freedom, the trustees and his colleagues had told him in effect that it would be unwise to exercise it on behalf of racial reform.

Why did Bassett go North? He did so, he told William E. Dodd of Randolph Macon College, because he "could not write history and direct public sentiment too."[187] He, however, probably went to the heart of the matter in a letter to his long-time confidant, William K. Boyd of Trinity. The decisive factor, he said, was not a larger salary, nor a lighter academic load, nor the desire to settle in a highly intellectual section of the country. "I merely wanted a peaceful atmosphere."[188]

Yet another dissenter from the white South's racial creed was Quincy Ewing, a clergyman of the Protestant Episcopal Church. Born on a Louisiana plantation in 1867, he completed his undergraduate and theological studies at the University of the South. In 1906, following short ministries in several cities, including Cleveland, Ohio; New Orleans, Louisiana; Greenville, Mississippi; and

---

185. "Editorial in the Archive," *ibid.*, 69. The *Archive* was a student publication, and the editorial was written by its editor-in-chief, W. P. Budd.
186. Bassett to Villard, November 17, 1905 (Villard Papers, Harvard University Library. Used by permission).
187. Bassett to Dodd, May 7, 1907 (Bassett Papers). For a similar explanation, see Bassett to Charles Francis Adams, November 3, 1911 (Bassett Papers).
188. Bassett to Boyd, January 2, 1912 (Bassett Papers).

Birmingham, Alabama, he took charge of Christ Church in the small town of Napoleonville, Louisiana, where he remained for twenty-three years.[189]

In the late summer of 1901, the racial heretic preached a scathing anti-lynching sermon to his congregation at St. James Church in Greenville, and the New York *Outlook* reprinted an extended extract from it in a commendatory editorial, entitled "The Epidemic of Savagery."[190] Among other courageous statements, Ewing declared that if Mississippi could not put an end to the lynching of Negroes, the national government "ought to take a hand in this business." Naturally, the rector quickly became a prime target for James K. Vardaman, the state's most notorious racist.

Responding to a request from the *Outlook*, Quincy Ewing expanded his views under the title, "How Can Lynching Be Checked in the South?" That barbarity could be stopped, he wrote, if public sentiment were strong enough to force the state legislatures to outlaw it. The press and the pulpit could generate that sentiment, if they only had the will and courage to speak out. After mildly criticizing the journalists for their moral apathy, Ewing severely chided the southern clergy. "And the pulpits—what is the matter with them? Are the men fit to fill them unfit to recognize murder when they see it? ... They must speak out, or have it written against them that their ministry is a mockery of the spirit of Jesus Christ."[191]

Since nothing came of his appeal, Ewing seems to have fallen silent on the subject. In 1905, while serving as rector of the Church of Advent in Birmingham, Alabama, he wrote George W. Cable a melancholy letter, saying that he often felt keenly "the loneliness" of his position "in regard to certain matters of social unrighteousness." In that remark he evidently had chiefly in mind the harsh treatment of black people, for he told Cable that he had just sent a manuscript to a northern publisher on "The Criminality of the Southern Negro: An Essay in Explanation and Rebuttal."[192]

189. For a full account of Ewing's family background and ministerial career, see Charles E. Wynes, "The Reverend Quincy Ewing: Southern Racial Heretic in the 'Cajun' Country," *Louisiana History,* VII (Summer, 1966), 221–28.
190. *Outlook*, September 7, 1901. According to the editorial, four Negroes had been "burned at the stake" during the preceding month.
191. *Outlook*, October 12, 1901.
192. Ewing to Cable, August 16, 1905 (Special Collections, Tulane University Library).

In 1909, after brooding several years, the lonely churchman published a keenly perceptive essay on the essence of the South's racial problem. He disagreed entirely with those who located that problem in what they termed the ignorance, indolence, and criminality of blacks.[193] Instead, said Ewing, the heart of the race problem consisted in the white southerner's determination to prevent the black man from disproving the dogma of Negro inferiority. "Friction between the races is entirely absent so long as the Negro justifies the white man's opinion of him as an inferior; is grateful for privileges and lays no claim to *rights.*" But trouble arises the moment the black man begins to manifest those qualities, tastes, and ambitions which supposedly belong exclusively to the white race and which, if not checked, would undermine the traditional doctrine of Negro inferiority.[194]

According to Ewing, the South's system of segregation was designed not so much to separate the races in space as to separate them in status. In other words, the dogma of black inferiority would be endangered if blacks and whites attended the same school, sat side by side on a train or in a bus, occupied the same pew in a church, competed for the same honor, or broke bread at a common table. When, for instance, President Theodore Roosevelt in 1901 dined with Booker T. Washington at the White House, many white southern spokesmen regarded it as a serious breach of social etiquette.[195] It mattered not at all that his guest was the distinguished principal of Tuskegee Institute; he was a Negro, and no Negro was fit to sit at a white man's table, least of all the table of the President of the United States. When, in July of 1908, a Negro girl won first prize in a national spelling contest, held at Cleveland, Ohio, there was a similar southern uproar. The superintendent of the New Orleans public schools was "roundly denounced" for allowing his white wards to compete with a Negro.[196] The frenzy was the result of one thing only: the girl's victory challenged the traditional stereotype of Negro inferiority.

193. "The Heart of the Race Problem," *Atlantic Monthly,* CIII (March, 1909), 390–92.
194. *Ibid.,* 393.
195. *Ibid.,* 395. See also Dewey W. Grantham, "Dinner at the White House: Theodore Roosevelt, Booker T. Washington, and the South," *Tennessee Historical Quarterly,* XVII (June, 1958), 112–30.
196. "The Heart of the Race Problem," *Atlantic Monthly,* CIII, 395.

V

There was, then, a native protest against the dominant racial creed of the post-reconstruction South, and those sharing in that protest had a profound understanding of the fundamental root of white racism. Yet they were a voice crying in the wilderness. For many years George Cable contended that there was a silent South in basic agreement with him, and he persistently urged this South to speak out against the increasing subjugation of the black man. If any such South existed, it kept discreetly silent. Cable finally stopped publicly agitating the sensitive subject, apparently concluding that his breath was being wasted. Lewis Harvie Blair at first seemed hopeful of persuading the white South to unloose the shackles of the minority race, but he finally capitulated to the anti-Negro movement which he had previously assailed. Dispirited and isolated, Quincy Ewing abandoned his public fight for racial justice long before leaving the parish at Napoleonville. John Spencer Bassett, a historian with a reforming impulse, tried to awaken his fellow whites to the social perils of oppressing black people, but when his prophetic article of 1903 triggered a heated reaction, he abandoned the role of racial reformer and soon left the South for calmer academic surroundings. In short, all four fought a losing battle.

The movement of racial orthodoxy, on the other hand, grew stronger every year through at least the first decade of the present century. Assuming that the racial theorists reviewed in this chapter typified the clerical thinking of their generation, it is clear that organized religion in the white South was dominated by spokesmen who held firmly to the dogma of Negro inferiority, and who thus maintained that the system of black-white separatism represented the normal development of a divinely implanted instinct. They furthermore defended the policy of segregation on the ground that it was necessary for the preservation of racial integrity. Moderates as well as extremists condemned the constitutional provision for Negro suffrage and heartily sanctioned the southern campaign to disfranchise blacks. When the twentieth century dawned, white churchmen of the South had largely lost ecclesiastical contact with their "brother in black." They were enslaved to the traditional spirit of color caste, and there was little prospect of their emancipation in the foreseeable future.

INDEX

Abbott, Lyman, 217
Abel, 131
Abolitionism. *See* Antislavery movements
Abraham, 13, 16, 131, 192, 213
Adam (first man), 157, 159–61, 164–65
Adam (slave), 17
Adams, Charles Francis, 301n
Adams, Herbert Baxter, 274–75, 297, 298, 299n
Adger, John B., 138n, 209, 243n
Adlam, Samuel, 115, 123–24
African Methodist Episcopal Church, 54, 223–24, 259
African Methodist Episcopal Zion Church, 223, 224–25
African Presbyterian Church, 242
Agassiz, Elizabeth C., 156n
Agassiz, Louis, 155–57, 161
Alabama, Baptists in, 126, 227, 281; secessionist stance, 175, 178, 179
Alabama Baptist, 253
Albright, Raymond W., 223n
Alderman, Edwin A., 281n, 286
Allen, Charles R., Jr., 49n
Allen, Ira M., 118
Alpha Synod (Lutheran), 245–46
Alvord, John W., 219
American Anti-Slavery Society, 74–75, 78, 96
American Baptist Anti-Slavery Convention, 118, 122, 125
American Baptist Free Mission Society, 124
American Baptist Home Mission Society, 120, 123–26, 221–22, 252
American Colonization Society, 8, 66–68, 71, 91, 95–96, 100, 106, 128
American Education Society, 83, 87
American Freedmen's Union Commission, 219
American Home Missionary Society, 83, 87
American Missionary Association, 218, 220–21, 251
American Missionary Society, 217

"American School" of ethnology, 154–65
"An Address to Christians Throughout the World," 197–98
Anderson, Hugh George, 244n, 246n
Andrew, James O., 102n, 108–111
Anglicans, as slaveholders, 9; attitude toward slavery, 8–11. *See also* Episcopalians
Anglo-Saxonism, 262–63, 276–77
Antislavery movements, Colonial period, 15–18; Revolutionary period, 18–73; ante-bellum period, 74–128
Anti-Slavery Society of Salem and Vicinity, 116
Antislavery societies, 69–77, 96, 116
Antonelli (Cardinal), 7
"Appeal" and "Counter Appeal," 97–99, 114
Aristotle, 140
Armstrong, George D., 145n
Asbury, Francis, 37–38, 40, 42n, 44, 46–47, 69
Asplund, John, 47n, 53n
Atlanta University, 221
Atlantic Monthly, 285
Atlantic Synod (Presbyterian), 243
Aycock, Charles B., 276, 299

Bachman, John, 161–64, 244–45
Bacon, Augustus B., 299
Bacon, Leonard W., 278n
Bacon, Thomas, 11–12
Bailey, Hugh C., 285n, 286n, 287n, 289n
Bailey, Rufus William, 154n
Bainbridge, Peter, 53
Baird, Samuel J., 82n, 89n
Baker, Paul M., 290
Baker, Ray Stannard, 271n
Baker, Robert A., 115n, 119n
Baker, William A., 180
Baker Institute, 221
Baldwin, William H., Jr., 286
Baltimore Conference (Methodist), 108
Bangs, Nathan, 97, 102
Banneker, Benjamin, 22

Banner of the South, 253
Baptist Board of Foreign Missions, 117–20
Baptist General Tract Society, 118
Baptists, abolitionism controversy, 114–27; as slaveholders, 53; attitude toward defeat of Confederacy, 210–11; freedmen's work, 221–22; opposed to slavery, 47–55; post-Reconstruction attitudes, 264–66, 273–74, 281–82; proslavery stance, 53–55; secessionist stance, 179; segregation of churches, 226–29
Barnes, Albert, 83
Barnes, Gilbert H., 75n, 77n
Barnes, William B., 127n
Barringer, Paul B., 286
Barrow, David, 49–53, 130–31
Bascom, Henry Bidleman, 45–46, 95–96, 100, 105, 110, 112, 144, 152
The Basis of Ascendancy, 287
Bassett, Ancel H., 190n
Bassett, John Spencer, 297–301, 304
Baudier, Roger, 178n, 251n
Baxter, George A., 65n, 84–89, 134n
Beard, Augustus F., 218n
Beecher, Charles, 89n
Bell, John, 184
Bell, John L., Jr., 228n, 244n
Beman, Nathan S. S., 78n
Benedict, David, 50, 52
Benezet, Anthony, 24–25, 29, 36–37
Bennett John B., 214n
Bentley, George R., 219n, 220n
Berkeley, George, 11
Berwanger, Eugene H., 152n
Biblical arguments for and against slavery, 17, 28, 42, 55, 84, 98, 129–36
Biblical Recorder, 185, 228
Biblical Repertory, 80
Biddle Memorial Institute, 223, 243
Bikle, Lucy L. C., 289n, 291n
Birney, James G., 75, 101n, 102n
Birney, William, 52n
Bishop, H. G., 247
Black churches, 54, 153, 223–25, 227–28, 279
"Black Republicans," 171, 194, 208
Blair, Lewis Harvie, 294–97, 304
Bledsoe, Albert Taylor, 132n, 134n, 138n, 143, 149n, 214–15, 216, 253
Blenk, James H., 251
Blied, Benjamin J., 190n, 199n
Bloomfield, Maxwell, 274n
Board of Baptist Ministers (London), 117–18

Board of Domestic and Indian Missions (Baptist), 226
Bolles, Lucius, 117
The Book and Slavery, 65–66
Boorstin, Daniel J., 21n
Bost, Raymond M., 161n, 164n, 244n, 245n
Botsford, Edmund, 53
Bourne, George, 61–66, 74, 88, 130
Bourne, Theodore, 61n, 65
Bowen, Henry C., 261
Bowen, William, 35
Boyce, James C., 278n
Boyce, James Petigru, 173n, 180
Boyd, William K., 41n, 301
Bracken Association (Baptist), 50
Bragg, George Freeman, Jr., 246n
Bray, Thomas, 8
Breckinridge, John C., 177, 184
Breckinridge, Robert J., 85–87
Brewer, H. Peers, 223n
Brisbane, William Henry, 75, 124
Broadus, John A., 173n
Brookes, George S., 23n, 24n, 33n, 36n, 37n
Brookes, Iveson L., 145, 169n
Brown, Edward, 145
Brown, John, 216
Brown, Morris, 54
Browne, William H., 10n
Brownlow, William G., 144n, 149n, 186
Bryan, T. Conn, 189n
Buchanan, James, 176, 186, 259
Bucke, Emory Stevens, 113n
Bureau of Refugees, Freedmen, and Abandoned Lands, 219–20
Burgess, Dyer, 65n
Burke, J. M., 231–32
Burks, Edward C., 186n, 188n
Butler, Benjamin F., 174n

Cabell, James L., 164n
Cable, George Washington, 289–94, 295, 302, 304
Cadbury, Henry J., 35n
Cain, 131
Caldwell, John H., 211–12
Calhoun, John C., 144n, 150, 158n, 166, 168, 173
Canaan, 16, 130–31, 157
Cannibals All, 150
Capers, William, 95, 102
Carmen, Joshua, 49
Carroll, Charles, 7–8, 20
Carroll, John, 7
Carroll, Kenneth L., 7n, 16n, 32n, 42n

Caskey, Thomas W., 177
Catholic Mirror (Baltimore), 199
Catholics. *See* Roman Catholics
Catterall, Helen T., 10n
Catton, Bruce, 195n
Central Methodist (Louisville), 271
Central Presbyterian (Richmond), 197
Central Tennessee College, 221
Channing, William Ellery, 137–39
Chapman, Stuart W., 190n
Charleston, S.C., 54, 171–72, 246–47
Charleston Association (Baptist), 116
Charleston Union Presbytery, 79
Chillicothe Presbytery, 77, 88
Chinese Exclusion Act (1882), 262
Christ in the Camp, 215
Christian Advocate (Nashville), 188, 213
Christian Advocate and Journal (New York), 97, 234
Christian Index, 264
Christian Monitor, 67
Christmas Conference, 1784 (Methodist), 38–39, 43, 103
Church Intelligencer, 185
Church of the People (New York), 275
Churches. *See* names of individual groups, e.g., Baptists
Cincinnati Antislavery Society, 101
Civil Rights Act (1866), 252
Civil Rights Act (1875), 255, 263, 291
Civil rights of blacks, 252–57, 258–64, 289–303
Civil War, 187–96
Claflin University, 221, 279
The Clansman, 277
Clapp, Theodore, 138n, 153
Clark, D. W., 103n
Clark, Elmer T., 37n, 46n, 69n
Clark University, 221
Clarkson, Thomas, 25
Clay, Henry, 167
Clebsch, William A., 189n, 197n
Clergymen in the Civil War, 188–96
Cleveland, Henry, 183n
Clinton, Joseph J., 225
Cochran, Bernard H., 47n
Codrington, Christopher, 9
Coffin, Joshua, 18n
Coffin, Levi, 219
Coke, Thomas, 37–40
Coles, Edward, 22n
Colonization of blacks, 8, 17, 21, 63, 66–68, 71, 78, 95–96, 100, 106, 143, 269–70

Colored Methodist Episcopal Church in America, 231, 279
Colquitt, Alfred H., 278n
Colver, Nathaniel, 121n, 222n
Comfort, Silas, 106
Commager, Henry S., 252n, 262n, 263n, 264n
Committee on Freedmen (Presbyterian), 223
Compromise of 1850, 167–68, 184
Compromise of 1877, 258
Compton, Henry, 8
Cone, Spencer H., 117, 121, 122
Confederate States, 180–96
Congregationalist (Boston), 216
Congregationalists, freedmen's work, 220–21, 251; opposed to slavery, 18–19, 218
Congress (U.S.), 75, 166, 214, 219–20, 252, 253, 255, 260, 262
Constitution (Confederate), 182–84
Constitution (U.S.), 75, 169–70, 173, 182–83, 186, 214–15, 253, 258, 263–64, 272, 288
Converse, Amasa, 80, 82
Conversion of slaves. *See* Evangelization
Cook, Harvey T., 173n
Cook, Raymond A., 275n
Corey, Charles H., 222
Coulter, E. Merton, 186n
Craig, William, 62
Crallé, Richard K., 144n, 150n, 166n
Crocker, Zebulon, 78n, 82n, 89n
Crutenden, Robert, 14
Cumberland Presbyterian Church, 190
Curd, Charles P., 273n
Curnock, Nehemiah, 36n
Curry, Daniel, 234
Curry, Jabez L. M., 257n, 258, 279n, 280–82
Curtis, Moses Ashley, 158
Cush, 16

Dabney, Charles W., 286
Dabney, Robert Lewis, 136, 180, 185, 187, 188, 189, 209–210, 214, 215, 216, 239–40, 242n, 266–67, 268, 278
Dagg, John L., 130n, 135n
Daily Delta (New Orleans), 175
Dalcho, Frederick, 130n, 149
Dana, William C., 171, 173
Daniel, W. Harrison, 153n, 185n, 186n, 189n
Daniels, Josephus, 298n, 300
Daniels, W. H., 236n

INDEX

Darwin, Charles, 163, 274
Davidson, A. B., 62
Davies, Samuel, 13–15
Davis, David Brion, 15n
Davis, Hugh, 3
Davis, Jefferson, 175, 182, 191, 215, 216n, 249n, 250
De Bow's Review, 150
Declaration of Independence, 137, 172, 265, 295
Declaration of Sentiments, 74–76
A Defence of Virginia, 209
Degler, Carl N., 3–4
Delaware Conference (Methodist), 232, 233, 235
De Santis, Vincent P., 259n
Dew, Thomas Roderick, 146–47, 148
Dexter, Henry M., 216
Dianna (slave), 41
Dickey, James H., 77n, 78n, 81
Dillon, Merton L., 70n
Dissent from racial orthodoxy, 289–305
Dixon, Thomas, Jr., 274–77, 278, 300n
Dodd, Dorothy, 176n
Dodd, William E., 301
Dodge, Josiah, 49
Doggett, David S., 230–31
Donald, David, 255n
Dover Association (Baptist), 229
Drake, Richard B., 218n, 219n, 220n
Drake, Thomas E., 6n, 15n, 16n, 29n, 31n, 32n, 34n, 35n, 72n, 73
Drinker, Joseph, 35
Drinkhouse, Edward J., 190n
Dromgoole, Edward, 39n
Duberman, Martin B., 97n
Du Bois, William E. B., 225–26
DuBose, William Porcher, 285
Dumond, Dwight L., 75n, 185n
Dunlap, William C., 34n
Dunwody, Samuel, 131n, 135n
Durbin, John P., 109, 111
Durden, Robert F., 298n
Duren, William L., 283n

Eaton, Clement, 20
Eaton, John Q., Jr., 257
Edmonds, Helen G., 298n
Education of blacks, 142, 202–205, 221–23, 250, 255–57, 267, 273–74, 279–80
Elder, William H., 250
Elements of Moral Philosophy, 270
Elements of Moral Science, 137, 140
Elkhorn Association (Baptist), 49–50

Elliott, Charles, 100n, 111
Elliott, Stephen, 191–95, 196, 206–207, 210, 226
Ellis, John Tracy, 7n, 253n
Ely, Richard T., 275
Emancipation, 20, 50, 57, 60, 66, 127, 198, 216
Emory, John, 99–100
Enfranchisement of blacks, 251–54, 259–62, 267, 272, 282, 288, 296, 299
England, John, 133
Engles, William M., 81
Episcopal Methodist (Richmond), 230, 231
Episcopalians, freedmen's work, 223; opposed to segregation, 301–303; participation in Civil War, 189; post-Reconstruction attitudes, 285–89; pro-slavery stance, 196–97; segregation of churches, 246–48. *See also* Anglicans
Estes, Matthew, 143n, 144n
Ethnology, 154–65
Eubank, Wayne C., 175n
Euclid, 21
Evangelical Lutheran Church of Freedmen in America, 245–46
Evangelical Lutheran General Synod in North America, 244
Evangelization of slaves, 8–15, 19, 46, 94, 152–54, 197
Evans, J. E., 232
Ewing, Quincy, 301–302, 304

Fairly, John S., 247n
Family Visitor (Richmond), 67
Farish, Hunter D., 40n
Fee, John G., 221n
Felton, Rebecca Latimer (Mrs. William H.), 284–85
Filler, Louis, 75n
Finley, James B., 108–110
Finley, Robert, 8n
Finnie, Gordon E., 72n, 75n
Fisher, John E., 278n
Fisk, Wilbur, 97, 99, 107
Fisk University, 221, 279
Fitzgerald, O. P., 170n
Fitzhugh, George, 150–51, 152n
The Flaming Sword, 277
Fleetwood, William, 9
Fletcher, John, 131, 150n
Florida, secessionist stance, 175–77, 179
Foote, William H., 60n, 87n
Ford, Paul L., 22n

Ford, Paul M., 201n
Foss, A. T., 115n, 117n, 118n, 121n–126n
Fothergill, John, 24n
Franklin, Benjamin, 25
Franklin, John Hope, 72n, 152n, 198n, 224n, 252n, 264n, 271
Fraser, Walter J., 257n
Fredrickson, George M., 155n
Free Negroes, 72, 152
Free Presbyterian Synod, 91
Free Will Baptists, 220, 225
Freedmen's aid societies, 218–26
Freedmen's Aid Society (Methodist), 221
Freedmen's Bureau, 219–20
Freedmen's Commission (Episcopal), 223
Freeman, George W., 135n, 139n
Fretz, J. Herbert, 15n
Friends, as slaveholders, 6; freedmen's work, 225; opposed to slavery, 15–16, 23–36, 69–73
Friends of Humanity, 50–52
Fry, Thomas, 245n
Fuller, Erasmus Q., 235–36, 256
Fuller, Richard, 122–24, 133, 134n, 135–36, 138, 143n, 153n
Furman, James Clement, 173
Furman, Richard, 53–55, 173

Galbraith, Robert C., 77n
Galloway, Charles Betts, 282–83
Galusha, Elon, 118–19, 122
Gannon, Michael V., 176n, 249n, 250n
Garber, Paul L., 196n
Garrettson, Freeborn, 41n, 42n
Garrison, Wendell P., 116n
Garrison, William Lloyd, 65, 74, 116
Gaston, William, 34
Genetic theories of racial origins, 154–65
George, Enoch, 45
Georgia, Baptists in, 121, 125–27; Methodists in, 104–105, 110, 235; participation in Civil War, 193
Georgia Colony, 13
Gewehr, Wesley M., 14n
Gibson, Edmund, 9–10
"Gideonites," 219
Gillard, John T., 7n, 248n, 251n
Gillett, Ezra H., 82n, 83n
Gilliland, James, 60, 77n
Gilman, Daniel C., 278n
Gilpatrick, James, 115
Girardeau, John L., 237–38, 240
Gladden, Washington, 261, 262
Gliddon, George R., 155, 156n, 164n

"God Save the South," 190–91
"God's dark providence," 208
Godwyn, Morgan, 11
The Gospel Among the Slaves, 213
Grady, Henry Woodfin, 292–94
Graham, Fay M., 115n
Graham, William, 136n
Grant, Ulysses S., 217, 255, 257
Grantham, Dewey W., 303n
Gravely, William B., 41n, 114n, 233n
Graves, John Temple, 286
Grayson, William J., 150, 153
Great Awakening, 12–15
Green, Ashbel, 65n
Greene, L. F., 47n
Greene, Lorenzo J., 5n, 8n
Greenwood, Leonora, 108
Grégoire, Henri, 22n
Griffith, Alfred, 108
Gross, William H., 250, 251
Grosvenor, Cyrus Pitt, 115, 117–18, 119n
Guilday, Peter, 248n
Gummere, Amelia Mott, 26n–31n

Habakkuk, 27
Hall, James D. S., 223
Ham, 16, 28, 130–31, 157, 271
Hamilton, William H., 298n
Hamilton, William T., 134n, 161
Hammond, James Henry, 148–49
Hamner, James G., 92
Hampton, Wade, 258–59, 260
Hampton Institute, 221, 279
Hancock Association (Baptist), 115
Handlin, Oscar and Mary F., 3n
Handy, Robert T., 15n, 55n, 74n, 114n
Harding, Francis A., 108
Hargrove, Dudley, 45
Harlan, Louis R., 271n, 286n, 287n, 288n
Harper, Thomas G., 247
Harper, William, 147
Harris, Marvin, 3n
Harris, Robert J., 263n
Harrison, William P., 94n, 213
Hartzell, J. C., 256
Haven, Gilbert, 114, 233–37, 256, 259, 279, 292
Hayes, Rutherford B., 258–60, 278n
Haygood, Atticus G., 277–80, 282
Haynes, Henry W., 6n
Hedding, Elijah, 98n, 99–100, 102n, 103
Hening, William W., 3n, 33n
Henkle, Moses M., 45n, 46n, 96n

Henry, Patrick, 23
Henry, Stuart C., 13n, 196n
Hepburn, John, 15
Herron, Robert, 62
Hewat, Alexander, 10n, 18n
Hickey, Doralyn J., 174n
Hickman, William, 50
Hill, Benjamin M., 121n
Hirshson, Stanley P., 259n, 260n
Historical Account of Guinea, 36
History, proslavery philosophy of, 143–65, 174, 192–95
Hodge, Charles, 77n, 78n, 80, 128
Hoge, James, 78, 81
Hoge, Moses Drury, 185n, 197n, 205n, 208, 217, 252
Hoge, Peyton H., 208n, 252n
Holland, Rupert S., 259n
Holmes, Edward D., 53n
Holt, William Stull, 298n
Hood, James W., 224–25
Hoole, W. Stanley, 175n
Hopewell Presbytery, 79
Hopkins, John H., 137n
Hopkins, Samuel, 18–19
Hopkins, Stephen, 31
Horton, Jotham, 107
Hosmer, William, 114
Houston, Samuel, 64n
Howard, Oliver Otis, 219
Howard, Victor B., 77n, 78n, 89n, 91n, 92n, 93n
Howe, George, 160
Howe, William B. W., 246–48
Huffam, James Dunn, 228
Hughes, John, 199n
Hundley, D. R., 148n
Hurd, John C., 3n, 7n

Ide, George B., 123
Independent (New York), 261, 294
Indians, 5, 229, 274
Inferiority of blacks (claimed by whites), 4, 5, 11, 21–22, 128, 137–45, 154–65, 210, 239–40, 262–63, 264–77, 279–80, 282–84, 303
Intermarriage, 3, 51–52, 57, 162, 240, 266, 270, 293
Isaac, 131
Ives, L. Silliman, 139n

Jackson, Thomas J. ("Stonewall"), 189, 193n
Jacob, 131
Jamaica, 35

James, E. S., 212n
James, Sydney V., 31n, 34n, 35n
Jamestown, Va., 3
Japheth, 130–31, 271
Jarratt, Devereaux, 39
Jefferson, Thomas, 20–22, 23, 24, 28, 137, 140–41, 150, 183
Jenkins, Courtney, 199
Jenkins, William S., 164n
Jernegan, Marcus W., 10n
Jesus' attitude toward slavery, 133–34
Jeter, Jeremiah Bell, 124, 210, 228–29, 253, 255–56, 257
Jim Crow laws, 254–55, 280, 299
Johnson, Andrew, 252
Johnson, Clifton H., 218n
Johnson, Thomas Cary, 136n, 180n, 185n, 187n, 210n, 239n, 242n
Johnson, William B., 122, 125, 127
Johnson C. Smith University, 223, 243
Jones, Charles Colcock, 154
Jones, John William, 214, 215–16
Jones, Rufus M., 29n, 30n, 31n
Jordan, Winthrop, 4, 22n
Joseph, 16, 152
Josephites, 249
Junkin, George, 136n

Kansas, 148–49
Keith, George, 15
Kelly, Alfred H., 255n
Kennebec Association (Baptist), 115
Kennedy, Lionel H., 54n
Kenrick, Francis Patrick, 176
Kentucky, Baptists in, 48–52; Methodists in, 100; Presbyterians in, 56–59
Ketocton Association (Baptist), 47
Ketring, Ruth Anna, 70n, 71n
Key, David M., 260
Key, V. O., 264n
Kirk, J. Allen, 299n
Klingberg, Frank J., 8n, 9n, 10n, 11n
Knoxville Whig, 186
Koontz, D. J., 245

Lamar, Lucius Q. C., 177
Laurens, Henry, 20
Laws concerning black-white relationships, 3, 6–7, 10, 13, 32–33, 252, 254, 263–64, 293–94, 299
Lay, Benjamin, 15, 18
Leacock, W. T., 173–74
Leberton, Dagmar Renshaw, 178n
Lee, Jesse, 40n
Lee, Luther, 102n, 107n

Lee, Robert E., 189, 190, 193, 195, 208, 300
Leftwich, William M., 269
Le Jau, Francis, 8–9, 11
Leland, John, 47–48
Lemen, James, 52n
The Leopard's Spots, 275–77
Letters on Slavery, 67
Levin, David, 6n
Lewis, T. Willard, 234
Lexington Presbytery, 62–65
Lexington (South) Presbytery, 92
Liberator, 74, 97, 116
Lincoln, Abraham, 171, 174, 175, 177–78, 180, 181, 184, 186, 187, 192, 198, 207, 215, 290
Lincoln, Heman, 120, 124
Linegar, Isaac, 35
Litwack, Leon F., 144n
Lockhart, Jesse, 71
Lockwood, Lewis C., 218
Lodge, Henry Cabot, 282n
Loetscher, Lefferts A., 15n, 55n, 74n, 114n
Logan, Frenise A., 281n, 296n
Logan, Rayford W., 271n
Longstreet, Augustus B., 135, 167, 170, 191
Lord, John C., 136n
Lord, Nathan, 131n
Louisiana, secessionist stance, 173–75
Luker, Ralph E., 158n
Lundy, Benjamin, 70–72
Lurie, Edward, 156n, 157n
Lutheran Church–Missouri Synod, 246
Lutherans, participation in Civil War, 189; segregation of churches, 244–46
Lynch, James, 223, 224
Lynch, Patrick N., 199n, 250–51
Lyon, James A., 180, 202–205

Malone, Dumas, 23n
Manire, B. F., 177n
Manly, Basil, 175
Mann, Harold W., 278n
Mansfield (Lord Chief Justice), 25
Manumission of slaves, 7, 30, 41, 55, 69–73
Marriage (among slaves), 27
Marriage (black-white). *See* Intermarriage
Martin, Asa Earl, 48n, 58n, 70n, 73n
Martin, Auguste, 199
Maryland, Friends in, 31–32
Maryland Colony, 4
Mason, George, 20

Mather, Cotton, 5–6
Mathews, Donald G., 38n, 94n, 97n, 99n, 105n, 106n, 109n, 113
Matlack, Lucius C., 97n, 99n, 102, 103n, 105n, 106n, 107n
Mattison, Hiram, 114n
Maxwell, William, 67n, 68n
May, John A., 180n, 181n
May, Samuel J., 74
McCaine, Alexander, 130n, 133n
McColley, Robert, 24n
McCue, John, 62
McElhenny, John, 81, 85, 87
McFeely, William S., 220n
McIver, Charles D., 286
McKendree, William, 45, 46n
McMurry, Vincent de Paul, 199n, 248n, 250n
McPherson, Edward, 182n
McPherson, James M., 198n, 219n, 225n, 226n, 254n, 255n
McTyeire, Holland N., 188, 231
Mead, Sidney E., 82n
Mebane, George Allen, 286n
Meier, August, 263n
Mell, Patrick Hues, 130n, 132n, 143, 149n
Memminger, C. G., 247n
Merritt, Elizabeth, 148n
Methodist Advocate (Atlanta), 235
Methodist Episcopal Church, South, 112
Methodist Protestant Church, 189
Methodist Quarterly Review (New York), 234
Methodists, abolitionism controversy, 94–114; as slaveholders, 95, 108, 111, 113; attitude toward defeat of Confederacy, 211–13; freedmen's work, 221; opposed to segregation, 297–301; opposed to slavery, 36–47; participation in Civil War, 189; post-Reconstruction attitudes, 268–71, 277–80, 283–85; proslavery stance, 197; segregation of churches, 229–37
Miles, James Warley, 158n
Miller, Charles W., 279
Miller, Samuel, 78, 80, 81, 85
Mims, Edwin, 300n
Missionaries in the South, 216–26
Mississippi, secessionist stance, 177
Missouri Question, 68, 166
Mitchell, Joseph, 108n, 111n
Monroe, Haskell, Jr., 178n, 186n
Moore, Edmund A., 87n, 89n
Moore, George H., 17n, 18n
Moore, John, 59

314 INDEX

Morehouse, Henry L., 222n
Morison, Samuel Eliot, 193n
Morris, Thomas A., 100, 102, 104
Morrow, Ralph E., 232n, 237n
Morton, Samuel George, 155–57, 161–63
Moseley, B. W., 237n
Moses, 196
Muller, Dorothea R., 262n, 263n
Murch, W. H., 115, 118n
Murphy, Edgar Gardner, 285–89
Murphy, John C., 248n
Murray, Andrew E., 92n, 244n

Nat Turner Insurrection, 146
National Freedmen's Relief Association of New York, 218
Natural rights doctrine, 18–22, 27–28, 51, 137–38
Negro Evangelization Fund, 242
New Brunswick Presbytery, 80–81
New England Anti-Slavery Society, 74
New England Conference (Methodist), 97, 99, 101, 103
New England Freedmen's Aid Society, 218, 220
New Hampshire Conference (Methodist), 97, 99, 101
New Orleans, 173–75
New Orleans Christian Advocate, 184, 213, 283
"New South," 212, 267, 277
New York Presbytery, 81
News and Observer (Raleigh), 300
Nicholls, Francis T., 258
Niles, Nathaniel, 18
Noah, 16, 28, 130–31
Norris, Samuel, 101–102
North Carolina, antislavery societies in, 70–72; Baptists in, 227–28; Friends in, 33–34; Lutherans in, 245; Presbyterians in, 60, 244; secessionist stance, 185–86
North Carolina Christian Advocate, 185–86, 187
North Carolina Manumission Society, 70–71
North Carolina Presbyterian, 185–86
North District Association (Baptist), 50
Norwood, John N., 112n
Notes on the State of Virginia, 20–22
Nott, Josiah Clark, 155, 157–61, 164
Nuesse, C. J., 7n

Ogden, Robert C., 286, 288
O'Kelly, James, 41–42

Onesimus, 135
Orr, Oliver H., Jr., 299n
Osborn, Charles, 70–71
Otey, James Hervey, 186, 187–88
Our Brother in Black, 278
Our Country, 262–63
Outlook (New York), 302

Paine, Robert, 46n
Paine Institute, 279
Pakenham, Richard, 144n
Palmer, Benjamin Morgan, 94n, 173n, 174–75, 176, 205–206, 207, 217, 241–42
Park, Edwards A., 19n
Parker, Linus, 213, 253, 256
Parmelee, Julius H., 218n, 219n, 220n
Patterson, Henry S., 156n
Pattillo, Henry, 60
Paul (Apostle), 11, 54, 98, 134–35, 159, 213, 289
Paxton, John D., 62, 66–67
Payne, Daniel A., 54n, 224
Peabody, George Foster, 257, 286
Peabody Education Fund, 257, 281
Peake, Mary, 218
Peck, George, 111
Peck, Jesse T., 237
Peck, Solomon, 122
Peden, William, 20n
Pendleton, J. M., 186
Pendleton, William N., 189
Penn, William, 6
Pennsylvania Colony, 6–7, 29–31
Pennsylvania Freedmen's Aid Commission, 218
Pennypacker, Samuel W., 15n
Perché, Napoleon Joseph, 176, 178
Perry, William Stevens, 8n
Pettus, John J., 177n
Philadelphia, 7, 12, 29, 35
Philadelphia Conference (Methodist), 102
Philadelphia Port Royal Relief Committee, 218
Philemon, 135, 192
Phillips, Ulrich B., 54n
Phoebus, George A., 41n
Pierce, Edward L., 219
Pierce, George Foster, 195, 200–201
Pilcher, George W., 14n
Pillar, James J., 177n, 190n
Pinkney, William, 20
Pitts, Charles F., 189n
Plan of Union, 82, 87, 90
Pleasants, Robert, 23, 25n, 33

Plenary Council, 2nd (Baltimore), 248
Plessy v. *Ferguson*, 263
Plumer, William Swan, 85–89
Polk, Leonidas, 189
Pollard, J. H. M., 247
Pope, John, 193
Porter, Earl W., 300n
Powell, Milton P., 114n
Prentice, George, 236n
Prentiss, William O., 171–73
Presbyterian (Philadelphia), 78, 84, 85
Presbyterians, abolitionism controversy, 77–93; as slaveholders, 59–60; attitude toward defeat of Confederacy, 208–210; freedmen's work, 222; old school-new school controversy, 82–93; opposed to segregation, 289–94; opposed to slavery, 55–69; participation in Civil War, 189; post-Reconstruction attitudes, 266–67, 271–73; proslavery stance, 196, 205–206; secessionist stance, 178; segregation of churches, 237–44
Price, P. B., 67n
Price, R. N., 45n
Le Propagateur Catholique, 178
Protestant Episcopalians. *See* Episcopalians
Public school segregation, 255–57, 267, 279–80, 282
Purifoy, Lewis M., 113n
Puritans, as slaveholders, 5–6; opposed to slavery, 16–17
Putnam, Mary B., 119n, 122n, 124n

Quakers. *See* Friends

Racism, definition of, viii; new term for old American malady, 3
Racial orthodoxy, exponents of, 264–89; critics of, 289–303
Raleigh Institute, 222
Ralston, Thomas N., 96n
Rankin, John, 71, 75, 77n
Raper, Arthur F., 271n
Redkey, Edwin S., 270n
Redpath, James, 261
Reed, John C., 278n
Reeve, James, 126
Reimers, David M., 289n
Religious Herald (Richmond), 210, 228–29
Religious instruction of slaves. *See* Evangelization
Revels, Hiram R., 224

Reynolds, J. L., 221
Rhett, Robert Barnwell, 171
Rhode Island Colony, 26–27
Rice, David, 56–58, 63n
Rice, Jessie Pearl, 281n
Rice, John Holt, 67–68
Rice, Madeline H., 178n
Rice, Nathan L., 136n
Richards, Leonard L., 76n
Rivers, Richard H., 149, 270–71
Roanoke Association (Baptist), 48
Robert, Joseph C., 146n
Roberts, Robert R., 102n
Robinson, John, 172n
Rockefeller, John D., 286n
Roman Catholics, as slaveholders, 7; proslavery stance, 198–200; segregation of churches, 248–51
Roosevelt, Theodore, 303
Rose, Willie Lee, 219n, 259n
Ross, Frederick A., 132
Roszel, Stephen G., 101
Rouquette, Adrien-Emmanuel, 178n, 180
Rubin, Louis D., Jr., 278n
Ruchames, Louis, 3n
Ruffin, Edmund, 175n
Ruffner, William H., 256, 257n
Rush, Benjamin, 25
Rust, Richard S., 221
Rutledge, Francis H., 175–76
Ryan, Abram J., 253

Sacred Congregation of Propaganda, 177
Saffin, John, 17
St Catherine's Church, New Orleans, 251
St. Francis Xavier Church, Baltimore, 248
St. Mark's Church, Charleston, S.C., 246–47
Salem Association (Baptist), 49
Sanders, B. M., 120
Sandiford, Ralph, 15
School segregation, 255–57, 267, 279–80, 282
Scott, Orange, 96–97, 99, 101–104, 106–107
Seabrook, E. M., 247n
Seabrook, Whitemarsh B., 143n, 168
Sears, Barnas, 257
Secessionism, 166–88, 213–16
Segregation of blacks, 226–57, 264–89
The Selling of Joseph, 16–17
Semple, Robert B., 47n
Sewall, Samuel, 16–17

Sexual relations between blacks and whites, 3, 51–52, 57
Shaftsbury Association (Baptist), 115
Sharp, Daniel, 119n, 126
Sharp, Granville, 25
Shaw, John W., 251
Shaw University, 222, 279
Shem, 130–31
Sherman, William T., 206
Shiloh Association (Baptist), 227
Short, William, 22
Silliman, Benjamin, 156
Silver, James W., 188n
Sisters of St. Joseph, 249–50
Slater, John F., 278
Slater Fund, 278–81
Slavery, ethnological arguments for, 154–65; religious arguments against, 16–22, 24–73, 99, 104, 127; religious arguments for, 5–6, 12–13, 17, 28, 80, 84, 93, 98, 129–36, 152–53, 164–65, 168, 172, 176, 197–98, 200–201
Slavery in America, Colonial period, 3–18; Revolutionary period, 18–73; ante-bellum period, 74–128; Civil War period, 166–207
Slavery reform, southern advocates of, 200–205
Slaves, numbers, 7, 25, 48, 72, 211; treatment of, 62, 203
Sledd, Andrew, 283–85
Sledd, R. N., 268–69
Sleeper, John, 32
Sloan, James A., 130n, 131n
Smith, Adam, 150
Smith, C. S., 54n
Smith, Ellen Hart, 7n, 8n
Smith, Elwyn A., 84n, 89n
Smith, H. Shelton, 15n, 55n, 74n, 82n, 114n
Smith, Whitefoord, 168
Smith, William A., 101, 108–109, 113, 133n, 134n, 140–43, 145, 152–53
Smylie, James, 86, 129, 132–33, 135n
Smyth, Thomas, 157n, 161, 172–73, 191, 214
Snead-Cox, John G., 249n
Snyder, Henry N., 273n
Social gospel, 262, 285
Society for the Propagation of the Gospel in Foreign Parts, 8–10, 14
Society of Friends. *See* Friends
Sociology for the South, 150
Some Considerations on the Keeping of Negroes, 27

Somerset, James, 25
Soule, Joshua, 102n
South Atlantic Quarterly, 298, 300
South Carolina, Baptists in, 53–55, 227; Lutherans in, 244–45; Presbyterians in, 60; secessionist stance, 168–73, 177–78, 179, 180–82
South Western Baptist, 178
Southeby, William, 15
Southern Baptist Convention, 127, 211, 226. *See also* Baptists
Southern Christian Advocate, 231
Southern Christian Herald, 84
Southern Education Board, 286–88
Southern Episcopalian, 177
Southern Presbyterian, 177
Southern Presbyterian Review, 204
Southern Religious Telegraph, 80
Southern Review, 214
Southern Society for the Promotion of the Study of Race Conditions and Problems in the South, 285–86
Spain, Rufus B., 211n, 226n, 265n, 282n
Spalding, Martin J., 248–49
Spanish-American War, 262
Speece, Conrad, 67, 68n
Spellman, Norman W., 113n
Spencer, J. H., 49n, 52n
Stagg, John W., 271–73
Staiger, C. Bruce, 77n, 83n, 84n, 89
Stampp, Kenneth M., 252n
Stanton, Robert L., 188n
Stanton, William, 155n, 156n, 161n, 163
State rights, 166–88, 214–16
Staudenraus, Philip J., 8n
Stephens, Alexander H., 182–84, 215n
Stephenson, Wendell H., 297n
Stevens, Abel, 97
Stiles, Joseph C., 136
Stillman, C. A., 243
Stokes, William H., 121
Storrs, George, 96–97, 99, 101–103
Stow, Baron, 115, 118n, 119n, 122
Straight University, 221
Straton, John Roach, 273–74, 281, 283, 286
Straub, Jean S., 24n
Strawberry Association (Baptist), 48
Stringfellow, Thornton W., 130n, 132n, 134, 135n
Strong, Josiah, 262–63, 274
Summers, Thomas O., 213
Sumner, Charles, 255
Sumner, William Graham, 261–62
Sunderland, La Roy, 96–98, 103, 107

Supreme Court decisions, 257, 263–64, 291
Sweet, Robert, 3
Sweet, William Warren, 8n, 40n, 43n, 50n, 52n, 89n, 90n, 109n
Swint, Henry Lee, 226n
Syracuse, N.Y., 76

Talladega College, 221, 279
Talmadge, John E., 284n
Tappan, Arthur, 74
Tappan, Lewis, 74
Tasmanians, 274
Taylor, Gilbert T., 45
Taylor, Nathaniel, 82, 83, 84
Taylor, Stephen, 134n
Telford, John, 37n
Tennessee, antislavery societies in, 70–72; Lutherans in, 245; Methodists in, 45–46; secessionist stance, 186–87
Tennessee Baptist, 186
Tennessee Manumission Society, 71
Texas Baptist, 178
Thompson, Ernest Trice, 14n, 56n, 82n, 84n, 89n, 90n, 93n, 154n, 179n
Thompson, H. P., 8n
Thomson Biblical Institute, 221
Thornwell, James Henley, 94, 134, 136n, 138, 151, 164–65, 169, 180–82, 196n
Thoughts upon Slavery, 36
Tillman, Ben, 271
Tillotson College, 221
Tilton, Theodore, 217
Tindall, George B., 246n, 296n
Todd, Willie Grier, 116n, 118n, 119n, 125n
Tougaloo College, 221
Towne, Laura, 259
Towner, Lawrence W., 17n
Townsend, Leah, 53
The Traitor, 277
Transylvania Presbytery, 58
Transylvania University, 56
Trinity College, 297, 300–301
Trinterud, Leonard J., 14n
Tucker, Henry Holcombe, 264–65
Tupper, Henry M., 222
Turner, Arlin, 289n, 290n, 291n
Turner, Edward R., 6n, 7n, 25n
Turner, Henry M., 224, 263, 269, 270n
Tuskegee Normal School, 279
Tyerman, Luke, 13n

Underwood Constitution, 267
Unitarians, freedmen's work, 225

United Synod of the Presbyterian Church in the U.S.A., 93
Ussher, James, 156n, 163

Vander Velde, Lewis G., 190n, 222n
Vardaman, James K., 271, 302
Vaughan, C. R., 185n, 266n
Vaughan, Herbert, 249
Vaux, Roberts, 24n
Verot, Augustin, 176, 199, 200, 249–50
Vesey, Denmark, 54
Villard, Oswald Garrison, 301
Virginia, Baptists in, 47–48, 227; Friends in, 32–33; Methodists in, 40–42, 231; Presbyterians in, 60–65, 79–80, 84, 238–41; secessionist stance, 184–85
Virginia Colony, 3–4
Virginia Evangelical and Literary Magazine, 67
Virginia Foreign Mission Society (Baptist), 126
Voting rights. *See* Enfranchisement

Waddell, Alfred M., 286
Wade, Richard C., 54n, 254n
Wagstaff, Henry M., 71n
Walmsley, James E., 186n, 188n
Warnock, Henry Y., 285n
Warren, Edwin R., 115
Washington, Booker T., 274, 286n, 299, 300, 303
Washington, Bushrod, 8
Washington Conference (Methodist), 232, 233, 235
Watts, Isaac, 14
Wax, Harold D., 6n, 29n
Wayland, Francis, 116–17, 133, 134n, 136n, 137–41, 143n, 153n
Webb, Robert A., 263
Webster, Alonzo, 234
Webster, Samuel, 18
Weeks, Louis, 68n
Weeks, Stephen B., 32n, 33n, 34n
Weld, Theodore Dwight, 77, 130, 137n
Wesley, John, 13n, 36–37, 112
Wesleyan Methodist Connection of America, 107, 110, 220, 225
West, Robert A., 108n, 109n, 110n
West Lexington Presbytery, 58–59
Western Christian Advocate, 100
Western Freedmen's Aid Commission, 219
Wharton, Vernol L., 224n, 254n
Wheatley, Phillis, 21
Whedon, Daniel D., 97, 234

INDEX

Whelan, James, 190
White, Charles L., 221n
White supremacy. *See* Inferiority of blacks
Whitefield, George, 12–13
Whitfield, Theodore M., 73n
Whitney, Janet, 26n, 29n
Whittier, John Greenleaf, 74
Wight, Willard E., 189n, 199n
Wightman, William M., 95n, 112n
Wilberforce, William, 37
Wiley, Bell I., 200n
Wiley, Calvin H., 201–202
Wiley University, 221
Willard, Samuel, 5
Willey, Austin, 75n, 115n
Williams, Charles R., 259n
Williams v. *Mississippi*, 264
Williamson, Joel, 254
Williamson, William, 60n
Wilmot, David, 166, 167
Wilson, Harold, 175n
Wilson, John L., 54–55
Wilson, Joshua L., 86
Wilson, Norval, 113
Winans, William, 101
Winkler, Edwin T., 253
Winthrop, Robert C., 257
Wish, Harvey, 150n
Witherspoon, John, 78n, 83, 86, 88
Wolf, Richard C., 189n
Woodward, C. Vann, 254n, 258n, 264n
Woolman, John, 16, 24–32, 35
Wooster, Ralph A., 181n, 182n, 184n, 187n
Wooten, Fred T., Jr., 189n
Worrell, Richard, 15
Wright, Elizur, 74, 77n
Wright, J. Zebulon, 275n
Wyatt-Brown, Bertram, 76n, 218n
Wynes, Charles E., 256n, 267n, 294n, 297n, 302n

Zion's Watchman, 96, 99